FORENSIC HYPNOSIS

Revised First Edition

FORENSIC HYPNOSIS

The Practical Application of Hypnosis in Criminal Investigations

By

WHITNEY S. HIBBARD, M.A.

Project Developer, Montana Board of Crime Control
Co-Director, Missoula City/County Crime Attack Team
Licensed Private Investigator

and

RAYMOND W. WORRING, M.A.

Director, Investigative Research Field Station
Project Developer, Montana Board of Crime Control
Co-Director, Missoula City/County Crime Attack Team
Licensed Private Investigator

With Contributions by
Richard K. King, M.S.
and
Daniel L. Falcon, J.D.

CHARLES C THOMAS • PUBLISHER
Springfield • Illinois • U.S.A.

Published and Distributed Throughout the World by

CHARLES C THOMAS • PUBLISHER
2600 South First Street
Springfield, Illinois 62794-9265

© *1996 by* CHARLES C THOMAS • PUBLISHER

ISBN 0-398-06575-6 (cloth)
ISBN 0-398-06576-4 (paper)

Library of Congress Catalog Card Number: 95-46882
First Edition, 1981

With THOMAS BOOKS *careful attention is given to all details of manufacturing
and design. It is the Publisher's desire to present books that are satisfactory as to their
physical qualities and artistic possibilities and appropriate for their particular use.*
THOMAS BOOKS *will be true to those laws of quality that assure a good name
and good will.*

Printed in the United States of America
SC-R-3

Library of Congress Cataloging-in-Publication Data

Hibbard, Whitney S.
    Forensic hypnosis : the practical application of hypnosis in
criminal investigations / by Whitney S. Hibbard and Raymond W.
Worring ; with contributions by Richard K. King and Daniel L.
Falcon. — Rev. 1st ed.
       p.   cm.
    Includes bibliographical references and index.
    ISBN 0-398-06575-6 (cloth). — ISBN 0-398-06576-4 (paper)
    1. Forensic hypnotism.   I. Worring, Raymond W.   II. Title.
HV8073.5.H5   1996
363.2′54—dc20   95-46882
                                                                     CIP

CONTRIBUTORS

Daniel L. Falcon, J.D. Deputy County Attorney, Cascade County Attorney's Office.

Whitney S. Hibbard, M.A. Project Developer, Montana Board of Crime Control. Co-Director, Missoula City/County Crime Attack Team. Licensed Private Investigator.

Richard K. King, M.S. Captain, Los Angeles Police Department. President, Society for Investigative and Forensic Hypnosis. Instructor at Law Enforcement Hypnosis Institute. Instructor at Rio Hondo Police Academy. Instructor at California State University at Los Angeles.

Raymond W. Worring, M.A. Director, Investigative Research Field Station. Project Developer, Montana Board of Crime Control. Co-Director, Missoula City/County Crime Attack Team. Licensed Private Investigator. Past Director, Technical Assistance Bureau, Institute for Social Science Research, University of Montana. Past Counselor, Counseling Center, University of Montana. Past Investigative Reporter, CBS.

to all our students and subjects
who taught us much

PREFACE
TO THE
REVISED EDITION

S ince the publication of *Forensic Hypnosis: The Practical Application of Hypnosis in Criminal Investigations* in 1981, a great deal has happened in the field, enough to warrant the publication of a revised edition. This edition reflects a survey of the professional activity in the field and a comprehensive review of the relevant case law that has been generated from 1981 to 1995. Chapter 6, **Case Law Analysis of Hypnotically-Related Evidence,** will prove especially valuable as it has been entirely updated with a comprehensive new section on the admissibility of hypnotically-influenced testimony. As such, it will prove invaluable to all investigators who already use or are considering the use of hypnosis as an investigative aid, and to any legal counsel that must defend that use in a court of law.

A nationwide review of the current status of forensic hypnosis has revealed that it is still a growing and maturing field. Although some court rulings have made it more difficult for the admissibility of hypnotically-enhanced testimony, other rulings have done just the opposite. Overall, there seems to be a resurgence of interest in the technique, and it is broadening to include more civil applications. In some quarters, practitioners in the field have differentiated between "investigative" and "forensic" hypnosis with the former being specific to the investigative phase and the latter being specific to the legal phase and testifying in court. In this edition, we generally use the term "forensic" as all inclusive. Training in forensic hypnosis is still available in various state law enforcement academies and there are several good courses taught by private consultants, most of whom are retired law enforcement personnel with extensive experience in hypno-investigation. In some states, there is virtually no activity in forensic hypnosis (e.g., Montana), whereas in other states (e.g., Texas) there is a great deal of organized activity in the field. For instance, in 1980 the **Texas Department of Public Safety/Texas Rangers** developed a comprehensive in-house hypnosis training program which trained veteran law enforcement officers in investigative and forensic hypnosis. Between July 1, 1980 and January 1, 1993 the **Texas Department of Public Safety** conducted 1341 hypnosis interviews in which additional information was obtained in 74 percent—a very admirable record. Texas is also the first state to enact legislation permitting the use of hypnosis in criminal investigations and requiring certification of law enforcement officers conducting hypnosis interviews. There is also an active state association in Texas, the **Texas Association for Investigative Hypnosis.** Other law enforcement agencies around the country interested in developing a hypnosis program should contact the **Texas Commission of Law Enforcement Officers Standards and Education** in Austin and the **International Society for Investigative and Forensic Hypnosis** currently in Reno, Nevada.

The authors are indebted to the many people who have been active in promoting the field of investigative and forensic hypnosis and to those who provided current information that helped us bring **Forensic Hypnosis** up-to-date: Dr. Martin Reiser, Paul Kincade, George Baranowski, Marx Howell, Phil Dunnigan, Jerry Brooks, Kathleen Burke, Harold Cottle, Dr. David Cheek and, Dr. George Mount.

W.S.H.
R.W.W.

PREFACE

THE SPECIFIC PURPOSE of this book is to fill the need that has long existed for a definitive and authoritative textbook on the use of hypnosis in criminal and civil investigations. It is a comprehensive technical manual on the principles, techniques, application, procedures, management, and legal aspects of forensic hypnosis. It also clearly defines the parameters of this new science and encourages the use of better techniques in its application and management than are generally taught and used. It is based on extensive research and experience in the field and is written by professional hypno-investigators for investigators, whether law enforcement officer, prosecutor, defense attorney, private or legal investigator, or consulting doctor.

In writing this book, it was the senior author's purpose to bring together a unique blend of expertise in the technical, practical, and legal areas of hypnosis and forensic hypnosis that would complement his own post-graduate training in clinical hypnosis and extensive experience with law enforcement and criminal justice. To this end, he utilized the technical assistance and consultation of an experienced hypnotist and hypno-investigator, Ray Worring; a contribution from one of the most experienced hypno-investigators in the country and original member of the L.A.P.D.'s pilot hypnosis project, Dick King; and a contribution from an experienced prosecutor knowledgeable in hypnosis, Dan Falcon.

The author wishes to express his appreciation and gratitude to Chief Jack Anderson of the Great Falls, Montana, Police Department and Sheriff Glenn Osborne of the Cascade County, Montana, Sheriff's Office for inviting myself and Ray Worring into their respective departments and for prompting us to design and teach a course on hypnosis in criminal investigation. I am also indebted to Scott G. Hibbard, Robert Rechlin, and FBI Special Agent Al Murphy (ret.) for their editorial comments and advice on the manuscript. Special thanks is given to Sergeant William Raynes, G.F.P.D., for the idea for the book and for his technical advice on the hypno-investigation room. Special thanks is also given to Doctor John G. Watkins of the Graduate School of Clinical Psychology, University of Montana, and to Helen Huth Watkins, Counseling Psychologist at the Center for Student Development, University of Montana, for training me in clinical hypnosis.

W.S.H.

ACKNOWLEDGMENTS

THE AUTHOR EXPRESSES appreciation for permission to quote and reprint material from the following sources:

Jack H. Anderson, Chief of Police, for permission to reprint the Great Falls Police Department's General Order on Investigative Hypnosis.

Harry Arons. *Hypnosis in Criminal Investigation.* Copyright © 1977 by Power Publishers, Inc. Reprinted by permission of the Publisher.

Leslie M. LeCron and Jean Bordeaux. *Hypnotism Today,* 1978 ed. Copyright © 1947 by Leslie M. LeCron and Jean Bordeaux. Reprinted by permission of Mrs. L. M. LeCron.

Milgram. Some conditions of obedience and disobedience to authority. *Human Relations, 18:*59–60, 1965. Quoted by permission of Stanley Milgram, Ph.D.

Reprinted by permission of Hawthorn Books, Inc. from *The Brain Book* by Peter Russell copyright © 1979 Peter Russell. All rights reserved.

Myron Teitelbaum. *Hypnosis Induction Technics.* Copyright © 1965 by Charles C Thomas, Publisher. Quoted by permission of the Publisher.

John G. Watkins. *Hypnotherapy of War Neuroses.* Copyright © 1949 by Ronald Press Co. Reprinted by permission of John Wiley & Sons, Inc.

André M. Weitzenhoffer. *General Techniques of Hypnotism.* Copyright © 1957 by Grune & Stratton, Inc. Quoted by permission of the Publisher and André M. Weitzenhoffer, Ph.D.

Lewis R. Wolberg. *Medical Hypnosis: The Principles of Hypnotherapy.* Copyright © 1948 by Grune & Stratton, Inc. Quoted by permission of Lewis R. Wolberg, M.D.

DISCLAIMER

F*orensic Hypnosis* is designed to provide information on the practical application of hypnosis in criminal and civil investigations. Its intention is educational. Its purpose is not to render legal or other professional advice. If such services are necessary, consult a competent professional in the desired field.

Every effort has been made to make this text as complete and accurate as possible. The information contained herein is believed to be accurate; however, each investigator must make individual decisions and assume responsibility for his/her own behavior.

The authors and publisher shall have neither liability or responsibility to any person or entity with respect to any loss or damage caused or alleged to be caused directly or indirectly by any information contained in this book. The authors and publisher cannot be held responsible for the results of your actions whether or not you follow the suggestions or rely on the information in this book.

CONTENTS

FORENSIC HYPNOSIS

INTRODUCTION TO FORENSIC HYPNOSIS

What Is Forensic Hypnosis?

*F*orensic hypnosis is the application and management of the science of hypnosis in criminal and civil investigations. The primary objective of forensic hypnosis is to enhance the recall of volunteer victims and witnesses to crimes and civil actions. Forensic hypnosis will be used interchangeably with *investigative hypnosis* and *hypno-investigation.*

What Is a Hypno-Investigator?

A legal professional, whether a law enforcement officer, prosecutor, private attorney, or private or legal investigator, who is trained in and utilizes hypnosis as an investigative tool to gather facts pertaining to an event that is likely to be subject to prosecution or litigation is commonly referred to as a hypno-investigator. *Hypno-investigator* is often used interchangeably with *hypnotechnician*, however, the latter term, as popularized since 1955 by the Association to Advance Ethical Hypnosis, generally refers to one who is trained in hypnosis techniques as a paramedical assistant. Hypno-investigator will be used interchangeably with *operator*, and *hypnotist.*

Why a Book on Forensic Hypnosis?

Forensic hypnosis is a new and blossoming field, as evidenced by numerous articles and a variety of courses on the subject now offered throughout the country for criminal justice personnel, but a comprehensive operator's manual does not exist. Anyone embarking on the study of investigative or forensic hypnosis will immediately become painfully aware that there is a tremendous lack of concise and centrally located information regarding its use and what does exist is scattered throughout a variety of texts, articles, case precedent, and within the minds of those experienced in the area. Furthermore, most hypnosis texts are written by doctors for doctors, which means that their central aim is therapeutic and that the terminology used is usually beyond that of the ordinary layman. It is rare that one of these texts will address the area of forensic hypnosis. Those that do usually do so only in passing, and the authors have usually had little or no experience and involvement with the criminal justice system. Due to the ever changing case law and legal status of hypnosis, what has been written is now largely out-of-date. Therefore, with the growing interest in and use of investigative hypnosis, the need for a comprehensive book on its principles, techniques, application, management, and legal aspects is evident.

Who Is This Book Meant For?

This book is designed and will have practical application for any professional who is involved in the legal establishment as an investigator, lawyer, or consulting doctor who is interested in hypnosis as it may apply to his work. Specifically, it is written primarily for law enforcement officers who are interested in adding a valuable investigative tool to their armamentarium and to the prosecutors who must ultimately defend its use in court. The book will, however, be of equal benefit to those professionals in the private sector who also are confronted with the poor memories of victims and witnesses, whether they be private civil or defense attorneys, legal or private investigators, or psychologists and psychiatrists doing criminal or civil case consulting. This book will also be valuable for those students of hypnosis who are interested in learning or teaching a comprehensive system of hypnotic induction techniques, but who are uninterested in forensic hypnosis itself.

What Is The Purpose of This Book?

Hypnosis is presently and rapidly becoming a practical and valued investigative tool. Until very recently, however, hypnosis was carefully controlled by select professions and was seldom used in law enforcement. The norm has usually been for law enforcement to seek the aid of a clinical hypnotist as a last resort on major cases. The results were often mixed, however, due to an unsympathetic hypnotist, or even good intentioned ones who had little or no understanding of law enforcement, crime-related interviewing procedures, rules of evidence, or information needed to solve cases. After a close working association with law enforcement over the past several years, it is the authors' purpose to make hypnosis much more accessible to law enforcement. By this we mean that carefully selected law enforcement officers, as they have been throughout the country, should be trained as hypnotists to function as hypno-investigators within their departments. Hypnosis has demonstrated its validity and effectiveness as an investigative tool to the point that it should be made a collateral and supportive service either within or available to every law enforcement agency in this country.

Forensic hypnosis is a special discipline and should be made a separate branch of the science of hypnosis, for reasons to be explained later. It is hoped that in some small way this book will aid in this development.

What Is The Scope of This Book?

Briefly, this book covers the history, theory, principles, practice, management, and legal aspects of hypnosis in criminal investigations. Although the emphasis is primarily on criminal investigation, the basic procedures for the application and management of hypnosis, as well as the case law regulating its use, hold equally for civil cases.

More specifically, the book is designed to function as:

1. A student's technical manual for learning investigative hypnosis techniques.
2. An instructor's manual for teaching investigative hypnosis techniques.
3. A technical manual on how to develop a hypno-investigation program within a law enforcement agency.
4. A technical manual on how to manage and regulate the use of investigative hypnosis.
5. A technical manual on how to lay the proper foundation in criminal cases so it will stand the test in court.
6. A comprehensive review of the legal standing of hypnosis.
7. An analytical survey of special topics and problems in forensic hypnosis.

What Is The Plan and Format of This Book?

The book is designed primarily for self-teaching. It is a *how-to-do-it* book in very readable form. Keeping in mind the audience the book addresses and recognizing the fact that most hypnosis literature is written in difficult psychological terms, the authors will make a conscious effort to avoid obscuring the material presented by utilizing abstruse and arcane words. Wherever possible, therefore, the authors will use simple, definitive terms. Necessarily difficult words and hypnosis terminology will be defined within the body of the text as they first appear.

Forensic Hypnosis is also designed to function as an instructor's manual and text, text, as well as a reference manual for hypno-investigators, prosecutors, and other attorneys who need a concise and consolidated reference on hypnosis and the law.

Where possible and appropriate, the authors will cite specific references for further inquiry for the interested student. Furthermore, in certain complex areas or topics, the authors will include more detailed and specific information in appendices so as not to detract from the simplicity and straightforwardness of the main text.

There are four basic stages and objectives in this book: (1) to orient the reader to the history, theory, and principles of hypnosis and forensic hypnosis, (2) to teach a comprehensive system of hypnosis techniques, (3) to thoroughly address the practical aspects of when and how to apply and manage investigative hypnosis, and (4) to thoroughly review the legal status of hypnosis.

The ultimate question, however, is if a law enforcement officer can become a good hypno-investigator just by reading and following the instructions in this book. *Forensic Hypnosis* was written in an attempt to answer this question in the affirmative.

What This Book Is Not

This book is not a collection of war stories and anecdotes. References to case histories will only be included to elucidate specific points.

This book is not meant to solve the controversies that continue to rage concerning hypnosis or to teach therapeutic techniques. It is meant to promote the science of forensic hypnosis and to persuade the investigator that the careful and discriminate use of hypnosis can enlarge his investigative effectiveness. The widespread use of hypnosis in criminal justice by laymen is inevitable, and it is the authors' concern that it be employed in a professional and judicious manner so that law enforcement will always have it as an investigative tool.

HOW TO USE THIS BOOK

This book can be used in several ways to fulfill several different purposes. It can be used by an interested criminal justice department or agency head, training officer, or individual to familiarize himself with the potential and practical aspects of investigative hypnosis. From this point, the interested party may choose not to use hypnosis, to utilize the services of an outside medical or psychological consultant experienced in forensic hypnosis, or to have himself and/or other individual investigators trained as hypnotists. If the latter is his choice, there are several ways to proceed, which are listed here in order of preference:

1. Obtain the services of a local sympathetic psychologist or psychiatrist trained in hypnosis and preferably experienced in forensic hypnosis to use the book as a teacher's manual and text for instructing departmental investigators.

2. Send an officer(s) to a recognized course in forensic hypnosis. The International Association for Forensic Hypnosis maintains a roster of trainers and training programs. The reader is cautioned against attending any forensic hypnosis course without first carefully examining the instructors, content and format of the course. Undoubtedly, other quality

courses will be developed and offered, but, unfortunately, many opportunists are cropping up who recognize the economic potential of offering such courses. Many of these lack the qualifications and greatly underestimate the amount of time and work that goes into learning hypnosis. For example, the authors are aware of a day-long forensic course that purports to teach hypnosis techniques for three hours in the morning and advanced hypnosis techniques in the afternoon, at which point the student is awarded a certificate of course completion. Other forensic hypnosis courses offer as little as twenty hours of instruction, yet make extravagant claims of superior course quality and effectiveness. Other courses teach as few as one induction technique.

The authors recommend that any officer trained in an established forensic hypnosis course attempt to enlist the aid of a local sympathetic clinician experienced in hypnosis for further training and supervision as in #1 above. Any short course in hypnosis is only the beginning.

3. Institute an interdepartmental self-training course using this book as a text. This can also be done in conjunction with #2 above.

This book is also designed to be used as a comprehensive reference manual on the legal aspects of hypno-investigation. Any legal professional who uses or intends to use hypnosis in his work or must defend the admissibility of hypnotically induced testimony and evidence in a court of law will find this book valuable.

Plan of Study for Beginning Hypno-Investigators

This book is designed to provide optimum training to the beginning hypno-investigator, either by self-teaching or as a text in an offered course. There are basically two steps in learning hypnosis:

(1) proper instruction and (2) practical experience. As mentioned previously, the ideal situation is to be trained and supervised by an experienced operator, but if this is not possible, do not hesitate to teach yourself. An historical survey would probably show that a sizeable percentage, if not the majority, of practicing hypnotists, whether lay or professional, were self-taught. If self-taught, however, the hypno-investigator should pick up certification as soon as possible by attending a formal course(s), as credentials are important for expert witness qualification.

Whichever approach is taken, there are some basic considerations to follow to maximize one's understanding and learning of hypnosis:

1. To be a successful practitioner, one must have a basic understanding of the principles of suggestion and hypnosis. In other words, you must know *how* it works before using it. Avoid the temptation, therefore, to begin directly with the induction techniques, but begin instead at page one so you obtain the proper foundation first.

2. Once each chapter has been digested up to Chapter 4 — The Seven Stages of Hypnosis — the reader is ready to begin learning the actual induction techniques. The techniques included progress from the simplest to the most complex and the reader should feel comfortable with each in its turn before moving on. The goal is to be able to deliver each technique without hesitation, major mistakes, or uncertainty. For such proficiency in each technique, five basic steps should be followed:

a. *Memorizing.* Although word for word memorization is not necessary, the essential components, verbalizations (patter), and their sequence must be memorized. Begin by memorizing the first induction and the first two deepening techniques (there are twice as many deepenings as inductions, which also progress from the simplest to most complex) as well as the waking procedure.

b. *Role-playing.* Once the induction technique (protocol) is memorized, act it out and see if it can be recited from memory. Do this by yourself either in front of a mirror while addressing an imaginary subject in a chair next to you, or by recording or videotaping your practice session which can then be reviewed. In this way you discover how you will appear and sound to a real subject. Periodically during the day, try to visualize yourself going through the whole protocol.

c. *Simulation with Classmates.* If more than one of you are learning at the same time, simulate the induction with each other, then critique each other's performance for technique, verbal and nonverbal communication, etc. This phase develops the smoothness, fluency, and proficiency necessary to be convincing to a subject. If your partner becomes hypnotized, don't panic, but continue normally through the protocol and awaken him.

d. *Practice with Subjects.* Now you are ready to actually induct a subject. Be sure that you have memorized, role-played, and simulated the awakening procedure so you can bring your subject out of hypnosis.

e. *Feedback.* If your subjects do not mind, tape record or videotape your practice sessions and listen to them immediately after doing a session. Critique your technique, patter, nonverbal behavior and verbal presentation. Try to observe and listen to yourself from your subject's point of view. You may even sit in his chair and role-play the induction as a subject as you listen to yourself. Have other classmates or experienced operators listen to or observe the tapes. All these methods of feedback will give you a tremendous amount of insight into the subtleties of hypnotic induction, which will greatly improve your effectiveness.

3. To maximize one's ability to empathize and be sensitive to a subject's experience, it is highly recommended that any trainee be hypnotized by the class instructor, if there is one. If not, attempt to seek out a professional hypnotist and undergo the experience, or at least practice with self-hypnosis.

4. It is important to emphasize at the outset that although hypnosis looks deceptively simple and easy to learn by the uninformed observer, its sophisticated and professional use actually involves the learning of an entire system of techniques as well as a sound theoretical understanding. Hypnosis is a science, a skill, and an art that demands a great deal of study, practice, and experience from those who wish to become proficient. With this in mind, anyone interested in learning hypnosis should take a close look at his motivation, his degree of commitment and seriousness, as well as the material to be covered. Some comments from trained hypno-investigators may help to elucidate this important point:

- "First he should look at his commitments. He should be totally committed. He must be committed to home study and commit a lot of time."
- "Probably the first thing I'd suggest to an officer is to try to get a good idea before you start of what you'd be looking at."
- "It's ten times more involved than it appears. It must be taken very seriously."
- "It's a labor of love. It's not easy. It's a lot of work and you're messing with other people's lives so you have to be ready for it."

5. It is highly recommended and well worth your while to keep going back over material learned previously. Each

time the beginner reviews, his understanding is increased in light of his experience, and he slowly becomes more of a professional. It takes hundreds of tests and years of study for a polygraph operator to become an expert, and hundreds of interrogations and much study to become a proficient interrogator. The same holds true for becoming an adept hypno-investigator.

Lesson Plan

In learning hypnosis, or any skill for that matter, it is essential that the student proceed in a step by step fashion to build the necessary foundation of basic knowledge upon which successive and more difficult material depends. This book is designed to first acquaint the student with the history, theory, principles, dynamics, and nature of hypnosis and suggestion before beginning to teach technique and practice with subjects. The techniques themselves progress from the simplest to the most complex and each should be learned in its turn.

The Contents page serves as an ideal outline for a course in forensic hypnosis. It is recommended that the course be taught using a format of one meeting per week of three-hours duration. In the authors' experience, this format is necessary to give the students adequate time between classes to read, study, and practice. Although the outline is specifically designed for a course being taught by an experienced hypnotist, it can be easily adapted for a self-teaching program.

The first session should begin with a comprehensive live demonstration of the hypnotic techniques to be taught. This will give the students an immediate and realistic impression and appreciation of the complexity of the material to be learned. Similarly, the course outline and objectives should be thoroughly reviewed, and the necessity for a sincere personal commitment by each student should be explained. The basic

purpose of the first session is to weed out those students who do not have a genuine interest and serious commitment.

During the second session, the material in Chapter 1 — Introduction to Forensic Hypnosis — can adequately be covered. Chapter 2 — Orientation to Hypnosis and Hypno-Investigation — and Chapter 3 — Principles and Dynamics of Hypnosis and Suggestion — will each require an additional two sessions apiece.

Having covered the fundamentals of hypnosis and suggestion, the students are ready to begin learning the techniques in Chapter 4 — The Seven Stages of Hypnosis. To give the student adequate time to learn and practice each technique, the following sequence should be utilized. The instructor reviews the protocol and demonstrates the first induction technique (eye fixation), the two simplest deepening techniques (silent period and breathing), and the awakening procedure. During the intervening week between classes, the students study and essentially memorize the protocols. During the first hour of the next class, they pair off and practice on each other in quiet rooms around the building. During the second hour, the practice subjects are brought in and one subject is assigned to each student pair. Each member of the pair then practices, in turn, the techniques on the subject. During the third hour, the instructor reviews the protocol and demonstrates the next induction technique (eye blink) and the next two deepening techniques (counting and rapid arm drop). During the intervening week the students continue to practice the first techniques while studying and memorizing the new ones. After the third or fourth week, the instructor can begin to review the protocols and demonstrate the tests and challenges the students will begin to use. This process will continue for approximately eight weeks until each induction, deepening, test, and challenge is learned. At this point, the protocols for hypermnesia and revivification are reviewed and demonstrated. When practicing on each other, the student pairs should change every week provided there are enough students. This will give each a greater range of experience, will facilitate their feeling comfortable doing hypnosis with different people, and will avoid the development of cliques.

Once the techniques are learned, the course reverts back to lecture, spending two sessions on Chapter 5 — Practical Aspects of Hypno-Investigation — then two sessions on Chapter 6 — Case Law Analysis of Hypnotically-Related Evidence — then two additional weeks on Chapter 7 — Special Problems and Topics in Forensic Hypnosis. During these last four weeks each student is required to do two videotapes with subjects. In the first tape, the student does an induction and deepenings of choice and all the tests and challenges. This tape is then reviewed with the instructor so both he and the student can critique it. Given an adequate performance by the student, he is cleared to tape a time regression with a subject. This tape is subsequently critiqued by the student and instructor. The videotapes serve not only as an exam, but also as a learning experience and competency evaluation for the student.

Each student is awarded a certificate when course requirements have been successfully completed. Considering the amount of work that has gone into the course, it is recommended that a quality certificate be designed, one that the hypno-investigator will be proud to display on his wall and one that will have a psychological impact upon future subjects. (See Appendix 1 for a sample certificate which has been reduced from an 11 by 14 inch blue on white parchment. The back of the certificate should specify exactly what the student has been taught.)

The total length of the course will be approximately sixty hours of instruction and supervised practice spread over four and one-half months, with additional time for videotaping, videotape critiques, and individual practice and study. The course can, however, be condensed or lengthened depending on individual or departmental constraints.

At this point, the hypno-investigators are ready to begin a designated period of supervised practice on actual cases before working independently on their own (see Chapter 5). During this phase it would be educational and beneficial for the class to continue to meet formally at approximately monthly intervals to review cases, critique tapes, and gain additional practice. At the end of this phase, the students have proven themselves as competent hypno-investigators and can henceforth operate without supervision.

Who and How Many Officers Should Be Trained?

As stated previously, it is the authors' belief that every law enforcement agency should either have within its own ranks the services of a hypno-investigator(s) or at least have access to such services outside the department or agency. The inevitable question is, "Who should be trained and how many?" Here are some general guidelines and considerations:

1. More important than quantity is quality.

2. A hypno-investigator must first and foremost be mature. He must also be intelligent, sensitive to others, observant, confident, conversant, and be easily liked.

3. Considering expert witness qualifications, a college degree and even a masters degree would be helpful, although certainly not necessary.

4. Some law enforcement agencies who have had hypno-investigators trained insist that those trained should

be functionally separate from any division having investigative follow-up, case development and prosecution responsibility, and that they be at least of the rank of lieutenant. This is meant to shortcircuit potential defense objections and to ensure the objectivity and credibility of the department's criminal investigators. Although seemingly valid, experience to date has not supported this position, as long as the hypno-investigator is not the primary investigator and all sessions are properly documented. Polygraph operators, however, are cautioned against being trained as hypno-investigators.

5. Both male and female officers should be trained to accommodate hypnosis subjects' gender preferences.

6. A general guide in selecting the number to be trained would be to have at least as many hypno-investigators as polygraph operators within the department. If the department does not have a polygraph examiner, a hypno-investigator should be trained anyway, or arrangements with another law enforcement agency should be made to make the service available. Due to the intense and intimate interpersonal nature of hypnosis, and recognizing the fact that success in hypnosis depends largely on the ability to establish rapport with a subject, it is highly recommended that any department of any size have a pool of hypno-investigators to draw upon to accommodate the individual differences and preferences of subjects. Furthermore, it is the authors' experience that less than half of those who begin a course in hypno-investigation will actually finish and become skilled in its use.

7. Of primary importance is the officer's motivation and commitment. The officer must be sincerely dedicated and committed to learning an investigative tool to be used strictly for that one purpose. Curiosity seekers, frustrated psychotherapists, credential hunters, would-be magicians, and others should be carefully screened and avoided.

8. Minority and bilingual operators should be trained if community demographics warrant it, i.e. significant populations of minorities and non-English speaking people.

WHY SHOULD LAW ENFORCEMENT OFFICERS BE TRAINED IN HYPNOSIS?

Hypnosis is too valuable an investigative tool to be used only sporadically and as a last resort, yet this is primarily the way in which it has been used. There are several reasons for this. First of all, there is the difficulty of finding a sympathetic and available clinical hypnotist. When law enforcement needs information, they want it now and often cannot wait for an appointment next week. Second, there is the problem of cost. Some clinical hypnotists have charged up to 500 dollars for a single session, and, with budgetary constraints, the additional costs are prohibitive. Third, clinicians are experts in therapy, not investigation, rules of evidence, and case-related interviewing. As a result, clinicians often fail to ask the questions that will give the needed information. Fourth, there is the problem of the reception given law enforcement by clinicians. It has been the experience of several jurisdictions with which the authors have worked, that clinicians conduct the hypnosis begrudgingly and treat the law enforcement officers condescendingly. Fifth, there is the additional problem of restrictions placed on the hypnotic interview by the clinicians. In a homicide case familiar to the authors in which a crucial witness was hypnotized, the clinician refused to permit the detectives to be present and refused to tape it. Incidentally, the bill was 300 dollars and all the detectives had was the psychologist's assurance that the witness knew nothing of value. Sixth, there is the additional problem that clinicians usually have not had experience with the media, and often bias a case by freely granting interviews to discuss the results of the hypnosis. Furthermore, some psychologists do not want to get involved because of the possibility of having to testify in court. Finally, there is the seemingly universal tendency on the part of law enforcement agencies to not want to go outside of the department for assistance.

Law enforcement officers, rather than the clinician, are the experts in investigating, rules of evidence, and case-related interviewing. This is probably the main reason why officers should be trained in hypnosis. The investigator can efficiently, but carefully, discover if the subject has the necessary information needed for the case. Clinicians will often obtain valid, but too often useless, information.

What Value Is Hypnosis to Law Enforcement?

Most authorities on hypnosis and researchers of human behavior believe that everything a human being takes in through the five senses is permanently recorded in his brain. They also recognize, however, that the vast majority of this information is perceived and registered only on a subconscious level, or, if registered consciously, quickly slips below the level of conscious awareness due to its sheer unimportance, or, is actively repressed because of its traumatic nature. These experts also agree, however, that this stored information can largely and accurately be retrieved through hypnosis (see "The Nature of Memory" in Chapter 7).

Modern law enforcement is being rapidly transformed by new electronic and other technical developments, by new information systems and management tools, and by the advent of special

tactics and teams. The major and most important source of evidence, however, is still the eyewitness. In this regard, the nemesis of the law enforcement officer is the unreliable and often blank memories of victims and witnesses. Every experienced officer has closed many a case for want of information from an eyewitness. He can also relate many incidences of spending numerous hours tracing down faulty leads given by poor witnesses. The eyewitness account will never be replaced or computerized, but it has been the one area of law enforcement that has undergone little or no improvement. The utilization and application of the science of hypnosis is the obvious remedy to this proverbial problem.

Hypnosis has been used in criminal cases sporadically over the past 100 years with some dramatic success, and is now being used ever more frequently. It should be stated at the onset, however, that hypnosis is not a panacea. Many variables affect its success, such as the hypnotic susceptibility of the subject, the amount of attention the subject originally paid to the stimulus or information, the skill and experience of the hypnotist, and depth of trance.

In terms of cost effectiveness, the use of hypnosis as an investigative tool has proven to be one of the best investments law enforcement has made, not only in terms of dollars, but in clearance rates as well. In fact, in a one year pilot study on the effectiveness of hypnosis as an investigative aid utilized by trained police officers, the Los Angeles Police Department found that out of a sample of sixty-seven criminal cases, new important information was obtained from witnesses that was otherwise unattainable through routine interviews in 77 percent of those cases. Of the sixty-seven cases, 16 percent were actually solved by the use of hypnosis.[1] In an evaluation of the 462 hypnoinvestigations conducted from 1975 through September of 1979, the hypnosis unit found that additional information was elicited from hypnotized witnesses in 80.3 percent of the cases. In only 19.7 percent of the cases was no additional information obtained. The information obtained was deemed valuable to the case investigator in 66.9 percent of these cases, and it was found to be accurate in 90.5 percent of the cases in which accuracy could be determined (180). One hundred and thirty five cases, or 30.9 percent, were solved, and hypnosis was deemed to be of value in 65.2 percent of them.[2] In an earlier study of nearly 300 of the 462 cases, the hypnosis unit found that information given by hypnotized witnesses was corroborated in all but 3.7 percent of them. The study also showed that witnesses were able to recall some new details in 91.8 percent of the cases, and hypno-induced information led to solving of the crime in almost one third of them.[3] The New York Police Department claims a 75 percent success rate in providing new information in over sixty major cases from November 1976 to October 1978.[4]

In conclusion, hypnosis is an efficient and effective investigative tool that is essential in saving valuable time, trimming costs, and providing new leads in difficult cases.

What Is The Difference Between Forensic Hypnosis and Clinical Hypnosis?

Forensic hypnosis and clinical hypnosis are separate and distinct branches of the science of hypnosis, each with its specific definition and objectives. We have previously defined *forensic hypnosis* as the application and management of the science of hypnosis in criminal and civil investigations. As such, its main objective is to carefully and discriminately use hypnosis with volunteer victims and witnesses of crimes and civil actions to enhance their recall within the confines of the law.

Clinical hypnosis is the application of hypnosis in a therapeutic encounter. Its main objective is to use hypnosis as a means of enhancing the process of therapy with a client, whether psychological or medical.

Consistent with professional ethics and courtesy, the authors believe that forensic hypnosis should ideally only be practiced by forensic hypnotists, just as clinical hypnosis should only be practiced by clinical hypnotists, unless they are trained in both fields. This position seems to be consistent with one of the major conclusions in the report of the Council on Mental Health of the American Medical Association which investigated the clinical use of hypnosis. The report, published by the Council in 1958 in the *Journal of the American Medical Association* following its approval by the AMA Board of Trustees and the House of Delegates, concludes, among other things, that "no physician or dentist should utilize hypnosis for purposes that are not related to his particular specialty and that are beyond the range of his ordinary competence."[5] Although this admonition was in specific reference to a physician or dentist utilizing hypnosis in a medical specialty in which he was not trained, it seems legitimate to presume that it would pertain equally to nonmedical specialties as well. This conclusion would seem to indicate that unless a clinical hypnotist, whether a psychologist or psychiatrist, is knowledgeable in forensic hypnosis, that he should not conduct hypno-investigations.

This may be an extreme position. The authors are not advocating that clinical hypnotists do not render their services and skills when requested, or for law enforcement not to seek these services if they do not have them within their departments. A point is made, however, that if clinical hypnotists are to become seriously involved in hypno-investigations, they had best educate themselves or take some formal instruction in forensic hypnosis to be of maximum benefit.

The authors do not intend to condemn all clinical hypnotists, as there are many fine ones among their ranks who are sympathetic to law enforcement and criminal justice. Some clinical hypnotists have even risked their professional reputation and standing among their colleagues by assisting and training lay hypno-investigators.

It is interesting and somewhat ironic to note that the current groundswell of interest and training of criminal justice personnel in forensic hypnosis is largely the result of this service not being readily available among the medical and psychological community. If such professionals had offered their services free of charge and allowed such basic and necessary procedures as audio recording and videotaping and the presence of the primary investigator, law enforcement would never have felt the need to train their own hypno-investigators. Where a vacuum exists, however, ...

What Is the Difference Between Clinical and Forensic Hypnotists?

The answer to this question can probably be best presented by listing the basic requirements, qualifications, education, and areas of training and expertise.

Clinical Hypnotist	Forensic Hypnotist
Advanced graduate degrees optional, but recommended*	Advanced graduate degrees optional, but unnecessary
Thorough and competent training in hypnosis	Thorough and competent training in hypnosis
Thorough knowledge in the following additional areas: a. hypnoanalytic techniques b. hypnotherapeutic techniques c. medical uses of hypnosis d. personality theory e. psychology and dynamics of personality f. psychopathology g. psychodynamics h. systems of psychotherapy i. physiological psychology j. psychological theories k. psychological evaluation and testing l. developmental psychology m. theories of learning n. children's behavioral disorders	Thorough knowledge in the following additional areas: a. rules of evidence b. legal aspects of hypnosis c. laying the proper foundation for hypno-induced testimony d. crime-related interviewing techniques for victims and witnesses e. hypnosis-related interviewing techniques for victims and witnesses f. criminal codes g. criminal case investigation procedures and techniques h. testifying in court i. report writing j. dealing with crime victims and witnesses k. taking statements l. dealing with the press m. using hypnosis with the polygraph n. using hypnosis with a composite artist or identi-kit o. conducting hypnosis with rape victims, sexually abused children, and other special types of victims

* Lay hypnotechnicians may practice in most states under the supervision of a licensed doctor.

By examining this list, it is obvious that the only qualifications that clinical and forensic hypnotists have in common is the thorough and competent training in hypnosis.

Not only do the qualifications differ, but there is a crucial difference between the way in which clinical and forensic hypnosis is conducted. Whereas clinical hypnotists enjoy the sanctity of the doctor-patient relationship and the security and comfort of working alone in a private office, forensic hypnotists must have their hypno-investigations recorded, videotaped, and witnessed. Maximum trance depth needs to be achieved and appropriate tests conducted for verification. The possibility of having the tapes scrutinized by opposing experts, and of eventually testifying and being cross-examined in court, are ever-present realities. Additional pressures of expectant investigators and persistent reporters must also be coped with. Frustration is also enchanced because of the time pressures of an investigation: as many as four to six hours may be spent with a subject in multiple back-to-back sessions without retrieving the forgotten information.

MYTHS AND MISCONCEPTIONS REGARDING THE USE OF HYPNOSIS BY LAW ENFORCEMENT

Whenever hypnosis is mentioned in conjunction with law enforcement, some myths and misconceptions immediately come to most people's minds, whether professionals or laymen. These myths and misconceptions badly need debunking, so the authors will discuss some of the more prevalent ones. Furthermore, this will enable the hypno-investigator to adequately respond when confronted with them.

Myth #1

Hypnosis will be used by law enforcement to force confessions out of unknowing or unwilling suspects and defendants. This is probably the first image that comes to most peoples' minds and it is probably the most common question that hypno-investigators will be faced with from uninformed critics. This myth is a hard · one to combat because it is difficult to convince people otherwise since it is based on such a profound lack of information and outright misinformation regarding the nature of hypnosis. In answering this question the hypno-investigator should stress several points:

A. HYPNOSIS IS ONLY USED BY LAW ENFORCEMENT ON VOLUNTEER VICTIMS AND WITNESSES TO CRIMES TO ENHANCE THEIR RECALL OF FORGOTTEN DETAILS. In the rare event that it is used with defendants or suspects, it will only be done so at the request of the defendant and with permission of defense counsel. Furthermore, in the case of suspects, the actual hypnosis will only be conducted by an outside independent expert, usually a psychologist or psychiatrist trained in hypnosis and experienced in forensic hypnosis, and both defense and prosecution will usually be present during the session. The public does not realize that the use of hypnosis on defendants is much like the polygraph in that it works just as often to the advantage of defense counsel as it does to the prosecution. In fact, experience has shown that when hypnosis is used on defendants it more often than not is to the advantage of the suspect. Based on a great deal of personal experience in using hypnosis on defendants, Arons concludes that "for one case in which the use of hypnosis in the investigation of a crime leads to a person's conviction, a dozen or more have contributed to exoneration."[6]

B. PEOPLE CANNOT BE FORCED TO SAY OR DO ANYTHING AGAINST THEIR WILL

UNDER HYPNOSIS; they are actually in control rather than the hypnotist (see "The Corpse in the Laboratory: The Possible Antisocial and Criminal Use of Hypnosis" in Chapter 7).

C. PEOPLE CANNOT BE HYPNOTIZED AGAINST THEIR WILL. Given the proper setting, relationship, motivation, and techniques, however, some authorities maintain that a person can be hypnotized unknowingly. For example, medical doctors can tell a patient they are just going to teach them how to relax and proceed into an actual induction. This type of induction requires a motivated subject in a legitimate setting such as a doctor's office, in which case the patient comes for help, and he does what the doctor says. It should be obvious that disguised techniques are not feasible in an interrogation room, and the fact that you cannot get a hypnotized person to violate his sense of self-preservation negates this possibility anyway. Furthermore, the induction techniques taught police officers are very obvious and visible and require the subject's complete cooperation. All sessions are also audiotaped and/or videotaped as well as witnessed. Any attempt at a disguised induction by an officer would be a definite violation of departmental ethics and grounds for suspension. Even assuming that a confession could be extracted under hypnosis, it would be inadmissible in court because it was nonvoluntary (see "The Corpse in the Laboratory: The Possible Antisocial and Criminal Use of Hypnosis" in Chapter 7).

D. AS THERE ARE FALSE CONFESSIONS TO MAJOR CRIMES BY INNOCENT BUT PSYCHOLOGICALLY DISTURBED INDIVIDUALS, THE POLICE ARE REQUIRED TO VERIFY CONFESSIONS WITH OBJECTIVE MATERIAL EVIDENCE. No defendant can be convicted on a confession alone. Hypno-induced confessions would be subject to the same scrutiny. Most experts in the field agree that no hypnotic subject can be forced to violate his in-

stinct of self-preservation or his moral or ethical code. Furthermore, the courts have not allowed cases to stand solely on hypno-induced testimony.

Myth #2

Police hypnotists may inadvertently suggest responses to victims and witnesses to confirm their suspicions of who is guilty of a crime. The Executive Council of the Society for Clinical and Experimental Hypnosis unanimously approved a resolution opposing the use of hypnosis by police officers in October of 1978, which said in part, "police officers usually have strong views as to who is likely to be guilty of a crime and may easily inadvertently bias the hypnotized subject's memories even without themselves being aware of their actions."[7] Although this admittedly is a possibility, concern for it happening is unfounded for the following reasons:

A. POLICE OFFICERS USUALLY DO NOT HAVE STRONG VIEWS AS TO WHO IS LIKELY TO BE GUILTY OF A CRIME. In most cases in which hypnosis is used, the primary investigators have little or no evidence from which to draw conclusions. This is precisely the reason why hypnosis is used.

B. THE HYPNO-INVESTIGATOR IS NEVER THE PRIMARY INVESTIGATOR and is therefore less likely to have a biased interest in the case.

C. THE HYPNO-INVESTIGATOR TAKES APPROPRIATE MEASURES TO PREVENT THE POSSIBILITY OF SUGGESTING ANSWERS TO THE HYPNOTIZED VICTIM OR WITNESS. He is trained in proper questioning, and his techniques can be reviewed on the tape made of the session.

D. THE MERE FACT THAT ALL HYPNO-INDUCED EVIDENCE IS CORROBORATED BY INDEPENDENT EVIDENCE BEFORE ARREST OR SEARCH WARRANTS ARE OBTAINED NEGATES THE CONCERN OF RELYING ON UNSUBSTANTIATED INFORMATION.

E. ALL HYPNOSIS SESSIONS ARE AUDIO AND/OR VIDEOTAPED FOR THE EXPLICIT

PURPOSE OF RENDERING THE SESSIONS EX-
AMINABLE BY A PARTY-OPPONENT.
Should the issue of hypnosis be raised,
the tapes can be scrutinized for any
biasing and suggestive influence.

F. THE MEMORIES OF VICTIMS AND
WITNESSES ARE EASILY INADVERTENTLY
BIASED WITHOUT HYPNOSIS, SO THERE IS
NO REASON TO SINGLE OUT AND INDICT
HYPNOSIS (see "The Nature of Memory"
in Chapter 7).

Myth #3

Hypnosis should not be used by law en-
forcement officers because they are not
trained to handle the repressed emotional
trauma that they are likely to uncover. This
myth was started and is still propagated
by a small group of psychologists,
psychiatrists, physicians, and dentists
who argue that hypnosis should only be
employed by these select professions
within the area of their expertise. If this
position is examined closely it becomes
obvious that it is not only absurd but
even negates itself. First of all, as was
discussed above, forensic hypnosis does
not fall within the expertise of any of
the above professions. Secondly, the
implicit assumption is that hypnosis is
inherently or potentially dangerous
and that these professionals, by virtue
of their training, are the only ones competent to deal with psychological and
emotional problems that it may uncover. The alleged dangers of hypnosis are
debunked in the next myth to be discussed, and as far as the competence
issue, it should be obvious that non-
psychiatric physicians and dentists have
no more training than police officers in
dealing with human problems. In
actuality, police officers have abundant
practical experience in dealing with every type of human problem and
trauma. Granted, psychologists and
psychiatrists are professionally trained
to deal with such problems (although
training in any discipline, including
hypnosis, is no guarantee of competence), but it is quite odd that they

would include their medical and dental
brothers, who are not trained to deal
with psychological trauma, among
those qualified to practice hypnosis.

This myth assumes that repressed
emotional traumas are inadvertently
uncovered under hypnosis. To fairly
examine this issue, one must look at the
source — psychologists and psychiatrists. These professionals, in citing the
triggering of repressed traumatic
psychological or emotional problems,
are ignoring several variables:

A. PSYCHOTHERAPISTS TREAT SICK
PEOPLE WHO COME TO THEM WITH
THE EXPLICIT PURPOSE OF WORKING
THROUGH PERSONAL PROBLEMS.

B. ONE OF THE PURPOSES OF PSY-
CHOTHERAPY IS TO UNCOVER AND ELIC-
IT REPRESSED TRAUMATIC PSYCHOLOG-
ICAL AND EMOTIONAL INCIDENCES.

C. SPONTANEOUS OUTBURSTS IN
NONTHERAPEUTIC SETTINGS ARE EX-
TREMELY RARE. Dentists and physicians
should ask themselves how many times
their hypnotized patients have spontaneously discharged a repressed
trauma. You would be hard pressed to
find a single one.

D. HYPNO-INVESTIGATORS WILL BY
AND LARGE BE HYPNOTIZING NORMAL
ADULTS IN A SITUATION IN WHICH THE
OBJECTIVES, PURPOSE, AND LIMITS OF
THE HYPNOSIS SESSION ARE CLEARLY
UNDERSTOOD. In other words, the subjects are motivated volunteer victims
and witnesses who wish to enhance
their memory to help with the case;
they are not there to undergo
psychotherapy.

E. THE TIME SPAN BETWEEN THE
ACTUAL CRIME EVENT AND THE HYPNOSIS
WILL IN MOST CASES BE ONLY A MATTER
OF DAYS OR WEEKS, HENCE GREATLY RE-
DUCING THE INADVERTENT TRIGGERING
OF PAST TRAUMA. Most repressed
psychological or emotional traumas
stem from early life experiences, so, by
merely regressing a victim or witness
back only a few days or weeks, the possibility of stumbling across such an ex-

perience is logically negated. As a safety precaution, however, specific instructions can be given to the subject before the regression to keep this from happening (see "Elicitation of Hypnotic Phenomena" in Chapter 4).

F. WHEN DEALING WITH ACTUAL TRAUMATIZED CRIME VICTIMS OR WITNESSES, DISSOCIATIVE TECHNIQUES ARE USED TO SEPARATE THE SCENE FROM THE TRAUMA SO THE SUBJECT DOES NOT HAVE TO RELIVE IT (see "Elicitation of Hypnotic Phenomena" in Chapter 4).

G. THE BENEFITS TO THE INVESTIGATION THROUGH NEW INFORMATION, AS WELL AS THE BENEFITS EXPERIENCED BY THE TRAUMATIZED VICTIMS THROUGH PROPER SUGGESTIONS, ARE OFTEN OVERLOOKED BY CRITICS. Most rape victims, for example, report feeling much better afterwards. In psychological terms, the experience is usually cathartic or therapeutic in and of itself.

H. IN THE AUTHORS' EXPERIENCE AND THAT OF THE L.A.P.D. HYPNOSIS UNIT, WHICH HAS DONE OVER 460 CASE-RELATED SESSIONS, THERE HAS NOT BEEN A SINGLE INSTANCE OF REPRESSED TRAUMATIC OUTBURSTS OR POSTHYPNOTIC PROBLEMS. In fact, of 180 hypnotized victims and witnesses questioned, 95 percent felt emotional relief after the hypnosis.

Another assumption in this myth is that police officers, by virtue of their lack of medical or psychological training, are not qualified to handle hypnosis. This has been clearly demonstrated a fallacy by the several thousand practicing hypno-investigators in this country. Granted, a police officer's training may not be in the classroom, but his training comes from direct experience from years of daily contact with people and their problems. From the authors' experience, we have found those police officers whom we have trained to be older, more mature and stable, much less naive, more conservative, practical, capable, and sensitive, and profoundly more enthusiastic and interested in the subject than hypnosis classes of graduate students in clinical psychology in doctoral programs.

Myth #4

Hypnosis is potentially dangerous. This myth is closely related to Myth #2 discussed above, the implication being that since it is potentially dangerous, anyone not trained in psychology or psychiatry should not be using it. André Weitzenhoffer, Ph.D., who has had many years of research and clinical practice and who is recognized as one of the leading experts on hypnosis, concludes that "hypnosis per se is no more dangerous than natural sleep. There is no evidence that hypnosis in itself weakens the will, damages the nervous system, or in any other way adversely affects the mental and physical well-being of individuals. The danger lies in its *misuse,*" especially "in the *mismanagement* of the hypnotic subject before, after and, particularly, during hypnosis."[8] Likewise, Lewis Wolberg, M.D., another eminent hypnotherapist, researcher, and author, states, "In competent hands hypnosis has no harmful effects, but where it is utilized to evoke nonsensical and dramatic phenomena by showmen and parlor pranksters, and where symptom removal is attempted without some understanding of the dynamics of the patient's illness, neurotic persons may be influenced adversely."[9] It would be hoped that hypno-investigators will be adequately and competently trained and that they will under no circumstance practice symptom removal or other forms of therapy, nor engage in nonprofessional uses of hypnosis outside of their respective departments.

Wolberg continues to say that he has "induced trances in patients and volunteer subjects virtually hundreds of times, and not in a single instance has any patient become overly dependent on me or has become addicted to the trance state. There is no justification for the fear that a hypnotic subject will remain under the influence of the operator who will be able to wield a Svengali-like power over him."[10] William Kroger, M.D., another well respected authority on hypnosis and hypnotherapy, quotes Platonov to summarize his views regarding the dangers of hypnosis: "Platonov, an associate of Pavlov, who has used hypnosis for over 50 years in over 50,000 cases, reports as follows in one of the most remarkable books written on hypnosis."[11]

We have never observed any harmful influence on the patient which could be ascribed to the method of hypnosuggestive therapy, presumably leading to the development of an "unstable personality," "slavish subordination," weakening of the will, increase in suggestibility, pathological urge for hypnosis, etc.[12]

Two other eminent psychiatrists and authors, Doctors Herbert and David Spiegel, conclude, "In our experience of using hypnosis with thousands of patients, we have had no case of a patient who became psychotic as a result of hypnosis. . . . Surprisingly, we have tested many frankly paranoid patients for hypnotizability with no adverse effect."[13]

Jacob H. Conn, M.D., one of the first Presidents of the Society for Clinical and Experimental Hypnosis, wrote, "In my own practice, over a period of 30 years, which includes the treatment of over 3,000 patients, I have not observed hypnosis 'precipitating a psychiatric illness.' Patients have been reported by others . . . as becoming psychotic *following* hypnosis, but never, in my opinion, *because* of hypnosis."[14] In a critical evaluation of the historical, experimental, and clinical data, Conn concluded that the answer to the question, "Is hypnosis really dangerous," was, in his opinion, an unqualified "No."[15]

A well-known lay hypno-therapist, researcher, and author, Leslie M. LeCron, believes that "it can be safely said,

and all authorities will agree, that hypnosis, in itself, is completely harmless. No bad effects, either mental or physical, from the mere fact of being hypnotized have ever been incurred by anyone."[16]

In spite of the general harmlessness of hypnosis, the authors deem it wise to leave the reader with an admonition from Ernest Hilgard, Ph.D., the Director of Stanford University's Laboratory of Hypnosis, who states, "The general harmlessness of hypnosis does not mean that it is something that should be treated lightly; it is an interpersonal relationship that involves intrusion into privacy and responsibility upon the part of the hypnotist to handle the relationship wisely and maturely."[17]

Myth #5

It takes an advanced degree in psychology or medicine to practice hypnosis. The use of hypnosis in most states is not regulated by law in this regard. A few states, however, have restricted the use of hypnosis to medical and psychological professionals under their Psychology Licensing Acts or Medical Practice Acts. Even so, most of these states permit lay hypnotechnicians to accept referrals and practice hypnosis under the supervision of a licensed doctor. Hypnosis is easy to learn and does not require an M.D. or Ph.D. for the limited purpose and use to which the hypno-investigator puts it. Furthermore, lack of an advanced degree does not diminish a hypnotist's expertise if he is well trained.

Myth #6

It takes years of study to learn hypnosis. The basic art of hypnosis is relatively straightforward and simple to learn, and as such, any layman can learn hypnosis just by reading a book on the subject. A major criticism of most forensic hypnosis courses levelled by many psychological and medical professionals is that they are too short; the reputable courses range from three or four days in length. Although the authors tend to agree with this criticism, believing that most courses fall particularly short in the area of supervised hands-on experience with practice subjects, it should be noted that a sizeable number of psychological and medical professionals themselves were taught hypnosis in three-day seminars. During the period of 1955 to 1961, a group of highly respected authorities, which included, among others, Leslie LeCron and William Kroger, M.D., organized a traveling teaching group that gave what were known as "Hypnosis Seminars," which were chaired by Milton Erickson, M.D. The purpose of the seminar was to make training in hypnosis available to as many physicians, psychologists, and dentists as possible as quickly as possible. Of importance here is the fact that the group "did not believe it essential that its students have intensive background study in basic psychology, psychopathology, or psychodynamics. They held that the average physician, psychologist, or dentist could, with this minimal three-day training, be trusted to use hypnotic techniques in his practice or research in a primarily beneficial way."[18] The authors stress, however, and we are sure that the "Hypnosis Seminars" group would readily agree, that although basic hypnosis is easy to learn, it takes years of study and practice to become an expert.

Myth #7

Hypnosis is practicing medicine or is a form of therapy. This is also not true. Hypnosis is only a tool or modality for many uses, including medicine and psychotherapy, but in itself it is not a form of therapy. As Doctor Hilgard stated in a recent interview, "Hypnosis is just a tool. You're not cured by hypnosis, but by other methods used with it."[19] Similarly, the Spiegels even "avoid the use of the term 'hypnotherapist' because by itself hypnosis is not therapy. . . . It may enhance therapeutic leverage but by itself it is not a treatment."[20] The use of hypnosis to treat physical or psychological problems, however, is regulated by law, which restricts it to licensed doctors.

In conclusion, the authors believe that an informed person, whether a layman or professional in the field, does not have a sound argument against the training of law enforcement officers in hypnosis. The authors draw this conclusion from a unique perspective: we have been on both sides of the fence. Prior to our intimate working relationship with law enforcement, we had some stereotyped characterizations of law enforcement and delusions of overzealous detectives and prosecutors. From personal acquaintants, we know for a fact that some authorities in the field of hypnosis who are ardent opponents share these same delusions. In fact, prior to our exposure to law enforcement, we would just as vehemently opposed and objected to hypnosis being in police hands. Once working directly with law enforcement on special Law Enforcement Assistance Administration crime control projects, however, the authors had these stereotyped characterizations and delusions quickly deflated. Five years of a continued working association has led us to the point of training officers in hypno-investigation with no reservations or regrets. We would ask, based on this personal experience, that critics and detractors do not judge too quickly from the isolation and security of academic and research enclaves. They should first experience law enforcement from the standpoint of the policeman.

It should be quite clear by now that hypnosis is only a tool and is consequently the property of no particular group. A knife in the hands of a surgeon is used to cure, in the hands of a soldier to kill, and in the hands of a cook to peel potatoes. Furthermore, it is in the interest of public safety that law enforcement utilize this safe, efficient, and effective investigative tool in their fight against crime. Ultimately, it is the taxpayer who will benefit.

HISTORICAL SIGNIFICANCE AND PRESENT STATUS OF HYPNOSIS

It is not our purpose here to give a detailed chronological narrative of the history of hypnosis, as the interested student can readily find ample sources on this subject elsewhere. Furthermore, the hypno-investigator will not be expected to have a thorough knowledge of the historical roots of hypnosis. History, however, has much to teach, and the history of hypnosis has some important lessons to give of which the hypno-investigator should be aware.

Those embarking upon the study and practice of forensic hypnosis will knowingly or unknowingly be tapping into an evolutionary struggle several thousands of years old. The history of hypnosis, which is one of the oldest medico-psychological and religious arts, clearly shows that the struggle for its acceptance, oppression, and ownership has often been a violent one. Any who would become involved in the use of hypnosis in whatever form, necessarily will be affected by this ancient history and the familiar course that it has charted. Forensic hypnosis, as a subscience of the broad field of hypnosis, will not be excluded from this struggle.

Since ancient times, hypnosis has been practiced in one form or another and under many different names throughout the world. Throughout its history, hypnosis has generally been closely held and controlled by the aristocracy and religious hierachy. Unauthorized persons employing the skill were often harshly dealt with, even burned at the stake as witches. Do not be fooled into believing that it is much different today in our enlightened and civilized world, for its use is still closely guarded by many professionals who severely criticize those who dare infringe on their territory and utilize their "mysterious" tools.

The people and events that have gone before us differ only by a factor of time and space, form and degree, from the kind of treatment hypno-investigators might expect today. The beliefs that led to persecution and suppression of hypnosis throughout its history are still with us, only the labels have changed.

The history of hypnosis describes a chilling process of overt and covert control. This process ranged from putting the eyes out and drawing and quartering a man for conducting hypnosis-like experiments circa 1468, to official commissions appointed by the King of France which investigated and condemned Franz Anton Mesmer, a Viennese physician and prominent figure in the resurgence of hypnotism, and his theory of "animal magnetism" in 1784 and again in 1837. (Only 15 years prior to the first of these official commissions, which was chaired by Benjamin Franklin, another commission claimed that meteorites did not exist.)

By ascribed authority, those in power are given or assume "blanket expertise" and control over processes that exist freely in nature and are not the property of any specific discipline or group. The pattern is clear; throughout history, those with official credentials have regarded hypnosis as exclusively theirs and so have attempted to insure this right of ownership. In the modern world, this is done first by suppressing its unofficial use by propagating the belief that only the professional elite is qualified to practice it, and later, when this fails, by actual legislation.

It would seem that any method or tool that could aid criminal justice in the performance of its mandate would be welcomed and perfected, but conflict has followed the uneven course of such a method or tool we now call hypnosis. During the preceding centuries, hypnosis and its supporters have periodically enjoyed enthusiastic support and then rigorous persecution. Oftentimes the cultural moods changed drastically in short periods of time. Prior to the King's commission of 1784, as many as 3,000 people a day came to see Mesmer, but, shortly after the commission's verdict, he left France in disgrace.

The historical development of hypnosis has another lesson to teach, which the acceptance and use of hypnosis has predictably followed. This is the familiar cycle of "boom and bust." The first stage of the cycle is one of skepticism, but with time and exposure the opponents "discover" its value and become proponents—the second stage. At the third stage the new proponents wholeheartedly and overenthusiastically embrace hypnosis and see it as their panacea. This eventually leads to a disillusionment when it fails to produce 100 percent all the time, which leads to abandonment—the fourth stage. The lesson to be learned here is to watch for this cycle in your own use of hypnosis. Discover it and use it, but don't abandon it at your first failure. Try to develop a fifth and final stage, that of a healthy balance. It would be wise to remember, as a precautionary note, that hypnosis has been hurt more by the excessive claims of its proponents than by its opponents.

Today, the use of medical hypnosis is approaching the fifth stage with an ever-growing number of universities and medical schools adding it to their curriculum and with the advent of several national societies and journals. According to one survey, over 40 percent of the graduate departments of clinical psychology, 35 percent of medical schools, and 30 per-

cent of dental schools, now offer courses or lectures in hypnosis. This represents a 100 percent increase in the last five years.[21] Professional clinical hypnotists first formally organized in 1949 when The Society for Clinical and Experimental Hypnosis was founded. The Society's present membership is composed primarily of physicians, psychiatrists, psychologists, and dentists, and it publishes a quarterly scientific journal, *The International Journal of Clinical and Experimental Hypnosis.* Another professional society, The American Society of Clinical Hypnosis, was formed in 1957 and currently has members who are primarily physicians, psychiatrists, psychologists, and dentists. The Society publishes a quarterly journal, *The American Journal of Clinical Hypnosis.* Other societies, such as the American Hypnodontic Society, have been formed to appeal to specialized interests and applications of hypnosis.

Forensic hypnosis is clearly entering the second stage—discovery—and has the potential of entering the third stage—overenthusiastic support and claims—which often ends in the fourth stage—abandonment. With its prudent development and management, however, it should find itself in the same theatre as the polygraph, photography, and fingerprinting as heavily relied-upon scientific investigative aids.

Historical Significance and Present Status of Forensic Hypnosis

Even in the absence of consistent gains, there is strong and abundant evidence of the developing and professional use of hypnosis in criminal and civil investigations, as well as its acceptance in the courts. Forensic hypnosis has come a long way from the court's position in 1895 (*People v. Ebanks*) that "The law of the United States does not recognize hypnosis." Appellate courts in recent years allow hypno-induced testimony as evidence, while leaving it to the trier of the fact to decide its weight.

The history of any new scientific investigative tool is inevitably and largely the story of court decisions that regulate its acceptance and use. The story of the use of hypnosis in criminal investigations is probably the most interesting and dramatic as it has suffered so long by its misassociation with occultism, the mysterious, and the mystical. More than any other scientific investigative tool, the legal course that hypnosis has charted has been woefully influenced by the personal prejudices and beliefs of misinformed courts. Some courts have even been outright misled by experts who have colored their testimony in the service of their own biases, erroneous beliefs, or professional goals. As the case analysis in Chapter 6 will clearly show, the spurious rulings of many courts set legal precedent that severely hampered and delayed hypnosis as an accepted investigative tool.

As mentioned in the previous section, forensic hypnosis is clearly entering the second stage of discovery in the boom and bust cycle. As such, it is a fledgling science and is suffering all the growing pains that all sciences inevitably must go through. The predictable pattern for any new science involves three basic phases leading to legitimacy and acceptance. First, any new science is almost automatically regarded by the established order as being illegitimate. Through many years of hard effort and good basic research, however, the fledgling slowly becomes recognized by the established authorities and disciplines. Third, the new science finally wins acceptance and status comparable to that of the established ones. (As Kuhn points out, however, in discussing scientific paradigm shifts, this is usually only after the old guard opponents die off.)[22]

The science of psychology is a perfect example of this process. In the late 1800s and early 1900s, when psychology was first developing, it was largely regarded by the established disciplines of physics, philosophy, theology, and medicine as the domain of crackpots. In spite of hard-nosed opposition, the crackpots continued to perform solid research, develop theories, and produce a body of professional published literature, all while emulating the scientific rigor of their idol — physics. Acceptance was slow, but finally by the mid-1900s the science of psychology was well recognized, although a little begrudgingly, by orthodox medicine and psychiatry. It is interesting to note that the advent of psychoanalysis in the early 1900s with Sigmund Freud paved a similarly rocky road from outright rejection and ridicule to eventual high acceptance and status.

It is important to note that the scorned reactionaries, visionaries, or crackpots of one generation or era become the established authorities of the next. One would think that the cycle discussed above would end at that time, but, ironically, those who went through it themselves make it most difficult for the underlings. It seems that they tend to forget the struggle their own science went through and to subconsciously, once their science gains acceptance and status in the scientific community, go to extremes to protect that cherished position from any possible encroachment. It seems to be a larger version of a phenomenon that most every experienced law enforcement officer is familiar with: the child beater was once a beaten child himself. As psychologists say, "Neurosis is inherited." On a broader historical scale, it is a familiar case of the oppressed turning into the oppressor, a continually reoccurring historical phenomenon, especially in the political history of the world.

Forensic hypnosis has and will continue to suffer from its confrontation with some of the scientific community and established order who have assumed or been ascribed the power to mediate the use of hypnosis. In one sense, this controversy is healthy in that it will foster rigorous experiments, thorough training, careful observation, and cautious application, all which should help lead to a gradual and general acceptance.

Forensic hypnosis will predictably follow a similar course that the use of hypnosis in the healing professions charted. In their struggle for legitimacy, the medico-psychological professionals that utilized hypnosis formed training programs, developed accreditation criteria, established professional organizations, and published newsletters and professional journals. All this while there were many internal frustrations which resulted in the formation of splinter groups, disagreements among themselves, and attacks from outsiders. As stated by Doctor John Watkins, a leading figure in this movement, "only those who could persevere in their programs in spite of isolation and adverse community attitudes could make the contributions and achievements which carried them to top positions of recognition by their associates."[23]

Those involved in the forensic hypnosis movement should heed these words as well as the struggles and experiences of psychology and clinical hypnosis in gaining recognition and acceptance. The ultimate irony is that it is and will continue to be members of the fields of psychology and psychiatry who oppose the development and recognition of forensic hypnosis as a separate science in general, but more specifically when applied by laymen. A further irony is the fact that a sizeable percentage of these were trained by laymen like Harry Arons, Dave Elman, and Leslie LeCron due to the fact that medical schools and graduate schools in psychology by and large had refused to teach it.

It is not just problems, criticism, and pressure from the outside that forensic hypnosis will have to deal with, but internal problems will likely develop as well, which will probably closely parallel those experienced in the medico-psychological realm. Controversies will likely arise over training, certification, education, and standards and guidelines of application and management of hypno-investigations. All this is likely to result in different societies with their respective newsletters or eventual published journals. What is probably unique to forensic hypnosis is that this will all be complicated by attempts at legislating investigative hypnosis and the ultimate impact of appellate court decisions.

In its struggle for recognition and acceptance, there have been some historical milestones in forensic hypnosis. The first officially approved course in hypno-investigation was conducted by Harry Arons and Harold Grey in the Ridgefield, New Jersey, Police Department, in 1962. As early as 1959, Arons was teaching hypnosis to detectives and prosecutors unofficially. The historical beginnings of forensic hypnosis for the lay hypno-investigator can probably legitimately and rightfully be dated at the time of this first official course. During this same year, W. J. Bryan Jr., M.D., J.D., director and founder of The American Institute of Hypnosis in Los Angeles which teaches courses in medical-dental-legal hypnosis, published his book *Legal Aspects of Hypnosis.* Between 1959 and 1967, when Arons published his book, *Hypnosis in Criminal Investigation,* he trained approximately 350 police officers in hypnosis. In 1954, Arons incorporated the Association to Advance Ethical Hypnosis, and in 1967, he incorporated the Ethical Hypnosis Training Center which offers a forensic course approved by the International Association for Forensic Hypnosis which was incorporated in 1979.

Probably the next most notable advance in forensic hypnosis for the lay hypno-investigator came in 1975 and 1976, when the L.A.P.D. developed, implemented, and evaluated a hypno-investigation program in which fifteen officers were trained. Doctor Martin Reiser, the Director of the Behavioral Science Services of the L.A.P.D. and the director of the hypno-investigation program, was so encouraged by the results that he founded the Law Enforcement Hypnosis Institute to train criminal justice personnel throughout the country. This course is also approved by the International Association for Forensic Hypnosis. As of this writing, over 700 criminal justice personnel from forty-two states and Canada have been trained. In 1976, hypno-investigators from the L.A.P.D. founded The Society for Investigative and Forensic Hypnosis complete with a Constitution, Board of Directors, Code of Ethics, minimum membership qualifications, and Standards and Principles of Practice that govern and regulate the members. The main objective and purpose of the Society is to further professional training and utilization of investigative hypnosis.

It is illuminating to review a statement by Harry Arons when he wrote his book, *Hypnosis in Criminal Investigation*, in 1967.

At this writing, hypnosis is at the crossroads. Whether or not its use in criminal investigation will become an accepted fact depends largely upon which road it will take. One road will lead to gradual restriction and eventual extinction. This road has been chosen by two small groups of physicians, dentists and psychologists who have been instigating restrictive legislation in a number of states. These groups have attempted to convince the legislators that only members of these three disciplines are qualified to use hypnosis.[24]

Recent legislative attempts to curb its use by police officers have failed, which indicates that the use of investigative hyp-

nosis has taken the correct road toward becoming an accepted and legitimate tool. In 1977, the American Civil Liberties Union in Oregon became alarmed at the growing use of hypnosis by police officers and introduced a bill in the legislature to severely limit and control its use. The bill would have outlawed the use of hypnosis by unsupervised police officers and would have placed numerous restrictions on when and how it could be used even under supervision. After much debate and expert testimony, an amended version of the original passed, but with only one remaining restriction—all hypnosis sessions must be videotaped or mechanically recorded.[25]

Similarly, in 1979, California Senate Bill 706 was introduced, which would have outlawed the use of hypnosis by anyone other than licensed medical doctors, psychologists, dentists, and marriage counselors. Intense pressure from various lobbies had police officers and other social service and health professionals excluded. As of this writing, the bill is tabled in committee, but could surface every legislative session until passed.

Opponents of hypno-investigation have also tried to get the courts to regulate the use of hypnosis in criminal cases. One of the most organized recent attempts was an appeal to the California Supreme Court in 1977 of the *People v. Quaglino* conviction, in which the defendant was convicted largely on testimony from the hypnotically refreshed memory of a witness. The defense attorneys, backed by the California Attorneys for Criminal Justice as well as by Doctor Martin Orne and Doctor Ernest Hilgard, two world-renowned authorities on hypnosis, asked the state supreme court to limit the use of hypnosis in criminal investigations. They wanted the technique to only be used under court order with medical supervision and videotaping.[26] The California Supreme Court refused to hear the case as did the United States Supreme Court, which denied certiorari on a later petition.

Professional hypnosis organizations have also objected to the training of lay hypno-investigators as evidenced by the resolution passed by The Society for Clinical and Experimental Hypnosis in October 1978. The Society, besides pointing out a legitimate concern of relying on uncorroborated hypno-induced testimony, recommended that hypno-investigations only be conducted by "trained psychiatrists or psychologists with experience in the forensic use of hypnosis." The Society also stated that it was considered unethical to train, collaborate with, or serve as a consultant to "laymen who are utilizing hypnosis."[27]

In a classic characterization of attempts to regulate the use of hypnosis, Former Judge Dewey Kelley of the Indiana Appellate Court stated in his Foreword to *Hypnosis in Criminal Investigation* —

... many of the so-called experts are members of the medical community who unwarrantedly assert that they are the only ones capable of utilizing and practicing the hypnotic art. In fact, the medical fraternity for centuries refused to admit the wonderful potentialities of hypnosis although, historically, it was successfully used and applied by many others, including religious leaders, psychologists, doctors, dentists, and even laymen. During the last score of years, when the economic possibilities of hypnosis became apparent, there has been a nationwide medical project to corner the practice of hypnotism, not for just therapeutic and medical proclivity, but for all purposes. In this effort they have sought to make it appear that hypnosis is a very dangerous thing and is a bizarre condition which they, alone, are competent to understand and safely handle. All of this, of course, belies the accurate and impartial history of hypnosis.

To any fair minded, qualified, and logical observer, it seems ridiculous to note how hypnosis is pictured, when applied to or practiced by anyone other than a member of the medical association, as similar to the fictional evil wielded by Svengali over Trilby, but, when practiced or utilized by the medical member, hypnosis becomes an agency of great human facility. No one can or may reasonably doubt that the use or application of the techniques leading to the hypnotic state for medical or therapeutic purposes should be restricted to those trained in and authorized to practice medicine. But to say that those so trained are the only ones who should be authorized to practice in the broad field of hypnotism is a demonstrated fallacy. . . .

Attempts to define hypnosis as anything but a suggestible state of normal human beings are doomed to failure. For this reason, it defies captivity by special interests or for special purposes. Efforts by legislation to confine the non-therapeutic aspects of hypnotism to exclusive groups are certain to encounter considerable legal entanglements. Chief among these is the self-evident fact that the indefinable natural mental state of an individual, known as hypnosis, cannot be defined, banned, or controlled by law.*

This position is shared by practicing hypno-investigators in the field. Sergeant Charles Diggett, an experienced hypnotist with the N.Y.P.D., stated the following in a recent interview in reference to some major New York cases in which he utilized hypnosis:

Most of the witnesses in these cases had no reticence about being hypnotized by us. In fact, some of them even volunteered before we ever approached them with the idea. The opposition doesn't come from them. It comes from doctors and psychiatrists who want to control hypnosis, and civil libertarians who don't know anything about it.[28]

Similarly, Doctor Reiser argues that the detractors of police officers being trained in hypnosis are "a small handful of psychiatrists and psychologists who feel that hypnosis should be lim-

---

* From Harry Arons, *Hypnosis in Criminal Investigation,* 1977. Courtesy of Power Publishers, Inc., South Orange, New Jersey.

ited to professionals. But their domain is *therapy,* and this is investigation, which is the domain of the investigator."[29] The present-day police officer, who is many times more educated and highly trained than his predecessors were, is a professional in his own area of competence, just as the psychologist or psychiatrist is a professional in his. The authors suggest that the police officer trained as a hypno-investigator is not a layman at all, but is a professional utilizing a tool in the service of his profession.

Forensic hypnosis is currently experiencing a rapid development and broadening application that should continue commensurate with the interest. With continued exposure and inevitable reports of substantial suc-cess, interest will grow even more, creating an ascending spiral of discovery and application.

As a precautionary note, however, it is likely that its continued growth and acceptance in the criminal justice arena will create an ever increasing encroachment and threat to certain established authorities and disciplines. As discussed above, their natural tendency will be to resist until they eventually capitulate and give in to a sound and properly developed new science. Hypno-investigators in any state would be wise to keep a vigilant watch over every legislative session and be able to counter any attempts at regulation with sufficient and competent expert testimony.

REFERENCES

1. Dellinger, R. W.: Special report: investigative hypnosis. *Human Behavior,* April 1978, p. 36.
2. L.A.P.D. Hypnosis Survey, 1975 thru September 1979. Compiled 11-7-79.
3. Hypnotic detectives: now more fact than fiction. *U.S. News & World Report, 85(13):*75, 1978.
4. Monrose, Renee: Justice with glazed eyes: the growing use of hypnotism in law enforcement. *Juris Doctor, 8(8):* 55, 1978.
5. Council on Mental Health: Medical use of hypnosis. *American Medical Association Journal, 168(2):*187, 1958.
6. Arons, Harry: *Hypnosis in Criminal Investigation.* South Orange, Power, 1977, p. 10.
7. Society for Clinical and Experimental Hypnosis, Executive Council: Resolution. Proposed by Martin T. Orne, approved October 19, 1978.
8. Weitzenhoffer, André M.: *General Techniques of Hypnotism.* New York, Grune & Stratton, 1957, pp. 4, 354-355.
9. Wolberg, Lewis R.: *Medical Hypnosis: The Principles of Hypnotherapy, vol. I.* New York, Grune & Stratton, 1948, pp. 415-416.
10. Ibid., p. 417.
11. Kroger, William S.: *Clinical and Experimental Hypnosis.* Philadelphia, Lippincott, 1963, p. 97.
12. Platonov, K.: *The Word: As a Physiological and Therapeutic Factor.* Moscow, Foreign Languages Publishing House, 1959. [Quoted in Kroger, William S.: *Clinical and Experimental Hypnosis.* Lippincott, 1963.]
13. Spiegel, Herbert and Spiegel, David: *Trance and Treatment: Clinical Uses of Hypnosis.* New York, Basic, 1978, p. 19.
14. Conn, Jacob H.: Is hypnosis really dangerous? *International Journal of Clinical and Experimental Hypnosis, 20:*70, 1972.
15. Ibid., p. 76.
16. LeCron, Leslie M. (Ed.): *Experimental Hypnosis,* 2nd ed. New York, Citadel, 1968, p. 370.
17. Hilgard, Ernest R.: *Hypnotic Susceptibility.* New York, Harcourt, Brace & World, 1965, p. 56.
18. Watkins, John G.: Hypnosis in the United States. In Marcuse, F. L. (Ed.): *Hypnosis Throughout the World.* Springfield, Thomas, 1964, p. 291.
19. Kagan, Julia: Healing through hypnosis. *McCalls, 106(7):*51, 1979.

20. Spiegel and Spiegel, p. 20.
21. Kagan, p. 51.
22. Kuhn, Thomas: *The Structure of Scientific Revolutions.* Chicago, University of Chicago Press, 1962.
23. Watkins, p. 289.
24. Arons, p. xx.
25. Oregon Legislative Assembly, 1977 Regular Session: House Bill 3125, Chapter 540.
26. Dellinger, p. 37.
27. Society for Clinical and Experimental Hypnosis, Executive Council: Resolution. Proposed by Martin T. Orne, approved October 19, 1978.
28. Monrose, p. 56.
29. Wilson, Rob: Hypnosis: investigating the subconscious. *Police Magazine,* January, 1979, p. 19.

Chapter 2

ORIENTATION TO HYPNOSIS AND HYPNO-INVESTIGATION

Introduction

As a HYPNO-INVESTIGATOR, you are called in to assist on a case in which the rape victim, who is partially amnesic of the experience and cannot adequately describe her assailant, has volunteered to undergo hypnosis. You make the victim as comfortable as possible physically and you put her at ease mentally and emotionally. You proceed to explain the phenomenon and experience of hypnosis and clear up any questions or misconceptions she may have. At this point, you ask her to direct her gaze and attention to her left hand and continue giving the appropriate graded suggestions as the hand floats up to and finally touches her face, putting her into a hypnotic trance. You continue by intermittently testing for trance depth and further deepening the trance by the appropriate techniques. When sufficiently deep, you give the subject a set of carefully worded instructions that regress her to the actual crime event. This enables her to accurately describe in minute detail everything that she saw and experienced, right down to the color of eyes, the crooked front teeth, and the class ring on the finger of her assailant. Once satisfied that she has described everything of possible importance, you reverse the regression procedure and bring her back to the present time, date, and location, and then awaken her. The time elapsed is one hour. The information provided leads to the identification of the suspect who the victim later picks out of a police line-up.

This is all very interesting and worthwhile, but what did the hypno-investigator do and how do you explain it theoretically? The next three chapters of this book will answer this question. To be a good hypno-investigator, one must first have a basic understanding and knowledge of the phenomenon of hypnosis. An effective hypnotist is much more than a mere technician who recites memorized formulas. Hypnosis is as much an art and a skill as it is a science, and it demands a flexibility and confidence that is developed only through understanding and experience. Experience comes with practice and illuminates and increases ones understanding. As such, experience is beyond the capability of this book. What this book can establish is the foundation of basic knowledge and understanding upon which experience rests. It is up to the reader to put into practice this foundation of knowledge and to build his own experiential base.

The purpose of Chapter 2 is to begin to lay this necessary foundation of basic knowledge for the actual mechanics and practice of hypnosis to come in Chapter 4. To this end, this chapter will discuss, among other things, the nature of hypnosis and suggestion, misconceptions and the hypnotic experience, who can be hypnotized, who cannot as well as should not be hypnotized, and practical psychodynamics and nonverbal behavior for the hypno-investigator.

THE NATURE OF HYPNOSIS: A DEFINITION/THEORY

Throughout your career as a hypno-investigator you will always be confronted with the question "What is hypnosis?" Out of sheer frustration you will probably memorize a convenient definition to tell, and hopefully satisfy, the questioner. In spite of its ancient history, the exhaustive research, the hundreds of books written, and thousands of subjects hypnotized, the true nature of hypnosis remains a mystery.

It is not the authors' intention to thoroughly review the major definitions and theories of hypnosis and to discuss the relative merits of each. This has been done exhaustively in some scholarly works. However, a brief review of the major definitions and theories is included in Appendices 2 and 3, respectively. Even though the hypno-investigator will not be expected to have a thorough grasp of the many definitions and theories of hypnosis, he nevertheless must have a basic conceptual understanding of what hypnosis is and how it is possible. Without a reasonable explanation or theory of hypnosis, the hypno-investigator is left without a satisfactory guiding principle in his task of inducing, maintaining, and managing hypnosis in his subjects. To this end, the authors will attempt to develop an understandable and practical definition/theory of hypnosis.

This is a difficult task since research has shown that none of the present theories of hypnosis can account for and adequately explain all the phenomena of hypnosis (see Appendix 3 for an explanation of the weaknesses of each major theory). From a practical standpoint, it is relatively unimportant whether hypnosis and the associated hypnotic phenomena, as the major theories maintain, are the result of a conditioned cortical inhibition, a state of hypersuggestibility, a regression to a child-parent relationship, a goal-directed striving, role-playing, dissociation, an interpersonal relationship, a regression to a primitive mode of mental functioning, an altered state of consciousness, an ideo-motor reaction, a manipulation of ego cathexis, or any

other theoretical explanation. Whatever the explanation, the experts agree on one thing — hypnosis works. For the busy hypno-investigator who is primarily interested in results, this is much more important than *why* it works. The fact that neither the electrical engineer, nor the physicist for that matter, knows exactly why electricity works does not prevent him from using it in his work. However, a general understanding of its nature and principles will ensure that he uses it properly. Since the true nature of hypnosis is yet to be theoretically explained and empirically proven, the hypno-investigator, as a practical man, must use it anyway and explain it in a functional way that makes sense to him. Just as Mesmer's theory of "animal magnetism" was formally discredited by official scientific commissions, "his followers carried on, recognizing that the phenomena were there, regardless of the falsity of the theory."[1] Each theory, regardless of its validity, will continue to have its ardent proponents who will conduct research and seek clinical experiences in such a fashion as to prove their respective positions, while disproving those of their opponents.[2]

The solution is not one of either/or, but all/and. Hypnosis is such a complex and multifaceted phenomenon that each theory is partially correct, as it explains a particular aspect or aspects of it. The reader is encouraged to review each of these basic theories in Appendix 3. This will undoubtedly add to his general knowledge and understanding of hypnosis and will give him an appreciation for the complexity of the phenomenon.

The task before us is to adequately explain what hypnosis is and how it works, so that the hypno-investigator will understand the logic of the principles of suggestion and hypnotic inductions. To begin the discussion, the authors will relate the hypnotic experience to some everyday personal experiences, as most experts will readily agree that the hypnotic state is largely an ex-aggeration of some common experiences and states of mind.

We have all experienced those moments when we are so involved in something of interest that we quite naturally ignore and tune out everything else, even to the point of not hearing someone call our name or not feeling the cold or pangs of hunger. When reading a good book or watching an exciting movie, how often have you identified with the hero to the point that you actually felt and experienced his triumphs and sorrows? Turn around and look at the blank stares the next time you are at a good movie. Similarly, we have all become so immersed in a thought or daydream when driving down the highway that we were not consciously aware of the scenery or of even driving, yet we successfully negotiated the road. Think for a moment of the selective awareness of parents who can sleep through a thunderstorm, but awaken at the sound of a muffled cry from their baby in the next room. Isn't it also interesting how you can be listening intently to someone while you are simultaneously forming your reply as well as thinking of a dozen other things and watching the passersby? We have all experienced the vivid recall of a long forgotten experience triggered by hearing an old song. We have all experienced unexplained lapses of memory, even momentarily forgetting our own or a friend's phone number. Have you ever appeared to be attentively listening to someone, yet you didn't hear a word? Did you, or anyone you know, ever walk in his sleep as a child? Did you have an imaginary childhood playmate? Were you ever surprised to have your spouse tell you in the morning that you were talking in your sleep? How many times have you awakened from sleep in a sweat, relieved to find that the nightmare was only a dream after all? Isn't it interest-

ing how dreams only seconds in duration can seem like hours? Have you ever wondered how you can awaken only seconds before the alarm goes off? How often have you been so totally immersed in a daydream of some bygone event that it was as if you were actually there? Most people, at one time or another, have cut or injured themselves, but were completely unaware of it, as they were so involved in what they were doing, until they later noticed the blood. Similarly, think of how easy it is to distract a hurt child with a toy until the crying stops and the pain is forgotten.

These everyday experiences and slips of awareness illustrate that man's consciousness is not the well integrated whole under his conscious control and direction that we erroneously assume. In fact, all that is known about the human mind and experience illustrates that this is far from the case. In a unique series of experiments utilizing hypnosis to study the nature of consciousness, Hilgard concludes that there are actually multiple levels of control in the human organism and that "the unity of consciousness is illusory."[3] Watkins arrived at a similar conclusion when he discovered, through years of hypnotherapy with clients, that most people's personalities are actually clusters of centers of thought and control (ego states) that may or may not be aware of each other. These ego states and their subconscious interaction largely determine a person's behavior.[4]

The above examples of naturally occurring fluctuations and alterations of human consciousness and experience are but shadows or brief glimpses of experiences on a more impressive scale. Modern science has studied individuals who, in the waking state, can consciously control what would normally produce intense pain and bleeding and who can also control infection and the rate of healing.[5] There are many well-documented cases of spontaneous remissions of cancer in terminally ill patients given only weeks or months to live. Thousands of diseased and crippled people have walked away healed from sacred shrines such as Lourdes. Another psychologically baffling phenomenon is the astounding mental feats performed by a small percentage of autistic children known as *autistic savants*. These children, characteristically noncommunicative and schizophrenic, when asked seemingly impossible questions will respond immediately with the correct answers. For example, when a boy of eight, who stares blankly into space without seeing anything, is asked how much is 6,427 times 4,234, he instantaneously gives the correct reply of 27,211,918. Or a giggly girl of thirteen, when asked what months during 1998 will the seventh be on a Wednesday, immediately responds with the correct answer of January and October.[6]

Similar mental feats have been studied and reported with normal functioning adults. In Russia, a newspaper reporter by the name of Solomon-Veniaminovich Sheresheveskii was studied from 1920 to 1950 by the Russian neurologist, A. R. Luria. Sheresheveskii has the unique ability to easily recall everything that has ever been said to him from the time that he was an infant. Russell summarizes Luria's studies with Sheresheveskii, called "S" for short, in the following manner:

Luria tested him in a number of ways, giving him lists of numbers, nonsense syllables, words, passages of foreign languages, and complex mathematical formula to remember. He found no difference in the ability of "S" to remember, whatever the material. Luria worked up from short lists of twenty to fifty items to lists containing hundreds of items, and found that "S" still continued to remember everything perfectly.

Not only was there no apparent limit to the capacity of his memory, there was no apparent limit to its durability. Luria would sometimes ask "S" to recall lists that he had tested him with fifteen to twenty years earlier.[7]

Needless to say, "S" could recall them in their entirety without error.

Another Russian, Mikhail Keuni, an artist, can perform mathematical calculations with forty-digit numbers faster than a computer.[8]

Looking to other cultures, there are such well-known scientifically studied and documented feats as firewalking in Ceylon. Faithful Hindus slowly walk barefooted and unharmed the length of a 20 by 6 foot charcoal bed with a surface temperature of 1328 degrees Fahrenheit. When asked what their secret is, the Hindus respond that it is total faith and belief.[9]

All this is to demonstrate that human potential is much greater than we normally believe it to be. In fact, psychologists generally agree that most people use less than 10 percent of their mental capacity, but serious researchers in the field believe that most people have a dramatic potential to self-regulate. The obvious question becomes, "Why don't they?" The answer seemingly is that people do not believe that they can, therefore they can't. In effect, man's experience is dictated and controlled by his belief system, as these beliefs place artificial limits upon his abilities. The four minute mile was long believed to be impossible until it was actually done. Once broken, many runners quickly followed suit. In the province of the mind, hypnosis is the means of breaking the conceptual four minute mile.

The point of this discussion is to demonstrate that man possesses multiple levels of control and has the potential for vastly different and creative experiences that are there for his asking, were it not for his self-limiting belief system. The problem, then, becomes one of relaxing or distracting one's belief system and temporarily suspending normal patterns of logical control and self-direction. This allows individuals to experience and accomplish things that are within their behavioral repertoire, but usually not available to voluntary control. The essential task is to free the person from his limiting belief system so that natural and pre-existing mental processes and mechanisms that normally lie outside a person's conscious range of control and experience can be evoked. These abilities and potentials reside in the domain of the subconscious and can be readily produced or elicited, provided the conscious mind does not interfere. "The wonder and fascination of hypnosis is that it enables us to control those responses that are usually mediated by unconscious mechanisms outside the normal range of consciousness."[10]

The task of the operator, then, is to sufficiently dissociate the subject's conscious mind, so that he can gain direct access to the person's subconscious and other levels of control without conscious interference and mediation. Hence, we arrive at a definition/theory of hypnosis:

> Hypnosis is a controlled dissociated state in which the conscious, critical, intellectual, and logical portion of one's mind is dissociated, inhibited, misdirected, or distracted, allowing for direct access to one's subconscious, thereby making the elicitation of natural and pre-existing subconscious mental mechanisms possible.

The primary means by which a hypnotic subject is led into this state is by the process of suggestion, which is generally recognized as the main psychological mechanism involved in the induction of hypnosis. We now turn to a discussion of the nature of suggestion.

THE NATURE OF SUGGESTION

The process of suggestion is so central and crucial to the induction of hypnosis that it is often used synonomously, and in fact, the trance state itself depends upon responsiveness to suggestion. In other words, in traditional hypnotic techniques, a subject must respond favorably to suggestions in order to be hypnotized.*

The word *suggestion* is commonly defined as an idea offered to another, either verbally or nonverbally, for uncritical acceptance. Meares states that "an idea may be accepted into the mind by either of two processes. On the one hand is the logical, intellectual process by which an idea is evaluated in a critical way and is accepted or rejected according to its merits. On the other hand is suggestion, the essential feature of which is that the idea is accepted in an uncritical way, not according to its logical merits."[11] In other words, a suggestion is phrased in such a nature, is of such a content, and is given in such a manner that it is accepted and acted upon by the recipient below his level of conscious awareness. In essence, he acts without thinking. Weitzenhoffer states,

An especially important characteristic of suggestion is that the response it elicits is nonvoluntary. The subject *never initiates* the suggested act; the act is *nonvoluntary* in its initiation; it never involves the conscious, active, volitional participation of the subject. ... The first action in any suggested behavior sequence is never conscious. ... It need not be one that the subject cannot appraise or could not control if he wanted to, ... but it is an act in which *he is a passive participant.* This is why we speak here of "nonvoluntary" and not "involuntary" behavior.[12]

---

* Milton Erickson, M.D., has developed induction techniques utilizing means other than direct suggestion to induce hypnosis. The predominant and most easily understood and mastered method, however, is that of suggestion.

It is this "nonvoluntary" quality of suggestion that differentiates it from persuasion, instructions, requests, commands, and orders. Whereas a response to persuasion, instructions, requests, commands, or orders is consciously evaluated, accepted, or rejected according to its logical merits and carried out volitionally, a response to a suggestion is not consciously evaluated, is accepted uncritically, and is essentially carried out automatically or without thought.

Perhaps some examples from the theoretical history of hypnosis will help to elucidate this process. Meares, in discussing Mesmer's almost ridiculous theory of animal magnetism, which was largely subscribed to by the flamboyant society of pre-revolution France, points out that it nonetheless has an important lesson to teach regarding the nature of suggestion:

It shows us that the act of making a pass with the hands carries with it very powerful suggestion. More than this, it serves to alert us to the very important fact that the non-verbal communication of suggestion is often more effective than the statement of the same idea in words. Furthermore, from a study of the way in which Mesmer treated his patients we come to realize that the hypnotized subject to a great extent behaves in the way in which he believes that a hypnotized subject does behave. Thus Mesmer's patients believed that the animal magnetism would throw them into a convulsion; so when they took hold of the handles of his famous baquet which they believed contained specially magnetized iron, they felt the animal magnetism working on them, and they were in fact thrown into a convulsion.[13]

In the same vein, Charcot, another early leading French hypnotist and famous psychiatrist, was seen by his patients to "rub the tops of his subjects' heads and the subjects immediately went into somnambulism. The patients, in turn, expected the same to occur to them, and thus by indirect sug-

gestion the same result was realized."[14]

In the middle of the nineteenth century, phrenology — the unfounded science of character and faculty analysis by means of studying the shape and protuberances of the skull — became so popular that it overshadowed hypnosis. People of the time believed in it so strongly that when certain protuberances representing specific faculties were pressed on hypnotized subjects, they would immediately display that faculty. For example, when Sir James Braid, an English physician and surgeon and prominent figure in the history of hypnosis, gave demonstrations with hypnotized subjects, he would apply pressure to the phrenological protuberance allegedly responsible for "veneration," the subject would immediately sink to his knees in prayer![15]

The significance of these historical anecdotes lies in their demonstration that the acceptance of a suggestion depends primarily upon belief. In fact, Gibbons states that the principle of suggestion is "presenting an idea in such a manner that it is perceived as literally true and therefore 'real.' If the suggestion is effective, you respond to it in the same way that you respond to any other aspect of the reality which you perceive. . . . "[16] Mesmer's magnetic passes, first done with magnetized iron bars and later with just his hands, Charcot's rubbing of patients' heads, and Braid's phrenology served as very powerful suggestions because they caused those who believed and accepted them to behave as though they were true.

Present day dramatic proof of the power of suggestion, as well as of the built-in subconscious creative mechanisms and potential for self-regulation spoken about previously, are demonstrated in medical studies done on the placebo effect. A *placebo* is a nonactive drug, usually a milk-and-sugar tablet disguised to look like an authentic pill, that is generally given to a patient with a psychosomatic ailment for its psychological effect. In a review of the placebo effect, Cousins has summarized some dramatic findings. In one study, it was shown that the placebo was 77 percent as effective as morphine in relieving postoperative wound pain. Interestingly enough, it was also discovered that the more severe the pain, the more effective the placebo. In another study, placebos proved to be equally as effective as aspirin and cortisone when administered to a group of eighty-eight arthritic patients. Not only was pain relieved, but some experienced improvement in eating, sleeping, elimination, and even reduction in swelling. Morphine addicts, who have been given saline injections as placebos, do not suffer withdrawal symptoms until the injections are stopped. A group of medical students were given what they were told to be stimulants and depressants, which were actually placebos. More than half the students exhibited specific psychological reactions to the placebos. For example, the pulse rate fell in 66 percent of the subjects and a decrease in arterial pressure was observed in 71 percent. Others experienced adverse side effects of dizziness, abdominal distress, and watery eyes. A patient with Parkinson's disease who was administered a placebo, but was told that it was a drug, experienced a marked decrease in tremors. Placebos have been shown to have profound effects on other organic illnesses, including incurable malignancies and rheumatoid and degenerative arthritis. Warts have spontaneously remitted after the administration of a placebo, and blood chemistry has also been dramatically affected. On the other hand, placebos have also been known to have serious toxic effects and produce physiological damage. In one case in which a placebo, believed to be the drug mephenesin, was given to subjects, one person collapsed in anaphylactic shock, and others exhibited such adverse reactions as nausea, dizziness, and palpitation, which are common side effects of mephenesin.[17]

As part of a larger study, eight Japanese high school students who were highly sensitive to a poisonous plant similar to poison oak, were simply told with eyes closed that they were being touched by the poisonous leaves. In actuality, they were touched by leaves from a harmless tree. All eight students developed some degree of the familiar poison oak-type inflammation. The same students were touched on the other arm by the poisonous leaves while being told the leaves were from a harmless plant. Seven of the eight students did not develop any inflammation on that arm.[18]

Kroger summarizes the placebo effect by stating that "the effect of placebos can be very powerful and often permanently modifies physiological functioning. These effects are not superficial or transient."[19] When examining these phenomena, one must reflect on the statement by Paracelsus, a famous sixteenth century German physician/mystic: "Whether the object of your faith is real or false, you will nevertheless obtain the same effects." Dramatic proof of this is the exposé of Margot, a famous evangelist. Throughout his career as a young evangelist, Margot performed many hundreds if not thousands of seemingly miraculous faith healings, yet one day he exposed himself as a complete fraud.

The positive response of a person to a placebo depends upon strong explicit and implicit suggestions coupled with the confident belief and anticipation of success. The authors, however, do not mean to give the impression that hypnosis is solely a placebo response, even though there is undoubtedly a great deal of placebo response in hypnosis. In fact, a study on the comparison of placebo-induced analgesia with hypnotically-induced analgesia indicated that the latter was superior.[20] Additional evidence of the differing nature of placebo response and hypnosis is the common experience of hypnotic subjects who do not believe in hypnosis and expect it to fail, yet who prove to be highly susceptible. Furthermore, whereas a placebo will never work if the patient knows it to be a placebo, this is not true for hypnosis. The authors have found that their students' increasing knowledge of the nature and principles of hypnosis and suggestion in no way hindered their hypnotic ability, i.e. those who were excellent hypnotic subjects remained so. In fact, one of the authors of this book is an excellent subject. Placebo response and hypnosis are further differentiated by the fact that "careful studies have failed to find any relationship between suggestibility, gullibility and sensitivity to placebo."[21]

What the placebo studies demonstrate is the reality and power of properly constructed and conveyed suggestions given under the proper conditions in the appropriate setting. The above studies give dramatic proof of the power of belief and the ability of the proper suggestions to create this belief. In this sense, the effectiveness of hypnosis "lies in its ability to influence how people interpret what they perceive, and therefore influence what they experience."[22] The role of suggestion is to create the belief in the subject that he is undergoing hypnosis and at some point is hypnotized. In this sense, "the power of hypnosis is the power of belief! Thus, hypnosis is merely a catalytic agent through which conviction phenomena can be established."[23] The experience of hypnosis, then, is largely dependent upon what people believe it to be and the way in which the culture and, more specifically, the hypnotist define it to the subject. This was convincingly illustrated by Orne in an experiment in which it was demonstrated to an introductory psychology class that hypnotized people cannot move their dominant hand, although this is just as untrue as people convulsing under hypnosis like Mesmer's patients. When members of this class were later hypnotized, the majority of them, with no further suggestions, could not move their dominant hand.[24]

In another study by Sarbin, subjects were asked to write down what they believed happened under hypnosis. They were subsequently hypnotized, and their experiences were then compared with their written expectations. The results indicated that each subject's hypnotic experience was closely linked with his expectations. For example, one subject took two inductions to be hypnotized. A look at his paper showed he had written, "Most people cannot be hypnotized the first time." Another subject could not follow hypnotic suggestions when standing. She had written, "The subject has to be reclining or sitting."[25]

On the basis of these and other studies, Orne concludes that hypnosis is largely an artifact of implicit and explicit "demand characteristics" of the hypnotic situation and relationship. However, he does not challenge the "genuineness of hypnosis or the subjective reality of the hypnotized individual's experiences."[26] Sarbin maintains that hypnotic behavior depends upon "favorable motivation, a perception of the role, and role-taking aptitude."[27] Individual susceptibility to hypnosis, as conceptualized by Sarbin, depends upon the degree to which a person can lose himself in the role that the hypnotist suggests; it is not merely voluntary cooperation or sham behavior, however.

The above studies show that subjects' hypnotic experiences are largely determined by demand characteristics and the way in which their role is defined to them, or how they believe their role to be. The problem is compounded, however, by experiences of subjects that are completely spontaneous and not a product of demand characteristics, role requirements, or beliefs and expectations. Very often, for example, even though the operator suggests heaviness and drowsiness during an induction, subjects will report completely different feelings, such as a light, floaty, alert feeling. Also, when asked what they experienced versus their expectations, hypnotic subjects will usually respond that they were totally wrong in their expectations. For example, the following responses to an interview question presented by the authors to experienced subjects are very typical:

• "I was very wrong in what did happen versus what I expected."

• "I think it was quite the opposite of what I expected."

Perhaps an even more enlightening and convincing, but often overlooked experience is that of hypnotized children as young as three years of age. These children will manifest all the phenomena normally associated with hypnosis even though they had never been exposed to it in any way, and did not even know what the word meant. These experiences seem to be indicative of an aspect or special quality of hypnosis as an independent state of mind and awareness.

Although there is quite often a great deal of influence by demand characteristics and role requirements, hypnotic subjects are not actively, purposefully, and willfully *trying* to behave in accordance with demand characteristics, role requirements, or even direct suggestions. "Suggested events are experienced as *happening to them* in ways that would require active effort to resist. Somehow, an altered state of consciousness helps to create this effortless involvement in the suggested state of affairs."[28]

The point to be made is that demand characteristics, role requirements, placebo-response, beliefs and expectations (all of which are subtle and implicit suggestions anyway), and direct suggestions, all converge on a subject's

thinking, perception, and experience in the induction process, until at some point he actually enters a hypnotic state. This state is characterized by a general reality reorientation in which the subject experiences himself as responding to the hypnotist's suggestions in a seemingly autonomous or automatic manner beyond his voluntary control. In essence, a hypnotic subject's consciousness becomes dissociated from its normal orientation so that his perceived and experiential world changes. At this point, suggestions take on a reality of their own, which lends proof to the subject that an altered state of consciousness has been produced. Furthermore, once reaching this point, hypnotic phenomena can be elicited or occur spontaneously for which demand characteristics, role requirements, placebo-response, beliefs and expectations, and direct suggestions can neither singly nor jointly account.

Factors Influencing Suggestion

Since the process of suggestion is so crucial to the induction of hypnosis, it is important to have a thorough understanding of it. To facilitate this, the authors have broken down the process of suggestion into the essential factors which determine its effectiveness. It is important to realize, however, that an effective suggestion depends upon the total impact of the combined factors, as the process of suggestion is a complex ongoing process involving an entire pattern of interaction between subject, hypnotist, and environment.

1. SETTING. The setting prepares the subject to receive the suggestion. Insure that the setting is quiet, professional, and secure from interruption. (Details of setting are discussed in "The Hypno-Investigation Room.")

2. AFFECTIVE RELATIONSHIP AND RAPPORT. The quality of the affective relationship and the degree of rapport established between hypnotist and subject are important factors in the accept-

ance of suggestions. This can be observed in our daily lives in which we tend to accept ideas from friends and loved ones uncritically while we may reject the same ideas from someone we do not know or of whom we are suspicious. Furthermore, the degree of faith and confidence engendered by the affective relationship and rapport will greatly affect the acceptance of suggestions.

3. PRESTIGE. The greater one's prestige, the more readily a subject will accept suggestions from him. Prestige, by indirect ways, creates an atmosphere of confidence and a subconscious desire on the part of the subject to meet the demands and expectations of the person in the prestige position. Persons of authority and high professional standing make very powerful suggestors. For example, we have all experienced ourselves following every directive of our doctor obediently and without question. In the same vein, the chief or sheriff may be a more powerful suggestor than a patrolman. In any case, one should try to maximize his prestige by his personal confidence, demeanor, vocal expression, etc. A hypno-investigator's prestige can be greatly enhanced in the eyes of a victim or witness if the referring investigator boasts of his reputation and great success with other victims and witnesses.

4. CONFIDENCE. According to Meares, "a suggestion may be accepted or rejected according to the way in which it is offered to the [subject]. An idea offered timidly or tentatively may be rejected, but the same idea expressed with confidence may be accepted. When the [operator] is giving a suggestion, he should always strive to do so in such a way as to convey to the [subject] that he assumes that the suggestion will be accepted and that there is no possible doubt in the matter whatsoever."[29]

5. VERBAL COMMUNICATION. The structure and verbal content of suggestions is very important and will be dealt with in detail in "Principles of Suggestion" in Chapter 3. It is important to realize that there are several levels of verbal communication. Verbal communication expresses ideas by logical sequences of words and sounds. For example, during an induction you say to your subject, "It's so easy to concentrate on the sound of my voice." The logical meaning of this sentence is easily accepted and understood by the subject. There is another level of meaning here, however, and that is the implied meaning that is independent of the logical meaning. This sentence, in an indirect fashion, implies or suggests to the subject that he *should* listen to the sound of your voice. This implied level of meaning is known as *extraverbal communication*.

The effectiveness of verbal suggestions can be greatly enhanced by the proper use of *intraverbal communication* or verbal expression. For example, in the above suggestion, put a pleading quality in your voice, for you are actually asking, in a disguised manner, that your subject listen to the sound of your voice. Similarly, if you suggest heaviness or even lightness, put a quality of heaviness or lightness respectively in your voice. In general, it is important that suggestions be given in a tone of conviction, self-assurance, and confidence in their effectiveness. A calm, positive, unhurried, monotonous, and rhythmic voice seems best. Developing a "hypnotic rhythm" is important as it has been found that even certain rhythmic poems can produce trance states when read to subjects.[30] Make your induction a lullaby.

6. NONVERBAL COMMUNICATION. The affective relationship and rapport, one's prestige and confidence, and the ease with which verbal suggestions are accepted, are all influenced by the hypnotist's expressions, gestures, and general demeanor. Research has shown that human beings are extreme-

ly sensitive and responsive to nonverbal behavior of others. Even though they are usually not consciously aware of or cannot describe this behavior, they nonetheless process and respond to it at a subconscious level. We have all had the experience of being introduced to someone we immediately did not like or vice versa, but could not explain our reasons why. If you had videotaped the encounter had then analyzed it with the aid of an expert on nonverbal behavior, you would discover behavioral clues in the other person to which you unconsciously reacted. Keep in mind that your hypnosis subjects will be reading and responding to you in the same manner. Therefore, it is important to mobilize your best nonverbal behavior. The primary consideration to follow in this endeavor is a concept known to psychologists as "congruence." This means that your nonverbal behavior should be congruent or consistent and harmonious with your verbal behavior. If it isn't, your subject will automatically and subconsciously pick this up and react negatively and defensively, which will hinder your chances for a successful induction. In essence, then, the affective relationship and rapport you establish, as well as the prestige and confidence you display, must be genuine. For example, if you are expressing confidence verbally, but your body is shaking and your teeth chattering, you may try to blame it on the cold, but your subject will know better. In addition, your best nonverbal behavior should be mobilized in support of your verbal communication and suggestions. For instance, if you are suggesting heaviness, be heavy! Likewise, if you are suggesting drowsiness, be drowsy! (See "Nonverbal Behavior for the Hypno-Investigator" for a more detailed discussion.)

7. MOTIVATION. A successful hypnotic induction will depend a great deal on the subject's willingness to be hypnotized, as poorly motivated subjects are relatively unsusceptible to hypnosis. Proper motivation, that is to say a high degree of motivation, will induce or create a favorable attitude and mental set for the acceptance of suggestions.* There are two basic approaches in establishing proper motivation: (1) overcoming existing negative motives and attitudes in the subject, and (2) creating new positive motives and attitudes. The basic means of overcoming or neutralizing the detrimental effects of negative motives is to clear up any misconceptions and questions the subject has regarding hypnosis during the preinduction (this is described in detail in "Misconceptions — What Hypnosis Is Not"). To further neutralize negative motives and attitudes and to create positive motivation, the hypnotist may continue by doing some suggestibility tests (see Appendix 4) to arouse the subject's curiosity and to give him an initial innocuous experience.

To create new positive motives and attitudes, which is usually easier than overcoming the negative ones, the hypnotist should stress that hypnosis is a very relaxing, pleasant, restful, creative, and beneficial state and that all subjects thoroughly enjoy it. The subject can be further motivated by telling him that once he has been successfully hypnotized by a professional, that it is very easy to learn self-hypnosis, which can be used as a personal development and therapeutic tool. If you notice that your subject smokes, is overweight, or bites his fingernails, you might get very

---

* White states that "it is unlikely that motivational factors alone determine susceptibility to hypnosis. Most workers agree that in addition to willingness there must be a suitable *aptitude*, perhaps a constitutional capacity, if the hypnotic trance is to take place. The best somnambulists do not always give evidence of being the most strongly motivated, and there is convincing genuineness in the disappointment not infrequently shown by eager subjects who cannot advance beyond a light state."[31] A study of 140 pairs of twins showed that there was a significant inherited or genetic component in hypnotizability.[32]

specific by indicating that he may even cure that habit with self-hypnosis. As a hypno-investigator, you can emphasize to your victim or witness the importance of the information you are after that they have forgotten.

8. EXPECTANCY. As with motivation, a successful hypnotic induction will depend a great deal on the subject's state of expectancy. When a subject is in a high state of expectancy, he will accept suggestions more readily. Mesmer's convulsing patients and Charcot's somnambulistic patients demonstrate the power of expectation. For this reason it is an excellent idea, although not always practical or feasible, to have a new subject watch you hypnotize an experienced good subject and to let him ask questions of the demonstration subject. This will obviously greatly enhance the subject's expectations and will also alleviate many fears and misconceptions. The authors can attest to the efficacy of this approach having used it on occasion themselves with fearful and resistant subjects. If a demonstration subject is not available or if time does not permit, the operator can at least give the subject a general idea of what is going to happen, what you expect of him, and what he may experience in the way of bodily and mental sensations. The state of expectancy itself may range from a general feeling that something is going to occur, to a specific expectation, such as his hand is going to levitate.

9. FACILITATION. "A successful suggestion always tends to increase the operator's prestige and to create in the subject a more positive attitude toward his ability to affect the subject."[33] As a result, each successful suggestion aids the acceptance of another suggestion, eventually leading to hypnosis. There is no suggestion more convincing to a subject than the advent of hypnosis.

10. GRADING. Closely related to the concept of facilitation is the process of grading. Recognizing that the induc-

tion of hypnosis depends largely upon one's belief that it is happening, it is extremely important not to damage that belief by taxing a subject's suggestibility. Therefore, it is imperative to build his belief by grading the suggestions offered from the easiest and simplest to the more difficult and complex. (Grading will be discussed in more detail in "Principles of Suggestion" in Chapter 3.)

In summary, it is important to keep in mind that the function and purpose of the process of suggestion is to bypass the logical and analytical portion of a subject's mind and to gain direct access to his subconscious by restructuring his perceived and experimental reality. As such, any gesture, word, inflection, body movement, etc. that tends to arouse the subject's critical or suspicious faculties militates against suggestion.

The actual mechanics of developing and placing suggestions is discussed in detail in "Principles of Suggestion" in Chapter 3.

Suggestibility

Suggestibility can be defined as that function, ability, or process of the mind, whether innate or learned, that determines the ease with which a person accepts suggestions. A great deal of research has been done on the nature of suggestibility and many scales have been developed for classifying people according to their degree of suggestibility. These researchers equated suggestibility with susceptibility to hypnosis, and they therefore were interested in being able to predict with a fair degree of accuracy whether or not a person could be hypnotized and to what depth. Some of these scales and research findings are mentioned in the next section. The authors' purpose here is to draw an important lesson from history and clinical experience by reviewing two basic approaches to suggestibility.

1. THE TRADITIONAL APPROACH. Historically, suggestibility was believed to be a character trait that was a relatively fixed and stable facet of one's personality. In other words, you either had it or you didn't. In this approach, if a subject proves to be unsuggestible and therefore unhypnotizable, the blame is essentially laid on him.

2. THE DYNAMIC APPROACH. Practical experience indicates that subjects who do not respond favorably to one induction may respond very well to another, and, likewise, a subject may not respond favorably to one operator, but will reach a deep trance level quickly with another using the same technique. This observation lead Meares to develop what he refers to as a Dynamic Concept of Suggestibility.[34] Basically stated, the above experience indicates that suggestibility is not a fixed quality or ability, but is largely determined by dynamic factors within the subject's own personality and between the subject and operator. In this approach, if a subject proves unsuggestible, the blame lies primarily with the operator. In other words, before dismissing the subject as unsuggestible, the operator had best take a close look at himself first, i.e. his induction technique, the various psychodynamic problems to be discussed later, and all the "Factors Influencing Suggestion" discussed above. Keep in mind, however, that research has conclusively shown that people do differ substantially in their hypnotic susceptibility, so do not be too harsh in your personal criticism.

WHO IS SUSCEPTIBLE TO HYPNOSIS?

Susceptibility to hypnosis refers to the ability of a person to respond to hypnosis induction techniques. Persons who are easily hypnotized and to considerable depth are said to be susceptible to hypnosis, whereas persons who are difficult to hypnotize and who only reach minimum depth, or who do not respond at all, are said to be unsusceptible to hypnosis.

Since 1843, when Braid attempted to classify his patients' hypnotic susceptibility according to a specific characteristic, many researchers have attempted to design measuring scales and tests that would accurately predict a person's susceptibility. Researchers and clinicians, such as the Hilgards and Weitzenhoffer, Davis and Husband, Friedlander and Sarbin, LeCron and Bordeaux, and the Spiegels, to name a few, have been wrestling with this problem for years. The product of their respective research has been several elaborate tests and scoring scales. The following are some of the more common ones:

• Davis and Husband Hypnotic Susceptibility Scoring System

• Friedlander-Sarbin Scale
• LeCron-Bordeaux Scoring System
• Stanford Hypnotic Susceptibility Scales
• Harvard Group Scale of Hypnotic Susceptibility
• Children's Hypnotic Susceptibility Scale
• Hypnotic Induction Profile

These tests and scoring scales are largely of academic and experimental interest and have little practical application or value for the hypno-investigator. Even most clinicians will readily agree that the best way to determine a person's susceptibility is to try to hypnotize him, which can largely be done in the time that it would take to administer one of the tests. Furthermore, the reliability of tests of hypnotic susceptibility are somewhat in question, and they do not take into account the dynamic concept of suggestibility discussed earlier. As Bowers cautions, it is conceivable that "a person can be high in hypnotic susceptibility one day and virtually unsusceptible the next day, just as his or her mood can change dramatically from day to day."[35] Susceptibility scales are largely used in laboratory settings where the induction techniques are standardized out of necessity for the experimental design. This appraoch, however, does not allow for "the use of diversified methods [which] can meaningfully increase the responsiveness of subjects initially resistant to hypnosis as well as those less resistant."[36]

There are some general characteristics, though, that the hypno-investigator should be aware of so that he can make a determination as to whether or not to accept a case for referral. Generally, people of average intelligence or above who can concentrate well, relax easily, and visualize well tend to make good subjects, especially if they are motivated. Males are no less susceptible than females, but susceptibility does vary with age, peaking at ages nine to twelve with a gradual decline thereafter. Children below the approximate age of six as well as the old, senile, mentally ill, or people of low intelligence can generally not concentrate well enough to be hypnotized.

Other variables indicative of high hypnotic susceptibility were studied by Hilgard.

1. Ability to become involved in reading and dramatic arts, as well as deep religious involvement, correlate with high susceptibility.
2. The ability for visual imagery correlates significantly with susceptibility.
3. Subjects who have had imaginary playmates as children are likely to be more susceptible than those who haven't.
4. Childhood punishment correlates positively with hypnotizability.
5. Highly motivated subjects tend to be more susceptible than the uninterested or resistant subject.[37]

In an analysis of motivations affecting hypnotic susceptibility, White came to several conclusions that refute some popular misconceptions of who are susceptible while reinforcing others.

1. Women do not exceed men in hypnotic susceptibility.
2. Introverts are no more susceptible to hypnosis than extroverts.
3. General submissiveness is not directly relevant to susceptibility.
4. Deference, which is the tendency to yield willingly to a superior person, is related directly to hypnotic susceptibility.
5. Passive individuals, who avoid or retreat from difficulties and who wait for others to assist them or overcome the problem for them, are sometimes more susceptible.
6. Tendencies of exhibitionism and self-dramatization seem to correlate positively with susceptibility [38]

A frequent question regards the effect of alcohol on susceptibility. Experience has shown and most experts agree that a small quantity of alcohol may enhance susceptibility as it lowers a person's defense mechanisms. Too much alcohol, though, will interfere with the person's ability to concentrate and follow suggestions and hence will be counterproductive. The same may hold true for drugs.

It should be kept in mind that the appearance of any one or combination of the above positive characteristics does not guarantee high hypnotic susceptibility, just as a cluster of negative characteristics does not mean the subject will always be unsusceptible. There are always exceptions to every rule so do not make any hasty judgments. For example, there is a type of person known as a *paradoxical reactor* and there is usually one in every group. Whenever the authors have given a lecture/demonstration or taught a course, there is always the highly skeptical, vocal, and almost critical individual in the audience. During the group suggestibility tests, or even during a demonstration with a single subject, this individual will often become hypnotized by merely watching. At some level of awareness, it seems that he either realizes that he is highly susceptible or has some unconscious need or desire for hypnosis that he consciously defends against with an openly critical attitude. Wolberg concludes in his review of susceptibility that "the existence of unconscious motives explains why hypnotizability is so difficult to predict."[39] Similarly, even though a direct correlation between vividness of imagery and hypnotic depth has been posited,[40] some excellent hypnotic subjects have great difficulty in visualizing. In much the same way, although relaxation facilitates the onset of hypnosis, some tense people who cannot relax prove to be highly hypnotizable while others who relax well are unsusceptible.

In conclusion, then, if there are no clear contraindications for attempting hypnosis, do it. You have everything to gain (if nothing else, practice and experience, all of which builds towards one's expert witness qualifications) and nothing to lose but a little time.

When examining susceptibility to hypnosis the obvious question, one that the tests and scoring scales tried to answer, is what percentage of the population is hypnotizable and to what depth? It seems that as with every aspect of hypnosis, this is also a matter of controversy. Although many experimenters and clinicians believe that susceptibility is a normal and relatively stable trait, they do not agree as to what percentage of the population has it and to what degree, i.e. what percentage falls into arbitrary categories of highly susceptible, moderately susceptible, susceptible, and not susceptible. This question will be examined in detail in "Depth of Hypnosis" in Chapter 3.

WHO IS SUGGESTIBLE?

Susceptibility and suggestibility, although often used interchangeably and considered synonomous by some authors, are actually different phenomena. As Hilgard states, however, "the subject must respond to suggestions in order to become hypnotized."[41] As mentioned above, susceptibility refers to the ability of a person to become hypnotized, whereas suggestibility refers to the ability of a person to respond to suggestion. The difference may seem largely semantic, but the essential difference is that suggestibility is a subcomponent of susceptibility, and, to a large extent, susceptibility to hypnosis depends upon a person's suggestibility. Yet, hypnosis is more than just hypersuggestibility. Bowers goes to considerable lengths in his discussion and review of hypnotic susceptibility and suggestibility studies to differentiate between the hypnotic state and mere hypersuggestibility. He concludes that hypersuggestibility outside of hypnosis, that is in the waking state, cannot account for all of the phenomena and subjective experience alterations of the trance state.[42] In fact, some authorities do not believe that hypersuggestibility is a necessary characteristic of trance.[43]

The important consideration here is that the standard hypnotic techniques outlined in this book are dependent upon the development of hypersuggestibility in a person, for it is through a gradual increase in response to suggestion that a person becomes hypnotized (see "Principles of Suggestion" in Chapter 3). Although most researchers agree that a person does not need to be hypersuggestible to be susceptible to hypnosis, it sure helps. "The correlations between waking and hypnotic suggestibility are impressive and suggest that, by and large, people who are responsive to hypnotic suggestions are also responsive to waking suggestions and people who are low in one tend to be low in the other."[44] From a practical point of view, then, some general guidelines to follow will aid the hypno-investigator in determining whether or not to accept a case referral.

People differ considerably in their degree of suggestibility and the difference seems to lie along a continuum of trust, acceptance, and mental flexibility. At one end of the spectrum are the people who basically trust and accept others and are relatively secure and open-minded. On the other end of the spectrum are those who are generally alert, insecure, and suspicious, with relatively closed minds and rigid personalities, or who intellectualize and analyze everything. These people are likely to interfere with the process of suggestion by constantly questioning it, but keep in mind that there are exceptions to the rule like the paradoxical reactor described above. Hysterical and impulsive people as well as neurotics and alcoholics are often very suggestible unless they have a subconscious resistance and defense. People in positions of authority who give orders are usually less suggestible than their subordinates who take orders. For this reason, police officers often make good subjects when being hypnotized by a superior, although more authoritative inductions may have to be used. Bullheaded people are generally too uncompromising to be suggestible. Overly flighty, capricious, or giddy persons, although generally very suggestible, are often unable to concentrate long enough on the operator's suggestions or to make themselves passive. Interestingly enough, studies have shown that there is little or no correlation between suggestibility and character traits or psychiatric diagnostic classifications.

There are many fairly easy and rapid tests of suggestibility that will give an operator a rough indication of a person's susceptibility (see Appendix 4). In effect, suggestibility tests are mini-inductions and their purpose is to see to what degree a person responds to suggestion. There are four basic circumstances in which a hypno-investigator

might want to use them.

1. To select suggestible persons from a group to be used for training purposes.

2. To help put a very nervous and fearful subject at ease. Specifically, the operator might say, "Well, we won't do the actual induction yet, but instead would you like to do some simple exercises which will give you a basic idea of what the experience is like? Then we'll go from there. Okay?" This maneuver accomplishes several things:

a. It serves as a release valve for the person's anxiety by temporarily letting him off-the-hook by postponing the feared situation.
b. It builds rapport and trust because it demonstrates concern and empathy for the person's feelings.
c. By asking the subject if he would like to do the exercises (very seldom will they refuse, but, if they do, just schedule another appointment), you subtly force the subject to commit himself to doing them by answering in the affirmative.
d. The exercises themselves will usually diminish the person's anxiety, hence facilitating the induction.

3. It helps to convince a skeptical, but cooperative, subject that he can follow and respond to suggestions. Successfully responding to some simple suggestions will tend to build the subject's suggestibility for the more complex and difficult induction suggestions.

4. If a beginning operator "doubts his ability to hypnotize a [subject], under the pretext of testing he can proceed immediately with an induction [technique] instead. If hypnosis is obtained, one can say, 'I started to test you, but I recognized that you would be an excellent subject. Therefore, I continued hypnotizing you.' Contrarily, this can be a welcome face-saving device for the novice in case hypnosis is not obtained."[45] Before continuing

with the induction, however, it might be wise in some cases to get the subject's permission by saying, "You are doing so well I'd like to continue by moving right into an induction. Okay?"

An inherent problem and risk factor in using suggestibility tests, which is nowhere answered satisfactorily, is what to do if they fail? Below are several recovery techniques that could be used depending on the subject and the personality of the operator.

1. Compliment your subject on responding favorably and indicate that you are certain now that he will be a good subject, then proceed to an induction of choice.

2. Subtlely and tactfully "blame" your subject for not cooperating fully and then discuss his resistance. For example, you might say, "You don't seem to be relaxing completely, or maybe you're having trouble visualizing or concentrating." This open statement should invite the subject to discuss his experience and any lingering misconceptions, concerns, or fears he may still have, at which point you can openly discuss them, reassure the subject, then proceed with more tests or an induction if he so desires. If he does not volunteer any useful information, ask him outright if he has any concerns or fears. (Additional recovery techniques are discussed in Appendix 4.)

THE TRANCE STATE AND THE EXPERIENCE OF HYPNOSIS

The trance state is a very private, personal, and individual experience. No two hypnosis subjects ever experience hypnosis in the exact same way. After interviewing hundreds of experienced subjects, the authors are still constantly amazed at the variability of the individual's experience. Even two subjects at approximately the same hypnotic depth, or even the same subject during different sessions, may have entirely different experiences. One subject may feel totally dissociated from his body as if he were spinning and floating up into the air, while another at the same depth will exclaim that he was not hypnotized upon waking because he felt no differently. Even though the subjective and physical experience of subjects varies tremendously, there are some basic characteristics of the trance state that are generally manifested and observable. These primary characteristics are listed below along with a typical response from an experienced subject.

PROFOUND PHYSICAL AND MENTAL RELAXATION. "One thing I remember very well is that I got so relaxed I started sliding off the chair."

SELECTIVE ATTENTION WITH HEIGHTENED CONCENTRATION AND ELIMINATION OF DISTRACTIONS. "I was totally involved. Pretty soon I couldn't hear the other voices or noises, just your voice."

UNCRITICAL ACCEPTANCE AND INCREASED RESPONSIVENESS TO SUGGESTIONS. "I felt what you were saying was happening. I felt heavier and heavier."

REDUCTION IN THE NEED FOR REALITY TESTING. "I felt it was just as you said it was. It didn't matter."

EFFECTS OF COGNITION ON BODILY FUNCTIONS ARE AMPLIFIED. "As soon as I thought of my hand getting lighter it started to float up."

HEIGHTENED ABILITY FOR VISUAL IMAGERY AND FANTASY PRODUCTION. "I really felt I was at my favorite place. I could see everything so clearly."

LOSS OF INITIATIVE OR DESIRE TO MAKE AND CARRY OUT PLANS OR IDEAS OF ONE'S OWN. "I just didn't feel like doing anything unless you said so."

AVAILABILITY OF PAST MEMORIES. "When you first started taking me back I thought of things, people, or scenes at each age. They just kind of flashed by as if on a screen."

DISINCLINATION TO SPEAK, MOVE, OR THINK. "I knew I could talk, but I just didn't want to. I felt too lazy."

FEELINGS OF HEAVINESS, NUMBNESS, BUZZING, FLOATING, SPINNING, ETC. "I felt a tingling numbness and a lightness like my body wasn't there."

It is apparent from the above that hypnotic subjects will experience a wide spectrum of physical and psychological sensations, but for some it is not a totally new experience. In some instances, it is basically a rediscovery of what one has experienced before under different circumstances. The trance experience can be much like being totally absorbed and involved in a good movie or book, or like hanging in the familiar twilight zone between waking and sleep. The above described experiences are by and large spontaneous and naturally occurring and are largely independent of the operator's suggestions. There is, however, a whole other category of hypnotic experiences — those that are triggered or created as a direct result of the operator's carefully constructed suggestions. These suggested experiences are virtually limitless for deeply hypnotized subjects. Some of these are as follows:

1. hallucinations in any or all of the senses
2. complete anesthesia
3. ability to carry out posthypnotic suggestions
4. complete body catalepsy (temporary muscular rigidity)
5. amnesia
6. control of involuntary bodily functions, i.e. heart beat, blood pressure, digestion, pain
7. time distortion and automatic writing
8. hypermnesia (enhanced recall)
9. age regression
10. revivification (reliving past events)

For the hypno-investigator, the last three phenomena listed are the ones of interest, and a substantial portion of this book is devoted to techniques for their elicitation.

Even though the hypno-investigator cannot use hypnosis for purposes other than eliciting information, he should be aware of some other purposes and uses for hypnosis so he can adequately and intelligently respond to some likely questions from subjects. Some of these other uses, although plainly for medical or psychological purposes, are listed below.

1. *internal medicine:* psychosomatic, cardiovascular and gastrointestinal disorders, asthma
2. *surgery:* general or topical anesthesia
3. *obstetrics:* control of labor and pain
4. *dermatology:* allergies, skin disorders
5. *pediatrics:* bed-wetting, thumb-sucking
6. *habit removal:* alcoholism, smoking, insomnia
7. *dentistry:* topical anesthesia, needle phobias
8. *hypnoanalysis:* diagnosis of neuroses and personality disorders
9. *hypnotherapy:* symptom removal, abreaction of early traumatic experiences, treating neuroses and personality disorders
10. *personal development:* improving concentration and recall, increasing will power and control over personal habits and problems, e.g. obesity, anxiety, stuttering, tics, nail-biting

Misconceptions: What Hypnosis Is Not

Unfortunately, hypnosis has suffered a great deal from a severe lack of information and an abundance of outright misinformation. Stage hypnotists and Hollywood have done hypnosis a great disservice by projecting and displaying wrong images. Interestingly enough, hypnosis is probably one of the most widely misunderstood yet sought after experiences. The hypno-investigator will be confronted by the misconceptions that every subject will have, and he must be able to adequately explain them to overcome the fears, anxieties, and reservations that they cause. No matter how thorough an explanation you provide, however, most subjects will still hold on to some of their previous doubts and beliefs until disproven by their first experience.

In a recent training program conducted by the authors on Hypnosis in Criminal Investigation in which selected officers were trained in hypno-investigation, each officer was instructed in six different hypnotic induction techniques. Each officer was required to practice each technique on a different subject. To examine some of the conventional misconceptions, the authors interviewed one practice group of six subjects about their beliefs before and after hypnosis, with the intent of giving the beginning hypno-investigator some idea of what to expect.

Each of ten commonly-held misconceptions are stated below, which is followed immediately by a typical statement from one of the six subjects interviewed. This statement is succeeded by the scientific belief, which is then followed by a typical statement from a subject after hypnosis.

1. CONVENTIONAL BELIEF. Hypnosis is a state of unconsciousness or sleep.

Typical Statement Before Hypnosis. "I expect to be kind of out of it and not to feel anything."

Scientific Belief. Physiological tests prove that hypnosis is not a state of sleep. Specifically, EEG and EKG measurements, base metabolism rates, the patellar reflex or knee jerk, as well as blood pressure, blood count, and chemical analysis all approximate the normal awake state and not sleep. Furthermore, self-reports of hypnotic subjects indicate that they are usually very much aware of themselves and their surroundings, and can talk, think, and act more or less normally.

Typical Statement After Hypnosis. "I was very wrong in what did happen versus

what I expected. I remembered everything and found that I was totally aware of everything that was going on."

2. CONVENTIONAL BELIEF. You surrender your will under hypnosis.

Typical Statement Before Hypnosis. "I am afraid of doing or saying something I don't want to. I don't think I'll be in control."

Scientific Belief. Hypnotic subjects are actually in control at all times and can refuse to do a requested act while in trance and can even come out of trance by themselves if the need arises. Hypnosis is actually a cooperative interpersonal venture as well as a natural state of mind which all normal people have the potential of entering.

Typical Statement After Hypnosis. "I thought that under hypnosis I'd just be a blank and that I'd do what I was told and that there wouldn't be all these thought processes. I was wrong."

3. CONVENTIONAL BELIEF. Hypnosis takes a weak-minded person.

Typical Statement Before Hypnosis. "It must take a weak-minded person to be hypnotized, or you will become weak-minded after being hypnotized a number of times."

Scientific Belief. Research studies on hypnotic susceptibility show that people of above average intelligence who can concentrate and visualize well make the best subjects. Weak-mindedness does not correlate with hypnotic susceptibility; weak-minded and strong-minded people are both hypnotizable. Although continued or multiple hypnosis sessions increases susceptibility, there is no evidence that it weakens a person's mind or will, in fact, the opposite is often true.

Typical Statement After Hypnosis. "Each time I'm hypnotized I go a little deeper, but I actually feel more in control. In fact, I've been doing self-hypnosis to increase my willpower."

4. CONVENTIONAL BELIEF. People reveal their secrets under hypnosis.

Typical Statement Before Hypnosis. "I'm

afraid you'll ask personal questions and I'll spill it."

Scientific Belief. People under hypnosis are aware of everything and as stated above, are fully conscious; therefore, they will not say anything under hypnosis that they don't want to.

Typical Statement After Hypnosis. "I'm sure I wouldn't have said anything I didn't want to."

5. CONVENTIONAL BELIEF. Some people under hypnosis might not wake up.

Typical Statement Before Hypnosis. "My biggest fear is that, if I went under and something happened, I won't come out of it."

Scientific Belief. There has never been a reported case of a hypnotized person not coming out of hypnosis. It is true and often the case, however, that the experience is so enjoyable that people do not want to come out when commanded to, but instead, wish to enjoy it further. Studies have shown that if the hypnotist leaves the room unbeknown to the subject, he will either awaken in a few minutes or will fall asleep and awaken when he is ready.

Typical Statement After Hypnosis. "I could awaken if I had to. In fact, I did once when startled by a noise."

6. CONVENTIONAL BELIEF. Hypnosis only works on gullible people.

Typical Statement Before Hypnosis. "I am very gullible. I believe everything anyone tells me, so I think I'll be a good subject."

Scientific Belief. Hypnosis works just as well on many people who are not gullible. The main variables are motivation, expectation, and trust. Gullible should not be confused with suggestible. *Gullible* is defined as easily cheated or tricked, whereas *suggestible* refers to the ability to respond to suggestion, a positive characteristic. People are not cheated or tricked in hypnosis. Gullible people, however, are very suggestible.

Typical Statement After Hypnosis. "I really don't think gullibility has any-

thing to do with it. I just followed your instructions and it happened."

7. CONVENTIONAL BELIEF. The hypnotist needs a dominant and strong personality.

Typical Statement Before Hypnosis. "I think it would take someone who is very aggressive and strong."

Scientific Belief. Experienced subjects report overwhelmingly that this is not true, but that the qualities of a good hypnotist are primarily confidence, calmness, and voice.

Typical Statement After Hypnosis. "Now I think it'd take someone who's soft-spoken and quiet."

8. CONVENTIONAL BELIEF. The hypnotist is in total control.

Typical Statement Before Hypnosis. "I don't think I'll have any control."

Scientific Belief. Studies show that hypnotic subjects cannot be made to do anything against their moral or ethical code. In reality, the subject is in control, not the hypnotist.

Typical Statement After Hypnosis. "I don't know why but I felt totally in control of myself."

9. CONVENTIONAL BELIEF. You do not remember anything that happened under hypnosis.

Typical Statement Before Hypnosis. "I expect not to know what is really going on or to remember it."

Scientific Belief. Unless posthypnotic amnesia is suggested as is sometimes done by clinicians for therapeutic reasons, and except for those rare occasions when an excellent subject will experience some posthypnotic amnesia, all subjects remember everything. To neutralize any anxiety regarding this belief, tell your subject that before awakening him you will instruct him to remember everything.

Typical Statement After Hypnosis. "I was aware of and remembered everything."

10. CONVENTIONAL BELIEF. You are not aware of anything during hypnosis.

Typical Statement Before Hypnosis. "I expect that under hypnosis I won't be aware of what will be said or what will happen."

Scientific Belief. Self-reports of experienced subjects indicate that they are very much aware. Some subjects may selectively tune out the external environment, noises, distractions, etc. and turn inward, even to the extent of losing awareness of their bodies, but they never lose awareness of the operator's voice.

Typical Statement After Hypnosis. "I didn't really know if I was under hypnosis because I was aware of everything."

Contraindications: Who Not to Hypnotize

Although the myth of the dangers of hypnotism were clearly dispelled in Chapter 1, there are some people that the hypno-investigator should not hypnotize.

Understanding that hypnosis is a tool to be utilized by the hypno-investigator only within the parameters of his expertise, he must make it very clear to his subjects, as well as to himself, peers, and public, that he does not practice therapy. To avoid any such charges or criticisms from the medico-psychological community, as well as out of good common sense, respect for other professionals, and regard for the subject, the hypno-investigator must ask his subject during the initial contact if he is presently under the care of a doctor, whether medical doctor, psychologist, or psychiatrist. If the subject is, the hypno-investigator should consult with the doctor first to get his permission before doing the hypnosis, unless of course he is merely being treated for a minor physical problem, such as a cold.

If the subject has a cardiac problem, it would be advisable to only conduct the hypnosis in the presence of his physician, even if you have permission from the doctor to do otherwise. This is to protect yourself in the exceedingly

remote coincidence of the hypnotized subject having a heart attack, which could not only be libelous, but embarrassing as well.* Do not think for a moment that hypnosis can actually trigger a heart attack: the experts agree that a hypnotized person is actually less likely to have one due to the profound relaxation. The presence of a physician, though, would insure immediate medical assistance.

As discussed previously, the critics claim that there is always a remote possibility that hypnosis could precipitate or cause an adverse psychological reaction in a prepsychotic or psychotic. These people, especially the psychotic, would normally be difficult or impossible to hypnotize anyway because of their general inability to concentrate. These people should be screened out before hypnosis is attempted. Psychotics are generally easy to recognize due to their behavioral and psychological aberrations, e.g. bizarre physical behaviors, gestures, and thinking patterns manifested in their conversation. The prepsychotic is more difficult to recognize, but the primary characteristic is usually a pathological mood condition, whether consistently depressive, consistently manic, or intense and frequent swings between the two. Other indicators might be showing inordinate amounts of fear, perspiration, shortness of breath, no eye contact, glassy eyes, or inappropriate behaviors.

---

* A well-known Hungarian lay hypnotist, Neukom, was alleged to have been able to hypnotize hundreds of people by merely showing himself and raising his hand. Unfortunately, in 1895, one of his clients collapsed during hypnosis and died shortly thereafter. Although the criminal court decided that the patient "had not died of hypnosis," a decree was issued that made Hungary the first country to restrict its use to physicians.[46] A similar incident occurred in Japan in 1906, when a patient died some days after she had been hypnotized by a physician. Although the patient died of her illness and not hypnosis, a decree was enacted in 1908 that severely restricted its use by laymen, psychologists, and physicians alike.[47]

Obviously, law enforcement officers have not been trained to diagnose and determine pathological conditions, yet they generally have a profound practical working understanding of people and their problems that develops over their years of experience in constantly dealing with all socioeconomic levels of people with every conceivable problem. Recognizing mentally unbalanced people, then, is no new trick for experienced peace officers. Besides watching for the above characteristics, rely on and trust your inner reaction to a potential subject. Even if you cannot attach a psychiatric diagnostic classification or label to him, you can judge by instinct whether or not the person is basically sound. As a precautionary note, the authors would suggest that when in doubt, **don't.** As an alternative, do what you are good at — background investigation — and then make your decision. If your department has a staff or consulting psychologist or psychiatrist, request his professional opinion before proceeding.

During the preinduction talk when the operator reviews the subject's answers to the Preinduction Questionnaire (see Appendix 5), he can further determine whether or not there are any contraindications. By examining the questionnaire, you will see that there are some loaded questions that will uncover potential problem subjects if answered truthfully. For example: (A) "Have you had any emotional problems within the past six months?" (B) "Do you have any problem sleeping at night, i.e. heavy dreaming, nightmares, etc.?"

If you believe the person is essentially normal and you have no qualms, then proceed unless there is a contraindication not to do it at that particular time, e.g. the person has a bad cold, headache, or other physical condition, or he has pressing concerns, such as job or family, that will interfere with the induction. If this is the case, it would be best to wait for the condition to clear up sufficiently or to make other arrangements so that job or family will not interfere.

Once deciding to hypnotize a subject, there are several contraindications that may be manifested during the induction, although these are exceedingly rare. First, the subject may experience bizarre muscular movements and contractions, such as trembling or twitching of various body parts, very heavy and labored breathing, or rocking of the head. The subject may also manifest, either in conjunction with these physical movements or alone, such psychological and hysterical reactions as crying or laughing. These types of incongruous behaviors may be indicative of an underlying prepsychotic or hysterical condition that manifests itself as the ego controls are lowered. If these signs are not overly bizarre, they may also be natural concomitants and reactions to profound relaxation in a generally uptight and tense person. In other words, chronically contracted muscles may relax for the first time in literally years under hypnosis, which may cause the subject to jerk, twitch, laugh, or even cry. These signs, therefore, could either be indicative of an underlying prepsychotic condition or of the natural onset of hypnosis. The determination as to which is the case can largely be made on their degree of disparity with the individual's normal waking state. It is recommended in this event that the subject be quizzed as to what he is experiencing, i.e. report the behavior to the subject and ask him what he is feeling. Depending on the response, the operator should be able to determine if it is safe to continue or if it is wise to terminate the session. For example, if the subject reports bizarre feelings and sensations and is frightened by them, discontinue the session, but reassure the subject that it is normal. On the other hand, the subject might just say that he hasn't relaxed like this since a child and that it feels great.

Second, a subject may be difficult to awaken. If this is the case, it may be symptomatic of some subconscious conflicts or neurotic process (see "Dehypnotization or Waking" in Chapter 4), in which case the subject should not be hypnotized again. On the other hand, the subject may feel so good while under hypnosis that he legitimately does not want to come out right away, but instead wants to enjoy it long-er. Clues to which situation is the case can be gained by quizzing the subject during the postinduction talk. For example, if the subject responds when asked why he didn't want to come out by explaining that he found a dark room in his head he wanted to hide in, further sessions would be contraindicated. On the other hand, a subject may say that he was so deep that you just brought him out too fast.

BASIC PSYCHODYNAMICS OF HYPNOSIS FOR THE HYPNO-INVESTIGATOR

Hypnosis is a very intensive and intimate interpersonal relationship, and the prospect of being hypnotized for the subject, as well as actually conducting the hypnosis for the operator, can stimulate a great deal of unconscious needs, fears, or desires that can affect the success of the induction. To be an effective operator, then, it is important to have a basic working understanding of these dynamics. The authors, therefore, will first present some basic principles and then offer some practical examples of some psychodynamically-related problems encountered, their explanations, and their solutions.

To begin with, *psychodynamics* refers to the intrapsychic complex of unconscious desires, needs, and anxieties that largely determine a person's behavior. Many psychologists regard our everyday life as a constant and never-ending endeavor to maintain our fragile egos and protect them from anxiety. The roots of anxiety lie not only in real or imagined threats from our environment and other people, but from within ourselves in the form of unacceptable desires, motives, and impulses. To protect itself against these potential threats and sources of anxiety, the ego develops and employs certain defense mechanisms. Since hypnosis necessitates the relaxing or surrendering of the intellectual, logical, and critical portion of one's mind, the ego is very likely to interpret this state of affairs as a loss of control and therefore threatening, which will cause it to employ certain defenses to prevent the onset of hypnosis. (These will be discussed later in "Common Defenses and Forms of Resistance" in Chapter 4.) It is important to realize that, by nature, defenses are (1) unconscious and (2) self-deceptive. Therefore, defenses operate below the level of awareness. In other words, the individual will not consciously realize that he is defending himself. In fact, if you confront him outright about defending himself, let's say by his overt restlessness which prevents hypnosis, he will probably vehemently deny it.

The specific unconscious needs, desires, and fears that are likely to be stimulated in an individual about to be hypnotized (or during the hypnosis itself, for that matter) depend primarily upon how the person interprets the hypnotic state. For example, some subjects may interpret hypnosis as a symbolic seduction, which may stimulate fears or wishes, depending on the person. Others may interpret a hypnotic trance as a state of unconsciousness, sleep, or even death, which also will stimulate fears or wishes. Other subjects may interpret the experience as a submission to another's will and authority, as an opportunity to freely fantasize, or to relinquish responsibility, all of which will also stimulate fears or desires depending again on the person. If the subject interprets hypnosis as potentially dangerous, or as an invasion of his mind and innermost thoughts, he will most likely be fearful and hence resistant.

The important lesson to be learned here is that a skillful operator will be sensitive to how his subject interprets the experience of hypnosis and will discuss that interpretation with him, or take other appropriate measures if it hinders depth of trance (see "The Dynamic Method: Dealing With Resistance" in Chapter 4). Watkins states that "it is the meaning of the inter-personal interaction implied in a so-called 'technique' and not the simple stimulus value of certain words which is of most significance in determining the kind and extent of the hypnotic response."[48]

The operator, as with the subject, is likely to interpret and behave in the hypnotic relationship in an unconscious manner. For example, it is likely to stimulate within him unconscious needs of dominance and control, or sexual needs and desires, which the subject will unconsciously pick up and react to, either positively or negatively. If you meet with a failed induction, therefore, examine yourself and see if you were unconsciously projecting something that the subject was reacting to adversely.

Once the actual induction begins and the trance becomes deeper, different desires or anxieties are likely to be stimulated, which often account for dramatic fluctuations in trance depth or even spontaneous awakenings. As hypnosis deepens and subjects begin to experience different physical or psychological phenomena and sensations that are seemingly spontaneous and beyond their control, some subjects will go with it and submit, while others will become fearful and rebel. Given two subjects having the same experience, one may suddenly go into a very

deep trance while the other spontaneously awakens.

The following are some situations that a hypno-investigator will probably encounter at one time or another when dealing with the complex conscious and unconscious processes present during the interpersonal relationship and communication with the subject during hypnosis. The examples are psychodynamically-related and are included here to illustrate some common and potential problems with their probable explanations and solutions.

1. COMMON PROBLEM. The subject seems a little hostile and says that he doesn't think you can hypnotize him.

Explanation. The subject probably interprets the hypnotic relationship as a control problem. He is actually very insecure and unconsciously views hypnosis as a submission to another's will, which is highly threatening. He is most likely to be unaware of this, however, believing himself to be well-adjusted with a strong personality.

Solution. Explain to your subject that hypnosis is not a battle of wills, but in fact is a cooperative venture in which you merely serve as a guide. Explain further that all hypnosis is actually self-hypnosis and that well-adjusted strong individuals make the best subjects. Also explain that contrary to popular belief, people do not lose control under hypnosis, but actually gain more control over their physiological and mental processes to the point of even controlling high blood pressure, migraines, and pain, as well as enhancing recall and concentration, etc. As operator you may also emphasize that if he really cooperates and proves to be a good subject, which you are certain he will, that he can easily learn self-hypnosis, which he can use as a personal development tool to make himself even better.

2. COMMON PROBLEM. Your subject is a very dependent, almost helpless, and seemingly very suggestible young woman. Much to your chagrin, she

proves to be very unsusceptible and your induction fails.

Explanation. Although dependent people are usually motivated for hypnosis, this particular one has an unconscious fear of being overwhelmed or controlled in a dependency relationship. She is what is known as a passive-aggressive personality in that her seeming dependency is actually a subtle means of controlling others. She perceived hypnosis as a loss of this control and therefore resisted.

Solution. Whenever an induction is unsuccessful, it is essential that the operator first "recover" in a manner that will salvage as much of his credibility and prestige as possible (see "Dynamic Method Sequence Chart" in Chapter 4). In this particular instance, as was the case discussed above, the problem is one of control. The operator should therefore go to considerable lengths to explain to the subject that she is actually in control and that you merely serve as a guide. Appeal to her need to control by explaining that people can actually gain more control over themselves as was done in the above case. If the subject is willing, proceed with another induction.

3. COMMON PROBLEM. The subject is a very enthusiastic, almost hysterical, attractive female who proves to be highly hypnotizable.

Explanation. For this subject, hypnosis is likely to be interpreted as a symbolic seduction which she unconsciously desires. This subject can quickly develop severe dependency needs. When frustrated, she can (1) sexualize the relationship, (2) experience posthypnotic amnesia, and (3) become very uncooperative in terminating the contact.

Solution. The hypno-investigator must clearly delineate the goals, expectations, and time range of contact before beginning. If she requests additional sessions you must either refuse or instruct her in self-hypnosis. Your role must be explicitly stated and reinforced, i.e. to only help the subject recall the needed information, or, if she has volunteered as a practice subject, make it clear that the hypnosis is just for your experience.

4. COMMON PROBLEM. A very dominant masculine male is your subject. You are apprehensive about being able to hypnotize him, yet he proves to be highly susceptible. Upon waking he is very surprised and a little unsettled.

Explanation. This person's dominant, aggressive personality is a front. Underneath there are very definite submissive and dependency needs. Unconsciously he interprets hypnosis as an opportunity to lay the front aside and temporarily turn control over to someone else. He is anxious upon waking because his conscious mind and ego are very surprised that he could seemingly give up so much control to another.

Solution. Simple reassurance is called for in this instance. Praise the subject for his cooperation and positive response while stressing the beneficial aspects of hypnosis. Also, reaffirm that hypnosis is not a battle of wills and that the operator does not control the subject.

5. COMMON PROBLEM. The rape victim is very nervous and sits on the edge of her chair. She says that she doesn't feel well, keeps looking at the clock, and feels that she shouldn't be away from her job. She insists, however, that she wants to assist in the investigation. A short and fairly unsuccessful induction is tried. At the moment of recall she comes up from a medium to light trance. She leaves and is late for her next appointment.

Explanation. In spite of her assurances to the contrary, the subject does not want to identify her assailant either out of fear of retaliation, apprehension about going to trial, or a subconscious resistance and defense against recalling the traumatic incident. At the same time, she desires to be a good citizen and assist in the investigation. Her inner conflict results in a variety of overt conflict responses.

Solution. The subject's conflict should be openly discussed. If it cannot be resolved, further sessions are contraindicated.

6. POTENTIAL PROBLEM. Your subject is in a deep trance and for no apparent reason spontaneously awakens.

Explanation. Usually this indicates that the person's ego had suddenly realized that it was losing control, so it terminated the session by immediately grabbing control. Occasionally, a subject will be startled by a vivid visualization or will rebel against an unusual physical or psychological sensation.

Solution. Discuss the person's experience with him while stressing its naturalness. Then continue with the same induction or another one if he agrees.

7. POTENTIAL PROBLEMS. A subject starts calling you daily. You begin to enjoy doing hypnosis regardless of how appropriate or necessary it might be to the case. You hypnotize only attractive subjects. You begin to feel very protective and fatherly to your subjects. The operator becomes a little tin god.

Explanation. These are problems of transference and countertransference. *Transference* is defined as the development of an emotional attitude, either positive or negative, on the part of the subject toward the operator which is based on childhood relationships with one's parents and not on the actual present interpersonal relationship. Similarly, *countertransference* refers to the development of special feelings towards one's subjects, especially strong parental attitudes and feelings. As such, the danger lies in the acting out of these infantile fantasies by the subject, and the parental fantasies by the operator, all of which can escalate into a very mutually dependent relationship. The very rare hypnotic aftereffects or complaints, such as headaches, problems sleeping, marital problems, nausea, etc., are sometimes due to transfer-

ence; the subject does not want to let go of the experience or the relationship. Hypnosis tends to trigger transference and countertransference-type reactions because, in the psychoanalytic sense, it is a re-enactment of a parent-child relationship.

Solution. The best way of dealing with transference problems is to avoid them, which is to say, recognize them and terminate the contact before they get out of hand. Dealing with transference and countertransference, then, is primarily a matter of awareness. Whenever you begin to have feelings for a subject, examine them closely. Transference and countertransference feelings or reactions can be recognized in that they are not appropriate to the situation because they are an artifact or carry-over from a previous relationship. In other words, they are incongruent and do not fit the present relationship. Do not try to work through these problems with your subject because that is the domain of the psychotherapist. In the rare event that an operator-subject relationship does begin to get out of hand, discuss it with another hypno-investigator or, more appropriately, the department psychologist if there is one.

8. POTENTIAL PROBLEM. Your subject is responding nicely, but seems to come up to a lighter stage and gets agitated and anxious during the descending stairs deepening technique.

Explanation. The visualization of descending the stairs has probably triggered a repressed traumatic incident or fear. Another likely possibility is that the subject interprets hypnosis as a state of unconsciousness, nonexistence, or death, and descending into a dark area may stimulate this fear.

Solution. As soon as your subject becomes agitated, interrupt the technique and ask if anything is the matter. The subject will probably reply with something like "I was pushed down the stairs once and broke my arm," or "My mother dragged me down the basement stairs once and locked me in a dark closet." At this point, the operator should show empathy and change techniques by saying, "Okay, well we won't go down any further but instead let's turn around and go up the stairs." Similar reactions may occur during any of the induction or deepening techniques if they become associated with a repressed traumatic experience.

Most hypno-investigations will be relatively trouble free as the subject has volunteered and is anxious to help solve the case; the hypno-investigator is motivated to gain the essential information needed by the primary investigator; and the objective, boundaries, and limits of the session and interpersonal contact are well-defined. Each session, however, will be unique.

Another dimension of psychodynamics involves the interpersonal interaction between the subject and operator. The hypnotic relationship is a continually changing and developing interaction. Both the operator and subject consciously as well as unconsciously "read" and evaluate or size up the other and subsequently act toward each other according to this information. Due to the relatively short-term and intense relationship, a lot is going to hinge and depend on first impressions. At the moment of introduction, the subject will be consciously and unconsciously computing your every action, gesture, expression, and word, including voice tone, sincerity, genuineness, etc. Likewise, the hypno-investigator will be doing the same with the subject.

This is all done naturally and instantaneously (probably out of an instinct for self-preservation) for the purpose of determining like or dislike and level of trust. Mehrabian refers to this as the *immediacy principle:* "People are drawn toward persons and things they like, evaluate highly, and prefer; and they avoid or move away from things they

dislike, evaluate negatively, or do not prefer."[49] These judgments are by and large made unconsciously and therefore are not acted upon consciously. Nevertheless, they produce behavioral consequence. The other party will consciously or unconsciously react to these behaviors causing the first party to consciously or unconsciously react to the latter's reaction. Very quickly, then, a vicious cycle can be developed. This often happens so quickly that it requires an ultra slow motion movie camera and detailed analysis to discover it.

Farina et al. conducted a number of experiments that lend further proof to the significance of first impressions. They conclude that "if an individual believes he is perceived in an unfavorable way by another person, his behavior in a subsequent interaction is affected independently of the other person's actions in the situation."[50] The important lesson to be learned here is the importance of the initial contact and the adverse effect an inadvertant negative impression, even if unconsciously displayed and transmitted, will have on the subject and, hence, on your chances of success in the induction. The hypno-investigator, then, must become sensitive to, aware of, and in control of his inadvertent impressions. Usually, these impressions are the result of a personal response to a stereotype.

To help illustrate some of these, some common stereotypical situations any hypno-investigator is likely to encounter are listed below. Read each one and imagine yourself confronted with having to hypnotize this person. Try to see how you would react and feel. Try to examine each situation psychodynamically, i.e. what are the reasons for your reaction? What kind of desires, needs, anxieties or fears are stimulated? Also, examine each from the point of view of your subject. Ask yourself if you could control your initial reaction and be genuine with this person in this situation.

1. Your subject is the victim of a gang-rape. Are you genuinely sympathetic or deep down do you despise her and think to yourself that she probably asked for and deserved it? Why do you feel the way you do? Do you actually hate women because your mother mistreated you as a child or your wife steps out? Your subject has obviously been traumatized by men, so how is this going to affect her perception of you? Can she trust you? Are you comforting?

2. Your subject is an effeminate male or even a known homosexual. What kinds of anxieties, opinions, or reactions does he stimulate? Are you overly hostile both because of attraction/repulsion impulses? On the other hand, how does he feel about being hypnotized by a male cop?

3. You are a relatively easy-going, quiet, and gentle person. Your subject is an aggressive dominate male. Do you feel inferior? Can you hypnotize him? Or should he be hypnotizing you?

4. Your subject is a very attractive seductive female. What kinds of anxieties, fears, or desires does she stimulate? Are you afraid of your desires? Can you control them? Do you feel guilty? If you are a female hypno-investigator, do you feel inadequate? How will she react to you?

5. In a similar fashion, analyze each of the following encounters:

A. Your subject is black, white, American Indian, or Spanish.
B. A witness in a wheelchair is rolled into your office.
C. A seventy-eight-year-old woman has been raped and you are asked to hypnotize her.
D Your subject is a professional person, i.e. doctor, lawyer, president of a bank, or even a psychologist.
E. The witness himself is always on the fringes of society.
F. The victim is a hooker.

In conclusion, there are some general rules to follow that will help you be aware of and control negative first impressions and stereotypical responses.

1. Avoid labeling. Once you have labeled a person as dumb, sexy, queer, minority, hooker, or whatever, all your behavior and perception will be colored by that label. A study of the effect of the negative labeling of people as mentally ill found that "believing an individual to be mentally ill strongly influences the perception of that individual; this is true in spite of the fact that his behavior in no way justifies these perceptions."[51] So, if you cannot overcome your prejudice or bias, refer the case.

2. Delay making personal judgments. Avoid the temptation of making personal judgments of others too soon. Keep in mind that you have to build rapport with your subject and that any negative evaluation you may have will be detrimental. You don't have to like the person, but respect him and be appreciative that he volunteered to aid in the investigation.

3. Examine your own stereotyped beliefs. What are your biases and feelings toward certain groups or types of people? What are your racial, religious, ethical, and national prejudices? Often we aren't really aware of them, so to find out, ask yourself some questions. For example: "How do I feel about Blacks? Whites? Chicanos? American Indians? Jews? Catholics? Protestants? Hookers? Bums? Poles? Italians?" Once aware of your beliefs, you are in a position to control your reaction upon meeting someone you have stereotyped. Keep in mind that the stigmatized are always keenly aware of how they are perceived.

NONVERBAL BEHAVIOR FOR THE HYPNO-INVESTIGATOR

A person's mouth can lie but his body cannot. Following this maxim, one key to a person's real desires, needs, and fears is in disparities and incongruencies between what he says and what his body does. In your own experience, has your voice ever been shaking, brow sweating, and hands trembling while insisting you're not scared? To adequately read your subject, look for these types of incongruencies. For example, if your subject says that she has no questions regarding hypnosis as her eyes dart to the floor, legs cross, and she opens her purse and starts fumbling inside, you know immediately that she has some unanswered misconceptions and fears that you had better uncover and neutralize. Keep in mind that some experts say there are over forty ways to say no, each with an entirely different meaning!

Any number of examples may be given from your own experience to support the importance of nonverbal cues in the hypno-investigative session. Observation is one of the most important skills you can learn and keep refining, both as an investigator and a hypno-investigator.

Consider the message a subject is giving in the following examples:

1. Hands clutching her purse to her bosom.
2. Rarely speaking and looking at the floor or out the window.
3. Sitting rigidly on the edge of the chair.
4. Bouncing around the room unable to sit still.
5. Legs crossed.

Likewise, consider the message you give the subject:

1. Hands clutched into fists.
2. Interrupt talking with the subject to answer the phone.
3. Standing, feet apart, hands in your pockets.
4. Little eye contact.
5. Folding your arms and crossing your legs.

Since we have stressed the importance of first impressions and of creating an atmosphere of trust, security, and acceptance, what are some nonverbal behaviors and guidelines to follow to facilitate this process? The following are some nonverbal movements to generate trust:

1. Moving forward or toward the subject but without haste.
2. Leaning forward.
3. Reaching out.
4. Turning your body toward the subject.
5. Arms open, hands relaxed (not clenched into fists), palms open and up if sitting down or open and turned toward the subject if you are standing.
6. Smiling.
7. Moderate eye contact.
8. Respect the subject's private space.
9. Move freely about the room.
10. Move towards the subject and don't force or wait for him to come to you. Be the initiator.

The following are some nonverbal movements to generate security:

1. Squarely face your subject (standing at an angle or facing away are signs of rejection).
2. Don't sit behind a desk or other barrier.
3. Your posture should be relaxed, but alert.
4. Shake hands firmly (there will be sex differences since some women don't shake hands).
5. Stay with the subject as you move through the building to the office or room where the session will take place.

The following are some nonverbal movements to generate acceptance:

1. Facial expressions should be friendly and relaxed, but interested.
2. Posture should be casual and relaxed, but not unprofessional — don't slouch or put feet up on your desk.
3. Eye contact should be as frequent as the subject seems to need (too much might be threatening, but too little may not show enough interest or acceptance).
4. Touching when appropriate.
5. Align your body so as to welcome the subject on to your turf. Give him a piece of your turf to use, i.e. hang his hat or coat, place her purse upon, sit, etc.
6. Be responsive. This involves a cluster of behaviors including facial expressions, postural changes, etc.

In conclusion, the hypno-investigator must remember that it is his responsibility and objective to maximize the chances for a successful induction. In doing so, he must do everything possible to establish the necessary rapport, including a sense of trust, security, and acceptance. Recognizing that every nonverbal movement projects meaning and is therefore important, the hypno-investigator should be aware of his own nonverbal behavior as well as that of the subject. Most importantly, the hypno-investigator must be the initiator, recognizing that all the above movements imply interest and help people to think of themselves as worthy and accepted.

Exercises

1. Whenever possible in a public place, observe people out of hearing range. Try to determine what is happening or being communicated by observing their gestures, posture, facial expressions, and movements. Observe your own nonverbal patterns and ask for feedback.
2. Observe how others receive you and how you receive them. Carefully watch the nonverbal behaviors, cues, and interchanges. Don't listen as much to the words as you do the voice and its tone, rhythm, pitch, and inflections. Likewise, listen more to the person's body as well as to your own body. Ask your body what it thinks of the person. Ask yourself how you feel about the person.

THE HYPNO-INVESTIGATION ROOM

The purpose of hypno-investigation is to enhance the recall of victims and witnesses of crimes. With this in mind, it is essential to mobilize as many factors as possible in support of a successful hypnotic session. One important factor is the actual physical setting for the session. A properly constructed and controlled settting is essential for three basic reasons.

1. THE SETTING PREPARES THE SUBJECT TO RECEIVE SUGGESTIONS. The actual physical environment either facilitates or militates against the receipt of suggestions. As such, its importance cannot be overemphasized. Such factors as general appearance, size, furniture, comfort level, lighting arrangements, colors, voice level, odors, and atmospheric conditions including temperature, humidity, and drafts all affect the induction process.

The following are some recommendations based on experience and research:

A. The room should not be too small or too large for the subject to feel comfortably secure. It should be professional, yet comfortable. Ideally, there should be two distinct areas, one professional with desk, bookcase, chairs, etc. and the other relaxed and intimate with a large easy chair for the subject and several smaller chairs for the operator and primary investigator.

B. The room should be very quiet and secure from interruptions. If there is an intercom system, the nearest speaker should have an off-on switch. The phone should also have a wall plug that can be disconnected unless all calls can be held by the switchboard operator and dispatch. If the operator has a pager he must turn it off. Either a "Hypnosis Session in Progress — Do Not Disturb" sign should be printed and available to hang on the door, or there should be an external red light with an internal off-on switch.

C. The subject's chair should be a large comfortable fabric chair or recliner that will support the head. Leather and vinyl should be avoided since they generally cause sweating. Any muscle tension or strain the subject becomes aware of will militate against the induction. A footstool should be available if the subject desires one. The operator's chair should be on rollers so he can easily move closer during the induction.

D. There should be no bright or distracting lights that shine in the subject's eyes. Variable lighting is ideal as best results are achieved with the room dimly lit. Consideration needs to be given to the video quality, however.

E. There should be windows to an outside view yet with curtains that can be drawn before the session. The floor should be carpeted.

F. The room should be comfortably warm (between 73 and 75 degrees) as hypnotized subjects are particularly sensitive to cold.

G. The room should be draft-free as hypnotized subjects have been known to spontaneously awaken when disturbed by a cool draft.

H. The walls should be painted a soothing color such as light blue or beige. Reds tend to be aggressive and yellows invigorating.

I. To enhance the operator's prestige as well as the subject's expectation, several hypnosis books and texts should be arranged on the desk, and the operator's hypnosis course and professional society certificates should be hung on the wall.

J. A painting or two and some plants will add to the atmosphere. They should be fairly unobtrusive and nondistracting, however.

K. A pendulum clock or an audibly ticking clock can be incorporated by the operator into an induction procedure.

2. THE SETTING PREPARES THE OPERATOR IN GIVING SUGGESTIONS. A sense of turf and personal work space will aid the hypno-investigator's confidence and support his role as operator. Similarly, when the subject enters *your* space, it enhances his role as subject. Much as the objectives and roles of the examiner-defendant relationship become clear and distinct within the confines of the polygraph room, so should it be with the operator-subject relationship within the confines of the hypno-investigation room.

An important consideration, if there is more than one hypno-investigator in a department, is for all to have equal access and ownership of the room.

3. THE ROOM MUST BE SO EQUIPPED AS TO ADEQUATELY DOCUMENT HYPNOSIS SESSIONS TO LAY THE PROPER FOUNDATION. Every hypnosis session with volunteer victims and witnesses of crimes must be adequately documented to stand the possible test of a court challenge. Even though this even-

tuality is rare, the foundation must be laid so that the admissibility of hypno-induced testimony is not excluded on the basis of faulty procedure (see Chapter 6). The hypno-investigator must approach each session in the recognition that this may be the one that goes all the way, and with the understanding that an oversight or mistake on his part could result in an adverse case precedent.

The hypno-investigation room, then, must be so equipped as to mechanically record the entire session from beginning to end. The pictures in Chapter 4 illustrate a recommended mechanical set-up for proper recording. The equipment shown is usually found within any department, regardless of size, and was not purchased especially for the hypno-investigation room shown. A breakdown of the equipment is as follows:

1. A cookie display stand from a local grocery store gives support and accessibility to all of the electronic equipment. It also is mobile and collapsible for transport.

2. The top unit is an FM/AM radio cassette player used to play soothing classical music at low volume from start to finish of the encounter. This is to ensure continuity on the audio tape, which will be retained as evidence, as well as to help put the subject at ease and facilitate the induction. The tapes should be 90 or 120 minutes long so as to provide continuous music without frequent changing. This procedure is optional, however, as some subjects may not like the music or find it distracting. The player can also be used to play a recording of a metronome or environmental sound, such as the ocean, as a deepening technique.

3. The second unit is an inexpensive reel-to-reel tape player with at least a two-hour capability per one side of tape. This unit is turned on as soon as the subject enters the room and runs continuously until he leaves. Upon completion of the session, the tape from this unit must be preserved and kept as evidence. This tape must never be erased or reused until all prosecution, litigation, and appeals in the case have been expired.

4. The bottom unit is a cassette recorder. This unit is turned on only during the actual interview or memory enhancement part of the session. Upon completion of the session, this tape can be conveniently given to the primary investigator allowing him to review it in detail and to determine if future sessions are needed. This tape is not entered into evidence.

5. A one-hour reel-to-reel or cassette videotape recorder with camera and monitoring screen should be positioned unobtrusively in the far corner of the room. If possible, the ideal arrangement is for the equipment to be in an adjacent room with the camera viewing through a special vent or one-way mirror. The equipment is then monitored by another party. The entire hypnosis session, from the beginning of the induction, is videotaped. If the camera is in the hypno-investigation room, it should face the subject at an angle so he does not have to look directly into it. The operator and subject both must be entirely in the picture.

6. To ensure high quality audio recording, two clip-on power microphones, one for the subject and the other for the operator, should be interconnected with patch cords such that they drive the two audio and the video recorders. Specifically, the microphone cords will terminate into a three-way plug unit. One leg of this plug is corded into the input side of the video recorder. The other leg goes into a patch cord that ties into the reel-to-reel unit and the cassette recorder. Prior to the arrival of the subject the operator should check the voice level and video capability.

7. Directly behind the subject's chair

in full view of the video camera should be a large clock and numbered calendar hanging on the wall. The clock ensures continuity of the videotape and documents the duration of the session. The calendar documents the date.

Granted, the above recommendations represent the ideal, and departmental budgetary and physical constraints will often dictate the degree to which the proper accommodations can be arranged. Nevertheless, it should be realized that if you are competing with a distracting environment for the subject's attention and concentration, success in the induction is contraindicated.

In fact, several cases have been reported where normally excellent subjects were unable to reach even a light trance due to an unusually dry and hot atmospheric condition in the room.[52] Recognizing that a case may stand or fall based on the documentation of the procedures used if challenged in court, every effort should be made to comply with the above recommendations.

This discussion has been concerned strictly with the architectural considerations of a hypno-investigation room. Practical aspects of dealing with subjects within that setting are discussed in "Logistics at the Scene" in Chapter 5.

RECRUITING AND MANAGING PRACTICE SUBJECTS

When learning the system of hypnosis put forth in this book, the hypno-investigator should have a pool of a minimum of six volunteer subjects to practice on. These subjects should be highly susceptible and should vary considerably as to age, personality, sex, race, etc. It is important to begin with highly susceptible subjects so the beginning operator can have an initial motivating taste of continual success, for even one early failure can literally destroy a budding confidence. Furthermore, it is important for the learning operator to see that hypnosis does work: most will still retain doubts about its authenticity and especially their ability to induce it.

The subject pool should be diverse as it is very easy to develop some self-limiting beliefs and habits regarding what types of people you can hypnotize, e.g. only members of the opposite sex, members of your own sex, but only if they are younger, etc. It is also recommended that the beginner not practice on members of his immediate family or close friends as he might lack the necessary prestige, which will usually preclude success. It is also very hard to be serious and keep from joking when practicing on family and friends. As a beginner, it is also recommended not to try to hypnotize anyone who challenges you, nor should you try to prove the reality and value of hypnosis to a skeptic. It is very important throughout your training period and on through your whole career to treat hypnosis very seriously and to never engage in practices that could be viewed as parlor games and cocktail party entertainment.

Once a beginning operator has become fairly proficient at the basic techniques of eye fixation, arm drop, hand levitation, postural sway, the deepenings, testing and challenging, and is ready to begin the more difficult techniques of dynamic and confusion methods, which are designed for difficult subjects, it is recommended that the operator practice on less susceptible subjects.

Hypnosis is one of the most misunderstood, yet sought-after, experiences. As a result, in recruiting subjects one will usually be met with some initial resistance. After a straightforward explanation of the true nature of hypnosis, however, most people become eager volunteers, although probably still a little skeptical. If the course in hypnosis is being conducted within your department, a number of subjects can readily be recruited among office personnel. More subjects can easily be recruited from auxiliary criminal justice agencies with whom you work closely. If more subjects are required, plenty can be screened from groups outside the criminal justice system such as grade school, high school, and college classes.

The following are the procedures to recruit and screen subjects from groups:

1. Identify potentially interested groups.

2. Approach the person in authority for permission.

3. Give the group a brief explanatory talk on your purpose and the nature of hypnosis. Telling the group that volunteer subjects will be taught self-hypnosis at the end of the course, which they can then use as a personal development tool, helps to recruit subjects.

4. Conduct some suggestibility tests to screen out the best subjects (see Appendix 4).

5. Talk to each interested susceptible subject to determine if there are any contraindications for using this person (see "Contraindications: Who Not to Hypnotize").

6. Take the names of some of the less susceptible, but interested, subjects to be used later in the course.

7. Be certain that each screened volunteer thoroughly understands the objectives of the course and their role in it.

8. Have each sign a release and go over the Preinduction Questionnaire (see Appendix 5).

9. Determine the motivation of each volunteer. Quite often, subjects desire therapy and believe that hypnosis is therapeutic. These subjects should be rejected.

When screening subjects, one should keep in mind that suggestibility tests are not absolute predictors of susceptibility to hypnosis. There will occasionally be what are known as "false positives" or "false negatives," which are individuals who respond falsely either extremely high or low, respectively, to the tests for any number of reasons.

Considerations in dealing with subjects

1. The subject's welfare must be your primary concern.

2. Treat the subjects with utmost respect and be sensitive to their experience and appreciative of their cooperation.

3. Maintain a hypnotist-subject confidentiality, and only share hypnotic experiences with subjects and other hypno-investigators if educational. Most hypnotic subjects are very sensitive and self-conscious about their personal hypnotic experiences, so never talk about your experiences with hypnotic subjects in front of other subjects except in generalities and without mentioning names.

4. Subjects who either display an emotional problem during hypnosis or talk about one after hypnosis should be terminated as subjects.

REFERENCES

1. Hilgard, Ernest R.: *Hypnotic Susceptibility.* New York, Harcourt, Brace & World, 1965, p. 3.
2. Rosenthal, Robert: *Experimenter Effects in Behavioral Research.* New York, Appleton-Century-Crofts, 1966.
3. Hilgard, Ernest R.: *Divided Consciousness: Multiple Controls in Human Thought and Action.* New York, Wiley, 1977, p. 1.
4. Watkins, John G.: *The Therapeutic Self: Developing Resonance – Key to Effective Relationships.* New York, Human Sciences, 1978.
5. Green, Elmer and Green, Alice: *Beyond Biofeedback.* New York, Delacorte, 1977.
6. Rimland, Bernard: The autistic savant. *Psychology Today,* August, 1978, p. 69.

7. Russell, Peter: *The Brain Book.* New York, Hawthorn, 1979, p. 131.
8. Ostrander, Sheila; Schroeder, Lynn; and Ostrander, Nancy: *Superlearning.* New York, Delacorte, 1979, pp. 13-14.
9. Pearce, Joseph C.: *The Crack in the Cosmic Egg: Challenging Constructs of Mind and Reality.* New York, Pocket, 1973, p. 107.
10. Erickson, Milton H., Rossi, Ernest L., and Rossi, Sheila I.: *Hypnotic Realities: The Induction of Clinical Hypnosis and Forms of Indirect Suggestion.* New York, Irvington, 1976, p. 309.
11. Meares, Ainslie: *A System of Medical Hypnosis.* New York, Julian, 1960, p. 7.
12. Weitzenhoffer, André M.: *General Techniques of Hypnotism.* New York, Grune & Stratton, 1957, p. 22.
13. Meares, Ainslie: Theories of hypnosis. In Schneck, Jerome M. (Ed.): *Hypnosis in Modern Medicine,* 3rd ed. Springfield, Thomas, 1963, pp. 390-391.
14. Teitelbaum, Myron: *Hypnosis Induction Technics.* Springfield, Thomas, 1965, p. 20.
15. Jaynes, Julian: *The Origin of Consciousness in the Breakdown of the Bicameral Mind.* Boston, Houghton Mifflin, 1976, pp. 383-384.
16. Gibbons, Don: *Beyond Hypnosis: Explorations in Hyperempiria.* South Orange, Power, 1973, p. 2.
17. Cousins, Norman: The mysterious placebo: How mind helps medicine work. *Saturday Review,* October 1, 1977.
18. Ikemi, Y. and Nakagawa, S.: A psychosomatic study of contagious dermatitis. *Kyushu Journal of Medical Science, 13:*335-350, 1962.
19. Kroger, William S.: *Clinical and Experimental Hypnosis.* Philadelphia, Lippincott, 1963, p. 122.
20. McGlashan, T. H., Evans, F. J., and Orne, M. T.: The nature of hypnotic analgesia and placebo response to experimental pain. *Psychosomatic Medicine, 31:*227-246, 1969.
21. Evans, Frederick J.: The power of a sugar pill. *Psychology Today,* April 1974, p. 56.
22. Gibbons, p. 8.
23. Kroger, p. 120.
24. Orne, Martin T.: The nature of hypnosis: Artifact and essence. *Journal of Abnormal and Social Psychology, 58:*277-299, 1959.
25. Sarbin, T. R.: Contributions to role-taking theory: I. Hypnotic behavior. *Psychological Review, 57:*255-270, 1950.
26. Orne, Martin T.: On the simulating subject as a quasi-control group in hypnosis research: What, why, and how? In Fromm, E. and Shor, R. E. (Eds.): *Hypnosis: Research Developments and Perspectives.* Chicago, Aldine-Atherton, 1972, p. 442.
27. Sarbin, p. 269.
28. Bowers, Kenneth S.: *Hypnosis for the Seriously Curious.* Monterey, Brooks/Cole, 1976, p. 108.
29. Meares, *Medical Hypnosis,* pp. 9-10.
30. Snyder, E. D.: *Hypnotic Poetry.* Philadelphia, University of Pennsylvania, 1930.
31. White, Robert W.: An analysis of motivation in hypnosis. In Kuhn, L., and Russo, S. (Eds.): *Modern Hypnosis,* 1977 ed. No. Hollywood, Wilshire, 1977, pp. 204-205.
32. Morgan, A. H.: The heritability of hypnotic susceptibility in twins. *Journal of Abnormal Psychology, 82:*55-61, 1973.
33. Weitzenhoffer, p. 156.
34. Meares, *Medical Hypnosis,* pp. 16-18.
35. Bowers, p. 63.
36. Frankel, Fred H.: *Hypnosis: Trance as a Coping Mechanism.* New York, Plenum, 1976, p. 27.
37. Hilgard, Josephine R.: *Personality and Hypnosis: A Study of Imaginative Involvement.* Chicago, U Chicago Pr, 1970.
38. White, pp. 204-224.
39. Wolberg, Lewis R.: *Medical Hypnosis: The Principles of Hypnotherapy,* Vol. I. New York, Grune & Stratton, 1948, p. 101.
40. Sarbin, p. 268.
41. Hilgard, Ernest, *Hypnotic Susceptibility,* p. 23.
42. Bowers, pp. 85-109.
43. Erickson, Rossi, and Rossi, p. 312.
44. Bowers, p. 89.
45. Kroger, p. 33.
46. Völgyesi, Francis A.: Hypnosis in Hungary. In Marcuse, F. L. (Ed.): *Hyp-*

nosis Throughout the World. Springfield, Thomas, 1964, p. 140.

47. Naruse, Gosaku: Hypnosis in Japan. In Marcuse, F. L. (Ed.): *Hypnosis Throughout the World.* Springfield, Thomas, 1964, p. 197.

48. Watkins, John G.: Psychodynamics of hypnotic induction and termination. In Schneck, Jerome M. (Ed.): *Hypnosis in Modern Medicine,* 3rd ed. Springfield, Thomas, 1963, p. 363.

49. Mehrabian, Albert: *Silent Messages.* Belmont, Wadsworth, 1971, p. 1.

50. Farina, A., Allen, J. G., and Saul, B. B.: The role of the stigmatized person in affecting social relationships. *Journal of Personality, 36:*178, 1968.

51. Farina, A. and Ring, K.: The influence of perceived mental illness on interpersonal relations. *Journal of Abnormal Psychology, 70:*50, 1965.

52. LeCron, Leslie M. and Bordeaux, Jean: *Hypnotism Today,* 1978 ed. No. Hollywood, Wilshire, 1978.

Chapter 3

PRINCIPLES AND DYNAMICS OF HYPNOSIS AND SUGGESTION

CRITICAL ELEMENTS AND PRINCIPLES OF INDUCTIONS

THE FORMAL PROCESS and procedure utilized to put an individual into a hypnotic state is known as a hypnotic induction. To induce hypnosis, several basic steps must be followed and a sequence of elements obtained. These are enumerated and discussed briefly below.

The essential purpose of a hypnotic induction is to direct the subject's experience in such a way as to make his conscious mind and ego passive to the receipt of suggestions. The induction itself can be broken down into four basic phases.

1. RESTRICTING THE SUBJECT'S FIELD OF CONSCIOUSNESS. This is generally achieved by the following:

a. Fixating the subject's attention on some perceptual, physical, or mental region, or on all three simultaneously. For example, in the "eye fixation" induction, the subject is asked to gaze intently at the tip of a pen (perceptual) as he feels his eyelids get heavier and heavier (physical) as if a force (mental) were pulling them down.

b. Limiting voluntary movement.

c. Monotony and repetition.

2. DEVELOPING A SET OF EXPECTATIONS. The operator plants the initial suggestions of what is going to occur using the future tense, e.g. "Your eyes will become heavy, and they will blink."

3. REINFORCING THE SET OF EXPECTATIONS. As the initial suggestions or predicted responses manifest, the operator comments upon this by using the present tense, e.g. "You see, your eyes just blinked."

4. SETTING A SPECIFIC BEHAVIORAL GOAL AND ESTABLISHING A CUE FOR ITS ELICITATION. Once the subject has responded to the initial suggestions and you have commented upon and reinforced them, the operator then plants a definite and final expectation or goal that will occur at the presentation of a given cue, e.g. "When the eyes finally close, but not before, you will go into a deep state of relaxation. When the eyes close I will also press down on your shoulder, which will help you to go deep."

5. PROVIDING THE CUE AS THE SUBJECT REACHES THE GOAL. In most inductions the cue is an actual behavioral response of the subject, such as his eyes closing. However, an additional cue provided by the operator, such as pressing down on the subject's shoulder, will reinforce the suggested effect.

If the sequence and logic of the above critical elements and principles are examined closely, it can be seen that the induction process is a carefully structured and controlled situation in which the subject is led to have certain expectations that something specific is going to occur, and providing that something, which leads to conviction and hence to hypnosis. The function of a hypnotic induction, then, is to provide a controlled context and structured framework that facilitates the receipt of suggestions.

PRINCIPLES OF SUGGESTION

Throughout the five critical elements of hypnotic inductions outlined above, the operator's primary concern and skill will be to properly develop and place suggestions. The properly worded suggestion, given at the right time in the correct manner, will largely determine the degree of success of an induction. Some general principles in the development and placement of suggestions are discussed below.

The Practical Art of Developing Suggestions

Dictum — *One must use what he sees and see what to use.*[1]

The development of suggestions essentially involves a process of observing and anticipating a subject's behavior, commenting upon the behavior, then anticipating subsequent behavior and commenting on it. The purpose of this three-fold sequence is to create the belief on the part of the subject that your suggestions are *causing* his experiences. For example, in the eye fixation induction, observe your subject's eyes as he stares at the tip of a pen you are holding in front of him. You suggest that soon his eyelids are going to get heavy. As you continue talking you observe his eyes watering slightly and the lids becoming heavy so you immediately comment on the heaviness and suggest that he will soon blink. As soon as he blinks you bring this fact to his attention and continue to suggest greater heaviness and more frequent blinking. As the lids become heavier and the blinking reflex slows, it is time to suggest it will get even slower and that his eyes will get heavier until they finally close, at which point his whole body will be heavy, tired, and relaxed. By this time, if you have timed the suggestions properly, the subject will be thinking to himself, "What this guy says is true." Kroger explains the process in this way:

> During induction, the subject's attention is fixed upon his eyelids by the remark, "Your eyes are getting very, very heavy." If his eyes actually become very heavy, then he is ready to believe other suggestions that he attributes to the operator's "powers." The subject does not realize that the lid heaviness actually was induced by the constant and fatiguing position of the eyes, staring upward at the ceiling. Rather, he believes that his eye fatigue resulted from the operator's suggestions of heaviness.[2]

Thus, the subject attributes "power" and "control" over his experience to the operator in a gradually increasing manner until he can actively direct the subject's experience. This process gradually escalates to the point that the subject is surprised to find that his experience and behavior are altered in a seemingly autonomous manner and that his experience *seems* to be outside his usual sense of control and self-direction. Bowers describes the subject's experience as follows:

> They are surprised because they do not experience themselves as making the behavior happen; instead, they experience the behavior as happening to them. For example, when suggestions are given to hypnotized persons that their arms levitate, they do not experience themselves as raising their arms; rather, they experience their arms as rising by themselves. Frequently, a subject new to hypnosis will smile in wonderment as the arm goes higher and higher without apparent aid or effort.[3]

Grading

In essence, the purpose of hypnotic induction and suggestion is to create a situation in which a predictable response is likely in a subject so that the operator can predict this response and comment on it when it occurs, which ratifies his prediction, thus creating in the subject the perception that the operator *caused* it. Once this initial belief is instilled, the subject is likely to follow more difficult suggestions. In placing suggestions, then, the operator must start with suggestions that are easy and build to those that are more complex and difficult. Since hypnosis depends primarily on the subject's *belief* that it *will* happen, suggestions must be given that will be accepted, thus *convincing* the subject that it *is* happening. As one suggestion is accepted, the operator's credibility increases and the subject's conviction increases, which allows for the acceptance of a more difficult suggestion. This escalating process increases the subject's suggestibility, eventually leading to hypnosis. In effect, an ascending spiral of belief and conviction is created.

To avoid taxing the subject's suggestibility, the operator must *grade* his suggestions properly. This means that during the initial phases of the induction, he should merely observe behavior, comment on it, and make some mild predictions of inevitable behavior, the inevitability of which is unknown to the subject. Until this time the operator has essentially been *following* the subject, but once the predicted behavior manifests itself and the operator comment's on it, he may begin to *lead* the subject by giving more difficult suggestions that are not inevitable, but which the subject is expected to follow. For example, heaviness and eventual eye closure are inevitable in the eye fixation induction, but going into a deep trance at eye closure is not.

In conclusion, Weitzenhoffer states that

> it is essential to give the subject only suggestions to which he will respond, preferably with a strong response. This is one reason for using a graded series. If we start with the easiest suggestions first we stand a better chance of getting a response. At the same time, if the subject responds, then the chances of his responding to the next harder suggestions may be improved. . . . The first few suggestions must be so chosen that they will either evoke responses or be associated with activities which are present at the time. In this way, then, we gradually build up the subject's suggestibility.[4]

Linking

Another key principle in the development and placement of suggestions is known as *linking,* which refers to the actual process or mechanism by which a graded series of suggestions is tied or linked together. In essence, as a subject carries out one suggestion, his positive response is used to reinforce and help cause the next more difficult suggestion. For example, in the hand levitation induction, it is suggested to the subject, after his hand begins to float up, that his eyes will begin to get heavy, tired, and drowsy. The operator continues with suggestions to this effect until the eyes actually become heavy, tired, and drowsy, all the while giving the impression that this would have come about in the natural course of events anyway. What the operator has done is to give the subject the impression that the manifestation of the first response will *cause* the second response. Once the hand begins floating up, it is suggested that the subject's eyes will begin to feel heavy, tired, and drowsy *because* the hand is floating up. Thus, the subject's successful response to a graded series of suggestions that resulted in the hand levitating was linked to an entirely different response. In essence, the process of linking is the glue that binds graded series of suggestions together.

Another form of linking is what the authors have called *reciprocal linking,* which involves the operator phrasing his suggestions in such a manner that the successful response to a linked suggestion is fed back and used to reinforce the first suggestion. For example, when the linked suggestion of heaviness, tiredness, and drowsiness of the eyes takes effect, the operator reinforces the levitation of the hand by saying, "The heavier, tireder, and drowsier your eyes become, the lighter the hand becomes and the more it wants to float up." To initiate a cycle of linking and reciprocal linking, the operator can continue with, "And the lighter the hand becomes and the more it wants to float up, the heavier, tireder, and drowsier your eyes become."

Practical Hints and General Rules of Suggestion

1. Keep up a steady flow of suggestions and patter. Don't give your subject time enough to critically analyze the suggestions or process. Unannounced pauses will give the subject the impression that you may not know what you are doing.

2. Each suggestion must be acted upon before proceeding. If a subject does not respond or responds only weakly to a leading suggestion, go back to easier suggestions until you build his suggestibility enough to eventually readminister the failed suggestion.

3. Use your voice to facilitate the acceptance of suggestions. As suggested behavior is manifested, become slightly more emphatic and dynamic. This builds expectancy on the part of the subject because it conveys to him that what you predicted is actually happening.

4. Express confidence in the effectiveness of all your suggestions by giving them in a tone of conviction.

5. The effectiveness of suggestions can be greatly enhanced by attempting to engage as many of the subject's senses as possible. The objective is

total involvement of the subject in your suggestions. To facilitate this involvement, make as much use as possible of (a) description, (b) metaphors, and (c) physiological reinforcement. For example, in the closed door deepening technique, thoroughly describe the subject's favorite place to engage sight, hearing, smell, touch, and even taste. In the hand levitation induction, suggest that the hand is becoming so light that it's as if a balloon were tied to it or as if a force were pulling it up, while reinforcing these metaphors by lightly stroking the hand. This last maneuver is based on Pierce's Law of Dominant Effect, part of which states that a psychological suggestion can be reinforced by a physiological sensation.[5]

6. Do not give commands, but manipulate and direct the subject's experience through his imagination. This is based on Coué's observation that, "When the will and the imagination are in conflict, the imagination always rules."[6] A common example of this is stage fright. You can tell yourself that giving a speech in front of a group is really no different than giving it to a friend while willing yourself to be calm, but try as you may you cannot control your imagination. Hence, when giving suggestions, engage the subject's imagination as much as possible. For example, in the eye fixation induction, suggest to the subject that his eyes are getting so heavy that it's as if a force were pulling them down, as if a heavy weight were attached to them, as heavy as lead, and that the thought crosses his mind as to how easy it will be just to let himself go completely and become very drowsy and sleepy.

7. Keep repeating suggestions until they take effect. This is based on Baudouin's Law of Concentrated Attention, which states, "When a person's attention is concentrated on an idea long enough, that idea automatically tends to realize itself."[7] This is also known as "ideomotor action," which is the tendency for thoughts and ideas to spontaneously result in a physical reaction. For example, as the mind keeps imagining the feared situation as in the above example of stage fright, the body automatically begins to perspire, the stomach becomes nervous, and the voice shaky. In the same vein, concentrating on the idea of lightness in one's hand as in hand levitation, the hand will indeed begin to feel light and float up unless the person is resisting. It is the job of the operator, then, to keep the subject concentrating on that image with a steady stream of suggestions.

8. Give the subject adequate time to reorient and respond to suggestions. Don't hurry.

9. Observe and report every behavior of the subject as being indicative of the onset of hypnosis. For example, if the subject takes a deep breath, say, "There, you just took a deep breath, and that's a good sign that you're relaxing." Also, periodically reassure the subject that he is doing well: most subjects, particularly the first time, have no idea how they are doing or if they are doing it correctly. Beginning hypnosis subjects are learning a new skill so they need reinforcement.

10. Attempt to make your suggestions as logical and believable as possi-

ble. This is in the recognition that the greater the illogic or unbelievability of a suggestion, the greater the risk of arousing the subject's critical judgment, which may reject the suggestion. Where possible, then, provide a sound reason for the acceptance of the suggestion. For example, when anesthetizing a hand as a test of a medium trance level, it is much more believable and hence acceptable and successful if the operator links his verbal suggestions of numbness with the cool swabbing of rubbing alcohol. This provides the subject with a ready-made reinforcement and explanation for anesthesia. Similarly, when eliciting eye catalepsy, indicate that the reason the subject cannot open his eyes is because the muscles are so relaxed.

DEPTH OF HYPNOSIS

The primary goal of the hypno-investigator is to obtain additional information from volunteer victims and witnesses to crimes. It is generally recognized, however, that the elicitation of certain hypnotic phenomena requires certain depths of hypnosis. For example, a deep trance is necessary for age regression and subsequent revivification.

In theory, determining the depth of trance should be straightforward. In practice, however, the response variability of subjects complicates the evaluation of depth of hypnosis. Fortunately, there are some guidelines reviewed below.

Many researchers have attempted to categorize various hypnotic phenomena according to the depth of trance necessary for their elicitation. One purpose of these endeavors was to answer the question of what percentage of the population is hypnotizable and to what depth. A number of different scoring systems resulted that were designed to measure a person's susceptibility to hypnosis by the number of different hypnotic phenomena that could be elicited. The most comprehensive scoring system and depth scale was designed by LeCron and Bordeaux[8] (see Table I). Kroger warns, however, that "it is difficult to measure the depth of hypnosis objectively. At best, all rating scales are arbitrary divisions."[9] A further problem is that it is very difficult to accurately determine where one stage begins and another ends, for they are not separate and distinct, but continuous. Accurate determinations of trance depth are further compounded by the response variability of different subjects as some characteristics of the "deep state may be shown by a person in only a medium trance (perhaps even in the light stage), and possibly some of those listed as characteristic of the light or medium trances may not be evidenced by some individuals in the deep trance."[10] It is obvious, therefore, that the different stages with their associated phenomena are only general indicators of hypnotic depth.

To address the question of what percentage of the population can be hypnotized and to what stage of hypnosis, LeCron and Bordeaux estimate the following statistics based on experience and reports of other studies in the literature:

Insusceptible   5%
Hypnoidal   10%
Light Trance   25%
Medium Trance   35%
Deep or Somnambulistic Trance 25%

These figures indicate that 85 percent of the population can reach at least a light trance, but LeCron and Bordeaux caution that these figures are intentionally conservative and that an adept operator devoting consider-

TABLE I*

LeCRON-BORDEAUX SCORING SYSTEM FOR INDICATING DEPTH OF HYPNOSIS

Insusceptible
  0 Subject fails to react in any way

Hypnoidal
  1 Physical relaxation
  2 Drowsiness apparent
  3 Fluttering of eyelids
  4 Closing of eyes
  5 Mental relaxation, partial lethargy of mind
  6 Heaviness of limbs

Light Trance
  7 Catalepsy of eyes
  8 Partial limb catalepsy
  9 Inhibition of small muscle groups
 10 Slower and deeper breathing, slower pulse
 11 Strong lassitude (disinclination to move, speak, think or act)
 12 Twitching of mouth or jaw during induction
 13 Rapport between subject and operator
 14 Simple posthypnotic suggestions heeded
 15 Involuntary start or eye twitch on awakening
 16 Personality changes
 17 Feeling of heaviness throughout entire body
 18 Partial feeling of detachment

Medium Trance
 19 Recognition of trance (difficult to describe but definitely felt)
 20 Complete muscular inhibitions (kinaesthetic illusions)
 21 Partial amnesia
 22 Glove anesthesia
 23 Tactile illusions
 24 Gustatory illusions
 25 Olfactory illusions
 26 Hyperacuity to atmospheric conditions
 27 Complete catalepsy of limbs or body

Deep or Somnambulistic Trance
 28 Ability to open eyes without affecting trance
 29 Fixed stare when eyes are open; pupillary dilation
 30 Somnambulism
 31 Complete amnesia
 32 Systematized posthypnotic amnesias
 33 Complete anesthesia
 34 Posthypnotic anesthesia
 35 Bizarre posthypnotic suggestions heeded
 36 Uncontrolled movement of eyeballs—eye co-ordination lost
 37 Sensation of lightness, floating, swinging, or being bloated or swollen; detached feeling
 38 Rigidity and lag in muscular movements and reactions
 39 Fading and increase in cycles of the sound of operator's voice (like radio station fading in and out)
 40 Control of organic body functions (heart beat, blood pressure, digestion)
 41 Recall of lost memories (hypermnesia)
 42 Age regression
 43 Positive visual hallucinations, posthypnotic
 44 Negative visual hallucinations; posthypnotic
 45 Positive auditory hallucinations; posthypnotic
 46 Negative auditory hallucinations; posthypnotic
 47 Stimulation of dreams (in trance or in natural sleep)
 48 Hyperesthesias
 49 Color sensations experienced

Plenary Trance
 50 Stuporous condition in which all spontaneous activity is inhibited. Somnambulism can be developed by suggestion to that effect.

* From Leslie M. LeCron and Jean Bordeaux, *Hypnotism Today*, 1978 ed. North Hollywood, Wilshire Book Co. Courtesy of Mrs. Leslie M. LeCron.

able time to the induction could probably hypnotize almost any normal person, in which case these figures would prove to be much too low. The authors, as well as most experts, would have to agree that most every normal person should be hypnotizable to a fairly deep trance, given the proper operator-subject relationship, the correct technique employed by a skilled operator, the proper mental set of the subject, and enough time for repeated inductions. Teitelbaum believes "that anywhere from fifty to seventy-five percent of all first attempt subjects can be inducted into a somnambulistic trance state" given the proper technique.[11] Weitzenhoffer, on the basis of his extensive experience, estimates "that the percentage of people who can reach a relatively stable deep trance may be as high as 70 to 80 percent, and at least 50 percent or better — provided of course that hypnotizing is made an individual problem and the proper amount of time is allowed."[12]

The issue of time is interesting and important, but controversial. There are two basic time factors: (1) time required to induce hypnosis and (2) number of times a person is hypnotized.

The time required to induce hypnosis will vary greatly depending upon the technique used, the susceptibility of the subject, and the depth of trance desired. If a rapid technique is used with a highly susceptible subject and a stable deep trance is not desired, the induction will often be less than sixty seconds. On the other hand, if a slower more passive technique is used with a less susceptible subject and a stable deep trance is desired, several hours are not unusual to spend on an induction, and sometimes even then with little success. The average induction time on first attempt subjects will be approximately thirty minutes.

As regards the number of times a person is hypnotized, it is well recognized that most subjects will go progressively deeper and faster up to a certain point with each successive induction. Hypnosis is largely a learning and conditioning process, so subjects can be taught to enter deep hypnosis. Except with the highly susceptible subject, the deepest trance and best results will not be attained the first session, but only with two, three, or more subsequent sessions. With the relatively unsusceptible, the induction of hypnosis can become somewhat of a marathon. Vogt, a nineteenth century German hypnotist, allegedly attempted six hundred separate inductions on one subject and seven hundred on another before being successful. Erickson reported spending on one subject a total of "300 hours of systematic labor before a trance was even induced."[13]

The practical function of the LeCron-Bordeaux scoring chart (Table I) for the hypno-investigator is that it gives him some general guideposts for determining hypnotic depth. This is extremely important for several reasons. In recognizing the importance of properly graded suggestions and the subsequent development of the operator's prestige and the subject's belief, conviction, and expectation, it is essential that the operator "always test to determine what depth of trance the subject has reached before attempting demonstrations of phenomena of a deeper trance state."[14] By so doing, the operator can avoid embarrassing failures by attempting to elicit hypermnesia (enhanced recall) or revivification (reliving) without first being relatively certain that the subject has reached the necessary depth. Furthermore, the operator will maximize his chances for obtaining complete, accurate, and reliable information. The authors have observed a number of experienced operators, and occasionally even an authority in the field, destroy their credibility with a subject and fail to obtain additional information because they did not make sure the subject was sufficiently deep. Such an oversight may not only result in a session's failure, but may also destroy a potentially good subject. With this in mind, "the cardinal rule of hypnotic induction is that the operator should not attempt deeper trance states without first determining that the subject has entered the lighter trance states."[15] Exactly how this is done will be discussed in detail in "Challenging and Testing: Determining Depth of Hypnosis" in Chapter 4.

The question remains of how deep the subject should be. The answer to this is largely dictated by the objective of the hypno-investigator and by the hypnotic phenomena that he needs to elicit. The hypno-investigator's objective is to obtain as complete, accurate, and reliable information from victims and witnesses to crimes as possible. To obtain this quality information, the hypnotic phenomena of hypermnesia or revivification normally require a deep trance level, although slight hypermnesia may be achieved in the lighter stages. The system of hypnosis put forth in this book was designed to maximize the hypno-investigator's chances of obtaining either complete hypermnesia or revivification. This position is based on the following essential proposition:

> Any phenomenon that manifests or is elicited in a lighter trance state will be manifested or elicited in a deeper trance state, but to a greater degree, commensurate with the increased depth. Therefore, the degree of hypermnesia or revivification will increase proportional to increased depth.

The task of the hypno-investigator, then, is to get his subject as deep as he is capable during any particular session, and hopefully to a deep or somnambulistic trance level.

The one remaining question is, "How do you know how deep a subject is?" As mentioned above, the practical value of the LeCron-Bordeaux scoring chart is that it gives the hypno-investigator some general guideposts for determining hypnotic depth. It is these guideposts that the authors will now discuss.

Hypnotic Phenomena and the Determination of Depth

For practical purposes, the light, medium, and deep or somnambulistic trance levels are those that are of interest to the hypno-investigator. The 5 percent of the population who are unsusceptible are obviously of no value or interest, the hypnoidal state is prehypnotic, and the plenary trance is essentially theoretical.

The phenomena listed in Table I can be divided into four basic types: (1) those that can be observed, (2) those that can be tested for, (3) those that can be elicited through challenging, and (4) those that can be obtained only through feedback from the subject. In the course of undergoing hypnosis, certain observable behavioral signs are fairly consistently manifested, such as deeper more rhythmic breathing. Other hypnotic experiences and behaviors cannot be observed without testing for their existence, such as the absence of startle reflex. There are also some hypnotic phenomena that are characteristic of specific depths, but that can only be determined to exist by challenging the subject to perform a certain behavior that cannot normally be carried out at a particular stage, such as opening his eyes in a light trance. Some hypnotic experiences of subjects are of a private subjective nature and can only be determined by feedback, either while still in hypnosis or once awake. For example, if a subject under hypnosis says he is feeling very light and is floating he is probably in a deep stage.

A combination of these four different means is used by the operator to determine the approximate depth of a subject at any particular time during the session. Although it is difficult to accurately determine depth, since all subjects respond differently, the experienced operator can make a close approximation. Some general characteristics of each trance level are reviewed below. The specific tests and challenges are presented in detail in Chapter 4.

As a subject enters a light trance, he will physically relax; his eyelids will become heavy, blink, and eventually close; his breathing will slow and deepen; pulse will slow as observed by the carotid artery; the mouth, jaw, and eyelids may twitch and tremble slightly as the muscles relax; and he becomes disinclined to move or talk. To determine if in fact the subject is in a light trance he can be challenged to open his eyes.

The following are observable signs of increasing depth and a medium trance level: total relaxation, loss of control of the neck muscles causing the head to roll to the side or forward, limpness of the jaw and relaxing facial muscles, and deeper more rhythmic breathing. To make sure he is in fact in a medium level trance, the subject can be tested for glove anesthesia, olfactory illusions, absence of startle reflex, and total physical relaxation. A good indication of a medium trance level is the challenge for arm catalepsy, which takes a much larger muscle group than the eye catalepsy.

Observable characteristics of a deep or somnambulistic trance include a total bodily relaxation to the point of immobility and the appearance of sleep. An arm may slip off the person's lap or arm of the chair and hang limply. If asked to move or perform any suggested task there will be an automatic and willing compliance (as long as it does not violate the person's moral or ethical code). There is, however, a detectable time lag in initiating the movement or task, which is also characterized by a certain mechanicalness or rigidity. Speech and gestures will be slightly slowed and the eyeballs may move uncontrollably and even independently of each other. The subject may also be asked to open his eyes at this stage, or he may do so spontaneously, without awakening. The pupils will be dilated and they will have an obvious glassy, dreamy, or starry appearance and the face will almost appear masklike. Upon command, however, somnambulistic subjects can walk, talk, and behave normally to the point where even an experienced operator cannot tell the difference between them and nonhypnotized subjects without doing direct tests. If suggestions are not continued, though, the somnambules will return to their chairs and fall back into the traditional somnambulistic state.[16] Occasionally a somnambule will spontaneously become very animated, open his eyes, talk, and act normally to the point where the operator may make the mistaken observation that he has awakened (which is a possibility). If this happens, assume the subject is still in a deep state (as he most likely is) and give appropriate suggestions for him to close his eyes and continue with the session. One of the best tests for a deep trance is "suggested amnesia" which, if successful, indicates to the operator that the subject is sufficiently deep to obtain hypermnesia or revivification.

Once the session has been terminated, or during the trance state itself, the operator can obtain clues of depth through feedback from the subject. Specifically, if the subject reports different physical sensations such as heaviness, numbness, tingling, or feelings of detachment or dissociation from his body, he is at least in a light trance and possibly deeper. The more profound and noticeable these feelings of detachment, the deeper the trance. At a deep trance state the subject may report sensations of floating, lightness, spinning, spiralling down, or total nonawareness of his body. He may also experience bizarre bodily distortions, such as feelings of bloating, swelling, or shrinking.

The phenomena in Table I are only general indicators and not absolute predictors of hypnotic depth, and there are always exceptions. For example, although twitching of the mouth and jaw muscles are usually indicative of the onset of hypnosis, it may be a sign of resistance in some subjects. Similarly, although most subjects' breathing deepens and slows with increasing depth, it may quicken and become shallow with others. Yet with others, it is a sign of resistance. Furthermore, some subjects in a deep trance will display few or none of the observable signs. Determining hypnotic depth, therefore, must be based on the entire constellation of observable signs, tests, challenges, and feedback. Any one of these by itself is relatively insignificant when judged apart form the entire behavioral pattern of the individual.

The Nature of Hypnotic Phenomena

Essential to the study of hypnosis is the thorough knowledge of hypnotic phenomena, their characteristics, and techniques for elicitation, for therein lies the uniqueness and value of hypnosis. Hypnotic phenomena have undergone considerable testing and experimentation throughout the last half century. Although there is still considerable disagreement as to their true nature and cause, their existence is beyond question. The purpose of this section is to thoroughly acquaint the hypno-investigator with these phenomena, but techniques for their elicitation will not be presented until later.

Catalepsy

The term *catalepsy* is used in reference to two distinctly different muscle conditions: (1) waxy flexibility and (2) rigid catalepsy. *Waxy flexibility* refers to a peculiar state of muscular tonicity in which any muscle group, especially the arms, hands, and fingers will remain for indefinite periods in any position in which they are placed. Fingers can be molded into certain positions or an arm placed in an awkward position, and they will remain there automatically and without effort. If pressure is applied, the appendage will spontaneously resist it. If a hypnotized person's head is turned to one side or up or down, the eyes will remain fixed in their original straight ahead position.

Rigid catalepsy refers to a suggested condition of muscular contraction of various parts of the body that will seemingly involuntarily become extremely rigid. Once elicited, the subject is challenged to break the catalepsy, but he cannot if sufficiently deep. This type of challenge serves three purposes: (1) it is an indicator of depth, (2) it convinces the subject he is hypnotized, and (3) it convinces the operator that the subject is hypnotized. The most common catalepsies are those of eye catalepsy, which is indicative of a light trance, and arm catalepsy, which is indicative of a medium trance.

A popular feat of the stage hypnotist is complete body catalepsy. Generally, he will select a highly susceptible female out of the audience, hypnotize and suspend her between two chairs while suggesting muscular rigidity. Once cataleptic, he selects two or three hefty males to sit on her extended body, which she effortlessly endures. Obviously, the hypno-investigator must never attempt this.

Although rigid catalepsy is usually the result of direct suggestion, there is some question as to whether waxy flexibility is an independent spontaneous hypnotic phenomenon or if it is actually the result of nonverbal suggestion. For example, lifting a subject's arm up over his head and giving it a slight pull may be interpreted as a suggestion that it is supposed to remain there, as it sometimes will, which is indicative of at least a medium level trance. In the authors' experience, however, the arm will usually drop to the subject's lap with a thud, which is also indicative of a medium or deeper trance. If only in a light trance, the subject will lower his arm with some degree of volitional control, which is readily observable.

Rapport

There are two separate and distinct types of rapport. In its common usage, *rapport* refers to a harmonious, close, and sympathetic interpersonal relationship. As will be discussed in the next section, the development of rapport between the subject and operator during the preinduction phase is very important in relation to the subsequent success of the hypnotic induction, especially in passive induction methods.

The other type of rapport, known as *hypnotic rapport,* refers to the intensified and selective attention and responsiveness of the hypnotized subject to the hypnotist and his suggestions. This increased responsiveness can vary from a slight increase in attentiveness to the hypnotist and his suggestions, but with a continued awareness of the environment and other stimuli, to the degree of total selective attentiveness to the hypnotist and his suggestions with a corresponding total selective inattention to the environment and other stimuli. Highly susceptible subjects will sometimes become totally unaware of their environment, and their experiential perceptual world will contain only themselves and the hypnotist. Psychoanalytically-oriented operators have referred to this condition as a merging of ego boundaries in which the subject's ego merges with that of the operator. The condition of hypnotic rapport can more readily be explained by the process of suggestion and hypnotic induction in which there is a gradual narrowing of the subject's field of awareness down to the primary source of the hypnotist, which is coupled with an increased responsiveness to his graded suggestions.

Another apparent aspect of hypnotic rapport is the obvious desire on the part of the subject to carry out the operator's suggestions and to please him by doing so. This aspect of hypnotic rapport helps to explain why subjects in stage shows will perform ridiculous acts — their performance is largely an effort to please the one to whom they have deferred. This also explains why some people will simulate or feign hypnosis.

Historically, it was believed in the time of the Mesmerists that hypnotized persons were only conscious of the hypnotist and consequently would only respond to his suggestions. It was believed, however, that this rapport could be transferred or shared with others present. Most present-day authorities believe that hypnotic rapport is not an essential characteristic of hypnosis (at least in its classical sense) as most subjects are aware of the presence of other persons and will even respond to their suggestions. Some experimenters maintain that if the subject believes that he is only supposed to respond to the hypnotist, he will act as if others do not exist. Other researchers, however, have shown that some hypnotized children who have no notion of hypnotic rapport will spontaneously respond only to the operator. Even the parents are unable to attract their attention.

Whatever the true nature of hypnotic rapport, it is important for the hypno-investigator to assume that it does exist. Therefore, during a hypno-investigation, if the operator wishes to have the primary investigator ask questions of the victim or witness, he must first transfer or generalize the rapport. This can be done by simply saying, "Now Mr. Jones, Detective Macek, who is the investigator in this case and who has been sitting here, wishes to ask you some questions. You can now listen to him and easily answer him."

Anesthesia

Anesthesia refers to the partial or complete loss of the sense of pain. Complete or total anesthesia of major parts or the entire body is indicative of a deep trance level. The reality and validity of complete anesthesia is beyond doubt. Major surgery, including amputation, is frequently performed with hypnotic anesthesia alone. People in waking consciousness can tolerate up to approximately 20 volts when applied to their skin before finding the pain unbearable. Hypnotic subjects with induced anesthesia can withstand 120 volts without flinching.[17] Furthermore, studies conducted on physiological stress reactions to painful stimuli, as registered by changes in respiration, pulse rate, and galvanic skin reflexes, concluded that hypnotic anesthesia was genuine.[18, 19]

When hypnotic anesthesia is induced on a limited portion of the body, such as a hand, it is referred to as *glove anesthesia*, which is indicative of a light medium stage.

Both anesthesia and glove anesthesia are often manifested spontaneously if a subject becomes dissociated from his body.

Anesthesia can also be extended to other senses. For example, functional blindness and deafness can be induced. In controlled experiments, subjects who had their sense of hearing hypnotically anesthetized did not flinch or report hearing a concealed starter pistol fired behind their heads. It is interesting and important to note that Hilgard has shown that at some level of awareness the person did actually hear the shot.[20] Hilgard has empirically shown that a dissociated portion of the personality serves as a hidden observer. Watkins, in his hypnotic examination of ego states, concludes that there are multiple levels of perceiving selves within an individual, but that the dominant personality or executive ego state may not be aware of these other selves.[21] These observations may help to explain how a completely drug anesthetized and unconscious surgery patient can recall under hypnosis everything that was said and done during the operation. Similarly, it may help explain how a subject made hypnotically blind to a chair will nevertheless walk around it.

The value of producing and testing for anesthesia for the hypno-investigator is primarily as an indication of hypnotic depth and simulation (see "Controls for Simulation and Lying" in Chapter 7).

Hyperesthesia

The reverse of anesthesia is referred to as *hyperesthesia*. As a result of direct suggestions to this effect, a hypnotic subject can become extremely sensitive in all of his senses. Many experiments have been reported where subjects with hypno-induced hyperesthesia have been able to seemingly greatly enhance their sense of touch, hearing, seeing, taste, and smell. Whether the increased sensitivity is due to an actual organic change or to intensified concentration is a matter of debate. Whatever the case, hyperesthesia is indicative of a deep trance, but has little practical value for the hypno-investigator.

Sensory Illusions

Tactile (touch), gustatory (taste), and olfactory (smell) illusions can readily be produced in a medium level of hypnosis. If handed a cold coin and told it is very hot, a subject will immediately drop it and a blister may even appear.[22] "Presented with a blotter and instructed that he is partaking of a tenderloin steak, the subject will proceed to eat and swallow the blotter with satisfaction as if he were actually eating a tenderloin."[23] Asked to take a deep whiff of his favorite cologne, a subject will delightfully inhale ammonia without even a physical reaction. Such sensory illusions, especially the ammonia test, are good indications of depth as well as controls against simulating or feigning of hypnosis.

Posthypnotic Suggestions

A suggestion given a hypnotized person that will not take effect until a specific time, or upon a certain cue, after dehypnotization, is a posthypnotic suggestion. Any phenomenon that can be elicited or produced during hypnosis can also be elicited posthypnotically, but it takes a deeper stage of hypnosis to produce the same phenomenon posthypnotically. For example, by examining Table I, you will find that glove anesthesia can be produced in a medium trance, yet posthypnotic anesthesia requires a deep trance. In spite of this general fact, many posthypnotic phenomena will be carried out regardless of the depth of trance. The degree, force, or conviction and deliberateness with which they are carried out, however, will depend on the depth of trance, the existence of amnesia for the suggestion, the degree to which the suggestion has been repeatedly given and conditioned, its compatibility with the person's needs and motivations, and the amount of time before its elicitation. For instance, if a posthypnotic suggestion is given to a subject in a deep trance, amnesia for it is suggested, it is repeated several times by the operator and subject alike, it is compatible with the person's needs and motivations, and it is to be carried out within several hours or days, then it will most surely be promptly and correctly carried out below the person's conscious awareness. If, however, any one of these conditions is not met, the posthypnotic suggestion may be resisted. This will usually cause considerable anxiety as the individual is compulsively driven to carry it out.

Depending upon the degree to which the above factors are met, poshypnotic suggestions vary in the length of time that they will remain effective. It is generally agreed by the experts that most posthypnotic suggestions, if not periodically reinforced, will lose their effectiveness in several months. Even so, there are many reported instances where they have lasted for years.

For the hypno-investigator, there are only several practical applications of posthypnotic suggestions: (1) establishing a posthypnotic cue for instant rehypnotization, (2) to induce a deeper trance faster on the next induction, (3) reducing crime-related anxiety or trauma, (4) as techniques for enhancing recall, and (5) to elicit behaviors as tests of depth and simulation. All these will be discussed later.

Amnesia

There are three basic types of hypnotic amnesia: (1) spontaneous post-hypnotic amnesia, (2) suggested posthypnotic amnesia, and (3) suggested amnesia, all of which are usually indicative of a deep trance.

Spontaneous posthypnotic amnesia refers to a partial or complete loss of awareness upon waking as to what transpired during hypnosis. Historically, complete spontaneous posthypnotic amnesia was long considered a primary characteristic of hypnosis by some authorities and it occurred with a surprising regularity. This was probably due to a prevalent popular belief at that time that complete posthypnotic amnesia was always a result of hypnosis, as well as a result of induction techniques that relied heavily on the word *sleep*. Many people associate sleep with not remembering and hence by indirect suggestion they are amnesic. With the use of modern techniques, the avoidance of the word *sleep*, and preinduction emphasis that the subject will be aware and conscious, spontaneous posthypnotic amnesia is very uncommon. It is the authors' experience that spontaneous posthypnotic amnesia is very rarely a sign of very deep hypnosis as many authorities still maintain, but is actually usually a result of (a) indirect suggestions conveyed by the operator, or (b) by the subject's implicit beliefs and expectations which equate hypnosis with loss of awareness and hence remembrance, and (c) in the absence of suggestions to the contrary by the operator.

To avoid this potential problem, the techniques in this book do not use the word *sleep*, and a specific suggestion is given in the dehypnotization protocol for the subject to remember everything. If for any reason a subject is amnesic posthypnotically, he should be rehypnotized and the amnesia lifted, which is easily done. There are two basic reasons why this should be done. First, spontaneous amnesia can be disconcerting to the subject. Second, it is a precautionary measure wisely taken to protect the operator's integrity, especially if he is male and the subject female. There have been cases reported of accusations of rape made by female hypnotic subjects. When analyzed, however, what generally happened was that the subject developed a positive transference reaction to the operator and experienced a vivid or lucid wish-fulfilling erotic dream. The dream aroused considerable guilt so the woman unconsciously projected or shifted the blame to the operator, hence absolving herself of responsibility. This is all quite unconscious and the woman will be convinced that the sexual act actually occurred.

There may be a few instances where a hypno-investigator will want to deliberately induce suggested posthypnotic amnesia, i.e. to test for depth, faking, and lying which will be discussed later. *Suggested posthypnotic amnesia* refers to an induced post trance amnesia for a specific trance experience, memory, or behavior, as the result of a posthypnotic suggestion. For example, as a test for depth, a subject may be told that he will be unable to remember his phone number upon awakening.

Suggested amnesia refers to a suggested temporary forgetting during the trance itself. It is used primarily as a test for depth and is indicative of a deep stage of hypnosis if complete (see "Suggested Amnesia" in Chapter 4).

Dissociation

Hypnotic subjects will often say that they felt dissociated, of which there are three basic types: (1) dissociation from the environment, (2) from one's body, and (3) from one's self. A hypnotic subject may feel dissociated in any one or all three of these areas at any particular time. The degree of dissociation will also vary proportional to depth. In the lighter stages, a subject may lose some awareness of, or at least interest in, his environment or body. In the deeper stages, he can lose total awareness of his environment except for the operator. The subject may not be aware of his body and may feel "outside" of himself. Dissociation from one's self is used as a technique for anesthesia, probably most commonly in obstetrics and dentistry. For example, a woman in labor is asked to visualize herself outside of her body so she can watch "that woman who looks like her" having a baby, or a dental patient is asked to "step outside" of himself and go to his favorite place. In the same manner, a traumatic crime victim can be dissociated from the actual event.

Automatic Writing

Automatic writing is an interesting phenomenon that can be useful to the hypno-investigator as a means of accessing a person's subconscious for buried information. Automatic writing is essentially a dissociative phenomenon that is induced by anesthetizing or otherwise dissociating the dominant hand while giving the subconscious suggestions to write on a specific topic and to answer questions truthfully. Essentially an exaggeration of everyday doodling, automatic writing can proceed quite on its own without the awareness of the subject, who may even be talking on an entirely different topic. It is often used by hypnotherapists as a means of eliciting repressed traumatic material and of determining a patient's true feelings regarding a particular personal matter. In a similar fashion, a victim or witness's subconscious may be able to write out a license plate number while he cannot remember it consciously.

Even though all people cannot learn to write automatically, it can easily be elicited in most people in a medium trance. As with all hypnotic phenomena it will be enhanced with increased depth.

Time Distortion

Time distortion is another interesting and useful phenomenon for the hypno-investigator. That the human brain has the potential to distort time is evidenced nightly by dreams that seem to last for hours, but in actuality are a matter of seconds. There are numerous reports of near death accidents in which people report that their lives literally and instantaneously "flashed before their eyes." During medium to deep hypnosis, such time distortions can be readily produced. If a hypno-investigator wants to be certain that the victim or witness is recalling all the details of the crime event, he can slow the hypermnesia down, stop, or even back up the action and let the subject zoom in on one particular scene. Conversely, he could have the subject re-experience a crime event instantaneously and then relate the details posthypnotically.

Hallucinations

In somnambulistic subjects, hallucinations in any or all of the senses can be readily produced that will be experienced either while in hypnosis or posthypnotically. A *negative hallucination* refers to the suggestion for the subject not to be able to see, hear, feel, smell, or taste something that is actually there. For example, a somnambule can be made to not see a chair. A *positive hallucination* refers to the suggestion of the subject to see, hear, feel, smell, or taste something that is actually *not* there. For example, a somnambule can be made to hallucinate a rabbit that he can even pick up and fondle.

It is generally among researchers that hallucinations are genuinely experienced by the subject, but at some level of awareness the subject knows they are not real. As mentioned previously, some research demonstrates that a subject instructed to walk across a room will walk around a negatively hallucinated chair. As with most hypnotic phenomena, however, there are conflicting reports and differing views. Cases have been reported in which subjects bloodied their noses by trying to walk through a hallucinated open doorway in a solid wall.

With one notable exception, hallucinations are of no practical value to the hypno-investigator, and they should not be experimented with. The exception is that hallucinations can be used as an effective test for simulation (see "Controls for Simulation and Lying" in Chapter 7).

Trance Logic

As first observed and conceptualized by Orne, *trance logic* refers to "the apparently simultaneous perception and response to both hallucinations and reality without any apparent attempts to satisfy a need for logical consistency."[24] For instance, in the example of the negatively hallucinated chair, the hypnotized subject both sees and does not see the chair, and has no difficulty resolving this paradox. The simulating subject, however, might purposefully bump into the chair "under the mistaken idea that this would inevitably happen to a genuinely hypnotized subject who was negatively hallucinating the chair. What the simulator does not realize is that it is possible to register reality at one level while remaining unaware of it at other levels of experience."[25]

Regression, Hypermnesia, and Revivification

These are the most interesting and important hypnotic phenomena for the hypno-investigator and a major section will be devoted to their discussion and techniques for their elicitation (see "Elicitation of Hypnotic Phenomena" in Chapter 4).

REFERENCES

1. Kroger, William S.: *Clinical and Experimental Hypnosis*. Philadelphia, Lippincott, 1963, p. 51.
2. Ibid., p. 8.
3. Bowers, Kenneth S.: *Hypnosis for the Seriously Curious*. Monterey, Brooks/Cole, 1976, p. 116.
4. Weitzenhoffer, André M.: *General Techniques of Hypnotism*. New York, Grune & Stratton, 1957, p. 204.
5. Pierce, F.: *Mobilizing the Mid-brain*. New York, Dutton, 1924.
6. Coué, Émile: *How to Practice Suggestion and Auto-Suggestion*. American Library Service, 1923.
7. Baudouin, Charles: *Suggestion and Auto Suggestion*. New York, Dodd Mead, 1922.
8. LeCron, Leslie M. and Bordeaux, Jean: *Hypnotism Today*, 1978 ed. No. Hollywood, Wilshire, 1978, pp. 64-67.
9. Kroger, p. 43.
10. LeCron and Bordeaux, p. 67.
11. Teitelbaum, Myron: *Hypnosis Induction Technics*. Springfield, Thomas, 1965, p. 30.
12. Weitzenhoffer, p. 269.
13. Erickson, Milton H.: Deep hypnosis and its induction. In LeCron, Leslie M. (Ed.): *Experimental Hypnosis*, 2nd ed. New York, Citadel, 1968, p. 76.
14. Teitelbaum, p. 29.
15. Ibid.
16. Hilgard, Ernest R.: *Hypnotic Susceptibility*. New York, Harcourt, Brace & World, 1965, p. 6.
17. Estabrooks, G. H.: *Hypnotism*. New York, Dutton, 1957, p. 63.
18. Sears, R. R.: An experimental study in hypnotic anesthesia. *Journal of Experimental Psychology, 15*:1-22, 1932.
19. Dynes, J. B.: An experimental study in hypnotic anesthesia. *Journal of Abnormal and Social Psychology, 27*:79-88, 1932.
20. Hilgard, Ernest R.: *Divided Consciousness: Multiple Controls in Human Thought and Action*. New York, Wiley, 1977.
21. Watkins, John G.: *The Therapeutic Self: Developing Resonance — Key to Effective Relationships*. New York, Human Sciences Press, 1978.
22. Pattie, F. A.: The production of blisters by hypnotic suggestion. *Journal of Abnormal and Social Psychology, 36*:62, 1941.
23. Wolberg, Lewis R.: *Medical Hypnosis: The Principles of Hypnotherapy, vol. I*. New York, Grune & Stratton, 1948, p. 35.
24. Orne, Martin T.: The nature of hypnosis: artifact and essence. *Journal of Abnormal and Social Psychology. 58*:295, 1959.
25. Bowers, p. 104.

Chapter 4

THE SEVEN STAGES OF HYPNOSIS

Introduction

N OW THAT THE READER has a basic understanding of hypnosis and suggestion, critical elements and principles of inductions, principles of suggestion, depth of trance and hypnotic phenomena, it is time to begin the study of the actual mechanics of hypnosis.

The complete cycle of hypnotic induction is composed of seven basic sequential stages: (1) preparation and preinduction talk, (2) induction proper, (3) deepening, (4) challenging and testing for trance depth, (5) elicitation of hypnotic phenomena, (6) awakening, and (7) postinduction. The first stage sets the scene and maximizes as many favorable factors and neutralizes as many unfavorable factors as possible. The second stage is the formal procedure utilized to put the subject into hypnosis, and the third stage is designed to maximize this state. In the fourth stage, the subject is tested for sufficient trance depth so the operator knows he can successfully proceed to elicit certain hypnotic phenomena, such as enhanced recall — the fifth stage. Upon completing this stage, the operator then proceeds to gradually awaken the subject — the sixth stage — and continues with a post induction briefing for the final stage. Each of these various stages will be treated in detail in the next seven sections. It should be stressed at this point that these stages form a continuous and sequential flow with each stage subtly merging into the next, often without a pause. To give the reader a concrete example of how all the stages flow together, a complete transcript of a live hypno-investigation is included in Appendix 6.

The system of hypnosis presented in this section was specifically designed and field-tested with one objective in mind: to maximize the chances of the hypno-investigator achieving maximum depth with each subject for the purpose of obtaining as complete a hypermnesia or revivification as possible. To this end, a variety of comprehensive preinduction, induction and deepening techniques are first presented to give the operator a sufficient arsenal of techniques for different types of subjects. A system of testing and challenging will then be presented so the operator can accurately assess subjects' depth and the progress of each session. Comprehensive protocols for hypermnesia and revivification designed to maximize the accuracy, reliability, and completeness of the information obtained will then be covered. Finally, the procedure for dehypnotization and the postinduction talk will be presented and discussed.

PREPARATION AND PREINDUCTION TALK

The induction of hypnosis begins long before the first hypnotic suggestions are given. It is first necessary to make the subject receptive for hypnosis by setting the stage and developing the proper mental set and emotional readiness, including development of rapport, motivation, and expectation. If done properly, a susceptible subject will often be partially hypnotized before the actual induction proper is begun, and the explanation of hypnosis itself is an important factor in the subsequent success of the induction. The importance of this stage has been stated well by Meares.

> Inadequate explanation of hypnosis has been one of the most frequent causes of difficulty in induction.
>   The degree to which the defenses against hypnosis come into operation is very often determined by the adequacy or inadequacy of the explanation of hypnosis. We must remember that it is the acceptance of the explanation by the [subject], and not its logic and clarity in the reality sense, which determines the adequacy of the explanation. A mere verbal acquiescence by the [subject] that he understands is insufficient. Likewise, a critical, intellectual understanding is not sufficient. Before we attempt to induce hypnosis, we must bring the [subject] to feel that he is really quite familiar with the process and that for him it holds no mysteries. Before he has ever experienced it, we bring him to feel that he is really a veteran. By this means anxiety is very much reduced, and there is a corresponding reduction of motivation for the defenses against hypnosis.[1]

During this stage the operator prepares the setting to make it conducive to hypnosis, prepares the subject to be receptive to the onset of hypnosis, makes him mentally and emotionally comfortable, and explains the nature of hypnosis. The preparation and the preinduction talk are not two distinct processes, but are continuously and intimately connected. They will be treated separately, however, as preparation involves those things that are done, whereas the preinduction talk involves those things that are said.

The following are some basic considerations and steps for preparation:

1. Secure the setting against noise, interruptions, and other distractions. Hold all phone calls and pages. Make sure the room is not too warm, cold, or drafty.

2. Make the subject as comfortable as possible both physically and emotionally. In other words, make him feel at home by being kind, empathetic, understanding, open verbally and nonverbally, etc.

3. Have coffee, water, cigarettes, and soft drinks available, and ask the subject if he wants any of them. Also ask the subject if he needs to use the lavatory.

4. Keeping in mind the powerful connotations and feelings some people have about law enforcement authorities and police stations, ask the subject if he would like a tour.

5. Introduce the subject to some department personnel.

6. Ask the subject beforehand if he wants a friend or family member to sit in. This should generally be discouraged, however, since that person is another variable with which the operator has to deal and his presence may be suggestive and influence the subject's independent recall. If the session is for practice and training purposes, third parties present no particular problems.

7. Appropriate and necessary permissions should also be obtained beforehand, e.g. from the subject's doctor if under medical care, his boss if he is missing work, the parents if he is a juvenile, etc.

8. Have the subject sign the release form and complete the Preinduction Questionnaire (see Appendix 5). Ideally, the primary investigator should have the subject sign the release before being introduced to the hypno-investigator while explaining it as routine, so that rapport with the operator is not jeopardized. The primary reason for the release is that some subjects may experience unrelated life problems subsequent to the session that they may conveniently "blame" on hypnosis.

9. Dress up or down depending upon the subject.

10. Avoid personal habits that may be objectionable, e.g. smoking, chewing tobacco, coughing, etc.

11. The operator must exhibit complete confidence and display an attitude of helpful cooperation, yet maintain his role of authority and prestige as operator and the role of the subject as subject.

Some basic considerations and steps in the preinduction talk follow:

1. Introduce yourself and take a little time to discuss your background and training in hypnosis.

2. Take time to talk about something of interest to the subject. Art Roberts, a famous police interrogation instructor from Calgary, Alberta, advises to get what he calls "2Me2s" in any interview, e.g. "Me too, I have two children," or "My mother died a year ago too." Joke a little if appropriate. At this point, the operator can also establish a "yes set," which involves asking the subject any number of questions (usually a half dozen or so) of which the answer is known to be yes. For example, "You're twenty-three years old, right? You were the victim in this crime? It says in the report you live at (address)? It also says in the report. . . . " The purpose of the "yes set" is to subtlely condition in the subject a receptive frame of mind that will say yes to hypnosis.[2]

3. Remove all misconceptions and allay the associated fears and anxieties (see "Misconceptions: What Hypnosis Is Not" in Chapter 2). These are discovered by asking the subject what he knows about hypnosis, if he has ever seen it done (most have seen it on stage or depicted in a movie), what his expectations are, and how he feels about being hypnotized. Removal of all misconceptions helps establish a closer rapport and proper motivation.

4. Emphasize the naturalness of hypnosis. This can be done by explaining that everyone is hypnotized at least twice per day — right before waking and right before falling asleep (these twilight zones are actually hypnoidal states). You can also mention "highway hypnosis," losing oneself in a good movie, a book, or daydream.

5. Motivate the subject by indicating that intelligent, mature, well-adjusted people make the best subjects, as most people like to be thought of as such. This can be a double-edged sword, however, in that it may stimulate a negative motivation for hypnosis in some subjects who subconsciously do not want to be hypnotized and who do not regard themselves as

intelligent, mature, or well-adjusted. What you may do, if you sense this to be the case, is to indicate that people of low intelligence make poor subjects, as most people do not like to think of themselves as such. It is also wise to ask the subject if he can concentrate and visualize well. If the answer is negative, move on, but if it is affirmative tell him that is an excellent sign because both of these qualities correlate positively with hypnotic suscepti-bility (always say susceptibility or hypnotizability and not suggestibility, as people do not like to be thought of as suggestible). In any event, tell the subject that you are certain that he will be a good subject and will be of great help to the investigation (or training, if he is being used as a practice subject).

6. To further motivate the subject, mention the beneficial aspects of hypnosis (see "Factors Influencing Suggestion" in Chapter 2). Stress that hypnosis is generally experienced by all subjects as a very pleasurable and rewarding experience.

7. Describe in general terms what is going to happen, what you expect the subject to do, and how he may feel.

8. Stress the need for concentration and cooperation, but instruct the subject to remain as passive as possible. You might say, "Neither help nor resist, but just let yourself go. Just let it happen." This is based on Baudouin's Law of Reversed Effect, which holds that the more one tries to voluntarily do something, the less he's apt to succeed.[3] A common example is the insomniac. The harder he tries to go to sleep, the more awake he becomes. Little does he know that if he tried to stay awake, he'd quickly go to sleep. In hypnotic induction, then, the subject should not try too hard as the more he tries to become hypnotized the less are his chances. Similarly, instruct the subject not to think about or analyze what you are doing or what he is experiencing. A passive unquestioning mind will accept sugges-tions easier than an intensely concentrating one. Hypnosis is a process of letting go.

9. Stress to the subject that his body may tend to work automatically, but that that is a good sign. Also encourage him to let any physical or mental sensations or urges develop.

10. Some authorities recommend that every subject be told that all hypnosis is actually self-hypnosis and that the operator merely serves as a guide. This is also a double-edged sword. For sophisticated, analytical, or skeptical subjects, or those who might interpret hypnosis as a battle of wills, this approach is advisable. It should also be emphasized that hypnosis is a natural state that all people have the ability of entering, but that it helps to have an expert show them how. On the other hand, with relatively unso-phisticated subjects who have definite expectations and beliefs, and who attribute a certain power and special knowledge to the hypnotist, a discus-sion to the contrary may be counterproductive, unless of course their beliefs create a negative motivation for hypnosis. Most people believe that hypnosis is the result of something the hypnotist does *to* them, and it's not always advisable to try to convince them otherwise.

11. Assure the subject that he can stop or awaken at any time as this will

increase rapport and reduce anxiety.

12. Attempt to maximize all of the "Factors Influencing Suggestion" discussed in Chapter 2.

13. In a case-related session, obtain the necessary information of date, time, and location of crime, etc. Stress to the subject that you will only ask questions regarding the specific event agreed upon and will seek no other information. It is the authors' experience that some subjects preparing to be hypnotized by a law enforcement officer are afraid that he might ask questions regarding the person's background, moral behavior, and criminal conduct, so it needs to be made clear that your only interest is the crime in question. Furthermore, the operator should explain that since the subject will be totally aware and conscious during the session, he will not reveal any information other than what he wants to anyway.

14. Explain the necessity and reasons for electronically recording the session.

15. Determine the subject's representational system. "One of the most important pieces of information that you can learn about the nature of individual experience is that people represent their experiences differently in terms of *representational systems*. Representational systems are, simply, those sense modalities which we as human beings have available and use to know (represent) the world around us. The ways in which we know (represent, experience) the world are through the sensory portals of sight, audition, kinesthesis, olfaction, and taste."[4] Although all of these systems are always operating, most people rely heavily on one of the systems and interpret all their experience via that primary sense modality. For example, some people experience the world primarily visually, others auditorily, and still others kinesthetically. When asked if they understand what you are saying, for example, these people will reply with the following, respectively: "I see what you mean," "I hear what you mean," and "I feel what you mean." In working with hypnotic subjects, then, it is important to determine the primary representational system and to appeal to that system in the induction and deepening techniques while minimizing the others. For example, if the subject is a "feeling" person, it is contraindicated to appeal heavily to his visual imagery. If suggesting hand levitation, concentrate on the feelings of the hand getting light and numb. On the other hand, if the subject is a "visual" person, concentrate on the sight and imagery of the hand moving and floating up. To do otherwise is to utilize a sense modality that is less dominant and meaningful to the subject, hence lessening the chances of a successful response and induction.

There are three basic ways to determine the primary representational system in a subject: (1) ask him which of his five senses he relies on most heavily, (2) listen carefully to his description of the crime event during the preinduction interview to determine his primary sense modality, and, similarly, (3) listen carefully to his response to the question "What is your favorite place to get away from stress" (number 11 on the Preinduction Questionnaire).

16. Now that you have established the proper setting and finished the

preinduction talk, it is time to begin the transition to the induction proper. Tell the subject that very soon you are going to begin. You may even have him change chairs (from a less comfortable to more comfortable one) to heighten the anticipation. In fact, it is often helpful in building the subject's expectancy and initial suggestibility by having him respond to a few basic procedural commands or instructions, e.g. "I think it will work better if you'd move your feet back just a bit, and now tilt your head back a little more, now take three deep breaths."

17. Avoid the tendency to express doubt in your ability to induce hypnosis out of fear of failure, but approach each session with the expectation of success and be positive and confident. Never say, "I am going to try (or attempt) the hand levitation induction," but instead say, "Now I *am* going to do the hand levitation induction." It is often helpful, as a potential face-saver, to tell the subject that hypnosis always works, and the degree to which it works depends upon his willingness, ability to concentrate, cooperate, etc. This places responsibility for entering hypnosis on the subject and heightens motivation.

18. Indicate that you are willing to take as much time as needed, as this shows sincerity and empathy. You might say, "We have lots of time, and I won't push you too fast," even if you don't actually have or take the time.

19. Recognizing that subjects often experience hypnosis according to the way it is described to them (see "The Nature of Suggestion" in Chapter 2), stress the naturalness with which people can remember, regress, and relive past events.

20. To relieve the pressure on both the subject and himself and to build the proper expectation for a second session if needed, the operator can say, "I'm sure we'll get the information you've temporarily forgotten this time, and, if for some reason we don't, we almost always do the second time."

The following are some points to remember:

• The subject, from the moment of introduction, examines the operator both consciously and unconsciously; he "reads" you to see if you can be trusted, if you know what you are doing and are confident, etc.

• It is the operator's responsibility to establish rapport, trust, the affective relationship, etc.

• During the preinduction, estimate the subject's suggestibility, determine what fears and consequent likely defenses against hypnosis he may have, and determine the best induction technique to use. (This will be discussed in detail in "The Dynamic Method: Dealing with Resistance.") If the subject has some definite preconceptions about how a person is hypnotized (usually this will be by eye fixation) or places some preconceived constraints on the experience as described in "The Nature of Suggestion" in Chapter 2, be sure to incorporate them into the induction.

• No matter how much preinduction you do, there is no teacher like experience. Many subjects will retain certain fears and misconceptions in spite of the preinduction talk and will only relinquish them when dis-

proven by personal experience.
• Before beginning an induction, the operator must have it planned out in his mind; as this will enable him to proceed smoothly.

A complete sample preinduction talk is included in Appendix 6.

It is important to stress at this point that these steps do not have to be sequentially followed with each subject. In doing so, the operator would risk coming off as too mechanical and unnatural. The thoroughness with which the operator conducts the preparation and preinduction talk will depend primarily upon the needs, fears, expectations, and experiences of the subject. For example, if the subject is extremely anxious and nervous, it might be best to talk for a short while, quiz him as to the cause of the apprehension, proceed with a brief suggestibility test or two, and then make an appointment for another day, letting him think about his experience. If the subject has had an experience with hypnosis before, quiz him regarding it and then immediately proceed. Obviously, in subsequent sessions with the same subject, no preinduction will be necessary except to quiz him regarding his last experience and to help him to relax initially with casual conversation. If the subject's expectations and demeanor warrant it, you may keep the preinduction very short, even to the extent of not having any at all. Some experts, in fact, maintain that a preinduction talk is normally not necessary. For example, Teitelbaum takes the following position:

> This suggestion of a general discussion of hypnosis is not meant to imply that a preinduction discussion is necessary in all cases. In fact, a discussion is not normally desired. Most subjects will enter the trance easily and a discussion will tend to make the process lengthy. Where resistance is encountered, the operator may then easily switch to a discussion. Sometimes a preinduction discussion may have an adverse effect on a normally good subject. The average person who understands that he is to be hypnotized, immediately builds up an expectation. Because of all of the existing literature on the subject, it is usually not necessary to explain the phenomena to be achieved in advance. The expectation has already stimulated his imagination.[5]

The authors would agree with this position in the rare event that a subject waltzes into your office, sits down, makes himself comfortable, takes off his glasses and says, "Let's begin." Normally this will not be the case. The point is made, however, that the operator should be flexible and that the preinduction may range from zero to sixty minutes or more, but that the length will essentially be dictated by the needs of the subject. The operator should avoid the temptation of unnecessarily prolonging the preinduction out of fear of beginning the induction proper. On the other hand, it is better too long than too short.

The length and thoroughness of the preinduction also depends upon the approach or style of hypnotic induction, which will be discussed next.

INDUCTION PROPER

Authoritative v. Passive

There are two basic approaches or styles in the induction of hypnosis: (1)

authoritative or directive and (2) passive or nondirective. Meares has concisely explained the difference:

> The word "authoritative" is applied to hypnosis when the [operator] assumes an attitude of authority toward the [subject]. The [subject] is overpowered, mastered and subdued by the authority of the [operator]. Sometimes this has been known as "prestige" hypnosis, because the build-up of prestige is an important factor in enabling the [operator] to command the necessary degree of authority. . . .
>
> "Passive" hypnosis is the antithesis of the authoritative method. In it the [operator] makes no display of authority, and the prestige is subtle, so that the [subject] is not consciously aware of it. The [subject] is merely encouraged to allow himself to drift of his own free will into the hypnotic state. The [operator] merely guides the [subject]. . . .
>
> Ferenczi recognized the difference between these two types of hypnosis and referred to them as "paternal" and "maternal" hypnosis, depending on whether the [operator] assumed an authoritative paternal attitude or a soothing maternal approach.[6]

The basic difference is a matter of personal style, with some implications for technique. Generally, authoritative techniques are faster and are exemplified by the stage hypnotist who assumes a very dominating attitude and who does not allow the subject to think that he is in control at any time. Passive techniques, on the other hand, are relatively slower and are exemplified by the medical or clinical hypnotist who assures the subject that he is actually in control and can even awaken at any time if he desires. The ramifications of these different approaches, however, are more for style than technique, because, in actual practice, authoritative techniques can be done passively and passive techniques can be done authoritatively. The techniques presented in this book are primarily of a lengthy passive approach, although they provide enough latitude to accommodate a mildly authoritative personality or to be used in an authoritative manner for subjects whose expectations require it.

The different approaches to the preinduction, then, as exemplified by Meares and Teitelbaum in the previous section, lies in their respective styles and approaches to hypnotic induction; Meares is almost exclusively passive, whereas Teitelbaum is predominantly authoritative.

The reasons for the relatively lengthy passive approach presented in this book have been well summarized by Weitzenhoffer who has examined the pros and cons of rapid inductions.

> 1. If it is not essential that you obtain a deep trance, a rapid method will often be satisfactory, but if a deep trance is desired, then it is safer to use the slower method.
>
> 2. Failure to induce a trance by one method can hinder subsequent attempts to hypnotize by other methods which would have been otherwise successful. Since the likelihood of failure is greater with rapid methods (which usually depend upon certain ideal or semi-ideal conditions) the slower method is indicated in cases where subjects are not expendable.
>
> 3. For therapeutic and experimental purposes the slow method is usually to be preferred because it allows for better control and for a greater overall yield of successful trance inductions; yet some individuals only respond well to certain techniques which for a particular person may turn out to be what are normally considered rapid methods.[7]

Considerations for Hypnotic Induction

1. Ask the subject if he wishes to remove his shoes, tie, suit coat, or loosen his belt to get more comfortable.

2. If the subject wears glasses or contacts and provided he can see well enough without them, have him remove them as they are likely to cause discomfort. If the subject cannot see well enough without them, use an induction that can be done with eyes closed, e.g. arm drop, hand levitation, or postural sway.

3. Seat the subject comfortably in a chair with feet either squarely on the floor or on a foot stool with hands in his lap, unclasped. Crossed arms are discouraged as many techniques require the operator or subject to move one or the other hand. Lying down is also discouraged as it is too conditioned with sleep, and in some prone subjects hypnosis will actually merge with sleep. When seated, the subject's back should have ample support to avoid becoming tense and tired, and the full weight of his thighs should be on the chair seat so they can become completely relaxed.

4. To enhance the subject's role as subject and yours as operator, and to facilitate the transition to the induction protocol, begin with the following: "To begin with I want to see how relaxed you are. I'm going to pick up your right arm by the wrist. I want you just to let me have it. *(Pick up the right hand by the wrist.)* Let it relax completely and become heavy, as heavy as lead. *(If the subject is holding on to it and there is some muscle tension, move the arm around a little and give further suggestions to help relax it.)* Now I'm going to let go of it and just let it drop to your lap. You're still holding on to it a little so let's do it again. *(Some subjects will be totally relaxed the first time so it will only take one trial. Most subjects will be a little tense, so continue lifting and dropping the arm until it is as relaxed as it will become. Then do the same with the other arm.)* Now I want you to take three deep breaths and exhale completely, letting all the tension flow out of your body, relaxing further with each one." Synchronize your breathing with the subject's to enhance rapport and resonance. Hyperventilation tends to promote deeper relaxation and some authorities believe there is some evidence indicating that it increases suggestibility. To enhance this effect, the subject may be instructed to hold each inhale for a moment before exhaling. This whole procedure can be dispensed with on experienced subjects.

5. To enhance the subject's expectancy, a number of statements can be made that convey an indirect or extraverbal suggestion that the subject will indeed enter hypnosis. For example:

- "If you get completely comfortable, then you can go into hypnosis easier."
- "Did you know people can go into hypnosis standing up?" (Use if you plan on doing the postural sway induction.)
- "If you put your hands in your lap (feet flat on the floor, etc.) then you can go into hypnosis easier."
- "Before you go into hypnosis, you ought to remove your glasses (take your shoes off, etc)."

6. To further facilitate the subject's mind set for the onset of hypnosis, he can be asked a few binding questions. *Binds* are questions that provide a person with two alternative answers, each of which is a desired response of the questioner. Milton Erickson, M.D., was a master of this type of indirect suggestion and the following examples are taken from his work:

• "Would you like to experience a light, medium, or deep trance?"
• "Would you like to go into trance sitting up or lying down?"
• "Do you want to enter trance quickly or slowly?"
• "Would you like to have your hands on your thighs or on the arms of the chair when you go into trance?"[8]

Extrapolating from these examples, some further binds follow:

• "Do you want to go into hypnosis standing up or sitting down?"
• "Do you want to recall the crime this first session or the second session?"
• "Do you want to just recall the crime or actually relive it?"

7. It is always a good idea in any induction to compliment the subject periodically as the first time they never know how they are doing. Even if he is responding poorly, tell him that he is doing fine as this will make him believe that all is well and happening as it should.

8. In all inductions it is a good idea to use the person's name periodically as this helps build rapport.

9. If and when the subject's head nods forward or to one side, or if he slumps into an awkward position, tell the subject that if he wants to he can straighten up, move, and get more comfortable without affecting his depth. Subjects often do not find the position awkward and will remain as they are. If this is the case, repeat the above statement later in the session and the subject may straighten up at that time. The purpose of this is to avoid the development of an uncomfortable and distracting neck strain. It is necessary to tell the subject that he can move without affecting his depth, because most people believe that movement will bring them out of hypnosis.

10. Occasionally a subject's eyes will not close when they are supposed to (upon reaching the goal), but will stare fixedly ahead. This is usually a sign of a somnambulistic trance, especially if the eyes have a glazed or glassy look. A simple test to determine if this is the case is to move your hand in front of the subject's face. If he is in a deep trance he will remain staring directly ahead. If only in a light trance, his eyes will track your hand or blink. If this ever happens, tell the subject to close his eyes. If he does not, either ask him why he won't or gently close them for him.

11. The operator must realize that each subject is going to respond differently to each induction, particularly in reference to time required. The operator must therefore be flexible and fluent with the patter and understand the principles of inductions and suggestion so he can adapt the protocol to the needs and responses of each individual subject. The operator should not be concerned about strictly binding himself to the sample

protocols as major portions may have to be deleted with highly susceptible subjects or extended considerably with the less susceptible.

12. When the operator asks a subject a question to which he wants a verbal reply, he should preface it with the following suggestion: "I'm going to ask you a question and you'll be able to talk easily without affecting your depth." This is necessary because most people either believe that hypnotized people cannot talk or, once hypnotized, they are concerned that talking may bring them out.

13. The operator must never startle a subject with his actions. Therefore, if you are going to touch the subject, stand up, change a tape, or any other incongruous movement, tell the subject of your intentions beforehand.

14. Begin each induction in a normal voice and gradually shift to a monotonous hypnotic drone. The change should be slow and imperceptible to the subject so it does not arouse his critical faculties. Remember that your voice is your greatest tool.

Each induction will be broken down into two basic parts: (1) General Instructions and Method and (2) Verbalization. Each verbalization will be accompanied by periodic explanations within parentheses to help clarify the reasoning behind the protocol. The reader is highly encouraged to review "Critical Elements and Principles of Inductions" and "Principles of Suggestion" in Chapter 3 and to apply those principles to each protocol. In so doing, the operator will come to thoroughly understand their logic and will be able to modify them accordingly to meet individual subject responses.

To give the reader some idea as to how the protocol would actually be verbalized, several changes in type and punctuation will be used to denote voice changes and points of emphasis. Capitalized words indicate that they should be given more emphasis and with a louder voice. Hyphenated words are to be said slower. Capitalized boldfaced words that are hyphenated are to be said slower and deeper.

The following inductions proceed from the simplest to the most difficult and hence each should be learned in its turn. The ideal lesson plan and methods of learning the techniques are discussed in Chapter 1.

Eye Fixation

General Instructions and Method

With the subject seated comfortably in a chair, stand to one side out of his direct field of vision, but facing him. Hold a pen approximately 6 to 8 inches in front and slightly above the subject's eyes. His head should be level, facing directly ahead, and relaxed comfortably on his shoulders so that he has to look up at the pen. Your right elbow should be tucked into your side in a comfortable position to avoid fatiguing your arm by holding it outstretched (see figure 1). Instruct the subject to stare at the tip of the pen and to focus his concentration on it. Proceed to suggest heaviness of the eyes and occasional blinking, which is reported to the subject as it

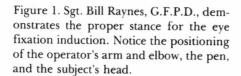

Figure 1. Sgt. Bill Raynes, G.F.P.D., demonstrates the proper stance for the eye fixation induction. Notice the positioning of the operator's arm and elbow, the pen, and the subject's head.

occurs. The suggestion continues that the longer the subject stares at the pen, the heavier and tireder his eyes will become and the more often they will blink. The goal is established to the effect that the eyes will become so heavy and tired that they will finally close tightly shut at which point the subject will go into a deeply relaxed state.

Verbalization

"As you sit there comfortably I'd like you to stare at the tip of this pen. Fix your eyes on it and also fix your concentration on it. As you do, breathe easily, naturally, and deeply and listen to the sound of my voice."

(By these three sentences the subject's attention and field of consciousness has been restricted to the tip of the pen, the operator's voice, and his own breathing. Relaxation has been extraverbally suggested by using the words "comfortably," "easily, naturally, and deeply." Voluntary movement has been completely restricted. The subject is directed to listen to the "sound" of your voice to make him aware of the rhythm and monotony while shifting his critical awareness away from the verbal content.)

"You will find that as you stare at the tip of this pen and concentrate on it, that your eyelids will have a tendency to get heavy, kind of a h–e–a–v–y, t–i–r–e–d, d–r–o–w–s–y feeling, as you become more relaxed and comfortable. You will notice that your eyes will occasionally blink." *(The subject's eyes blink.)*

(The operator has established a set of expectations of behavior that he has predicted

will occur by using the future tense. Immediately after the first blink of his eyes, report this behavior to the subject.)

"You see, your eyes occasionally blink."

(The initial prediction is reinforced using the present tense. The subject responded positively to the first graded suggestion – which was inevitable in the natural course of events — which increased the operator's prestige and the subject's confidence and expectation. As a result, the next more difficult suggestion can be given.)

"The longer you stare at the tip of this pen, the heavier your eyelids will become and the more often they will blink." *(The eyes are blinking more frequently and obviously getting heavier.)*

(Another prediction. The operator is also becoming monotonous and repetitious. If the subject's eyes ever look away from the pen, say, "Your eyes may occasionally look away, but they will always return.")

"Getting kind of t–i–r–e–d, h–e–a–v–y, and d–r–o–w–s–y. Blinking more and more, almost as if a force is pulling them d–o–w–n, as if a heavy weight is attached to them."

(Another ratification of the prediction and the subject's imagination is engaged through the use of metaphors. The operator should begin to move the pen gradually closer to the eyes to increase strain.)

"It's as if the eyes wanted to slowly close. It becomes more and more difficult to keep the eyes open as it gets harder to see, and the thought crosses your mind of how e–a–s–y it will be to just let yourself go and become so d–r–o–w–s–y and s–l–e–e–p–y."

(The operator starts referring to the subject's eyes as "the eyes" instead of "your eyes" to facilitate dissociating them from his conscious control. He is also careful not to say directly that "the eyes want to slowly close," but instead he says "it's as if the eyes. . . . " The reason behind this is that it is more of a suggestion and less of a command, thereby less likely to mobilize any resistance. Difficulty in keeping the eyes open is also linked to getting harder to see, which is most likely true. The operator extraverbally suggests that the subject should let himself go by saying "the thought crosses your mind . . . ," which it most likely will if it hasn't already. This maneuver also gives the subject more ownership for his responses.)

"In fact, the eyes are becoming so h–e–a–v–y, t–i–r–e–d, and d–r–o–w–-s–y, that you probably will not want to bother keeping them open anymore. You just want to enjoy this peaceful relaxed feeling. At some point along the way they will be s–o h–e–a–v–y and s–o t–i–r–e–d that you'll want to let them close, but you know that when they do close you will go into a deeply relaxed state." *(The eyes are only kept open with great difficulty.)*

(The operator is extraverbally suggesting eye closure by gently coaxing the subject to let go. The goal of going into a deeply relaxed state is established and paired with the cue of eye closure.)

"You feel as if they are slowly closing, slowly closing and getting h–e–a–v–i–e–r, and t–i–r–e–d–e–r, and when they finally do close how good you'll feel. You notice that it's more and more difficult to keep the eyes open as they become h–e–a–v–i–e–r and h–e–a–v–i–e–r each time they close. D–r–o–w–s–y, h–e–a–v–y, pulling down harder and harder. They're slowly closing and it's getting harder to see. S–o very hard to keep them open and feeling that very soon they will close tightly and you'll go way down." *(The eyes are almost closed.)*

(The operator continues the monotony and repetition, and he reinforces the goal.)

"Almost closing, ALMOST TIGHTLY CLOSING, ready to go WAY DOWN, TIGHTLY CLOSING, CLOSED! Going **D–E–E–P, D–E–E–P, D–E–E–P.**"

(As soon as the eyes close, the operator should reinforce the verbal suggestion with the nonverbal physical sensation of putting his hand squarely on the subject's shoulder and pressing firmly down in unison with a deep voiced command of going **"D–E–E–P, D–E–E–P, D–E–E–P."***)*

"The eyes are tightly closed, you feel relaxed, comfortable, heavy, and tired all over, as you let yourself drift deeper and deeper. You may find that this heavy, tired, relaxed feeling goes through your whole head and neck and they may just let go and nod forward slightly in a relaxed, comfortable position. The feelings magnify now, become more profound, and spread through your whole body. You've done very well, 'John.'"

(The operator attempts to maximize the relaxation and effect of the induction through a few continued suggestions. At eye closure, the subject's head may have spontaneously nodded forward or to one side. If not, the above suggestion to this effect is often enough to make it happen. If the head and neck lets go it is a good sign of increasing depth. You are now ready to proceed to deepening techniques or the eye catalepsy challenge.)

Considerations

1. If the subject wears glasses or contacts he should remove them for comfort unless his vision is too poor to see without them. If this is the case or if he has other eye problems, this technique may be contraindicated.

2. Once you position the pen, ask the subject if he can see it alright. You may have to move it closer or further away to where he can focus on it. Do not, however, let the subject look up at the pen with his whole head as this will reduce the necessary eye strain.

3. Some beginning operators have a tendency to watch the pen instead of the subject's eyes.

4. If the subject begins to blink several times before you have time to comment on it, remark, "You've probably been noticing that your eyes have been blinking."

5. Towards the latter end of the induction when the subject's eyes are held open only with difficulty, you may have to lower the pen slightly (an

inch or two) in order for the subject to still see it.

6. It is important to use a pen or other object held close to the subject's eyes in order to produce the requisite eye strain. If a far point on a wall or ceiling is used it will unnecessarily prolong the induction. Another commonly used object for eye fixation is a ring on your finger. If the latter is used and the subject responds poorly, move your hand within about 3 or 4 inches of his eyes and rhythmically move your hand up and down, suggesting that your subject "follow the ring, up and down, up and down, as your eyes become heavier and heavier. . . . "

7. An effective classical variation of the eye fixation is the use of a hypno-disc or strobe light. A very effective and often faster alternative is the use of a wrist watch with a sweep hand. The subject is instructed to watch the sweep hand as you use the same eye fixation patter. You must make certain, however, that the subject can see the sweep hand. A digital watch with a seconds register can also be used.

8. When the operator establishes the goal of going deep at eye closure, he may also pair the "single shoulder press" with this response by saying, "And when the eyes finally close, I will push down on your right shoulder which will help you to go way down." Making this suggestion explicit may have the added advantage of building expectancy (see "Shoulder Press" in "Deepening Techniques").

Eye Blink

General Instructions and Method

If the eye fixation does not produce an adequate response — the subject's eyes are not fatiguing, he continues to stare indefinitely, and it's taking too long — switch to the *eye blink* without breaking stride. This gives the subject the impression that everything is proceeding fine. The subject is complimented and then asked to continue staring at the pen as the operator begins an alternative counting sequence to which the subject synchronizes opening and closing his eyes. This maneuver enhances eye fatigue, at which point the operator continues with the eye fixation pattern and establishes the same goal.

Verbalization

"That's it, you're doing fine, but now we're going to do something that will help you to relax even further. As you continue to stare at the tip of this pen, I am going to begin counting 'one, two, one, two,' and with each count of 'one,' close your eyes, and with each count of 'two,' open your eyes. Alright, counting now, 'one, two, one, two, . . . '"

(Continue at a fairly rapid pace – about one count per second – until the subject's eyes begin to fatigue.)

"Continue counting to yourself, opening and closing your eyes as I talk to you. You will notice that the more you open and close your eyes the heavier the eyelids become. In fact, each time you close the eyes it will seem to become more and more difficult to open them again. Getting h–e–a–v–i–e–r, and t–i–r–e–d–e–r, and s–l–e–e–p–i–e–r. 'One, two, one, two, . . . ' " *(The subject's eyelids are getting more difficult to open.)*

(The operator has the subject continue on his own so that he can give additional suggestions. The obvious and inevitable is reported to the subject to enhance his suggestibility. The operator should take up the count again when the subject's eyes begin to fatigue. Begin slowing the count as it becomes harder for the subject to open his eyes.)

"That's it, you're doing fine. Just let yourself go and become more and more relaxed as the eyes become h–e–a–v–i–e–r and t–i–r–e–d–e–r. Very soon now the eyes will be so difficult to open that at some point you probably won't want to bother anymore; so just let yourself go into a deep state. They will be so difficult to open that they will finally just stick tightly shut, and you know that when they do you'll go into a very deeply relaxed state. . . . "

(The operator sets the goal and continues with the proper eye fixation patter until eye closure is obtained.)

Arm Drop*

General Instructions and Method

The arm drop induction is essentially an eye fixation coupled with an added physiological response. Seated beside the subject, instruct him to raise his left arm straight out in front of him and slightly above eye level as

---

* This induction technique was originally developed by Helen Huth Watkins, a staff psychologist at the Center for Student Development, University of Montana, and it is used here with her permission.

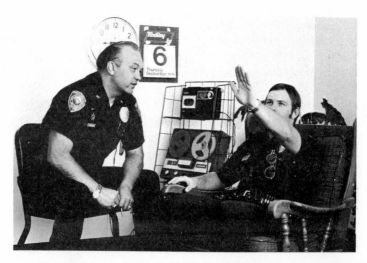

Figure 2. Asst. Chief Bill Steele, G.F.P.D., demonstrates the proper beginning position for the arm drop induction.

you demonstrate the proper position. Then ask the subject to choose either the index or middle finger and to fix his gaze and concentration on that finger (see figure 2). Proceed to suggest heaviness of the arm, which increases the longer the subject gazes at the selected finger, and suggest that the longer he gazes, the heavier and tireder his eyes become. The suggestion continues that as the arm and hand become heavier, the hand begins to move down, and, as the hand moves down, he begins to move down into a state of relaxation, but he will not enter a deep state until the hand touches the leg, at which point the eyes will be so heavy and tired that they will close tightly shut.

Verbalization

"As you sit there comfortably, raise your left arm straight out and slightly above eye level and cock your wrist back slightly like this (demonstrate) so that you can easily see your fingers. Now select either your index or middle finger and fix your gaze and concentration on that finger. You may even want to pick a particular spot on the finger you've chosen, but just keep your gaze and concentration on it as you breathe easily, naturally, and deeply, and listen to the sound of my voice."

(As in the eye fixation induction, the subject's attention and field of consciousness have been restricted to a particular visual object, the operator's voice, and his own breathing. The subject is asked to choose either the index or middle finger as if there was a logical reason (which there isn't), which is likely to increase his expectation and confidence in the operator and technique. Relaxation has also been extraverbally suggested by using the words "comfortably," "easily, naturally, and deeply." Voluntary movement has also been completely restricted, and the subject is asked to listen to the rhythm and monotony of your voice and not the logical content of the words.)

"You will notice that as you gaze at that finger the other fingers and the background may tend to fade into the periphery. As you gaze at that finger you will also notice that the arm has a tendency to get heavy, and the longer you gaze at that finger the heavier the arm becomes."

(The operator comments on and reports the obvious and the inevitable – the background will fade into the periphery, and the arm will become heavier. The operator is careful at this point to start referring to the subject's arm as "the arm" and not "your arm" in an attempt to dissociate it from his conscious self and control.)

"In fact, with each breath you take the heavier the arm becomes and it becomes s–o h–e–a–v–y that it will begin to move d–o–w–n. As if a force were pulling it down, as if it were as heavy as lead." *(The arm begins to lower.)*

(The operator predicts the inevitable, links the added physiological process of breathing to increasing heaviness, and engages the subject's imagination with some metaphors.)

"Getting h–e–a–v–i–e–r and h–e–a–v–i–e–r and moving d–o–w–n. You see, it is moving down and you move down with it, becoming more and more relaxed. A h–e–a–v–y, relaxing, pleasant feeling comes over you. If your eyes or concentration wander they will always return." *(The eyes are beginning to become heavy and blink.)*

(The operator ratifies the prediction, associates or links the subject going down with the arm, and becomes very monotonous and repetitious. The operator noticed the eyes look away from the finger so he added the additional suggestion that they would always return.)

"The longer you gaze at that finger, the heavier and tireder the eyes become. In fact, you've probably been noticing that your eyes have been blinking. With each movement down, the arm gets h–e–a–v–i–e–r and h–e–a–v–i–e–r, the eyes become h–e–a–v–i–e–r and t–i–r–e–d–e–r and d–r–o–w–s–i–e–r, and you become more and more relaxed." *(The arm is about halfway down.)*

(The eye fixation patter is now combined with the arm dropping and several suggestions are linked together.)

"The thought crosses your mind that when the hand finally touches your leg, but not before, the eyes will be s–o h–e–a–v–y and t–i–r–e–d that they will close tightly shut and you will go into a very deeply relaxed state. At that time, I will press down on your right shoulder, which will help you go deep. You think how easy it will be just to let yourself go completely and become s–o h–e–a–v–y and s–o d–r–o–w–s–y."

(The goal is set by pairing the cue of the arm touching the leg with eye closure. Notice, however, that the operator extraverbally reinforces the importance of the goal and the cue by implying that it will happen only at that time and not before. The additional behavioral cue of your hand on his shoulder will build expectancy.)

"Getting closer, about 6 inches away and getting h–e–a–v–i–e–r and t–i–r–e–d–e–r and s–o r–e–l–a–x–e–d and moving d–o–w–n. The eyes becoming h–e–a–v–i–e–r and t–i–r–e–d–e–r and they're so hard to keep open. Moving down now, and going down with it. Almost touching, getting ready to go with it. Almost touching, the eyes closing tightly shut, getting ready to go **W–A–Y D–O–W–N,** ALMOST TOUCHING, TOUCHING! Going **D–E–E–P, D–E–E–P, D–E–E–P."**

(As the hand touches and the eyes close, the operator reinforces this by pressing firmly down on the subject's shoulder.)

"You've done very well, Dick. Now the arm is completely relaxed, the eyes are heavy and closed tightly, and your whole body is heavy and relaxed. Just let yourself drift deeper and deeper relaxed as this feeling goes all through you."

(The subject is praised and some additional suggestions are given to maximize the effect of the induction. Notice that the operator does not specify exactly what the

subject is feeling. If the operator is too specific as to what the feeling is and is wrong, it may alert the subject's critical faculties. The subject is left to determine for himself just what the exact feeling is. You are now ready to proceed to deepening techniques or the eye catalepsy challenge.)

Considerations

1. This induction can also be done with eyes closed for those with exceedingly poor eyesight and other eye problems. If this is the case, have the subject start out with eyes open until he selects a finger. Have him gaze at the finger for a moment and then instruct him to close his eyes and continue to gaze at the image of that finger in his mind's eye. Of course the eye fixation patter will have to be omitted.

2. Some subjects will struggle to hold the arm up and to prevent it from going down. This is often due to a misunderstanding of what is desired of them. These subjects often believe that they are supposed to hold it up as long as possible. If you detect this to be the case (the arm might start trembling slightly or if it's held up for more than a minute or two without moving down), the following simple instruction will clear up this misunderstanding: "Don't try to hold the arm up; just let it slowly go down as it gets heavier. Don't try too hard; just let yourself go. The arm is a vehicle for relaxing." If the subject continues to hold the arm up, you have a resistance problem, which will be dealt with in "The Dynamic Method: Dealing with Resistance."

3. The left arm is used for several specific reasons. First, it is generally the weaker arm and hence will fatigue and lower sooner. Second, specifying a particular arm conveys that there is a particular reason which tends to build expectancy. To enhance this effect the operator can ask at the beginning of the induction, "Are you right-handed or left-handed? (Right-handed). Okay, I want you to raise your left arm. . . . " Third, recent research on the brain indicates that there is a special reason — the two hemispheres of the brain have different functions and qualities. The left hemisphere, which controls the right side of the body, is the seat of the intellectual, logical, rational, and technical aspects of a person, whereas the right hemisphere, which controls the left side of the body, is the seat of the creative, intuitive, artistic, nonrational, or nonlogical aspects. From the model of hypnosis presented in Chapter 2, it is the left hemisphere that hypnosis is designed to bypass, thus gaining direct access to the right hemisphere. Hence, the emphasis upon the left hand.

Hand Levitation*

General Instructions and Method

Instruct the subject to sit comfortably in a straight-backed chair with his

---

* This induction technique was first described by Milton H. Erickson, M.D. The verbalization is largely paraphrased from Lewis R. Wolberg, M.D., *Medical Hypnosis: The Principles of Hypnotherapy,* 1948, Grune & Stratton, Inc. Used with permission of Doctor Wolberg.

hands resting in his lap or on a table, desk, or arms of his chair. (As hand levitation depends on muscle tension, do not do the initial preparatory deep breathing or arm relaxation exercises.) The subject is then asked to gaze and concentrate on the hand closest to the operator (ideally this will be the left hand, but seating arrangements do not always permit this) and to become very aware of all the feelings and sensations in that hand. It is suggested that soon one of his fingers will feel differently and move. As soon as the first movement is detected, it is reported to the subject. Suggestions follow to the effect that that feeling and movement are spreading to the other fingers and the entire hand and that it begins to feel light and floats up. As the hand floats upward, suggestions of relaxation are given along with heaviness and tiredness in the eyes (use eye fixation patter). The relaxation and tiredness are suggested as increasing with each movement upward, and it is also suggested that when the hand finally touches the face, but not before, the eyes will close and the subject will go into a very deeply relaxed state.

Verbalization

"As you sit there comfortably, would you mind placing your hands on the table in front of you like this (demonstrate) and focus your gaze on your left hand as it rests lightly on the table. Now concentrate all your attention on that hand, and, as you do, you become very aware of all the sensations and feelings in that hand, no matter what they might be. For example, you may be aware that it is lightly sitting on the table and you feel its weight there. You can feel the texture of the table and the temperature of the table and possibly the temperature of the air in the room and maybe even an occasional little puff or breeze of air across the hand. You're keenly aware of the position of each finger in relation to the other fingers, as well as the color and shape of each finger. Now we know from experience that there is a great deal of muscular movement in our bodies and especially in the minute muscles of our hands. It is always there, but we are normally unaware of it. Now that you are gazing and concentrating on that hand you can become very aware of what movement and motion is actually there. It may not be noticeable yet, but, if you concentrate well enough, you will become aware of it, and it will manifest itself. If your concentration wanders from the hand it will always return. You keep gazing and concentrating on that hand and you're wondering when that movement will show itself and in which finger, which finger may feel differently and move first. It may be the index finger, the middle finger, the ring finger, the little finger, or even the thumb, but, whichever one it will be, it will feel distinctly different from the others, and it will move. It could be that it tingles a little, feels a little numb or light, and it may twitch or jerk a little, but if you concentrate well enough you will know what that feeling is and in which finger. You're probably kind of wondering which one it will be. It will be interesting to see just which finger moves first."

(At this point the subject's attention is fixed on his hand. He is curious about what

will happen, and sensations such as any person might experience are suggested to him as possibilities. No attempt is being made to force any suggestions on him, and, if he observes any sensations or feelings, he incorporates them as a product of his own experience. The object is to eventually get him to respond to the suggestions of the hypnotist as if these too are parts of his own experiences. A subtle attempt is being made to get him to associate his sensations with the words spoken to him so that words uttered by the hypnotist will evoke sensory or motor responses later on. Unless the subject is consciously resisting, a slight motion or jerking will develop in one of the fingers or in the hand. As soon as this happens, the hypnotist mentions it and remarks that the motion will probably increase. The hypnotist must also comment on any other objective reaction of the subject, such as motion of the legs or deep breathing. The result of this linking of the subject's reactions with comments of the hypnotist is an association of the two in the subject's mind.)

"There, it's the (index) finger! Now concentrate on that finger and you'll notice an interesting thing; the hand tends to work automatically, and that feeling of light numbness spreads through the whole finger, and it begins to straighten out as if it wanted to arch up and float upwards and raise off the table. *(The finger straightens and raises off the table.)* Now you'll notice another interesting thing; that feeling is beginning to spread to the adjacent fingers as if they wanted to follow. That's it, spreading into the middle finger and over into the thumb, and now over into the ring finger and little finger." *(All the subject's fingers are beginning to move.)*

(This is the first real suggestion to which the subject is expected to respond. If the fingers all start to arch up, they do so because the subject is reacting to suggestion. The hypnotist continues to talk as if the response is one that would have come about by itself in the natural course of events.)

"Getting numb and light and straightening out and lifting up. Spreading back into the whole hand and wrist now, getting lighter and lighter and the whole hand wants to float up and leave the table. That's it, you're doing fine, John. Getting lighter and lighter and floating up. Almost as if you feel a pull from above, as if a force is pulling it up, as light as a feather. It's moving by itself and without effort as if it wants to raise up into the air." *(The subject's hand has moved several inches off the table, and he is gazing at it fixedly.* See figure 3.)

(Depending on the speed with which the hand raises, the operator may have to resort to suggested visualizations or nonverbal suggestions to enhance the process. For example, if you determine in the preinduction that the subject can visualize well, you may describe a balloon of his favorite color above his head, which you are filling with helium, and that a string is tied between the balloon and wrist. The more you fill the balloon the lighter it gets and the harder it pulls on the wrist. As operator you can also make passes with your own hand over that of the subject's while suggesting that his hand and arm will get lighter and lighter with each pass. As a variation of this theme you can merely hold your hand several inches above the subject's and suggest that a force is attracting the subject's hand to yours and that as you raise your hand his will also raise.)

"Now as the hand and arm get lighter and lighter and rise higher and higher you will notice that your eyes will soon become kind of tired and heavy and drowsy. As the hand and arm continue to rise, the tireder and heavier and drowsier your eyes will become, and this feeling will begin to spread through your whole body. Now the hand begins to change direction, the arm bends at the elbow and it begins floating toward your face and it's as if your head and hand are like two magnets and the head being the larger magnet attracts the hand toward your face." *(The arm is about halfway up to the subject's face and his eyes are becoming visibly heavy and tired, and they begin to blink.)*

(As the subject executes one suggestion, his positive response is used to reinforce the next suggestion. For instance, as his arm rises, it is suggested in essence that he will get drowsy because his arm is rising. An additional metaphor is used to engage the subject's imagination, hence facilitating the levitation.)

"It's as if you can see and feel the lines of force between them, an irresistible force pulling harder and harder. The closer it gets, the harder it pulls, and the closer it gets, the heavier and tireder and drowsier the eyes become. The heavier and tireder the eyes become, the lighter the hand becomes as it pulls harder and harder toward your face. Your whole body is getting heavy and tired and relaxed and your breathing is becoming slow and regular. It's getting harder to see; everything but the hand is fading into the periphery. Blinking more and more as the eyes get heavier, the thought crosses your mind that when the hand finally touches your face the eyes will be so h–e–a–v–y and t–i–r–e–d and d–r–o–w–s–y that they will close tightly shut and you will go into a very deep and profound state of relaxation, but not before. In fact, the hand should not touch until you are ready to go real deep. About 6 inches away and moving closer. Pulling harder and HARDER, and moving closer and CLOSER, about 3 inches away and getting read to go way down. Almost touching, ALMOST TOUCHING, ready go go WAY DOWN, TOUCHING, going **D–E–E–P, D–E–E–P, D–E–E–P.**" *(The operator presses firmly down on the subject's closest shoulder.* See figure 4.)

(The operator continues to link hand levitation with eye fixation. He then sets the goal, but in such a manner as to properly align the subject's motivation, cooperation, and sense of participation in inducing hypnosis, i.e. "the hand should not touch until you are ready to go real deep." To build expectancy, the operator may add the single shoulder press as part of the verbal suggestions for the goal, as was done in the arm drop induction.)

"Let this feeling of relaxation go all through your body now. You've done very well 'John,' and now you can let the hand float gently back down to the table, and, as it moves down, you will move down with it, letting this deep state of relaxation become more and more profound. That's it, floating down now, going deeper and deeper down, and, when it touches, you will be twice as deep as you are now. Floating down, effortlessly drifting deeper and deeper down, almost touching, about 6 inches away and ready to go twice as deep. Moving down, almost touching, about 3 inches away and ready to go all the way down. Almost touching, almost touching, touching! Going **D–E–E–P, D–E–E–P, D–E–E–P.**"

(To maximize the impact of the induction, the operator utilizes the return of the hand to the table as a deepening technique.)

Figure 3. Capt. Keith Wolverton, C.C.S.O., demonstrates the hand levitation induction. The subject's hand has levitated several inches off her leg and she is gazing at it fixedly. The operator observes her eyes for signs of fatigue so that he can begin to tie in eye fixation suggestions.

Figure 4. After the subject's hand touches her face and as her eyes close, the operator simultaneously applies the single shoulder press and catches her hand which he then lowers to her lap while giving deepening suggestions.

Considerations

1. Wolberg believes that hand levitation is the best of all induction procedures because it permits an active participation in the induction process by the subject; he enters trance with his own participation. He warns, however, that it is "the most difficult of methods and calls for greater endurance on the part of the hypnotist."[9] It is also generally believed that hand levitation takes a greater degree of suggestibility because it is not "inevitable" that the hand will get light and float up.

2. The operator should be sure to have the subject place his elbows at his sides and not allow them to rest on the arms of the chair which militates against free movement of the arm and makes levitation more difficult.

3. Occasionally, a highly susceptible subject will enter somnambulism just by gazing at his hand before it begins to levitate. This can readily be observed by either the characteristic somnambulistic glazed eyes or rapid eye closure. In this event, the operator should instruct the subject to close his eyes, if they are not already closed, and dispense with the levitation suggestions. At this point, the subject should be praised, and the operator can continue with a deepening technique.

Similarly, some subjects will not close their eyes when the hand touches their face, but will gaze fixedly ahead in an eyes-open somnambulistic state. In this event, the operator should merely ask the subject to close his eyes. If the subject does not do so immediately, the instruction may have to be repeated, or the operator may close the subject's eyes for him.

An occasional subject may close his eyes before his hand touches his face. In this event the operator will have to determine through careful observation whether eye closure is due to hypnosis, is a sign of resistance, or a misinterpretation of the suggestions. If the former is the case, the subject's eyes will obviously be so heavy that he can no longer keep them open, at which point the operator merely reports this behavior and praises the subject. If it is due to resistance or a misinterpretation, the subject will voluntarily close his eyes before they become heavy and tired. In this event the operator should suggest that the subject keep his eyes open, i.e. "Even though you want to close the eyes, continue to gaze at that hand as it floats up toward your face."

4. If the operator decides beforehand that he is going to use the rapid arm drop deepening technique, he will have to seat the subject with his hands on his legs away from a table. This is to avoid the obvious, but often overlooked, problem of the table serving as a barrier that precludes the use of the rapid arm drop.

5. If the operator uses hand levitation with the subject seated at a desk or table, he may put the subject's hands in his lap for comfort at the end of the induction, if he has not done so on his own.

6. The operator should be positioned such that he can catch the subject's hand once it touches his face (see figure 4). With some subjects, the hand will continue to stay in a levitated position while others will lower their hands immediately or drop them with a thud to their lap. To be ready for

this eventuality, the operator should be prepared to catch the hand by the wrist after it touches the face so that he can lower it slowly while giving deepening suggestions. It is for this reason that the hand closest to the operator should be used. If the hand continues to levitate, the operator can give suggestions of it gently floating back to the subject's leg as in the above verbalization.

7. If the hand is slow to levitate and the operator is running short of suggestions, he can use a physiological sensation of lightly stroking the subject's fingers and back of the hand to reinforce his verbal suggestions. For example, the operator may say, "In a moment, I am going to lightly stroke the hand with mine, and, as I do, that feeling that you are now experiencing (do not commit yourself to a specific feeling) will begin to spread rapidly through the rest of the hand." (This is another reason why the closest hand should be used.) Often this nonverbal suggestion will result in a rapid levitation response. Occasionally, however, it can have the reverse effect with a subject who interprets the maneuver negatively, i.e. as too dramatic or showy, in which case it should be immediately discontinued.

8. The operator should observe and report other noticeable behavior that will help to build the subject's conviction and hence suggestibility. For example, if the operator notices that the head is moving slightly toward the hand as it approaches the face, he should remark, "You notice that your head is moving downward ever so slightly to meet the hand."

9. Many subjects will exhibit a considerable amount of trembling and movement in their fingers and hand as it levitates. Do not let this concern you: it is quite natural and common, and the operator should assure the subject of this. For example, he can say, "You notice the fingers twitch and move a lot, but that's a good sign. That shows that you are letting go, and it is very natural and common."

10. The hands of susceptible subjects will usually begin to move and levitate within several minutes. It is not unusual to spend five to ten minutes with less susceptible subjects before the hand begins to levitate.

Postural Sway*

General Instructions and Method

The subject is asked to stand in front of his chair with his feet together, shoulders back, and hands at his side. The operator must make certain that the subject is close enough and aligned properly with the chair so he will fall directly into it at the onset of hypnosis. The operator stands to one side of the subject. The subject is asked to close his eyes and then suggestions of swaying are given. As the subject becomes unsteady and begins to sway back and forth, the operator reports this motion to him. Once the swaying

---

* This induction technique was first described by John G. Watkins, Ph.D., and the verbalization is reprinted here from his text, *Hypnotherapy of War Neuroses*, 1949. Reprinted by permission of John Wiley & Sons, Inc. The words *operator, subject,* and *state* have been substituted for *therapist, patient,* and *sleep,* respectively, with permission of the Publisher.

Figure 5. The senior author demonstrates the proper positioning for the postural sway induction. In this picture the subject is swaying forward. Notice her position in relation to the chair and the placement of the operator's hands, i.e., he lightly touches the subject's shoulder to assure her that he will not let her fall.

Figure 6. The subject sways backwards and the operator again assures her by lightly supporting her with his left hand.

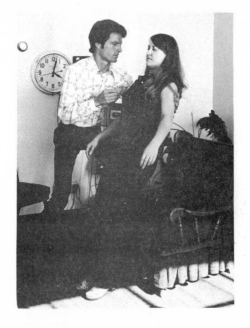

Figure 7. After a degree of hypnosis is induced and the swaying arc is substantial, the operator braces himself by extending his left leg back and puts his arm around the subject's shoulders to lower her into the chair.

arc is substantial, the operator begins to lead the subject to determine if he is sufficiently suggestible to interrupt the natural sway to follow his suggestions. The operator continues leading the subject and increasing the arc of the sway until the subject falls back into the chair. As the amplitude of the swaying arc increases the operator becomes more dominant and controlling with his voice. Swaying suggestions are continued in a firmer, more rapid voice in an attempt to get him to fall over backwards into the chair. When the subject is ready to fall, the operator places his arm around his back and gently lowers him into the chair (see figure 5, 6, and 7).

Verbalization

"Now Jones, I'd like to have you stand here with your heals and your toes together and your body erect, shoulders back. That's right. Breathe comfortably and easily with your hands at your sides. Now close your eyes. Just imagine that your feet are hinged to the floor and your body is like a stick pointing upward in the air, free to move back and forth. You will probably find after awhile, you will become unsteady. Don't worry, if you should fall, I'll catch you." *(This last remark is given in a rather matter-of-fact way, almost as a side comment. If previous suggestibility tests have been given, and the operator is quite certain the subject will enter trance, he may modify this statement by saying, "Don't worry, I will catch you when you fall.")*

The operator then continues: "Now while you are standing there, breathe very calmly and easily. Just imagine that your body is floating up into space. Don't try to do anything, and don't try *not* to do anything. Just stand there and let yourself drift." The operator is then silent for a time, perhaps fifteen seconds up to a minute. If the subject is suggestible he will sway back and forth slightly.

The operator should place himself at the side of the subject where he can line the back of the subject's head or the tip of his nose against a mark on the opposite wall so that a slight backward or forward swaying movement can be easily detected and measured. It is even convenient to have a card against the wall on which black vertical lines have been ruled about an inch apart, thus making it easier to determine the amount of sway. Usually the operator will soon detect the rhythm of the swaying, since it is almost impossible for anybody to stand perfectly still. There will always be some swaying, although it may be slight in the more unsuggestible subjects. One will generally find that the more suggestible the subject, the greater will be the amplitude of the swaying arc.

The operator next begins to reinforce this swaying by timing his remarks to coincide with it. As soon as the subject has reached the extreme forward part of the arc and begins to sway backward the operator says, "Now you are drifting backward." Frequently this will cause the subject immediately to catch himself and to reverse the direction, whereupon the operator instantly follows it with, "Now you are drifting over forward." As the swaying continues the operator reinforces it with "Drifting forward, drifting backward and forward, backward, forward, backward," etc. The tone is low, soft, and firm. The operator should be about one to two feet away from the subject's ear and should repeat the suggestions in a low, soft monotone from which all harshness has been deleted. It should have an almost pleading quality, monotonous like the drone of a bee. There should be no change of pitch, and the patter should be continued steadily. Occasionally it may be varied from "drifting forward" to "Swaying forward, swaying backward, swaying over backward, now swaying forward," or "Leaning forward, backward, forward, backward," etc. — on and on in a monotonous, repetitious voice.

As the operator observes the amplitude of the swaying arc increasing, he may make his voice somewhat less pleading, less soft and more dominant and controlling, even injecting some emotional pitch into the "forward backward, forward, backward."

When the amplitude of the swaying arc has become quite substantial — six or more inches — it is probable that some light degree of trance has been induced. Suggestibility should then be checked by beginning a command of "forward, backward" a little before the subject has reached the maximum sway of the arc. If the subject is suggestible, and there is a degree of hypnotic trance, he will interrupt the natural sway in order to follow the operator's suggestion. The past remarks of the operator have so closely followed the subject's swaying behavior that the subject begins to think to himself, "What this man says is true, I am swaying backward. Then I do sway forward." Consequently, the operator's prestige is increased, and the subject begins to follow the suggestions instead of leading them. From this point on the operator can generally assume the more dominating role and direct rather than follow the swaying of the subject.

To induce deeper trance the voice tone is now made much firmer, and the swaying suggestions are given somewhat more rapidly. *"Swaying forward, swaying backward, forward, backward,"* the volume of the voice growing stronger and stronger. Finally, attempt is made to induce the subject to fall over backward into a deep trance. The emphasis on the "backward" is increased, and on the "forward" diminished, and the verb is changed from "drifting" or "swaying" to "falling, *falling backward,* falling forward, *falling backward,* falling forward, *falling over backward,* falling, falling, *falling, falling*" rather rapidly and in a higher-pitched and more emotional tone. If a deep trance has been induced, the subject will increase the amplitude of his sway until he can no longer stand erect. He will then fall over backward in a deep trance state where he may be caught by the operator and eased into a waiting chair.

If the subject is in a light trance only he may start to fall backward, but catch himself by placing one of his feet back, or attempt to sway sideways or steady himself voluntarily in some manner. This indicates to the operator that a deep trance has not yet been induced, and he can then do one of two things: he may either continue the monotonous repetition of "falling forward, falling backward," etc., to induce a deeper degree of trance; or he may reassure the subject that he will not fall by placing a hand lightly behind his shoulder. This allays fears which might arise and interrupt the hypnotic process. After the subject realizes that he will not be permitted to fall and hurt himself, he tends to lose the signs of anxiety which may have begun to appear. He may then allow himself to fall back against the operator's arm, whereupon the operator continues the suggestions, "Falling over backward, falling backward, falling back into a deep state, back into a deep state, deep state, deep state," and then eases the subject gradually over into a chair. This, preferably an arm chair, should have been placed behind the subject. He can also be gradually lowered back upon a couch which has been located conveniently near. If the subject is either completely limp or in a stiff catatonic state when he is placed back on the chair or cot, it is evidence that a fairly deep degree of trance has been induced. If, however, he is able to help himself either by taking steps backward or by putting his hands on the armchair and guiding himself into it, then only a light or hypnoidal trance has been induced.

Considerations

1. Use a plush high-backed chair or a couch. If the chair is not secure enough, another person will have to hold it from the rear.

2. Put your hands lightly on the front and back of the subject's shoulder to assure him that you will catch him (see figure 5). As the arc of the sway increases, brace yourself and extend your arm around the back of the subject so that you can catch him and lower him into the chair (see figure 7).

3. The subject's perception of swaying can be amplified by moving or swaying your own body in the opposite direction, hence making your voice appear to be farther away. This increases the subject's conviction that it is working, hence this technique seems to work well for resistant subjects.

4. To help initiate the swaying, suggest to the subject that it's as if he is gently swaying in the breeze or rocking back and forth on the deck of a ship.

5. To aid the onset of hypnosis, periodically suggest to the subject that he drifts deeper relaxed with each sway. Also engage his imagination by suggesting that it's as if a force is pulling him backwards.

6. Towards the final phase of the induction when the operator is actively leading the subject, establish a definite goal, i.e. "When I finally lower you into the chair you will go into a very deep state of relaxation."

Confusion Methods

There are two basic approaches to confusion methods, but their goal is the same: to literally confuse the resistant or overly analytical and critical subject to the point where he desires escape into hypnosis.

The first approach may be called the *semantic approach* and it relies on the use of sophisticated forms of indirect suggestion often coupled with a rapid sequence of contradictory behavioral suggestions. This approach is very difficult and requires a thorough understanding not only of hypnosis, but of psychology and human behavior in general, semantics, and psycholinguistics. To be successful, the operator must be able to convincingly give the subject a continuous barrage of seemingly contradictory suggestions in a manner that will not arouse his logical faculties. As such, it is not recommended for the hypno-investigator. However, once an operator is thoroughly proficient with the other techniques outlined in this book and has had considerable experience, he may wish to explore the semantic approach further.

As an example of the semantic approach, Erickson would proceed in the hand levitation induction in the following manner:

> Emphatic suggestions directed to the levitation of the right hand are offered together with suggestions of the immobility of the left hand. Shortly, the subject becomes aware that the hypnotist is apparently misspeaking, since levitation of the left hand and immobility of the right are then suggested. As the subject accommodates himself to the seeming confusion of the hypnotist, thereby unwittingly cooperating in a significant fashion, suggestions of immobility of both hands are given, together with others of the simultaneous lifting of one and pressing down of the other. These are followed by a return to the initial suggestions. . . .
>
> Or, while successfully inducing levitation, one may systematically build up a state of confusion as to which hand is moving, which more rapidly or more laterally, which will become arrested in movement, and which will continue and in what direction, until a retreat from the confusion by a complete acceptance of the suggestions of the moment becomes a greatly desired goal.[10]

During the time that Erickson was giving these contradictory suggestions, which require a constant reorientation by the subject, he may have enhanced the confusion by subtlely placing the subject in a series of double-binds that provided him with a forced choice, either of which aids the onset of hypnosis. For example, Erickson would often say:

- "Will your right hand or your left begin to feel light first? Or will they both feel that lightness at the same time?"
- "Will your right hand move or lift or shift to the side or press down first? Or will it be your left hand?"
- "Do you begin to experience a numbness in the fingers or the back of the hand first?"
- "If your unconscious wants to enter trance, your right hand will lift. Otherwise your left hand will lift."[11]

The second approach to confusion methods may be called the "overload approach" which is considerably easier, faster, and probably as effective as the semantic approach. The basic rationale of the overload approach is to sufficiently confuse the subject by giving him multiple tasks or suggestions to carry out so that he either escapes into hypnosis on his own, or his conscious mind becomes passive so the subconscious can receive and respond to a simple predetermined suggestion. In the first instance, a subject may spontaneously "give up the battle," so to speak, and go into hypnosis. This is easily recognized by the subject suddenly letting go. If this does not happen, the operator must continue the suggestions until he believes the subject's conscious mind is sufficiently confused and fatigued to accept and respond to a simple suggestion that will let him escape into hypnosis to bring an end to the confusion. For example, the operator might say, "Finally, it crosses your mind as to how e–a–s–y it would be just to let yourself go now, and to feel your eyelids grow s–o h–e–a–v–y that they stick tightly shut and you let yourself go into a d–e–e–p pleasant state." This last suggestion is the goal you are trying to establish and achieve.

Overload Confusion Techniques

Overload confusion techniques generally consist of various combinations of inductions and deepenings. The operator will usually begin with a standard induction, but, if the subject responds poorly, he will introduce different techniques one at a time to the point where the subject is performing multiple tasks. One overload confusion technique will be presented for each of the major standard inductions. They are meant to be examples only, and the reader is encouraged to design some of his own; one's imagination is the only limit. In working with difficult subjects, the operator must remain flexible and be alert to the subject's individual responses as these will largely determine the exact nature of the technique to develop and use.

Eye Blink

If a subject continues to display resistance after switching from eye fixation to eye blink, instruct him to begin saying the count of one out loud as he opens his eyes, and the count of two to himself as he closes his eyes. Once this is firmly established, instruct the subject that you are going to alternate having the pen high and then low on the count of one and that he is to follow it with his eyes.

Arm Drop

Combine the arm drop with the eye blink and institute a difficult counting sequence.

Hand Levitation

Combine hand levitation on one hand with the arm drop on the other. Also incorporate the eye blink with the subject staring at a spot on a finger. Suggest that as the one arm lowers it's as if it was a lever that pushes the other up.

Postural Sway

Instruct the subject to tilt his head back (this changes the angle of the semicircular canals, which affects equilibrium and helps produce a state of mental confusion), roll his eyes up into his head, breathe deeply and hold the inhales as long as possible without undue strain (hyperventilation will produce lightheadedness), suggest hand levitation, and institute a difficult or repetitive counting sequence, e.g. one, two, three, four, three, two, one, etc.

Deepening Techniques

The standard deepening techniques may be turned into confusion techniques also. For example, while counting from twenty to one or descending the stairs, alter the count, e.g. twenty, nineteen, eighteen, sixteen, seventeen, fifteen, sixteen, seventeen, eighteen, nineteen, nine, eight, seven, six, etc.

Confusion Technique Patter

The operator can periodically use certain phrases that will enhance the subject's mental confusion.

- "Do not listen to the sound of my voice."
- "Pay no attention to the words that I am speaking."
- "You do not need to listen for it is your subconscious that I am talking to."
- "You do not need to know what's really happening."
- "No matter what you do you cannot stop it. It will happen all by itself."
- "You're probably noticing how bored you're becoming."
- "I'm really talking to your ears."
- "You actually have no conscious control over what happens."
- "You don't have to do anything as it will happen all by itself. You don't even have to prevent yourself from going into hypnosis."
- "Finally, it crosses your mind how easy it would be to just let yourself go."

The Dynamic Method: Dealing with Resistance

The tendency for most operators is to become proficient in one or two of the above induction techniques and to restrict themselves to their use. In learning the inductions in this book, the reader will quite naturally find those with which he is most comfortable. As long as the beginning operator practices on highly susceptible subjects screened from groups, one or two basic induction techniques would be adequate to meet his needs. The hypno-investigator must realize, however, that not all victims and witnesses will be highly susceptible to hypnosis. Even though they are volunteers and usually highly motivated and cooperative, a variety of subconscious needs, desires, fears, and other psychodynamic problems engendered by the hypnotic inter- and intrapersonal relationship may be stimulated (see "Basic Psychodynamics of Hypnosis" in Chapter 2). Even though the subject consciously desires to be hypnotized, subconscious conflicts may force him to defend against hypnosis.

To be successful with these subjects, the operator must recognize the subject's defenses as they manifest in behavior during the induction, and adapt his technique to either circumvent or enlist the aid of the defense. In this manner, the operator can maximize his chances of a successful induction. If, however, the operator limits himself to one or two techniques, he is likely to end in a failed session, and his tendency will be to dismiss the subject as unsusceptible.

Theoretically, the dynamic method is based on a dynamic approach to susceptibility. Essentially, susceptibility should be regarded not as a fixed and static attribute as is traditionally believed, but instead as a dynamic function of one's personality. Ordinarily, if a subject does not respond adequately to a standard induction he is dismissed as being unsusceptible.

This static approach, however, does not allow for subconscious psychodynamic mechanisms that may be preventing the onset of hypnosis. If these defense mechanisms are recognized and properly dealt with, the subject can enter hypnosis. Theoretically, the dynamic approach to susceptibility posits that every normal adult has the potential for entering a deep trance level, provided a way is found to utilize this potential. The dynamic method is the way.

When ready to hypnotize a subject, the operator is faced with a choice of method. It is always wise to begin by utilizing the presenting behavior of the subject. If he is relaxed or relaxes easily, begin with techniques involving relaxation, i.e. eye fixation or arm drop. If he is tense, begin with hand levitation. If the subject displays an overly critical or analytical attitude, start with a confusion technique. If the operator suspects the subject to be resistant, he can begin with the postural sway. If the subject responds favorably to the induction of choice, carry on with that particular technique, for there is no need to use the dynamic method. On the other hand, if the subject responds less than adequately and displays continued resistance, the operator should switch to the dynamic method.

The dynamic method is not a single technique, but is actually a method of changing or combining techniques based on the response of the subject. In the dynamic method, the exact form of the induction must be determined by the subject's behavior, which necessitates careful observation. When beginning an induction, the operator will never know if it will be necessary to proceed to the dynamic method. He will only know once the subject begins to respond or not respond to the induction. In essence, the dynamic method involves making a smooth transition to another technique if the first one fails. If the second technique also fails, the operator continues switching until he finds one that the subject responds to adequately.

The dynamic method presupposes that much of the subject's behavior in the induction phase is purposeful and, in many cases, is unconsciously directed to ward off the onset of hypnosis. For example, when giving suggestions for hand levitation, a subject is observed to relax his hand and arm completely. Instead of continuing futile suggestions of movement and lightness, the operator recognizes the behavior as a purposeful subconscious defense against entering hypnosis and changes his approach to utilize this behavior in a constructive manner. For example, the operator might say, "That's good, you're doing fine. You notice how the hand and arm become so relaxed that they don't move in the slightest. In fact, they are so relaxed that they are probably becoming heavy, and that's good. To show you just how relaxed and heavy that hand and arm are becoming, I am going to raise them straight up and out in front of you like this." The operator then continues with the arm drop induction which constructively mobilizes the subject's presenting defense in the induction itself. If the subject responds favorably to the arm drop, the operator continues with it to completion. The subject may continue to defend himself, however, by defiantly holding his arm out. To exploit this defense the operator can appeal to the subject's resistance by saying, "As you hold the arm up, you begin to resist it getting heavy. You say to yourself, 'It isn't possible for it to become heavy. It won't go down.' You will find that the more you resist, the harder it is to hold up. The harder you try the heavier it gets. Try it and you will find that the harder you try to hold it up the heavier it becomes. Try hard not to let it get heavy, but the harder you try the heavier it gets. Fight hard to keep it up, but the more you fight the heavier it becomes. Try to beat me, try to defy me, but no matter what you do you can't stop it. . . . "

The practical art of the dynamic method is predicated upon the ability to observe behavior and tie suggestions to those observations. If one induction is being met with resistance, concentrate on the subject's immediate functioning behavior and switch to a technique that will further develop and utilize the observed behavior. To be effective, the operator must be a shrewd observer as well as be conversant with the various inductions and methods of transition. (See the "Dynamic Method Sequence Chart" for specific examples.) The transitions must be done in such a manner as to make the subject think that he is progressing nicely and according to plan and that you are pleased with the way in which he is responding. This ability develops with experience. Beginning operators have a tendency to become disconcerted when met with an inadequate response and view the induction as a failure. It is important, however, that the subject does not detect his discomfort.

The successful use of the dynamic method demands adaptability on the part of the operator. He must be ready to change the nature of his suggestion according to the subject's defenses. The dynamic method is rather difficult to learn at first, but is really the answer to the flow of possibilities each operator may run into during each new session. It answers the questions even experienced operators ask, "What do I do now?" and "What do I do if . . . ?"

Common Defenses and Forms of Resistance

Most of the likely defenses and resistances can effectively be defused, circumvented, or eliminated during the preinduction talk through adequate explanation of the common misconceptions. If existing resistances are not neutralized during the preinduction talk, they may manifest themselves during the induction, in several forms, as the threat of the loss of ego control increases. To be proficient at the dynamic method, the operator must be able to recognize the most common forms of defense and resistance against hypnosis as they manifest and be able to adequately deal with them. Resistances and defenses may manifest singly or in different combinations. A subject should not be dismissed due to the manifestation of any of the following as his susceptibility and expectation will often outweigh them.

1. RESTLESSNESS. Restlessness is probably the most common defense against the onset of hypnosis and may occur at any time during the induction. Often at a critical point in the induction the subject may begin to

fidget, move his hands or feet, cough or clear his throat, sniff, shiver, talk, open his eyes, or any other behavior that will avert the onset of hypnosis. If the restlessness is only mild it may sometimes be adequately countered by direct suggestions of relaxation and letting go. If restlessness is persistent and well sustained, however, the operator should switch to hand levitation.

2. SIMULATION. Although infrequent, simulation of hypnosis is an ever-present possibility engendered by the hypnotic interpersonal relationship, and it may occur during any part of the session for any number of reasons. A consistent feature of hypnosis is the desire of the subject to please the hypnotist: he will sometimes pretend or feign hypnosis so as not to disappoint the operator.

When quizzed afterwards, a simulating subject will sometimes remark that he really wasn't hypnotized, but was just playing along. The interesting question, however, is whether the simulator was truly simulating hypnosis or was actually hypnotized and only thought that he was simulating. In the former instance, the subject is either nonhypnotizable and just wants to please the hypnotist or voluntarily carries out the suggestions to defend against hypnosis. In the latter instance the subject defends against the awareness that he was actually hypnotized by insisting that he was only cooperating fully and didn't want to let you down. This is usually the case with the person who says at the outset that he cannot be hypnotized, and hence finds it necessary to defend against the realization of a successful trance experience. Many truly hypnotized subjects believe upon waking that they only simulated hypnosis because they did not feel qualitatively different and no tests or challenges were performed to convince them otherwise.

Simulation may not only occur during an induction, but at any point during the session. For example, an occasional subject will feign eye or arm catalepsy and even role-play a revivification for the same reasons listed above.

Simulation of hypnosis is generally and most easily recognized by the promptness with which suggestions are carried out, by the lack of the almost mechanical deliberateness of hypnotic behavior, and by the lack of the general observable signs of hypnosis, i.e. slower and deeper breathing, twitching of the eyelids, total relaxation, drooping of the head, lethargy and passivity, time lag in response, etc. For example, in the hand levitation induction, the hand will raise quickly and smoothly without the usual display of tension or automatism, and the characteristic hypnotic gaze will be absent as the subject casually observes the hand. If the challenges for catalepsy are simulated the subject will usually not honestly try to beat the challenge even when prompted to do so. Besides these observable signs of simulation, there are some direct and foolproof tests which will be discussed in "Controls for Simulation and Lying" in Chapter 7.

The most effective means of coping with this defense seems to be to play along with the subject and keep repeating the induction over a number of sessions until he becomes progressively more involved in the procedure that eventually leads to hypnosis. It should be remembered that the desire or need to simulate hypnosis is actually an indication of suggestibility, and it does not mean that the subject will not eventually be a good hypnotic subject.

3. NEGATIVISM. In this defense the subject "defends himself against hypnosis by doing the opposite to what is suggested to him. By this means he is sure that he will not become hypnotized and that he will not lose control."[12] Hence, when hand levitation is suggested, the subject actually pushes his hand down. When heaviness of the eyes is suggested they actually open wider. It is important to realize that this contrary behavior is usually not consciously executed, but is subconsciously activated to avert the onset of hypnosis. Hence, the subject can legitimately claim he is cooperating while subconsciously sabotaging the induction. Meares stresses that the important thing about subjects "who react negativistically to suggestions is that they are in fact influenced by the suggestions, although in the wrong direction. The fact that they are influenced means that they are suggestible, and they can be hypnotized provided their defense can be circumvented."[13] To circumvent the defense, Meares recommends establishing a repetitive movement of an arm as an induction technique. Essentially, forward movement of the arm is suggested to which the subject will respond negatively by doing the opposite. The operator then suggests moving the arm backward to which the subject moves it forward again. This continues until the movement becomes automatic and the subject is hypnotized. Another means is to appeal to the subject's resistance by accepting it and making use of it to reinforce your suggestion. The subject is essentially told that the more he resists the more he is impelled to carry out the suggestion. (For specific verbalizations for the "repetitive movement" and "appeal to resistance," see the "Dynamic Method Sequence Chart.")

4. SLEEP. An occasional subject, especially if in a prone position, will escape hypnosis by going to sleep. It can be quite embarrassing when a subject begins to snore after the operator has earnestly been giving suggestions and deepening the trance. In seated positions, the defense of sleep is uncommon. In the event of hypnosis merging with sleep (which may also occur not as a defense, but during a silent period due to the lack of stimulation), the operator should report this to the subject in a manner that conveys that it was expected and a sign of hypnosis. Suggestions to this effect should be repeated several times in a soft voice, but close to the subject's ear. Then continue by saying, "I'm going to touch your hand and count to three and when I do you will automatically come back up out of sleep, but you will *not* wake up. . . . "

5. STARTLE REACTION. Sometimes when a subject is on the verge of letting go and lapsing into hypnosis he will suddenly startle awake. This can result from an unusually vivid fantasy that startles the subject, or it can be a defensive maneuver of an ego that suddenly realizes it is about to lose control. In either case, the operator should discuss the subject's experience

while stressing its naturalness, and then proceed with the same induction or another one if the subject agrees to continue.

6. DEPRECIATION. Subjects, who perceive hypnosis as a threat to their ego, fear the loss of control, or fear the domination of another, may depreciate the situation, the techniques, and you as hypnotist in an effort to falsely bolster their ego and reduce anxiety. This defense manifests verbally as well as nonverbally in subtle condescending, condemnatory, or sarcastic statements, questions, and facial expressions. Although this defense can be largely neutralized with explanations during the preinduction, it may manifest during the induction with continued facial expressions and even comments. Throughout the preinduction and induction the operator should continually stress to the subject that all hypnosis is actually self-hypnosis, that it is a very natural and positive state of mind, and that it takes 100 percent of his cooperation.

In an attempt to mobilize his resistance against himself, the operator may challenge the subject's ability to enter hypnosis. The subject can be told that it takes a considerable amount of intelligence and concentration, and all suggestions should be phrased in such a manner as to question his ability to perform. For example, the operator can phrase hand levitation in the following manner: "Let's see if you can make the hand so light that it will actually begin to move upward. If you try properly you can let yourself go to the point where your body will work automatically, but it takes a great deal of concentration and intelligence to do so. So I'll just keep talking as we see if you have the ability to make the hand so light that it will float up. . . . "

7. DEFIANCE. Occasionally a person will defy the operator to hypnotize him. This defense is usually exhibited by an individual who defends against a deep seated feeling of insecurity by displaying the opposite. There is usually little point in attempting to hypnotize this individual unless the operator can successfully get him to ventilate and talk through his defiance and hostility prior to the induction. This subject may prove a challenge, however, for the experienced operator who is proficient with the confusion and dynamic methods. When confronted with this type of subject, the operator should keep in mind the paradoxical reactor mentioned in "Who Is Susceptible to Hypnosis" in Chapter 2 and not dismiss him outright.

8. DISTRACTIBILITY. An occasional subject will defend against the onset of hypnosis by seemingly paying attention to anything and everything but the operator's suggestions. His eyes may continually dart away from the object of fixation; his concentration wanders; he may fidget and ask questions during the induction, all in an obvious attempt to avert hypnosis. Some individuals, however, may be quite naturally distractible, nervous, and flighty. In either case, the operator should switch to an active confusion technique such as hand levitation or postural sway to impel the subject to escape into hypnosis by overloading his fluctuating attention.

9. FEAR OF FAILURE. As paradoxical as it may seem, some people have

such a chronic fear of failure that when faced with a performance test of any kind, they will actually fail deliberately to stave off the greater anxiety caused by an expected eventual failure. In other words, they fail to prevent failure. In so doing they retain a degree of voluntary control and self-esteem by causing failure, which prevents the conscious traumatic realization that they would have failed in spite of their best efforts. During an induction, then, this person will be so fearful of failing at hypnosis that he will subconsciously deliberately bring an end to the session by prematurely giving up or failing.

This defense may be recognized by severe tension and anxiety, by the subject seemingly giving up at some point during the induction, or a statement like, "I really don't think I can do it." For example, as the subject's arm is lowering to his leg in the arm drop induction, he may quite suddenly give up and voluntarily retract the arm and terminate the induction while saying, "I just can't do it."

To capitalize on this defense the operator should circumvent the subject's fear of failure by saying, "Alright, we won't try hypnosis as yet. Let me just teach you how to relax," then proceeding to another induction. In so doing, the operator removes the feared situation of attaining hypnosis, merely by changing labels. An attitude and expression of constant and supportive reassurance may also aid the subject in overcoming this defense.

This same basic approach can often be used effectively in other defenses in which the subject displays an inordinate fear.

10. SECOND SESSION RESISTANCE. Although most subjects will go into hypnosis easier and faster with subsequent sessions as their resistances weaken and they learn to undergo hypnosis, some "will prove to be harder to hypnotize in the second session, some to show their strength of will to the [operator], and others to convince themselves that they can resist the process if they wish. Once they have shown that they can resist, this reaction ordinarily disappears."[14]

11. OVERCOOPERATION AND OVERENTHUSIASM. Quite frequently subjects will try too hard to enter hypnosis. The resultant tension is not conducive to the letting go necessary for hypnosis. A vicious cycle can easily develop as the subject tries harder and harder the more it doesn't work. Either overcooperation or overenthusiasm can also lead to simulation of hypnosis to please the operator. To combat this problem, the operator needs to continually reaffirm that the subject not try too hard and that he does not have to do anything or not do anything, but just let himself go.

12. OVERMOTIVATION. Although many people will be seemingly very interested in and motivated for hypnosis, not all will prove to be highly susceptible. In fact, some of these people may prove to be refractory because they lack the necessary aptitude and susceptibility or other defenses have been stimulated. On occasion a subject will actually use an overt display of interest and motivation as a defense against hypnosis. It seems that this person has no actual desire to enter hypnosis, but shows apparent interest and motivation for several reasons: (1) to please the

operator, (2) to live up to his self-image of being outgoing and game for anything, or (3) as the result of an ambiguous or conflicting interest in the case, e.g. the rape victim wishes to help the hypno-investigator to catch her assailant, but fears either recalling the incident or retaliation.

13. LACK OF MOTIVATION. Although many people will be genuinely not interested in or motivated for hypnosis, some individuals may use this as a defense against hypnosis and will prove to be very susceptible. For this reason, potential subjects should not be dismissed on the sole basis of lack of motivation. To help overcome the apparent lack of interest and motivation, the operator can stress the beneficial and positive aspects and uses for hypnosis, i.e. personal development, habit breaking, anesthesia, etc.

14. OVERCURIOSITY. Curiosity about hypnosis is generally a positive indication of susceptibility. Some people, however, are so curious about hypnosis that they interfere with the process by actively watching it as it occurs. Their motivation is usually to try to figure out how it works or to remember everything so they can do it themselves. To circumvent this problem, the operator should resort to a confusion technique while stressing the need for letting go.

15. AMNESIA. As stated previously, some subjects may experience posthypnotic amnesia as the result of an explicit or implicit suggestion from the operator, an inherent belief and expectation that people do not remember what transpired under hypnosis, or as a spontaneous result of very deep hypnosis. Another reason for posthypnotic amnesia is as a defense against the realization that one has in fact been under hypnosis. To avoid this remote possibility, the operator should be sure to include in the waking suggestions that the subject remember everything.

Behavior Utilization

The essential purpose of the dynamic method is to effectively circumvent or utilize a subject's defense(s) and forms of resistance in the service of the induction. The basic principle of the dynamic method is that the operator must carefully observe a subject's behavioral responses during an induction and adapt the procedure and suggestions accordingly if defenses and resistances manifest. Milton Erickson, M.D., probably *the* master of handling resistance, believed it was a grave, but common, mistake of the inexperienced hypnotist to try to "direct or bend the subject's behavior to fit his conception of how the subject 'should' behave."[15] Based on decades of clinical experience and experimentation, Erickson firmly believed that "whatever the behavior offered by the subject, it should be accepted and utilized to develop further responsive behavior. Any attempt to 'correct' or alter the subject's behavior, or to force him to do things he is not interested in, militates against trance induction and certainly against deep trances."[16]

Accordingly, the function of the dynamic method is to provide the operator with a theoretical as well as practical model and approach for recognizing, accepting, and utilizing a subject's defenses and resistances in a constructive fashion that will aid the onset of hypnosis.

Dynamic Method Sequence Chart

Induction	*When Indicated*	*Recovering and Dealing With Resistance*
I. Eye Fixation	When the subject can relax well and has no visual problems. For experienced subjects who feel tired, drowsy, and heavy.	
	1. When the subject is not adequately responding.	**a.** Switch to Eye Blink.
	2. When the subject appears to be defying or challenging you.	**a.** Appeal to Resistance: "As you sit there staring at the tip of this pen, you begin to resist getting tired and drowsy and you say to yourself, 'It isn't possible for this to happen. My eyes won't get heavy and tired and drowsy.' But you find that the more you resist and the harder you fight it, the more difficult it is to keep it from happening. Try it, and you will find that the more you resist getting tired and drowsy, the sleepier you become. Fight hard against becoming drowsy. Try not to become drowsy, but the harder you try the drowsier you become. Fight hard to keep awake. Try to defy me, but the more you do the sleepier you become. In fact, no matter what you do the eyes will become heavy and sleepy and finally close. You cannot stop them from closing. . . . "

Induction	*When Indicated*	*Recovering and Dealing With Resistance*
II. Arm Drop	For subjects who relax well and have no visual problems. Use with eyes closed for subjects who have visual problems. For experienced subjects who feel heavy.	

1. When the subject holds his arm out indefinitely.

   a. Switch to Hand Levitation: "That's good, you're doing fine. This was a technique to help you to concentrate, and now I'm going to take your arm and lower it to your leg, and now we can successfully move on to the next phase. Now I want you to switch your gaze and concentration to your right hand. ... " Continue with hand levitation patter.

   b. Appeal to Resistance (see I.2.a. above).

2. When the hand moves down but stops before reaching the leg.

   a. Switch to Hand Clasp: "That's good, you're doing fine, but now I want you to lift your other arm directly opposite this arm and turn your hands so they face each other like this (demonstrate). Now I want you to imagine that the hands are like two magnets and it's as if you can see and feel the lines of force between them. And if you concentrate well enough you will be able to feel them pull together, and the closer they get the harder it pulls." Continue this suggestion and establish the goal by suggest-

Induction	*When Indicated*	*Recovering and Dealing With Resistance*
II. Arm Drop (continued)		ing that the subject will go into a very deeply relaxed state when the hands finally touch. If this fails have the subject close his eyes and fantasize it as in the "Fantasized Hand Levitation" (see below), or switch to repetitive movement (see below).
III. Hand Levitation	When the subject exhibits some degree of muscle tension or nervousness. For experienced subjects who feel light.	
	1. When the subject appears to be relaxing so completely that his hand is unlikely to move and may in fact be getting heavier.	**a.** Switch to Arm Drop: "That's good, you're doing fine, but now I want you to pick a point on either the index finger or middle finger (or on a finger that moved) and fix your gaze on that point. Now I am going to pick up the arm and raise it straight out in front of you and, as I do, continue to stare at that point. . . ."
	2. If you determine during the preinduction phase that the subject can visualize well.	**a.** Switch to Fantasized Hand Levitation: "That's good, you're doing fine, but, now that you are very familiar with that hand, I want you to close your eyes and hold the image of that hand in your mind's eye and continue to gaze and concentrate on that hand in your mind's eye. As you do this, I want you to imagine, see, and feel that hand becoming lighter and lighter as if it wants to float

Induction	*When Indicated*	*Recovering and Dealing With Resistance*
		up. . . . " If the hand begins to raise, continue with the normal patter until it touches. If the hand still does not move, continue by stating, "That's good, now as the hand continues to rest lightly on the table (or leg) I want you to imagine and feel the *image* of that hand getting lighter and floating up." Continue with the normal patter, but instruct the subject to signal you when the image touches by letting his head nod forward.
	3. When the subject is visibly pushing his hand down.	**a.** Switch to Opposed Hand Levitation: Place your hand on the subject's and suggest that no matter how hard you try you cannot hold it down, that it is getting so light that it pushes your hand up. Continue to appeal to the subject's resistance by suggesting that no matter how hard you try you cannot hold it down. The idea is to mobilize the subject's resistance against himself; he will follow the suggestions to beat you, but little does he know that he is actually following suggestions that will lead him into hypnosis.
		b. Switch to Repetitive Movement: Pick up the subject's forearm so that it is straight up and resting on the chair or table. Take the arm by the wrist or cuff very loosely and suggest relaxation of the arm and the tendency for the body to work automatically.

Induction	*When Indicated*	*Recovering and Dealing With Resistance*
III. Hand Levitation (continued)		Move the arm back and forth slowly as you maintain a monotonous stream of suggestions. "The arm goes back and forth, back and forth, back and forth." Synchronize the verbal suggestions with the rate of movement of the arm. "Back and forth, everything lets go, your body works automatically, back and forth automatically, it keeps going on." Instruct the subject to stare at his thumbnail, hence incorporating eye fixation. When the arm takes up the movement gradually withdraw your contact, although you may need to maintain a suggestive shadowing or pacing with your own arm. Proceed to challenge the movement. "The arm goes back and forth automatically, you don't need to move it, it moves itself, you don't move it. It moves automatically. You don't move it and you cannot stop it. No matter how hard you try you can't stop it. Try hard but you can't stop it! In fact, the harder you try the harder it is to stop! That's good. Now I'll take the arm and as I do it stops and gently lowers to your leg and as it does you feel that deep relaxation come all through you." If the arm does not take up automatic movement and becomes very relaxed and flaccid, say, "The arm goes back and forth and everything lets go. Becoming

Induction	*When Indicated*	*Recovering and Dealing With Resistance*
		more and more relaxed. Now I take the arm and it flops down and as it does this deep relaxation goes all through you."
		c. Appeal to Resistance: "The right hand will levitate, the left hand will not." To resist successfully, contrary behavior must be manifested. The result is that the subject finds himself responding to suggestion, but to his own satisfaction.
IV. Postural Sway	For subjects who are resistant. Watkins lists several advantages of this technique: a. It is usually fairly rapid and results in a deeper trance. b. It can begin as a susceptibility test and turned into an induction if successful. c. It appears inoffensive to the subject. d. It is not generally known to the public and consequently its use is not likely to cause anxiety or apprehension as the standard techniques might do.[17] An additional advantage is that it is so easy to turn into a confusion technique.	If begun as a mere susceptibility test and the subject responds poorly, nothing is lost. The operator can proceed with another induction. If, however, the operator begins with this technique as an induction and the subject responds poorly (no or little swaying), he can attempt to induce swaying by increasing the subject's disorientation by doing some or all of the following: (a) have the subject look up towards the ceiling with eyes closed, (b) couple this with the suggestion of rolling his eyes back up into his head as if he were looking at his forehead, (c) instruct him to hold his arms straight up overhead, (d) deliberately induce swaying by placing your hands on the subject's shoulders and gently rocking him back and forth or in a circular motion, (e) have him hyperventilate by inhaling deeply, holding the breath, and then exhaling in a continuous sequence while suggesting light-headedness, and (f) insti-

Induction	*When Indicated*	*Recovering and Dealing With Resistance*
IV. Postural Sway (continued)		tute a difficult counting sequence such as counting backwards from 199 by threes.
V. Confusion Method	1. If all else fails. 2. If the subject is obviously very intelligent and openly displays an analytical or critical attitude.	If this fails, try again! If deemed necessary, tactfully discuss the subject's resistance.

Techniques for Children

Occasionally the hypno-investigator will be asked to hypnotize a child victim or witness. Although most children are easily hypnotized by relatively simple techniques, the operator's approach to the child and induction procedure will vary depending upon the child's age, mental development, intelligence, and maturity. For this reason the operator must have a basic understanding of hypnosis with children.

Most children are easily hypnotized due to their vivid imaginations, their willingness to defer to the omnipotence of the adult, their tendency to believe the statements of adults, and to the plasticity of their minds. Generally, children below the approximate age of five can neither concentrate well enough nor understand the vocabulary of induction techniques used with older children and adults. Hypnotizability peaks between the ages of nine to twelve and gradually declines thereafter as infantile suggestibility decreases and the powers of logic and rational judgment increase.

Considerations

1. The operator must adapt himself, his behavior, and vocabulary to the mentality of the child. He must be able to communicate in the language of the child yet behave in a manner that is natural and will not cause anxiety in the child. The operator should observe and talk with the child at length before the induction so he can accustom himself to his language and mode of thinking. The operator, however, should not overly accommodate himself to the child's level as this will be perceived as unnatural and may put the child on the defensive.

2. The operator must be relaxed and at ease with children as they are generally much more sensitive to anxiety and nervousness in others than adults.

3. The younger the child, the simpler the vocabulary and induction technique must be. Always attempt to talk to the child at his intellectual level. A hypnotized child may awaken to ask you what a word means.

4. Capitalize on the child's vivid imagination, his desire and willingness

to play games, and his personal wishful fantasies when designing induction techniques. In other words, make the induction sort of a game in which the child fantasizes himself involved in his favorite activity or identifies with an imaginary or real-life hero. The techniques should be naturalistic and not predesigned. "Let's pretend" or "Let's play a game" approaches work well with young children. The word *sleep* should generally be avoided because most children often resist sleep.

5. Induction techniques should be tailored to the age, intellectual, and maturation level of the child. With older children and young adolescents, the standard formalized inductions can be used successfully.

6. "Probably the most common source of failure [in hypnosis with children] stems from inability to resonate with the child's experience," and "failing to stay within the realm of what is familiar to the child, either in reality or fantasy. This is true not only in the general sense of adapting to the child's cognitive level and emotional needs, but also in the more specific sense of the particular experiences" of each child.[18]

Induction Techniques

TELEVISION TECHNIQUE. Determine during the preinduction the child's favorite TV program. Have the subject close his eyes and imagine himself playing a part in the program and continue with naturalistic suggestions enhancing the child's involvement.

HERO TECHNIQUE. Determine during the preinduction the child's favorite imaginary or real life hero. Have the subject close his eyes and imagine that he is in fact that person.

REPETITIVE TECHNIQUE. With a younger child whose vocabulary is very limited, a mere repetition of one or two easily understood ideas is often very effective. For example, "As you listen to me, you get very tired, sleepy, t–i–r–e–d, s–l–e–e–p–y, t–i–r–e–d, s–l–e–e–p–y, t–i–i–r–r–e–e–d, s–l–e–e–e–p–y–y–y. You close your eyes and go to sleep, go to s–l–e–e–p, s–l–e–e–p." Sleep suggestions can be used with children as they relate easily to known behavioral experiences. If a rocking recliner is available it may greatly facilitate this approach as monotonous rocking is a very primal hypnotic experience for young children and is associated with sleeping.

STORY TECHNIQUE. Common children's stories can be effective for inducing hypnosis if the child can actively imagine the story with either himself taking part or identifying with a character. Once the child becomes involved in the fantasy and he relaxes to the point where all fidgeting stops, suggestions of sleep may be woven in.

DISSOCIATIVE VISUALIZATION. The child is asked to close his eyes and visualize himself asleep in bed and to think how it feels to be nice and warm and comfortable under the covers. The operator continues suggesting to the child that he visualize this image of himself and then he slowly begins to associate or merge the image with the subject himself, i.e. "Now you are beginning to feel just like the picture of yourself under the covers, becoming more and more comfortable and going to sleep."

Two Finger Technique. This technique can be used with young children. The operator puts the child's hand flat on the arm of the chair or his leg, but raises the middle and ring finger. He then continues by saying as he touches the forefinger and little finger, "Look at these two fingers and let's play a game, okay? These two fingers have gotten tired and gone to sleep. They lie down on the chair and they are asleep. Now look at these other two fingers." *(Touch the two middle fingers.)* "They will soon get tired too and want to go to sleep like the others. Getting heavy and tired and going down to bed. As they go down your eyes get heavy and tired and will close. All of you is getting t–i–r–e–d, and h–e–a–v–y and s–l–e–e–p–y, s–l–e–e–e–p–y–y."

Mechanical Aids

The hypnosis literature is filled with references to various mechanical aids to trance induction. Metronomes, hypnodisks, pendulums, strobe lights, rotating mirrors, tape recordings, stethoscopes for magnifying heartbeat and respiratory sounds, electronic brain wave synchronizers, and many other gadgets have been developed to aid the induction of hypnosis with varying degrees of success. In essence, such mechanical and electronic devices are hypnotic placebos.

Mechanical aids may be of value to the hypno-investigator under two basic sets of circumstances, and he should not hesitate to use them if deemed appropriate: (1) when the subject has a preconceived notion that hypnosis is inducted by the aid of a mechanical device and (2) when the subject is not sufficiently intelligent or otherwise has difficulty understanding the standard inductions. Mechanical aids may also be of benefit with impressionable or distractible subjects. They must be used with discretion, however, as they will be too artificial, theatrical, or simplistic for some subjects.

The principle behind mechanical aids is that any rhythmic and monotonous stimuli has a tendency to induce relaxation and make the conscious mind passive through boredom. Although hypnosis can be induced in a susceptible subject who expects to be hypnotized by a mechanical device, appropriate verbal suggestions should be given for maximal effect, e.g. "With each beat of the metronome you will go deeper relaxed."

The most practical mechanical aid for the hypno-investigator will probably be the metronome (or a cassette recording of a metronome), which can be used in several ways. The metronome can either be placed out of sight of the subject in a cabinet or desk drawer (some subjects are irritated by the loud click) while appropriate verbal suggestions are given, or placed directly in front and slightly above the subject so eye fixation on the striker can be combined. In either approach, the metronome should be set at one beat per second so it approximates the resting heartbeat.

To further restrict the subject's field of consciousness, he may be instructed to count to the clicking, time his breathing with every three or four beats, or imagine himself stepping down an endless flight of stairs. For resistant subjects the eye blink induction can effectively be combined with the alternate beat of the metronome.

The metronome can also be used as a deepening technique after a standard induction or in combination with a confusion technique.

An interesting and important consideration in the use of mechanical aids was reported by Erickson after conducting a series of experiments. He found that more rapid trance induction and profounder trance states resulted from merely imagining looking at a crystal ball or pendulum, or listening to soft music or a metronome instead of the actual apparatus. Erickson believed that imagery is more effective because the subject does not have to be dependent on and restricted to distractingly consistent nonessential externalities, but instead utilizes his own actual and flexible capabilities that allow the stimulus to change according to his needs and trance experience. "At best, apparatus is only an incidental aid, to be discarded at the earliest possible moment in favor of the utilization of the subject's behavior which may be initiated but not developed by the apparatus."[19]

The determining factor as to whether to use the actual apparatus or its imagined counterpart would likely hinge on the subject's ability to visualize. As a viable alternative, a combination of the two approaches would likely work best for most subjects. Specifically, the operator should begin with the mechanical apparatus for a few minutes until the subject is thoroughly conditioned to it, then switch it off while asking the subject to continue imagining it for a specified time period.

DEEPENING TECHNIQUES

The essential purpose of the deepening process is to maximize hypnotic depth. Generally speaking, the process consists of giving suggestions to the effect that the trance is getting progressively deeper. In effect, each deepening technique, of which there are many, is a mini-induction in that the same critical elements and principles of inductions outlined in Chapter 3 hold equally true for each deepening technique, although in a condensed form. Specifically, each technique further restricts the subject's field of consciousness by fixating his attention on some physical, mental, or perceptual region. A specific expectation and a goal are set using the future tense, which are reinforced as they occur using the present tense. For example, in the simple counting technique, the subject's attention is fixated on the mental region of numbers and the perceptual region of your voice as he passively listens to you monotonously count backward from twenty to one. At the outset you develop a specific expectation that he will be twice as deep when you reach one. As you count backwards, you reinforce the initial expectation by telling the subject that he is going deeper with each count, and you build his expectancy of reaching the goal.

Since the reader has a working understanding of the critical elements and the principles of inductions and the principles of suggestion, the following deepening techniques will not be broken down and commented on at length as were the inductions. Depending on the technique, a few general instructions and considerations may be given with a sample verbalization.

The cardinal rule of deepening is to remain flexible and adapt the techniques to best suit the personal needs, desires, and hypnotic experiences of the subject. Deepening, to be effective, must be an individual process that incorporates the subject's physiological processes and sensations, his psychological experiences, and his experiential background. Although this is a little difficult to do during the first session, the subject should be thoroughly quizzed in the postinduction regarding his experience so that the deepenings can be altered to incorporate these individual experiences in the next induction. For example, you may discover through trial and error that the subject does not like silent periods, he prefers to count to himself, he thinks walking up the stairs would be better than going down, and he feels light and floaty. Hence, the next session can incorporate these preferences and experiences for maximum deepening.

Several techniques are presented that allow for and capitalize on these individual differences and experiences even during the first session, e.g. "fractionation." Furthermore, several questions in the Preinduction Questionnaire are designed to give some clues as to which deepenings to use, i.e. "Can you visualize readily with your eyes closed? What is your favorite place to get away from stress?"

As with the inductions, it is recommended that the novice operator begin with the easiest deepening techniques and not move on until he feels comfortable with each in its turn (see "Lesson Plan" in Chapter 1).

Regardless of which technique is used, each deepening should be prefaced with the following remark which facilitates the transition and heightens expectancy: "You've done very well John, but now we're going to do something else that will help to take you even deeper."

Silent Periods

Most experts believe that silent periods are effective, because hypnosis tends to deepen spontaneously and suggestions require time to take their full effect. Periods of silence can be used between the induction proper and the first deepening technique and between successive deepening techniques. They generally range in length from one minute to a maximum of ten minutes, although some clinicians leave their subjects for an hour or more while they work on another patient. For practical purposes, experience has indicated that silent periods of two to five minutes are generally preferred by subjects who enjoy them; not all subjects like silent periods and others come up to lighter stages during silence. With experienced subjects who like them, a definite time can be agreed upon in the preinduction. For the first induction, the operator can either specify the duration or he can shift the responsibility to the subject as we shall see.

Introduce the silent period in the following manner: "In a moment I am going to stop talking to you for (two) minutes so you can have some time to take yourself deeper." *(This shifts the responsibility to the subject for deepening.)* "You do this by letting whatever feelings you're having magnify, become more profound, and pervade your whole body. The feeling may be one of heaviness, numbness, or a buzzing, tingling feeling. It may also be one of spinning, floating, or lightness, or you may even become totally unaware of your body and feel dissociated from it." *(A wide range of options are covered as the operator does not know how the subject is feeling. This prevents the operator from making a wrong guess that would damage his credibility. An alternative approach is to ask the subject how he is feeling and then instruct him to concentrate on that feeling and suggest that it will increase during the silence, which will take him deeper.)* "Whatever that feeling is, let it increase and take yourself deeper. The deeper you go the more it increases and the better you feel; the better you feel, the more it increases and the deeper you go. Just let yourself go and let it happen. When I speak to you again at the end of these two minutes you will be much deeper and more relaxed and comfortable. Also, it will not surprise you when I speak to you again. Ready to take yourself down now, begin."

As an alternative to specifying the length of the silent period beforehand, the operator may choose to shift this responsibility to the subject. For instance, he may say, "In a moment I am going to stop talking to you for awhile so that you can take yourself deeper. When you feel that you have taken yourself as deep as you can without my help, signal me by raising this finger." *(Touch either index finger. Do not say, "the left index finger," as this may unnecessarily begin the subject thinking again.)* "You do this by letting whatever feelings. . . . "

For experienced subjects, you can determine what feelings they experience beforehand and directly incorporate them in the silent period. Experienced subjects may also have a preference as to time duration. Unless otherwise requested by the subject, it is recommended that only one or two silent periods be used per session.

During silent periods it is important for the operator to maintain rapport by resonating with the subject. This is done by synchronizing your breathing with the subject's and also periodically whispering "d–e–e–p--e–r," which also reinforces the goal. When the operator next speaks to the subject at the end of the silent period, he should do so in a soft voice so it does not startle him. Silent periods are also excellent times for the operator to collect himself and plan for the next step.

Breathing

Instruct the subject to take a designated number of deep inhales while suggesting that he will go deeper with each exhale. This technique can also be used in conjunction with other techniques that require counting by synchronizing the counting and exhaling. The operator should coordinate his own breathing with that of the subject as it increases resonance and rapport. He should also time some suggestions with occasional exhales, such as "d–e–e–p–e–r relaxed." The rationale for deep breathing is that some experts believe that it increases suggestibility and relaxation, hence helping to deepen hypnosis.

Research into the effect of breathing on hypnosis has shown that coordinating appropriate breathing phases with suggestions can be utilized to evoke and enhance special effects. In general, long, slow, and deep exhalations result in relaxation with accompanying feelings and sensations of sinking, comfort, heaviness, and warmth. Inhalations tend to evoke feelings and sensations of lightness, invigoration, and levitation. Therefore, the operator should time his suggestions with the breathing phase that is conducive to the desired effect. For example, if he is attempting hand levitation, the operator should coincide his suggestions of lightness and levitation with the subject's inhales. To do so during the inappropriate breathing phase of exhaling may counteract the suggested response. If suggesting relaxation and heaviness, the operator should observe and coincide his suggestions with the subject's exhales, which will invariably induce deeper relaxation. "Utilization of the breathing phases is especially indicated for subjects who are unwilling, or seem unable, to enter a hypnotic state."[20]

Counting

This simple technique is often very effective, and it can be used in a variety of ways.

1. "When I tell you to, I want you to count backwards to yourself at your own pace from twenty to one, and with each count backwards you will take yourself deeper relaxed, and when you reach 'one,' you will be twice as deep as you are now. When you reach 'one,' signal me by lifting this finger *(touch either index finger)*. Ready to go deeper now, begin."

2. A variation of number one involves coupling the counting with breathing, which has the added advantage of an ongoing physiological process reinforcing the psychological suggestion. "When I tell you to, I want you to count backwards to yourself from twenty to one, and to synchronize each count backwards with each exhale. With each count backwards you will take yourself deeper and deeper down; with each exhale, let yourself become more and more relaxed, and when you reach 'one' you will be twice as deep as you are now. Begin."

3. A variation of both of the above techniques is for the operator to count out loud. The advantage of this approach is that most subjects seem to believe it is more effective. Merely modify the above instructions to include you counting out loud.

4. Another variation of numbers one and two is for the subject to count out loud. The advantage of this approach is that the operator can gauge increasing depth by the subject's voice, i.e. if it lessens in volume and becomes harder to speak as the subject approaches one, the technique has been effective, whereas if the voice is the same all the way through, it probably was not effective. The disadvantage is that many subjects do not like to count out loud; they are too self-conscious. An experienced subject's preference can be determined in the preinduction. A novice subject could

also be asked in the preinduction if he would prefer to count to himself, out loud, or have you count.

5. For resistant or too analytical subjects a more difficult and longer counting sequence can be used. For example, counting backwards from forty-nine to one by twos, or from ninety-nine back to zero by threes. A repetitive counting sequence can also greatly add to monotony, hence making the intellect passive, e.g. one, two, three, four, three, two, one, etc. This approach to counting works especially well in conjunction with the confusion methods.

6. For highly susceptible and responsive subjects an abbreviated rapid sequence may be effective. "At the count of three you will be twice as deep as you are now. One, two, three, **D–E–E–P, D–E–E–P.**"

7. As a periodic indicator of depth as gauged by the subject's voice, the operator may ask him at the termination of each deepening to count out loud from three to one. As mentioned above, if the subject is going deeper, his voice should soften and it will be more difficult for him to speak.

Rapid Arm Drop

"I am now going to do something that will take you even deeper, I'm going to pick up this arm by the wrist." *(Pick up the closest arm using your thumb and middle finger.)* "In a moment I am going to count to twenty, and, as I do, the arm will become more relaxed and heavier with each count; so, by the time I reach twenty, it will be like a dead weight. At that time I will let go of it and it will drop with a thud to your lap and you'll drop down with it into a deep state, much deeper than you are now. Now just let me have the arm completely; don't try to hold it at all; just let it go and relax totally. Counting now, one, two, . . ." *(Continue counting and as you do you can test for the degree of involvement, i.e. the arm should get increasingly heavy and limp. If it does not, stop periodically and give additional suggestions aimed at relaxing the arm. A good maneuver is bobbing the arm just a little at each count to help loosen it up. When pausing, always do so at a major count such as five, ten, or fifteen as it is very easy to lose count otherwise.)* "That's it, getting heavier and heavier, almost like a dead weight, like a wet dishtowel, and getting ready to drop way down." *(Slow down as you go, and become more dramatic. Success depends on mobilizing the subject's expectancy and readiness.)* "Eighteen, ALMOST THERE, NINETEEN, READY TO GO **W–A–Y** DOWN, TWENTY going **D–E–E–P, D–E–E–P, D–E–E–P.**"

Patter

Some subjects, particularly if they like your voice, deepen just by listening to the sound of your voice. For these subjects, you can effectively spend several minutes providing them with a continuous stream of the hypnotic induction patter in your best hypnotic drone, all of which is designed to coax them deeper.

Besides being an effective deepening technique, it is helpful to memorize some phrases that can utilized in any induction technique when you are running short of things to say with resistant subjects and that are designed to facilitate the induction itself. They are also helpful to fill the inevitable gaps when learning hypnosis that occur when you need time to plan your next move. Their importance was probably best summed up by a subject, who said, in reference to different operators, "They have to give me confidence in that they know what they are doing. If they keep talking while I'm under I get the feeling of continuity, that they know what they're doing, but when they pause, I get the feeling they don't know what to do next."

By memorizing a number of these stock phrases the operator can mechanically recite them while he unhurriedly plans his next step. Once deciding on his next deepening technique or move, he can make a subtle transition so that the subject will never realize that there was any indecision. In this manner, the operator always *seems* to know what he is doing although he may not. If the operator runs out of patter and still needs time to plan, he can always introduce a silent period or let the subject go to his favorite place through the "closed door" (see below).

Some examples are listed below, but be creative and design some of your own. The following can be formulated in any number of combinations:

• "So pleasant and so relaxing. So pleasantly heavy."
• "A vague pleasant numbness pervading your body."
• "Kind of a heavy, drowsy, sleepy feeling."
• "Kind of a tingling, dreamy, drifting feeling."
• "So relaxed and so comfortable."
• "It's so easy just to let yourself go."
• "It's so easy just to let it happen."
• "It's so easy to concentrate on the sound of my voice."
• "It's so easy to allow yourself to drift deeper and deeper (further and further away)."
• "Drifting further and further away on the sound of my voice."
• "Drifting (sliding, sinking) deeper and deeper on the sound of my voice."
• "Effortlessly you drift deeper and deeper (further and further away)."
• "With each breath you take (beat of your heart, tick of the clock, each minute that rolls by) you drift deeper and deeper (further and further away)."
• "Don't do anything or not do anything; just let it happen. Neither help nor resist."
• "You can let yourself go so completely that your body will tend to work automatically, and that's a good sign."
• "You let yourself go, you let yourself go completely."
• "It is really so very simple and easy."
• "Feeling very good in every way. Feeling safe and secure and comfortable."
• "The deeper you go the better you feel, and the better you feel the deeper you go."
• "Gradually losing more and more awareness of your surroundings."

- "Neither too hot nor too cold, but just right."
- "Notice how relaxed your breathing is becoming."
- "You have no desire to even move. You just want to drift deeper."
- "You want to go as deep as you can because it's a very enjoyable pleasant experience."
- "My voice makes you want to go deeper."
- "You hear nothing but my voice, which may sound as if it were coming from far away."
- "It's going all through you. Let it go all through you."
- "That's good, you're doing fine."
- "It is your privilege to go as deep as you wish."
- "If you really want to go deeper and by your own efforts. . . . "
- "If you concentrate well enough. . . . "
- "If your mind wanders it will always return."
- "Experiencing yourself as you never have before."

Descending Stairs

"Now I want you to imagine in your mind's eye and to the best of your ability something that I am going to describe to you. I want you to imagine a staircase unlike any you've ever seen before." *(It is important to begin with these carefully constructed phrases that are designed to mobilize the subject's imagination yet hold it in abeyance until you can describe the staircase. Experience has shown that if you begin with, "I want you to imagine a staircase" and then proceed to describe one, your description will often clash with one that the subject has already pictured.)* "It's as if this staircase were in a misty cloud just kind of floating or suspended in midair, and you and I are standing at the head of this staircase and you look down and see that there are twenty stairs." *(Through description the operator tries to enhance its dreamy, unreal character.)* "These stairs are carpeted in a thick plush carpet of your favorite color and you're standing in your bare feet and you can feel the carpet around your feet and around your toes. I'm standing to one side and to the other side is a hardwood banister and you place your hand on that banister and you can feel its hard, smooth texture." *(The operator continues the description to try to involve as many of the subject's senses as possible. His favorite color is used as it is something he can easily visualize and relate to. The operator should observe the subject's toes and hand to see if they move at the mention of feeling the carpet and banister. If the subject is fairly deep, visualizes well, and is involved in the scene, they will usually move. Lack of movement, however, does not necessarily mean that the subject is not deep. The operator can also specify the favorite color of the subject, which he determined in the Preinduction Questionnaire.)* "When you can visualize this scene as best you can, signal me by raising this finger *(touch either index finger).*" *(The operator remains silent until the signal is given. Its purpose is to give those who don't visualize as readily more time to secure the scene in their mind's eye.)* "Good. In a moment we are going to step down these stairs from the twentieth down to the first, and, with each step down, you will go deeper and deeper relaxed and when we reach the first step you will be twice as deep as you are now. Alright, getting ready to go down, stepping down now from the twentieth to nineteenth, eighteenth, seventeenth, sixteenth, feeling your feet on the carpet and your hand sliding down the banister, going deeper and deeper. Stepping down again to fifteenth, fourteenth, thirteenth, twelveth, eleventh, halfway there as we pause for a moment. Going deeper and deeper with each step down and you know that when you reach the first step you'll be twice as deep. Stepping down again to tenth, ninth, eighth, seventh, sixth, five more steps and you'll be all the way **D–O–W–N,** fifth, fourth, third, second, first, going **D–E–E–P, D–E–E–P, D–E–E–P.**"

There are many variations of this theme limited only by your imagination. For example, ascending stairs work better for some subjects; some may prefer a familiar staircase such as one in their home; an ascending or descending elevator may work better for some subjects; varying the number of stairs, etc. The degree of elaboration can also vary greatly, but the specific technique can be determined by experimenting and quizzing the subject as to what works best. This technique usually works well for subjects who can visualize well and is containdicated for poor visualizers. The counting should coincide with the subject's exhaling unless it is too slow or erratic, in which case the operator sets the rhythm and pace.

Closed Door

This technique is best used in conjunction with the descending stairs. Once the subject has reached the bottom stair, describe a door off to the side. Instruct the subject to walk over and open the door, at which point he will find himself in his favorite scene. This requires quizzing the subject in the preinduction talk so you know the details of his favorite scene; a question to this effect is included in the Preinduction Questionnaire.

"Now I want you to look off to your left *(if the subject's head turns this is a good indication of depth)* and you will notice a door there, a large intricately carved oak door with a shiny brass doorknob. Now in a moment I am going to have you go over and open that door and on the other side you will find your favorite place on the beach. Alright, you go over and place your hand on that shiny brass doorknob and slowly open the door. And now you step out onto the beach and you can f–e–e–l the warmth of the sun on your body and you can feel the sand on your feet. You look out over the shimmering water and you can smell the fresh air and salt water. You have no worries or responsibilities: just enjoy yourself completely. Now I'm going to leave you here for two minutes during which time you will just enjoy this experience and take yourself even deeper, so that by the time I speak to you again you will be much deeper than you are now. Alright, begin." *(During the visualization the operator should maintain rapport by synchronizing his breathing with the subject's and occasionally whispering "d–e–e–p–e–r" on an exhale.)*

This technique works well for subjects who can visualize well and is contraindicated for poor visualizers. The rationale behind this technique is that the more involved a subject can become in a fantasy, the deeper he goes into hypnosis.

As a precautionary note, an occasional somnambule may act out the fantasy to some degree. Although rare, these subjects may open their eyes and begin talking. Although this is somewhat disconcerting, the operator must act in the realization that this happens and is a normal response. The recommended procedure at this point is to deepen the subject by saying, "Okay, 'Jan,' you're doing fine, but I now want you to go **D–E–E–P, D–E–E–P, D–E–E–P,**" which is syncronized with the single shoulder press. This will generally break the subject's involvement with the fantasy, but to be sure walk him back through the door before proceeding.

Shoulder Press

There are two variations of the shoulder press, which will be discussed separately. The first variation may be referred to as the *single shoulder press,* which is essentially a conditioned cue for immediate deepening. The actual technique involves firmly pressing down on the subject's nearest shoulder at the exact moment of reaching the goal in either an induction or other deepenings (see figure 4). This technique is based on Pierce's Law of Dominant Effect, referred to previously, which states in part that a strong physiological sensation will reinforce a psychological suggestion. Hence, to maximize the effect of an induction, for example, the operator should coincide the single shoulder press with eye closure and the suggestion of "going **D–E–E–P, D–E–E–P, D–E–E–P.**" Most subjects report that this really aids them in going deeper.

When applying the single shoulder press the subject's head may "let go" and fall forward or to one side. If the head leans towards the operator, it is a sign of good rapport and trust. If the head leans away from the operator, the reverse is probably true.

There are two different ways in which to introduce this technique: (1) the operator can make no mention of it to the subject and just do it, or (2) he can incorporate it in the induction itself when he establishes the goal by making it a cue for the elicitation of the goal. In the latter case, for example, the operator can say in the eye fixation, "When the eyes close tightly, you'll go way down. To help you go deep at that time, I will press firmly down on your left shoulder, which will push you deeper d–o–w–n." At this same time, the operator can condition the subject to automatically respond to this cue by suggesting to him that this will indeed be the case. Specifically, the operator may continue in the eye fixation suggestion given above by saying, "Only during the course of this session, each time I press down on your shoulder you will automatically and spontaneously go deeper." It is important to specify that this cue will work "*only* during the course of this session" because, if left unspecified, the subject may interpret it as a posthypnotic suggestion and go under sometime in the future when the operator or someone else inadvertently places a hand on his shoulder. As a

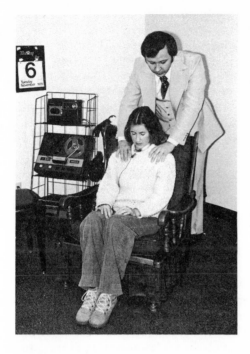

Figure 8. Dan Falcon demonstrates the proper positioning for the double shoulder press. Notice that the subject's arms are at her side and not braced on the arms of the chair.

further precaution, the operator should erase this cue in the waking suggestions.

The second variation of the shoulder press may be referred to as the *double shoulder press* which can be a very rapid and effective deepening for most subjects. "Now 'Penny,' I'm going to do something else that is very effective in taking all subjects much deeper." *(This phrase, which can be used with other techniques as well, will build expectancy.)* "I am going to stand up and move behind your chair and place both my hands on your shoulders like this." *(Move into position as you are talking. See figure 8.)* "In a moment I am going to press down on your shoulders to the count of three, and with each count you will go deeper and deeper down. Alright, one, two, three, d–e–e–p–e–r and d–e–e–p–e–r **D–O–W–N**." *(Apply a firm and steadily increasing pressure synchronized with each count on exhales only. Also use a lower, deeper, more dominating voice as this approach is fairly authoritative.)* "Now in a moment when I release the pressure, you will feel so light and floaty that it's as if you want to float away." *(Hold the pressure on the shoulders and then suddenly release it as you mention "light and floaty." The pressure should be released as the subject inhales. Continue by repeating the same procedure two or three times.)*

This technique capitalizes on the stimulation of inevitable physical sensations that the operator predicts to occur but that the subject attributes to your suggestions, hence your prestige increases commensurate with his conviction. Pressing firmly down on a person's shoulders will inevitably make him feel as if he were sinking down, just as suddenly releasing the pressure will make him feel light and floaty. In fact, hand levitation suggestions can effectively be given each time the pressure is released. Have someone try this on yourself. You can also use such phrases as, "It's as if you were sinking d–o–w–n," "As if you were going right through the chair."

An important consideration for using this technique is that the subject must be seated firmly in a solid, large, preferably fabric chair, as it is very easy to push a subject out of a small hard-surfaced chair onto the floor with very little pressure. Furthermore, if a subject is not seated securely, he may brace himself against the pressure, which will be counterproductive, and you won't be able to apply enough pressure for the technique to be effective. Also, be certain that the subject's elbows are not braced on the arms of the chair as this will hamper the full effect.

The use of either the single or double shoulder press will depend largely on how you read your subject's feelings about being touched. Some people like to be touched or are ambivalent, in which case these techniques are indicated. Other people dislike being touched, in which case these techniques are contraindicated. Psychodynamically, touching may be interpreted as an invasion of personal space, as a seductive move, as a homosexual advance, etc. An excellent maneuver and good indicator of a person's feelings about being touched is to ask him during the preinduction talk and simultaneously reach out and touch his shoulder as you carefully observe his eyes. If there is any startle reaction and the eyes dilate, even if the subject replies that he does not mind being touched, these techniques would probably be contraindicated as the subject responded defensively.

Repeating Induction

An easy and effective technique is to simply repeat the same induction or do a different induction. Repeating the same induction is most practical with either the arm drop or hand levitation, as the opposite arm can be used. No matter what the induction, a different one can be used as a deepening. For example, after eye closure is obtained with the eye fixation, the operator could easily proceed with either the arm drop (eyes closed version) or the hand levitation. Once a subject has fallen back into the chair with the postural sway, the operator could do the hand levitation or arm drop with eyes either open or closed, depending on how the subject responded, i.e. if only in a light trance as gauged by the degree of control the subject exerted in falling, the other inductions could be done with eyes open, otherwise they should be left closed. If the subject was only in a very light trance and could easily open his eyes, the operator could use the eye fixation or eye blink.

This technique seems to be particularly indicated and effective when the operator believes through observation or testing and challenging that the subject is only in a hypnoidal or light trance and a concerted effort is likely to be necessary to get him much deeper. If this is the case, a lengthy formal induction may be most effective at this stage, after which the operator could proceed with the other standard deepening techniques.

Progressive Anesthesia

This technique is best used with subjects that experience a numbness or bodily dissociation. This can be determined during the session, by asking the subject how he is feeling, or during the postinduction. To induce progressive anesthesia, the operator capitalizes on the numb feeling by suggesting that it is magnifying and spreading throughout the entire body. For example, the operator may say, "I'm going to ask you a question now and you'll be able to talk and answer me easily. How are you feeling now? *(The subject replies that he is feeling kind of heavy and numb and dissociated from his body.)* That's good; that's a good sign. You're letting yourself go and your body has a tendency to work automatically. What part of your body is most numb? *(The subject replies that he feels heavy and that he can't feel his hands.)* Now you're going to notice something interesting happen. That heavy numb feeling in the hands is going to spread back into the forearms, and I am going to help it spread by lightly stroking that forearm. As I do, that feeling, that heavy n–u–m–b feeling spreads back through the forearm and it continues up into the upper arm and shoulder. Now it's spreading through the other forearm as I gently stroke it. It is as if I'm stroking the feeling right out of it. That numb feeling moves right up that upper arm and shoulder and now down your back and over your chest. It's kind of like those times you have been numb before, like maybe when you were anesthetized or put to sleep for surgery or when you received a shot of Novocain® in your gums for dental work. It continues to spread through the whole trunk of your body, and you become h–e–a–v–i–e–r. Now it goes down into the legs, which are growing n–u–m–b. You might think of the times when you've sat on a leg wrong, and it went to sleep. *(The operator enhances the feeling by giving the subject personal experiences that he can relate to, hence enlisting the aid of his imagination.)* The whole body is s–o h–e–a–v–y and n–u–m–b, almost as if you were sinking right through the chair, as heavy as lead and losing all awareness of and interest in the body."

This technique is often very effective, but remember that glove anesthesia is indicative of a medium trance, and complete anesthesia is indicative of a deep trance, so the operator should be persistent with his suggestions and try to maximize the degree of anesthosis.

Visualization

The use of visualization follows the same basic principle as progressive anesthesia. The important thing to remember with all subjects is to incorporate and design techniques that you believe will work well for them or that they prefer based on their experience. For subjects who can visualize well, there is a great deal of room for innovation on your part by trying to develop a visualization that will enhance an already elicited feeling or experience. For example, some subjects feel a floating sensation. If so, maximize it by having them imagine they are floating on top of a fleecy white cloud. Some subjects experience a tumbling or spinning feeling along with the floating. In this case you can suggest they visualize and feel themselves tumbling or spinning in the middle of a cloud as they float along.

Self-reporting Scale

For experienced subjects who you intend to rehypnotize a number of times, you can incorporate a self-reporting scale of depth. For example, instruct the subject at the outset that he is to notify you upon request as to the depth of trance by a numerical representation, such as one being very light and ten being very deep. Between deepening techniques or before eliciting a hypnotic phenomenon, such as age regression, ask the subject how deep he is.

Fractionation

Fractionation involves dehypnotizing and rehypnotizing the subject in a fairly rapid succession. The basic procedure involves six steps: (1) induce hypnosis and deepen by standard procedures, (2) establish a posthypnotic cue such as the single shoulder press for rehypnotization, (3) rapidly waken the subject, (4) quiz him regarding his subjective experience and physical sensations, (5) rehypnotize him with the posthypnotic cue, and (6) give suggestions that will magnify his reported feelings.

As a sample verbalization, the operator can proceed in the following manner once he has induced and deepened hypnosis: "Now 'Diane,' we're going to do something kind of interesting. In a moment, I am going to count from one to three and tell you to waken, at which point you will open your eyes and be awake. Before I do this, however, I want you to know that all I'll have to do to rehypnotize you is to put my hand on your left shoulder and press down and you will immediately and automatically go back under hypnosis, but even deeper than you are now. Do you understand? *(The operator gives both the waking and rehypnotization suggestions and asks the subject if he understands. This is important because hypnotized people take the hypnotist's words and suggestions literally and at face value, therefore you should make certain that they are understood correctly. Furthermore, by replying yes, the subject implicitly commits himself to complying with the suggestions.)* Okay, getting ready to come awake, coming up now, one, two, three, AWAKE! There you go, how do you feel? How did you feel both mentally and physically when you were under? Was there a point when you felt deepest? *(The operator elicits as much information regarding the subject's thoughts, feelings and sensations as possible, particularly those experienced at maximum depth.)* Now I want you to go **D–E–E–P, D–E–E–P, D–E–E–P.**" As this is being said, the operator applies the single shoulder press. The subject will usually look you right in the eye and you can readily observe his eyes "fog over" and become "glassy-eyed" as the posthypnotic suggestion takes effect. Since this is a fairly authoritative technique, the operator should express as much dominance, control, and confidence as possible. To this end, the touch and voice should be firm and the operator should return the subject's gaze with equal command. The operator should be aware that it generally takes a few seconds for the cue to take effect, although some subjects will respond instantaneously (see figure 9).

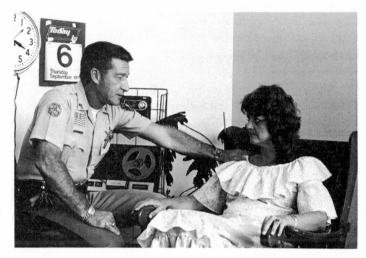

Figure 9. Sgt. Dick Donovan, C.C.S.O., demonstrates the proper positioning for fractionation.

Once rehypnotized, the operator can proceed to give suggestions built around the information elicited during the waking period, much as is done in the progressive anesthesia and visualization techniques. For example, if the subject reports feeling light, continue by saying, "Good. Now I'm going to use a special technique that will help you to become very light, much more so than you are now." Continue by counting from one to twenty and suggesting lightness on each inhale. If, on the other hand, the subject reports feeling heavy, merely reverse the procedure.

Weitzenhoffer states that fractionation "is one of the most effective methods for inducing a very deep trance state, and it often succeeds when every other method has failed. It is especially indicated when you expect the subject to enter a light to medium trance at best. It also offers an effective method for handling subjects who, because they experience at first only a light hypnosis, doubt that they have been hypnotized."[21]

An additional advantage of this technique is that it utilizes the actual feelings and sensations of the subject, which avoids the possibility of suggesting those that aren't manifest. Furthermore, the mere magnification of the subject's actual feelings and sensations through direct suggestion is conducive to the onset of deep hypnosis.

There is, however, one major disadvantage of fractionation — there is always a risk of failure. In this sense it is actually a test to see if the subject is sufficiently deep to follow a posthypnotic suggestion. Although there is some disagreement as to how deep a trance is necessary for fractionation to work effectively, most experts agree that simple posthypnotic suggestions will be heeded in a light trance, and most certainly in a medium trance. This coupled with the fact that the hypnotic state seems to "hang over" a short while upon awakening, particularly if the awakening is sudden, makes this technique much easier and more likely to succeed than one would suspect.

Due to the inherent risk of failure, the operator must be discriminate in its application and know how to recover. Once waking a subject according to the above instructions, the operator should observe his eyes and general appearance and behavior for signs of the hangover effect, i.e. glassy-eyed, sleepy countenance. If this is apparent, the operator can be assured of success, provided he does not let the subject become totally awake before rehypnotizing with the posthypnotic cue. If the subject awakens easily at the count of three and appears totally awake, he is probably not deep enough for the posthypnotic cue to take effect, in which case the operator had best move on to another formal induction or terminate the session altogether.

If the operator attempts fractionation and it fails, i.e. he applies the posthypnotic cue, but the subject continues to look him in the eye, he is faced with a potentially embarrassing situation. In the event of this happening, look the subject straight in the eye and say, "You really think you are awake, don't you?" If the subject responds yes, the implication of the question is that although he thinks he is awake he really isn't. If he responds no, the subject does not think he is awake. Either answer, therefore, has the same net effect. From this point, the operator continues: "Let me show you that you aren't awake. Switch your gaze to your left hand. . . . " The operator subtlely switches to the hand levitation or arm drop.

As an added precaution, the operator can give the following additional suggestion prior to waking to test for the likely effect of the rehypnotization cue: "When I awaken you at the count of three, your eyes will immediately begin to get heavy and tired again and they will begin to blink. As we talk after you awaken the eyes will get heavier and heavier as you listen to the sound of my voice, and you won't be able to help yourself from becoming so tired and drowsy again that you'll just want to close the eyes and go even deeper than before." Proceed to waken the subject and observe his eyes carefully. If they begin to get heavy and drowsy and blink, you know the posthypnotic suggestion is taking effect, which insures the success of the rehypnotization cue. This cue must be erased during the final waking suggestions at the end of the session.

Considerations and Helpful Hints for Deepening

1. Be flexible and attempt to make the deepening process an individual experience.

2. In all the induction and deepening techniques the word *sleep* is avoided for several reasons: (a) it is not necessary, (b) it tends to produce a more lethargic state of hypnosis that is not desirable with victims and witnesses who need to talk at length, and (c) some subjects may resist sleep suggestions. If, however, a subject says in the preinduction that he believes hypnosis to be a sleep state, the operator could capitalize on this expectation by using "*as if* you were going to sleep" periodically.

3. With subjects who are fearful, nervous, and anxious, the operator should avoid the use of the words *hypnosis* and *trance* during the preinduc-

tion and induction. Once the deepenings are begun, however, and signs of trance are appearing, the operator may begin substituting the words *relaxation* and *state* for *hypnosis* and *trance*. For example, in the goal of the induction the operator states, "And you'll go into a deeply relaxed state," but in the later deepening techniques the operator may state, "When you reach one you'll be much deeper in hypnosis than you are now." Or periodically he may say, "Going deeper into trance." The reason for this is that hypnosis is more than mere relaxation; there is an altered state of consciousness involved and the more powerful loaded words can be used to reinforce the belief and expectation of the subject that he is in fact entering an altered state. The operator must be careful and use his discretion, however, so he does not mobilize any resistance.

4. The goal of the last deepening technique used in any one session should be, " . . . and you will be as deep as you can go this time, as deep as you want to go." This statement implies to the subject that this is the last deepening and hence if he wishes to go deeper he had best cooperate to the fullest. Furthermore, it may stimulate the subject to "plunge," which is discussed later in "Dehypnotization or Waking."

5. The subject should occasionally be told that he can straighten up and get comfortable, cough, sneeze, scratch, brush his hair out of his face, or move in any way without affecting depth. Many subjects ask in the postinduction if they could have tickled their nose, swallowed, moved or whatever without coming out. They often say that they wanted to but were afraid to, thus creating a situation in which the physical annoyance is competing with you for their attention.

If observant, the operator can usually tell if something of this nature is bothering the subject, e.g. he has relaxed into an obviously uncomfortable position, he's twitching his nose, his hair is hanging in his face, etc. At this time, if not before, the operator should make the appropriate suggestion to remedy the situation. This suggestion not only allows the subject to get more comfortable and ensures against the movement interfering with depth, but it has the added advantage of displaying concern and empathy, which enhances rapport.

6. Some other recommended suggestions which should be interspersed with deepening are as follows:

a. "No matter how deep you go you can always hear my voice." This is not only a wise safety suggestion, but it will also help ease any anxiety the subject may have regarding losing contact.

b. "You will be aware of everything and remember everything." This suggestion will also tend to relieve anxiety.

c. "Any sounds you may hear will just kind of fade away and not bother you or may even take you deeper. In fact, sounds you may hear will remind you to relax further and go deeper." It is recommended that this suggestion be worked in fairly early in the session as there always seem to be some distracting noises. If the operator forgets to give this suggestion he should do so at the first significant disruptive noise.

7. The operator should attempt to put himself in his subject's place during the deepening process and ask himself such questions as "Am I convincing?" and "Would this work on me if I were the subject?"

CHALLENGING AND TESTING: DETERMINING DEPTH OF HYPNOSIS

The importance of challenging and testing for hypnotic depth cannot be overemphasized. The cardinal rule for the hypno-investigator is to not attempt hypermnesia or revivification without first determining that the subject is deep enough. To do otherwise will be to invite failure. Many operators experience failed sessions because they make the obvious mistake of attempting deeper trance phenomena before determining that the subject has reached the next lighter stage. For example, there is no doubt that if the subject cannot experience complete suggested amnesia, he will not be able to revivify. If the operator attempts to elicit revivification without first testing for the above, he is very likely to fail, which severely damages the confidence of the subject and the operator's prestige, hence rendering future success unlikely.

As mentioned previously, the system of hypnosis put forth in this book was designed specifically to maximize hypnotic depth for any given subject in support of the hypno-investigator's objective of obtaining complete, reliable, and accurate information from victims and witnesses. In its pure form, the system consists of a systematic and formalized seven-step procedure to induce maximum depth and obtain the necessary information: (1) induce hypnosis, (2) test for light trance, (3) deepen, (4) test for medium trance, (5) deepen, (6) test for deep trance, and (7) elicit hypermnesia or revivification (see Table II). Depending of course on subject susceptibility and response variability, this sequence may be substantially shortened or lengthened, which will be discussed later. The essential principle of the sequence, however, must be maintained by not attempting to elicit phenomena of a deeper trance state until the operator is certain the subject is at least in the next lighter trance state.

The rationale of this sequence is the following: if the operator determines the subject to be insufficiently deep by a poor response to a challenge or test, he necessarily backs up and gives additional suggestions and deepenings, eventually retesting the subject with the same challenge or test, or with a new one of similar difficulty. To do otherwise would be to violate one of the major principles of suggestion — grading. Challenges and tests are graded as to their difficulty just as any other suggestion, and, therefore, a subject's suggestibility should not be taxed by premature challenging and testing.

A challenge is a form of testing, and a test is a form of challenging. As we have seen, there are specific hypnotic phenomena that can be elicited through suggestion or manifested spontaneously at certain levels of trance. As a test of hypnotic depth, a subject is asked to attempt to voluntarily overcome the elicited or manifested phenomenon while simultaneously being told that he cannot. If the subject is at the sufficient depth

TABLE II

INDUCTION, DEEPENING, TESTING, AND CHALLENGING SEQUENCE
FLOW CHART

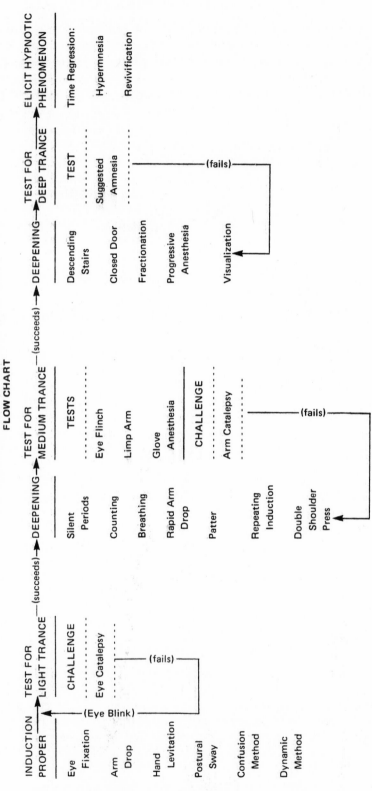

of hypnosis, he will not be able to voluntarily overcome the elicited or manifested phenomenon while simultaneously being told that he cannot. If the subject is at the sufficient depth of hypnosis, he will not be able to voluntarily control the phenomenon. Hence, a challenge is a carefully formulated suggestion in which the nonvoluntary quality of a hypnotic phenomenon is tested. For example, as a test of a medium depth of hypnosis the operator can suggest arm catalepsy and proceed to challenge the subject to bend his arm while suggesting that he cannot. If the subject is unable to bend his arm, he is at least in a medium level of hypnosis.

A test is a mild unobstrusive form of challenging in which the genuineness of elicited or manifested hypnotic phenomena are either demonstrated to the subject and operator alike, or just to the operator without the subject's awareness and active participation. For example, glove anesthesia can be elicited and demonstrated to the subject or just to the operator alone.

Challenges and tests serve several functions. First, they are indicators of hypnotic depth and they convince the operator that the subject is in fact hypnotized and to what degree. If challenges and tests are not done, it is virtually impossible to tell if in fact a subject is hypnotized. Operators who do not test or challenge, usually assume that a person becomes hypnotized at the moment of eye closure. This may or may not be true. A somnambulistic subject may become hypnotized with his eyes still wide open, and an unsusceptible subject may close his eyes from fatigue and not be hypnotized at all. Second, they convince the subject that he is hypnotized. Unless challenged, the vast majority of subjects upon waking will be uncertain if they were actually hypnotized. A sizeable percentage of these will believe that they were not hypnotized, just playing along. This disbelief will hinder increased depth because hypnosis depends largely upon belief and conviction. Hence, a third function of challenges and tests is to serve as deepening techniques. Until the subject is convinced that he is hypnotized, maximal hypnotic depth cannot be achieved. Teitelbaum believes it is important to bring about the "essential element of capitulation" through challenging, which refers to the realization by the subject that his desire to cooperate could not possibly account for his experience. The subject "will not be truly entranced until he in effect capitulates."[22] Similarly, Erickson believed it is necessary to strongly reinforce and "ratify" all hypnotic phenomena as they become manifest in order to demonstrate to the subject that hypnosis is in fact different from the ordinary awake state. To do this he would, among other things, bring all hypnotic behavior and phenomena to the subjects attention, such as alterations in pulse and respiration. Erickson believed a particularly effective means of ratifying trance is to induce an arm catalepsy and then awaken the subject with the arm still cataleptic.[23]

The reader may have rightfully asked by now, "What if the challenges or tests fail? Aren't they awful risky? Won't a failure destroy one's credibility and prestige?" The answer to these questions is yes and that is the reason why many hypnotists do not use them. It is the skillful use of challenges and tests, however, that separate sophisticated from unsophisticated operators.

It is the authors' belief and experience, as well as the unanimous opinion of numerous experienced subjects, that the advantages in the skillful use of challenges and tests far outweigh the disadvantages. With proper technique in applying a graded series of challenges and tests, the risk of failure can be minimized. In the event of failure, certain recovery techniques will by and large prevent any loss of confidence and prestige. The importance of challenging and testing is best stated by some experienced subjects themselves:

- "I think they're absolutely necessary because they not only prove to you that I am hypnotized, but they prove it to me. You know, sometimes I'm not sure I am where I'm supposed to be, but when I know through the challenges it makes me deeper."
- "They very definitely convinced me that I was hypnotized! I can forget my little fears that it's not working, and they make me go deeper because of the reassurance."
- "I think they really convinced me that I was under, as I was a little skeptical. When I couldn't open my eyes I thought to myself, 'Man, I really am under!' They're real necessary, especially with novice subjects. They're convincers."

Interviews with experienced subjects have shown that challenges are almost unanimously believed to be interesting, convincing, deepening, and necessary. In addition, no subjects found them frightening or indicative of the hypnotist having control over them.

A sufficient number of challenges and tests will be taught in this section to provide the hypno-investigator with the necessary tools to accurately estimate depth for any given subject. The reader is urged to review "Depth of Hypnosis" in Chapter 3, however, to become conversant with other observable signs of depth.

There are several types of challenges and tests: (1) direct challenges, (2) indirect challenges, (3) obtrusive tests, and (4) unobtrusive tests. The sophisticated use of challenges and tests requires that the operator be proficient in all four types.

Direct challenges are those that directly challenge a subject to break a suggestion. A subject may make one of two responses to a direct suggestion; he may attempt to break the suggestion and fail, or he will attempt to break the suggestion and succeed. If the subject fails to break the suggestion, he drifts deeper into hypnosis, but if he succeeds in breaking the suggestion, the whole induction is likely to fail unless the operator skillfully uses one of the recovery techniques. To minimize or entirely avoid the possibility of failure the operator must follow the cardinal rule of direct challenging: never directly challenge a subject unless reasonably certain of success. When uncertain of success, the operator should use an indirect challenge.

In an *indirect challenge* the subject is not directly challenged to break the suggestion. In essence, a hypnotic phenomenon is elicited and the subject is brought to realize that it is probably beyond his voluntary control, but he is not exhorted to test it. In this manner, the challenge is implicit and not explicit. A subject may make one of three responses to an indirect suggestion; he can ignore it, act on the challenge and fail, or accept it and succeed. If the subject ignores it he may drift a little deeper into hypnosis. If he accepts the challenge and fails, he will usually drift much deeper into hypnosis. If, however, he accepts it (which is unlikely), and succeeds the operator is in a much less vulnerable position. Since the challenge was only implied and not an explicit statement of fact, the operator is not confronted with an outright rejection of his challenge. In effect, then, direct challenges carry a greater risk, but also a greater potential for gain, whereas indirect challenges are less risky, but carry a lesser potential for gain.

For either type of challenge there are several recovery techniques that can be used to neutralize any potential damage to the session, or even to turn a failure to your advantage.

Obtrusive tests are those that are performed with the subject's cooperation and awareness. They are done for the purpose of convincing the subject and operator alike that he is hypnotized. As with direct challenges, they either succeed or fail, although the degree of risk and potential loss of face is more similar to that of the indirect challenges. As with challenges, certain techniques can be used effectively for recovering.

Unobtrusive tests are those that are performed without the direct knowledge and participation of the subject and whose sole purpose is a test of depth for the operator.

Eye Catalepsy

Direct

WHEN INDICATED. The *eye catalepsy* challenge is a test for a light trance and hence should be conducted immediately after eye closure is obtained by any of the inductions, or at the end of an induction done with eyes closed. The direct form of the challenge should be used if the subject responded positively to the induction as gauged by the observable signs, and the operator is certain of success.

VERBALIZATION. "The eyelids are so heavy and tired now that they are shut tight. In fact they are so relaxed that they're as heavy as lead, as if they were glued tightly shut — so relaxed and so heavy and sticking tighter and tighter. Now, with the eyelids closed tightly, roll the eyes up into your head as if you were looking at the top of your forehead and hold that position."

(This is the eyeball-set, i.e. it is very difficult to open the lids with the eyeballs rolled upward. The subject does not know this, however, and will attribute his inability to open his eyes to your suggestions. By this time some subjects may already be attempting to open their eyes and, if unsuccessful, this insures success.)

"You'll notice that the longer you hold this position the tighter the lids stick shut, as if they were glued together, sticking tighter and tighter. They are STUCK FAST!"

(The operator becomes a little more dramatic and authoritative as he approaches the actual challenge. This has the effect of creating a better response: it implies that what you predicted is actually occurring.)

"If you tried to open the eyes, you could not, and this is a good sign. If you really wish to go deeper you won't be able to open them."

(These two suggestions are important because they are subtle motivators that will maximize the subject's cooperation. Now the subject is ready for the actual challenge.)

"Go ahead and try to open the eyes, but you CANNOT! TRY HARD! In fact the more you try the more they stick! *(The subject struggles for a moment to open his eyes, but cannot.)* That's good, you've done well. Now let the eyes return to their normal position and relax. You see, the eyes are so relaxed that they are so heavy and tired that you cannot open them, and that's a good sign."

(The operator praises the subject, lets his eyes relax, and then explains the phenomenon to alleviate any possible anxiety that not being able to open his eyes may have stimulated.)

Indirect

WHEN INDICATED. If the subject responded with a less than adequate response to the induction and appears to be only in a hypnoidal or very light trance, an indirect approach should be used. Upon achieving eye closure and having continued suggestions of heaviness and establishing the eyeball-set as in the direct approach, continue with the following verbalization.

VERBALIZATION. "The eyes are so heavy and tired and relaxed now that they could only be opened with great difficulty. If you tried to open them you could not, but you have NO desire to even try. It would be too great an effort to even try. You just want to relax more and more and drift deeper and deeper." *(The operator must say this indirect challenge in a passive manner by using his same hypnotic monotone. It is important that you convey to the subject that he is not to try to open his eyes, but that you are making a mere statement of fact.)*

Recovering

If the subject begins to open his eyes in either of the above approaches, the operator has two avenues of recovery. First, he can remark at the first indication that the subject may open his eyes, "That's good, you've done fine. Now let your eyes relax. . . . " The operator terminates the challenge before the subject has a chance to break it. Second, if it appears that the subject is going to actually get them open and the operator does not have time to terminate the challenge, he can remark, "Now you can open your eyes, go ahead and open them. You see how difficult that was? I didn't want to let you strain too long." This approach will leave the subject uncertain as to whether the challenge was a success or failure. The operator should then proceed to the eye blink. At the moment of the challenge, the operator must carefully observe the subject's response to determine exactly which form he is going to use. It should be noted that many subjects can open their eyes just slightly, but will be unable to open them completely.

If the subject opens his eyes with either approach described above, say "That's good. I wanted to prove to you that you are in control and that I have no 'powers' over you." This tactic is indicated because the subject probably interprets hypnosis as a battle of wills or he is otherwise unable to let go and give up control. "You are in control. You can make the decision to let yourself go so completely and to relax the eye muscles so completely that you will be unable to open them. You must understand that you actually do this by your own efforts and you have the privilege of going deeper and deeper relaxed. O.K.? Do you want to proceed?" If the subject responds no, terminate the session and discuss his resistance. If he responds yes, move on to the eye blink and eventually retest for eye catalepsy.

Considerations

1. For subjects who have either responded very favorably to the induction and who are probably in a medium or deep trance or with those who are already trying to open their eyes but cannot, the eyeball-set is unnecessary.

2. Do not have the subject attempt to open his eyes too long, i.e. more than five seconds. The longer the subject tries the more likely he will succeed.

3. If the subject responds less than adequately to the induction and the operator is uncertain of success even with the indirect approach, he may opt to do a deepening technique before attempting eye catalepsy.

Eye Flinch

Once eye catalepsy is successful, the subject should be deepened with a standard deepening technique, and then tested with the unobtrusive *eye flinch* test that is an indicator of a medium level trance. To conduct the test, the operator very gently and noiselessly reaches up and touches the eyelashes of the nearest eye. There is normally an involuntary flinch or reflex if only in a light trance or above, but, in a medium or deeper trance, a person loses this startle reaction. If the operator is not sure of the reaction, he can do the test on the other eye or on the same one a little later. The operator must be very careful to keep talking, unless done during a silent period, and to not change his body position substantially as the subject is very attuned to his actions, and any unnecessary movement may make him anticipate the test.

To help ratify or prove to the subject that he is in fact hypnotized, this test may be turned into an obtrusive test by simply explaining it to him immediately afterwards if successful.

Limp Arm

Another medium trance test is the *limp arm* drop. At this stage of hypnosis, the larger muscle groups should be totally relaxed. As an easy unobtrusive test, the operator can tell the subject, "Now I want to see how relaxed you are. As we did at the very beginning, I am again going to pick ıp the left arm by the wrist and just let it drop." *(Pick up the arm and drop it. The subject should never be surprised or startled by your actions so always announce your intentions before touching him. If the arm drops with a thud to the lap or the cushioned arm of the chair, this indicates total relaxation and at least a medium trance. The degree of relaxation can be brought to the subject's attention if substantially different from the test at the beginning of the induction.)* "You see how much more relaxed you are now? That's a good sign."

If the arms are not totally relaxed, the operator had best attempt to completely relax them before proceeding, as muscle tension is an indication that a medium trance has not been reached. "You're doing fine 'Greg,' but you need to relax the arms a little more. Now, as I pick up the arm I want you to relax it completely. Just let it go and let me have it. Make it like a dead weight. Relax it completely, like you never have before. *(Let the arm drop to his lap.)* That's better. Now relax it even more as I drop it again." Continue lifting and dropping the arm while giving appropriate suggestions until it is completely relaxed. Then do the same with the other arm.

Arm Catalepsy

Direct

WHEN INDICATED. If both the eye flinch and limp arm drop are successful, the operator can proceed with relative certainty to the direct *arm catalepsy*, which is indicative of a deep medium trance according to the LeCron-Bordeaux scoring chart.

VERBALIZATION. "Now I'm going to take this arm *(pick up the closest arm)* and stretch it straight out in front of you and as I move it up you go deeper and deeper relaxed. In fact, with each motion that the arm moves upward you can think, feel, and imagine yourself going deeper."

(As you are saying this, take the subject's arm and gently guide it out straight in front of him or to the side. As you lift the arm slowly, you give additional suggestions for deepening by linking the physical action with going deeper.)

"That's it, extend it straight, and now make a fist, a tight fist, tighter and tighter."

(When the arm is extended straight out, the operator should support it at the elbow with one hand and give it a little tug from the subject's fist, which is a nonverbal suggestion implying that the arm is supposed to be straight and stiff. At this point the operator can test for spontaneous waxy flexibility (see "Catalepsy" in "The Nature of Hypnotic Phenomena" in Chapter 3) by trying to release his support under the elbow. With some subjects, the arm will stay in position with seemingly

no effort. If this is the case, the operator can proceed with the direct approach with confidence.)

"Now I am going to gently pass my hand over the arm, and with each pass the whole arm will become tighter and tighter."

(The operator begins to gently stroke the arm from shoulder to fist. See figure 10. It is recommended that the operator actually lightly grasp the arm in his fingers and to increase the tension slightly with each pass. This will impart a strong nonverbal suggestion to the subject that the muscles are supposed to tighten. The operator can also test for the degree to which his suggestions are taking hold by feeling the muscles tighten.)

"The arm is stiffening, automatically and spontaneously. With each pass of my hand it's getting stiffer and stiffer. I can feel it! The entire arm is becoming like a bar of iron! Rigid! So stiff it's like a bar of iron! So stiff you won't be able to bend it, and that's a good sign. If you really wish to go deeper you won't be able to bend it. The elbow is LOCKED! So still you cannot bend it! Go ahead and try! TRY HARD! The harder you try the stiffer it gets! That's good, you're doing good. Now as I take the arm you can let it relax and bend. And as it relaxes and slowly lowers to your lap you will go deeper and deeper relaxed, and when it touches you will be much deeper than you are now."

(The operator turns the lowering of the arm into a deepening.)

"You see, you are deep enough into hypnosis to where the body can work automatically, and that's a good sign."

(The operator gives a simple explanation of the phenomenon to alleviate any possible anxiety the cataleptic arm may have stimulated.)

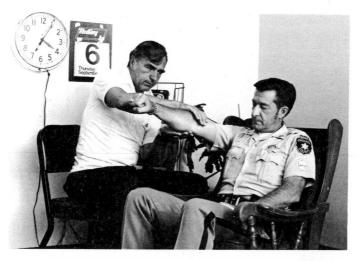

Figure 10. Ray Worring induces arm catalepsy in Sgt. Donovan. Notice how he gently supports the elbow with his fingertips as he lightly strokes the arm from shoulder to fist.

Indirect

When Indicated. If the arm does not tighten sufficiently as gauged by the feel (this is readily determined through even a light touch) and the operator is uncertain of success, he should use the indirect approach. Before using the following verbalization, continue giving additional suggestions for stiffness in an attempt to maximize the rigidity.

Verbalization. In a passive monotone voice, the operator says the following: "The arm is so stiff and rigid that you could bend it only with great difficulty. If you tried to bend it you could not, but you will NOT try to bend it, you have no desire to even try. It would be much too great an effort to even try. You just want to relax further and further as the arm relaxes now as I lower it to your lap. . . . "

Recovering

Immediately before challenging the subject with either of the above approaches, the operator should position his hands near the subject's elbow and wrist so he can grab the arm if the subject succeeds in bending it (see figure 11). This requires discrimination, however, because some subjects will be able to bend the arm slightly (approximately 1 inch), but no further. The deciding factor is generally the level of observable tension in the arm; the greater the tension the less chance of bending. If the subject does succeed in bending his arm and the operator catches it as it bends, he can recover in the same manner as indicated for eye catalepsy, i.e. terminate the challenge before the subject has an opportunity to break it. If the subject bends the arm completely, the operator can resort to the discussion of "control" as done for eye catalepsy. Another option is to catch the arm while remarking, "You see how difficult it is to bend it. That's a good sign. Now as I continue to bend the arm and lower it to your lap you just want to drift deeper and deeper relaxed. When it touches your leg you'll be much deeper than you are now."

Whichever technique is used to recover, the operator should proceed to another deepening technique while assuring the subject that he will do much better next time. After deepening further, eventually retest for catalepsy in the opposite arm or do another medium trance test, e.g. glove anesthesia (see "Controls for Simulation and Lying" in Chapter 7). Before testing for arm catalepsy, enlist the subject's cooperation by saying, "Let's see how stiff and rigid you can make it this time."

Considerations

1. Always test for arm catalepsy on the closest arm as it is much more convenient and less awkward for the operator.

2. Depending on the degree of tension, the operator should either shorten or lengthen the suggestions. Some subjects' arms become so tight and rigid so fast that unnecessarily drawing out the suggestions will result in a sore arm. On the other hand, some subjects' arms tighten only slowly so

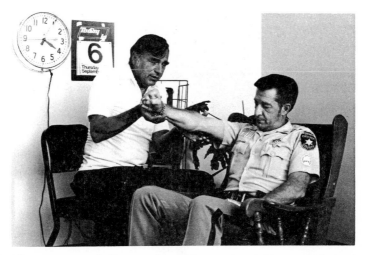

Figure 11. The operator challenges the subject to bend his arm. Notice how he has positioned his hands so he can grasp the arm should the subject succeed in bending it.

the suggestions may have to be deliberately prolonged to elicit sufficient tension before challenging.

3. Don't let the subject try to bend his arm too long, as, given enough time, he is likely to succeed.

4. The operator may have to give several countersuggestions to make the arm relax, i.e. "Now as I take the arm you let it relax. Let it relax completely now as I lower it to your lap."

Suggested Amnesia*

When Indicated

If the arm catalepsy is successful, the operator proceeds with one or two more deepening techniques and then tests for *suggested amnesia,* an obtrusive test for a deep trance. If successful, this will be the last test for depth before eliciting hypermnesia or revivification.

Verbalization

"Now that your body is completely relaxed, we must make sure that your mind is completely relaxed before we can proceed to obtain the regression, which you really want most."

(The operator subtlely motivates the subject while making a smooth transition to the test.)

---

* This technique was designed by Myron Teitelbaum, M.D., J.D., and the verbalization is largely paraphrased from his book, *Hypnosis Induction Technics,* 1965. Courtesy of Charles C Thomas, Publisher, Springfield, Illinois.

"I want you to imagine that you are in front of a blackboard. It can be any blackboard. One that you are familiar with or maybe one that you've never seen before. On this blackboard I want you to see the numbers going backwards from one hundred. That is, one hundred, ninety-nine, ninety-eight, ninety-seven, and on down to zero. It may be convenient to place them in five rows of twenty each. When you can see the blackboard and numbers clearly, signal me by raising your finger *(touch an index finger).* Here's what I want you to do. When I tell you to, I want you to begin calling off out loud these numbers from the blackboard, beginning with 100. As you call off each number, I want you to mentally erase the number off of the blackboard and out of your mind. When you get down to the number ninety-seven, I want you to erase all the remaining numbers off of the blackboard and out of your mind so that you cannot think of another number. All right, I want you to look at those numbers and begin starting with 100 to erase all those numbers. One hundred, now wipe it off the blackboard and out of your mind. Ninety-nine, now erase it off the blackboard and out of your mind. Ninety-eight, now the last number you will be able to find — 97. Now wipe it away completely and all the rest of the numbers so that they are completely gone. All you can see is a smudge there. You cannot think of another number. Your mind is a blank, and that's a good sign. You cannot find any more numbers, and that's what we both want. What is the next number? See, you cannot tell me the next number, can you? What is the next number?"

(At this point the subject should either move his lips to indicate the negative, or just shake his head. The operator must then determine whether the subject has true suggested amnesia or merely aphasia. He must obtain a response as to whether or not the subject can find the number. With aphasia the subject will be able to see the number, but will be unable to speak. With true suggested amnesia, a deeper stage, he will be unable to find the number at all.)

"You are now able to speak, and I want you to tell me if you can find any more numbers. 'No.' That's good. See, you have obtained complete mental relaxation, as your mind has become a blank."

Recovering

This test is very similar to a challenge in that the operator runs the risk of losing face and damaging the session if the subject continues to call off numbers below ninety-seven. As with the challenges, therefore, it is necessary that the operator be prepared for this eventuality. Teitelbaum recommends that this problem can be recognized and dealt with in the following manner:

If the subject glibly calls off the numbers from 100 through 97, he will almost always be able to continue on down past 97. This would indicate that the subject has not passed beyond the light trance state. Where the subject goes very slowly, and the voice volume drops, the indications are that the subject will have considerable difficulty recalling any more numbers. If the subject is able to go below 97, the operator should immediately stop him. To allow the subject to keep on going down to 90 and below, will bring him out of any trance state achieved. The moment the number 96 is called out, the operator should explain to the subject, that the subject was not relaxing his mind sufficiently. In this way, the operator does not place himself in an awkward position of telling the subject that something will happen, when it won't. Sometimes the subject may get down to 96 and then will be unable to proceed any further. The allowing of the subject to try further will depend upon the difficulty he has in finding and speaking any numbers below 97.[24]

If the subject is counting very slowly and with great difficulty, the operator could let him continue for a few more numbers while reaffirming the suggestions of making his mind a blank, i.e. "You see, with each number it's getting more and more difficult. They're fading fast as your mind is becoming a blank, and that's a good sign. That's what we both want."

If the operator deemed it necessary to stop the subject from counting below ninety-six, he can continue with the following verbalization: "Okay, you're doing fine, Leslie, you see how difficult it's becoming to see any other numbers. You need to go just a little deeper, however, so that you can make you mind a complete blank before we can move on to do what you want most, to recall the license number. Now to take yourself deeper what I am going to do is to count backward from ninety-six to eighty synchronizing each count with each exhale, and with each count backward you will go deeper and deeper than you are now." The operator has turned the test into a simple counting deepening technique. When he reaches eighty he does the single shoulder press timed with **"D–E–E–P, D–E–E–P, D–E–E–P."** At this point the operator repeats the exact initial suggested amnesia instructions but substituting the numbers eighty, seventy-nine, seventy-eight, and seventy-seven. He then redoes the exact same test. If it fails again, he continues on down in a cycle of deepening and testing.

If necessary, the operator may also use other deepening techniques, and he could repeat the arm catalepsy in the opposite arm. If the subject is young and naive enough, the operator may also use what may be called the *Chinese Acupressure Technique.* As the subject continues to count down, the operator may say to the subject, "Now I'm going to do something that will help you to make your mind a blank. I am going to press on a special acupuncture point known as the "third-eye," which is just below the middle of your forehead. Now as I start to apply pressure there *(the operator starts pushing gently)* you will find it harder and harder to find any other numbers, your mind is becoming more of a blank the harder I push. Go ahead and try to continue counting down, but the harder I press the more difficult it becomes. The numbers are vanishing. . . . " The operator continues fairly authoritatively until the subject can no longer see any other numbers.

If all these techniques fail the operator can only explain to the subject that he has not relaxed his mind sufficiently. He should emphasize, however, that most people are unable to the first time, but that almost all can the second time. At that point the operator may induce fractionation giving the subject a posthypnotic suggestion that he will not only go deeper each time he is rehypnotized, but that it will become more and more difficult to recall those numbers until his mind will finally be a blank. The operator can then proceed to retest for suggested amnesia.

As an alternative retest for suggested amnesia, the operator may induce fractionation, but give the subject a posthypnotic suggestion to the effect that he will not be able to count the even numbers when asked to count to ten. This particular retest is indicated if the operator suspects that either the subject did not understand the suggested amnesia instructions or could not visualize the blackboard and numbers sufficiently.

The suggested amnesia test is important for two reasons. First, a subject must be able to produce amnesia in order to revivify; he must be able to temporarily forget everything that happened subsequent to the regression event. Second, the instructions and format of the suggested amnesia test are very similar to those used to elicit regression, therefore the test preconditions the subject for regression.

Glove Anesthesia and Ammonia Test

These two tests can easily and effectively be used as either obtrusive or unobtrusive tests of a medium level trance. Their particular advantage and use are as tests for simulation of hypnosis and for lying. They will therefore be discussed later in "Controls for Simulation and Lying" in Chapter 7.

Helpful Hints and General Rules for Challenging and Testing

1. The operator must rehearse each direct, indirect, and recovery technique for each challenge so he is prepared to use them instantaneously.

2. Do not challenge or use obtrusive tests unless reasonably certain of success.

3. When a challenge or test is failed, always back up and deepen further and eventually retest for the failed challenge or test or with one of similar difficulty.

4. Always praise the subject's efforts and briefly explain the phenomenon once successful.

5. Challenges can be done either authoritatively or passively. For example, the suggestion, "The arm is so stiff you won't be able to bend it," can be spoken in such a manner as to be a provocative challenge to try to bend the arm, or as a mere statement of fact. The authoritative approach will generally lead to a larger reaction, but it is not suited for all subjects or all operators. For example, the authoritative approach may smack too much of showmanship for a sophisticated subject. Similarly, some operators may be uncomfortable with the authoritative approach. If this is the case, a challenge may be introduced by saying, "Now I'm going to show you something interesting that you can do under hypnosis." The operator then proceeds with the challenge in a passive manner.

ELICITATION OF HYPNOTIC PHENOMENA: TIME REGRESSION, HYPERMNESIA, AND REVIVIFICATION

Once hypnosis has been induced, deepened, and tested for depth of trance, the operator is ready to elicit the specific hypnotic phenomena that will allow him to fulfill his objective: time regression, hypermnesia, and revivification. It is these phenomena that form the cornerstone of forensic hypnosis, and it is their skilled elicitation and management that is the trademark of the successful hypno-investigator.

There are considerable differences of opinion in the hypnotic literature as to exactly what is meant by regression, hypermnesia, and revivification. Different authorities, although using the same terminology, may be referring to entirely different phenomena. There are no universally accepted standard definitions for regression, hypermnesia, and revivification, yet it is essential that they be specifically defined in order to be intelligently discussed. For the purpose of this book, therefore, they will be defined within the context of forensic hypnosis.

Hypermnesia is the opposite of amnesia. It refers to the enhanced recall of memories not subject to voluntary or nonhypnotic recall. There are basically two types of hypermnesia. Traditionally, hypermnesia is regarded as being enhanced recall from a nonregressed hypnotic state in which the subject is merely asked to remember the forgotten event from his present age and perspective. For the purposes of this book, this will be designated as hypermnesia Type II.

The other type of hypermnesia involves recall from a regressed hypnotic state in which the subject is asked to unemotionally and objectively describe what is happening using the present tense as he views it. For the purposes of this book, this will be designated as hypermnesia Type I. In effect, hypermnesia Type I is a detached experience of a past event in which the subject is not aware of the present.

For reasons to be made apparent in the following discussion of the research, hypermnesia Type I is far superior to Type II. Hypermnesia Type I is seldom complete, however, but often fluctuates to varying degrees between Type I and Type II as the subject's present biographical awareness intrudes.

Revivification, on the other hand, is an actual reliving or psychophysiological reproduction of a past event with amnesia for all subsequent events. In other words, a memory complex of a specific biographical event is totally activated and the individual has no awareness of any events or experiences occurring after that time. For all intents and purposes they are totally forgotten, erased, or ablated and therefore have no influence on the individual's regressed behavior. This is revivification in its true sense and will be referred to as Type I.

Revivifications are seldom complete, however. Sometimes the revivification will resemble more of a role-played or acting out of an adult's version of what the regressed level is imagined, remembered, or believed to be. This will be called a Type II or *pseudo-revivification.*

Time regression is the mechanism, technique, or process by which hypermnesia Type I and revivification Type I are produced. In the hypnotic literature, *regression* is often used loosely to refer to both hypermnesia and revivification and various combinations thereof. In its therapeutic usage, *regression* is usually referred to by clinicians as *age regression*, which refers to the technique of regressing clients to early traumatic incidences in their lives for therapeutic purposes. To avoid the therapeutic connotation, and recognizing that most regressions to crime incidents will be a matter of days or weeks, the authors deemed it appropriate to use the term *time regression*. In essence, then, time regression is the road to follow, and hypermnesia and revivification are what you do when you get there; they are your destination.

It is important to recognize that hypermnesia and revivification are not separate and distinct phenomena, but rather lie along a continuum and that a subject may exhibit a blend of the two. In fact, only with the most highly susceptible subjects at very deep trance levels will a complete revivification be possible. With the majority of subjects, regardless of whether a revivification or hypermnesia is attempted, some elements will be relived, others role-played, while others may only be described unemotionally in

TABLE III

**TIME REGRESSION, HYPERMNESIA, REVIVIFICATION:
INTERRELATIONSHIPS**

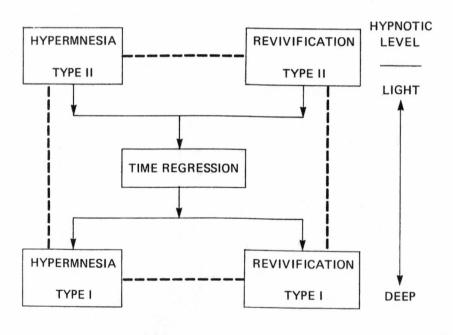

—————— Direct line relationship

— — — — Lines of fluctuation

the past tense. Table III is a graphic conception of how hypermnesia Type I and II and revivification Type I and II are interrelated. Unless otherwise specified, *hypermnesia* will refer to hypermnesia Type I and *revivification* will refer to revivification Type I.

The Nature of Hypermnesia and Revivification

Once the beginning operator induces his first time regression, and particularly when he elicits a revivification, he cannot help but be immensely impressed with its realism. If the operator was a skeptic until this point, he will probably no longer be one, and he will be quite surprised to discover that some experts question the genuineness of hypermnesia and revivification.

The hypno-investigator must have a working knowledge, understanding, and appreciation for time regression, hypermnesia, and revivification. To this end, some of the major studies will be cited to convince the operator of what a powerful tool he has in his hands, and to elucidate some important ramifications the studies have for technique.

The major question and center of controversy, which has a direct import for forensic hypnosis, is whether or not it is possible to recall or revivify past experiences without the intrusion and alteration of subsequent experience. In other words, does regression involve an actual psychophysiological return and reproduction of the original event, or is it merely the role-played version of the subject's present waking remembrance of an earlier event? Although the majority of the experts agree that the former is the case, the detractors maintain that hypermnesia and revivification are artifacts of the demand characteristics and role-requirements of the hypnotic situation. For example, in a regression of an adult to childhood, these experts maintain that the subject essentially hallucinates his adult conception of what he was like as a child, and acts out the hallucination.

In an attempt to prove their respective positions while disproving those of the other side, each camp has tended to conduct research that supports their respective positions.

In a study in which nine hypnotized subjects were compared with seven unhypnotizable simulators on a real versus simulated regression to their third birthday and tested on the Stanford-Binet Intelligence Test, Young found that the simulators came nearer a three-year-old performance than the regressed subjects. Young concludes that "role playing would more likely explain the phenomena. Hypnosis is playing the role with all one's heart but not with all one's mind."[25] In an attempt to replicate this study, Sarbin concludes, "There is no authentic and complete regression to earlier age-roles insofar as intelligence tests are concerned."[26]

Similarly, Orne tested ten university student somnambules regressed to the age of six on the Rorschach (ink-blot) and took drawing and handwriting samples. These results were compared with the simulated regressed test and samples of the same students' handwriting done in the awake state. Orne concludes, on the basis of the comparison, that important aspects of the adult personality were still present and functioning in the regressed state and that, although the personality does seem to change, "at all times we are dealing with the personality organization of the adult."[27]

In an attempt to distinguish clearly between true versus simulated regression as gauged by performance on the Goodenough drawings, Taylor concludes in part that the total group showed "no significant difference between the hypnotic and waking drawings."[28]

What is interesting, however, is that other researchers using the same tests in similar experiments derived opposite conclusions. Mercer and Gibson administered the Stanford-Binet, the Rorschach, and the Goodenough drawing to one subject regressed to various age levels. The researchers' conclusion was that the test findings reflected accurately the regressed age levels to the point that they could not doubt that a true regression had taken place.[29]

Another research team utilizing the Rorschach on an individual regressed to various age levels concludes that more is involved in regression than mere remembering.[30]

Handwriting samples and drawings by regressed adults have been found, in certain instances, to be completely identical to old specimens obtained from parents.[31]

Kline and Haggerty compared the responses of a subject on the Thematic Apperception Test first during the simulation of a regression and then during an actual hypnotic regression. The experimenters conclude that the simulation was statistically and qualitatively adultlike, whereas, in the actual regression, the subject's perceptual mechanism was convincingly that of the regressed age level.[32]

Kline also tested ten male college students at various regressed age levels on the Otis Self-Administering Tests of Mental Ability and compared the results with their responses on the test during the waking state. The results indicated that hypnotic age regression involves more than just recall or accurate simulation.[33]

These contradictory results, although initially confusing and perhaps a bit disheartening, are ultimately enlightening as they force a critical evaluation of methodology and technique. When closely scrutinized, all the above studies suffer from several basic weaknesses:

1. The samples are much too small; they ranged from one subject to a maximum of ten.

2. There is no control for depth of trance, hypnotic susceptibility, or technique used.

3. They rely on the external administration of a standardized test that compares the regressed adult to a statistical norm for the age to which the adult returns. No consideration is given to the fact that that same adult may have deviated either high or low from the norm when actually that age, but when he deviates in the regressed state it is interpreted as being significant.

These considerations render the above results, both positive and negative, essentially meaningless. As has been noted by others, any review of hypnosis research inevitably becomes a story of how not to do research.

So the question remains, "Is hypnotic regression genuine?" Fortunately, some researchers who have examined this question have used methodologies and techniques that preclude criticism, and their experimental results have been very conclusive indeed.

The authorities who believe that hypnotic regression is genuine theorize that in actual revivifications, not only are previous experiences and behavior reactivated in totality, but all subsequent experiences and behavior are ablated. In other words, the revivifying individual has no awareness of any experiences after his regressed age, and they, therefore, do not influence his regressed behavior. For all intents and purposes he *is* the regressed age. The subject is not acting as he believes and imagines a person of that age to act, but actual memory schemata are activated and re-experienced. Obviously, the individual cannot return morphologically, although, as some studies show, it is possible to reactivate infantile reflexes in a regressed adult.

The ultimate test of this position is to determine whether or not earlier organic responses and conditions beyond voluntary control and conscious remembrance can be activated by regressing to their original time of manifestation. Such tests would preclude the possibility of simulation.

One of the most convincing tests of this type was conducted by Gidro-Frank and Bowersbuch, in 1948, who gradually regressed three adult subjects, who knew nothing of the nature or purpose of the experiment, to less than six months of age to test for a Babinski reflex. The Babinski reflex refers to the automatic response in infants less than approximately seven months of age to involuntarily upturn (dorsiflexion) the big toe when the sole of the foot is tickled or stroked. After the approximate age of seven months, the reflex reverses; upon stimulation, the big toe involuntarily turns down (plantarflexion). Once the response reverses, it remains for the rest of the person's life. The subjects were regressed at month intervals and the soles of the feet were stimulated at each month. With each subject the adult response of plantarflexion reversed below the age of six months to the infantile response of dorsiflexion. Interestingly enough, when the age regression was reversed and the subjects were brought back at month intervals, the Babinski reflex again reversed to its adult form at five or six months. Furthermore, upon waking, none of the subjects could voluntarily produce or simulate the infantile response of dorsiflexion when the soles of their feet were stimulated.[34]

In 1951, this same study was conducted by another team of researchers who reported a positive Babinski reflex in five out of six subjects regressed to the age of one month.[35]

A similar physiological response manifested by very young infants and which is impossible to simulate is the unassociated or uncoordinated eyeball movements of the newly born. Lozanov, a Bulgarian psychiatrist, regressed five subjects between the ages of twenty and thirty to the age of two days. In three of the subjects unassociated eyeball movements were observed clearly and to a less degree in the other two. Lozanov was unable to elicit unassociated eyeball movement through direct suggestion to the subjects in hypnosis without age regression. The direct suggestion of, "Your eyes begin to move each one for itself, each independent of the other," did not result in unassociated eyeball movements under hypnosis, whereas they spontaneously manifested without suggestion at the regressed age of two days.[36]

Similarly, in a personal communication to LeCron, Erickson described a case in which he regressed a thirty-year-old male to just prior to one year. The subject was seated in a chair with a hinged back that would fall back into a horizontal position at the release of a latch. Once regressed, the latch was released. The involuntary reaction by an adult to such a loss of support is to extend both arms and legs to catch oneself and maintain balance. The regressed subject, however, "squalled in fright, made no movement of the limbs, and fell backward with the chair. A reaction quite unexpected and embarrassing to both Erickson and the subject was an accompanying urination which soaked the man's trousers! Certainly such behavior is not acting and is an impressive indication of the actuality of regression."[37]

Kline conducted a regression experiment that ended in a similarly embarrassing involuntary reaction. He exposed a twenty-five-year-old female subject to six normally fear producing situations for children, first in the waking state and then under hypnosis. The subject responded with no fear to any of the situations. Once regressed to the age of three, however, the subject exhibited intense crying and screaming and involuntarily urinated when shown a decapitated doll. The sight of the snake produced a "paroxism of terror."[38] The degree and spontaneity of these reactions as compared to the nonreaction in waking or hypnosis without regression appears to be quite beyond the possibility of simulation.

Other subjects, when regressed to infantile levels display seemingly involuntary sucking and grasping movements.[39] Similarly, David Cheek, an obstetrician, found that distinctive sequential head and shoulder movements and other fetal postural changes occurred during hypnosis in ten obstetrically naive adults regressed to their births.[40] Other biographical behaviors, such as nail biting, may also spontaneously reappear when regressed to the age of the original behavior.

Several cases have been reported of actual organic reproductions or reoccurrences characteristic of earlier periods in individual's lives. In one case report, a subject who had a condition of partial blindness corrected as the result of surgery was regressed to a time prior to the operation. During the regression the partial blindness returned.[41] Other similar organic responses and conditions have been reported as spontaneously occurring during regression to the particular time at which they were manifest. A case of actual improvement in vision as tested by an optometrist in a woman during a regression to an age when she still had normal vision was reported, [42] and actual hemorrages and bruising developed in another woman when regressed to the time of an accident.[43] Similarly, another man who had experienced a convulsive seizure at the age of eighteen was regressed to twelve years of age while monitored by an electroencephalogram. Brain tracings were normal until the subject was progressed up to his eighteenth year when the EEG measured definite cortical abnormalities.[44]

There are numerous examples of people raised in bilingual families who have literally forgotten the minority language as they switched to the dominant cultural language as adults. When regressed to childhood, however, many of these people spontaneously begin to speak fluently in the "forgotten" language, quite to the surprise of the operator.[45]

LeCron established a conditioned reflex in the waking state with two subjects by pairing a buzzer to an electric shock to a hand. The shock was sufficient to cause involuntary retraction or jerk of the hand. It was thoroughly conditioned and paired with the buzzer so that the sound of the buzzer alone would trigger the reflex. The subjects were hypnotized and the buzzer sounded; both involuntarily jerked the hand. The subjects were then regressed to ten years of age and the buzzer sounded; neither retracted the hand. Once the subjects were dehypnotized, the buzzer was again sounded and each responded with a definite hand jerk.[46]

In a similar conditioned reflex study, Edmonston concluded, "The ablation theory of hypnotic age-regression is substantiated. Hypnotic age-regression appears to be authentic rather than simulated."[47] Another research team also concludes, in a study of a conditioned GSR, that a functional separation of age levels can occur when a subject is regressed. This also supports the functional ablation theory.[48] The important finding of these studies is that behavior in a regressed state is not affected by subsequent experience and knowledge.

Enhanced recall from a regressed state has also been convincingly demonstrated under experimental conditions by regressing subjects and eliciting earlier verifiable information not available in the waking state. R. M. True regressed a total of forty men and ten women ranging from twenty to twenty-four years of age to the ages of ten, seven, and four using Christmas and their birthdays of each year as chronological landmarks. On each date they were asked, "What day is this?," referring to what day of the week the regressed Christmas or birthday fell on. The answers of the fifty subjects were later scored against a calendar and the results showed that 93 percent of the subjects' answers were correct at the age level of ten, 82 percent at the age of seven, and 69 percent at the age of four.[49]

In a very carefully controlled set of experiments in which hypermnesia was correlated in hypnotically regressed subjects with simulators, Reiff and Scheerer reported that the regressed subjects exhibited a statistically significant greater percentage of memories than in the normal waking state, but that there was no such increase with simulating subjects. Furthermore, they showed that under hypnotic age regression, that "recall is almost equally as good for the remote as for the more recent ages."[50]

In a single subject tested by Wolberg, "an eight digit series, repeated during hypnosis, was recalled in a trance two years later."[51]

A most convincing and important experiment on the extent of hypnotic recall was conducted by Cheek. To test his hypothesis that "the uncon-scious mind can hear and remember careless operating room conversa-tion," Doctor Cheek regressed postoperative patients to the time of surgery to determine whether or not his hypothesis was true. He con-cludes, on the basis of tape recordings and interviews with doctors and dentists, that "The anesthetized patient may lose all motor reflexes, lose all ability to communicate with the outside world, lose all sense of pain, but the anesthetized patient is able to hear and remember important events at a deep level of subconscious thought. This level can be uncovered and the events recalled by hypnotic techniques."[52]

The important implication of this finding is that a victim or potential witness should not be dismissed as unable to provide relevant information on the basis that he was in an inebriated or drug-induced state or even unconscious at the time. Similarly, victims or witnesses should not be dismissed as potential hypnotic subjects on the basis that they said they did not see anything of importance. In a regressed state, information that was recorded only on a subliminal or subconscious level can often be retrieved.

In conclusion, the consensus at the present time among the vast majority of authorities in the field is that regression with subsequent revivification is an actual psychophysiological reproduction that obviates all possibility of simulation. The answer to the original question posed at the beginning of this discussion would, on the basis of the above research, have to be "Yes, it is possible to recall or revivify past experiences without the intrusion and alteration by subsequent experience." It must be remembered, however, that genuine regressive behavior often coexists with subsequent develop-mental levels. In their thorough review of this problem, Reiff and Scheerer contend that, "where the memory trace is available, the hypnotically re-gressed subject will function on the basis of an actual revivification of earlier functional schemata; and where the memories are not available, he will utilize other available memories from later stages of development, or he will fabulize."[53]

As with the first experiments mentioned in this section, most of the above studies, as dramatic and convincing as they are, have been attempted to be duplicated by other researchers, but with negative results. For exam-ple, in testing alleged enhanced recall under hypnosis, numerous re-searchers have found no statistically significant difference over waking recall. In a study of memory enhancement of learned nonsense-syllables after a twenty-four hour delay, Huse found no statistical improvement.[54] In a similar experiment, another group of researchers also found that hypnosis did not improve recall of paired nonsense-syllables learned the previous day.[55] In an effort to replicate LeCron's study of a conditioned response as proof of age regression, McCranie and Crasilneck concluded that there is "no neurophysiologic proof of the reality of this phenomenon."[56]

So the question remains of how contradictory results can be reached on seemingly identical experiments. The answer involves a critical evaluation of methodology, which has been done by Reiff and Scheerer, but there are important ramifications for technique for the hypno-investigator.

When examined closely, the studies that yielded inconclusive or negative results suffered from some or all of the following major weaknesses:

1. Trance depth was not sufficient, i.e. tests were not made for somnambulism.

2. Inadequate induction and deepening techniques were used, tests and challenges were not performed, and the skill of the operator was not considered.

3. The regressions were too rapidly induced with inadequate instructions, e.g. "You are now three years old."

4. The subjects were not given time to reorient to the regressed state.

5. The hypnotist was not fitted into the regression situation, i.e. if the subject is regressed to a time prior to knowing the hypnotist, the latter theoretically cannot exist.

6. Instructions were not given to insure little or no deviation from the regressed age level, i.e. "You will think like you thought at the age of X, you will act like you acted at the age of X, you will feel and talk like you felt and talked at that age. You are not to invent or imagine anything that did not actually occur," etc.

7. Major chronological landmarks were not used which makes it difficult for the subject to reorient, e.g. "You are now three years old," instead of, "You will find yourself on your third birthday."

8. Subjects were not carefully selected according to susceptibility and motivational factors.

9. The continual problem of fluctuation in the regressed state was not considered, i.e. regressions are seldom stationary but fluctuate between hypermnesia Types I and II and revivification Types I and II as the subjects' depth changes. In other words, simple recall, imagined regressive behavior, and genuine regressive behavior often coexist in varying degrees. Specific suggestions need to be given to the regressed subject to remain at a depth level or else the mere performance of the requested task may bring him up to a lighter trance level.

10. The operator had a negative attitude. "Subjects have a remarkable ability in hypnosis to sense the attitude of the hypnotist through minimal cues and will respond accordingly. If the operator believes a negative result will ensue, the subject will probably respond negatively."[57] An informal clinical study by Wolberg showed clearly that symptomatic relief in patients treated with hypnotherapy is directly proportional to the doctor's positiveness and enthusiasm about the curative power of hypnosis.[58] Similarly, studies have shown that the effectiveness of placebos is directly proportional to doctor attitude.

11. The subjects were not trained in regression through repeated trials, i.e. subjects learn how to regress through experience, hence better results are attained with subsequent sessions.

12. Subjects were asked to talk, but were not instructed that they could

do so without affecting the depth of trance, i.e. most people believe they cannot talk while hypnotized so being asked to do so can bring them up to a lighter trance or even awaken. Some subjects regressed to a preverbal age were asked to describe their experience. Obviously, this invalidates the regression.

13. Sterile laboratory settings were used which is not conducive to deep hypnosis.

14. The experimenter-subject relationship is generally much less authentic and relevant than either the clinician-patient or hypno-investigator-witness relationship, i.e. the role of the experimentalist is necessarily detached and mechanical, and individual needs, motivations, desires, and fears are not taken into account.

15. The level of regression is not validated by asking some initial questions to determine if the subject is actually at the regressed age, i.e. if the subject is not, the trance should first be deepened before proceeding.

16. The material to be recalled in experiments on hypermnesia is not meaningful, i.e. recalling of nonsense syllables, etc. Research has clearly shown that "meaningful and emotionally stressed material is more readily available under hypnosis than in the waking state," whereas recall of nonmeaningful material is not significantly increased.[59] Recall of meaningful material, such as poetry, learned one year previously was shown to be increased by 54 percent under hypnosis in twelve subjects.[60] One study showed that recall under hypnosis, when compared to waking recall, increased 15.7 percent for nonsense syllables learned twenty-four hours earlier by eight subjects, 53.1 percent for poetry, and 83.1 percent for movie scene.[61] Another study showed that even hypnotic recall of nonsense syllables could be significantly increased if learned under stress.[62] Similarly, Spiegel et al. found that hypnotic regression was easier to obtain for emotionally significant events or days.[63] The obvious conclusion of these studies for the hypno-investigator is that hypnotic recall of crime scene material, and in particular visual scenes, witnessed under stress will be significantly increased over waking recall.

17. Studies of hypnotic hypermnesia were conducted in a nonregressed hypnotic state. In a carefully controlled set of experiments, Reiff and Scheerer concluded that "the somnambulistic state without regression resulted in no statistically significant improvement in percentage scores of memories over the normal waking state." When the experimental subjects were regressed, however, *"there was a statistically significant greater percentage score of memories than in the normal waking state"* (their italics).[64]

The techniques to be presented shortly were specifically designed to overcome the above weaknesses. In support of the hypno-investigator's objective of obtaining complete, accurate, and reliable information, the authors have designed a system of techniques to maximize the operator's chances of obtaining as complete a hypermnesia or revivification as possible with little or no fluctuation and intrusion of later developmental stages.

Considerations

1. In the preinduction phase, explain to the subject that the purpose of the hypnotic session is to obtain the wanted information. Also explain to the subject that the mind works much like a giant computerized videotape recorder and that everything perceived by the sensory system is recorded and stored permanently in the brain at a subconscious level. Much of this information, however, is momentarily not relevant and hence slips out of conscious remembrance, or it is actively repressed due to emotional trauma. With hypnosis this suppressed or repressed material can be recovered.

2. The operator should always establish a safety cue for regaining contact with the regressed subject should it be lost, i.e. "If for any reason you should lose contact with me, all I'll have to do is touch your hand, and you will immediately come back to where you can hear me." If for any reason contact is lost or the subject begins to become emotionally involved in a hypermnesia of a traumatic crime event, the operator should deepen the subject by the conditioned single shoulder press to break the involvement with the scene while simultaneously touching his hand. Occasionally, when attempting a hypermnesia, the subject may begin to slip into a revivification. To prevent this, the operator may have to reassert the hypermnesia instructions, i.e. "You are not to relive this event: just to describe it to me without emotion as you watch it." These instructions should be reaffirmed immediately upon the first indication of emotional involvement. If they are not sufficient in detaching the subject from the crime event, the operator at that point should use the deepening and recontact cues along with suggestions of calm and serentiy. In the event of an emotional outburst, be empathic and accepting, and do not bring the subject out of hypnosis until the reaction is under control.

3. If the crime event is not of a traumatic nature, revivification should be attempted. If the crime was of a traumatic nature hypermnesia should be used. During the preinduction, the subject should be asked if he wishes to merely recall or actually relive the event in question. If the subject does not have a preferance, the choice is the hypno-investigator's. It must be remembered that the well-being of the subject is the operator's primary concern. In this regard, the operator must recognize that certain victims and witnesses to traumatic crimes will have erected subconscious defense mechanisms to repress the event and block it from conscious recollection. These protective mechanisms must be respected and not violated. Doctor Cheek, in his studies of hypermnesia with postoperative patients, cautioned, "In exploring possible traumatic memories with age regression it is necessary to respect the decision of the subconscious mind regarding release of information."[65] Therefore, if the regressed subject exhibits any undue emotional involvement or conflict responses (fidgeting, sighing, etc.) the operator should ask him if he wants to continue, i.e. "We will

continue only if both your conscious and subconscious mind wants to, otherwise we can terminate the session if you wish."

4. It may be a good idea to regress the subject to a pleasant verifiable event in his life prior to the crime incident and then progress to the actual incident. This achieves several purposes. First, it convinces the subject as well as yourself that he is hypnotized. Second, it demonstrates to you the degree of regression. Third, it gives the subject a pleasant experience. Fourth, it may help to overcome any subconscious resistance that the subject may have for recalling a negative crime experience. Fifth, if the hypno-induced testimony may be a factor in a trial, it will lend credibility to the evidence.

Regardless of whether or not this is done, it is always advisable to regress a victim or witness to a short while before the actual crime, e.g. an hour or two earlier or that morning. This is important for several reasons. First, it enables the operator to test for the degree of regression. If not sufficient, he can deepen further before proceeding. Second, it gives the subject time to reorient to the regressed state. Third, it ensures that the subject will be able to chronologically report the event as it occurred, instead of finding himself in the middle of the action once regressed.

5. Many regressed subjects will be very lethargic due to the depth of hypnosis. There is no reason or advantage to this, so the operator should tell them that they can speak up and be alert and act more or less normally. This suggestion is usually sufficient, but, if need be, it can be repeated several times.

6. If any difficulty of any kind is encountered, simply ask the subject what is wrong and what you can do about it.

7. If the subject was the victim or witness of a serious crime against a person, the waking instruction to remember everything that occurred during the session may be qualified by stating, "You will remember only what you want to," unless of course the subject must remember everything for a possible trial. This gives the subject the choice of remembering or not remembering. This could also be negotiated with the subject in the preinduction.

8. Always be sure to bring the subject all the way back to the present date, time, and location before awakening.

9. Crime victims and witnesses can be given a pleasant experience before waking, if deemed appropriate, by having them imagine or go to their favorite place, especially if the closed door visualization deepening technique was used. This may be especially indicated for victims of traumatic crimes who will appreciate the concern and it will leave them with a good experience as a token of your appreciation.

10. Before doing a regression, it is essential that the operator plan it and write down critical information, such as the current date, time, and age; the regressed date, time, age, and location; critical details of the regressed event; information forgotten; and questions to ask. The operator should also decide beforehand if he is going to do a hypermnesia or revivification, exactly what technique he is going to use, and how he is going to regress the

subject, i.e. by days, weeks, months, or years. Whatever his decision, the operator should list the days, weeks, or whatever so that he can check them off as he regresses the subject. This is to avoid the all too common problem of becoming mixed up and confused and to ensure returning or "progressing" the subject the same way he was regressed. The hypno-investigator may find it helpful to develop a checklist of critical information to facilitate the session. The sheer amount of information he has to keep in mind can be quite overwhelming, so a concise checklist can ease the burden on his memory and ensure that he follows the correct procedure (see Appendix 7 for a sample checklist.) As a fine point of technique, the operator should keep his checklist or notes in approximate line of sight with the subject so he can always see him and his voice is always directed toward him. Fumbling through notes and talking away from a subject can be disconcerting to him.

11. There are some special considerations for selecting and working with practice regression subjects.

    a. Before ever attempting a regression, the beginning hypno-investigator should be proficient at all the basic induction, deepening, testing and challenging, and waking techniques. He should also have had considerable experience in working with subjects so that he feels comfortable and competent in managing hypnosis in subjects.

    b. Carefully select practice regression subjects. Select those from your practice pool who seem to be the most susceptible, mature, stable, and who want the experience. Make certain they are not doing it for therapeutic reasons.

    c. Make sure the subject has signed a release.

    d. Decide on an earlier event with the subject to which he wishes to return. Make certain that it is a pleasurable experience. Obtain the necessary regression information such as the subject's present age and the age, date, and location to which he wants to return. Preferably, all this information should be obtained at least a day in advance so the operator can plan the regression.

    e. During the preinduction, stress to the subject that you want this to be a pleasurable and enjoyable experience and that he must take responsibility for his own experience.

    f. Include additional suggestions in the regression instructions to the effect that it will be a good experience and that he is only to review pleasant memories and experiences during the regression itself. Also specify that during the actual return to the decided upon event, the subject will skip bad or negative experiences and years; these can also be uncovered during the preinduction by asking the subject.

12. Although the alleged dangers of hypnosis and the possibility of inadvertently triggering a repressed traumatic experience during regressions were put into perspective in Chapter 1, the hypno-investigator must realize that hypnosis and particularly regression are not toys; they both must be treated with utmost respect and practiced with professionalism.

13. It should be remembered that some experts maintain that there is "substantial room for error in the use of temporal regression to recall previous events; for if the memory is still unavailable, the subject may easily supply some fantasized event or experience in its place, without being aware that a substitution has occurred."[66] If the above considerations and the following regression instructions are followed closely, this potential problem can generally be avoided. To further minimize this possibility, as well as likely defense objections, the operator must be extremely careful to not ask any leading questions (see "Guidelines for Interviewing" in "The Nature of Memory" in Chapter 7).

14. In cases where the crime victim has been severely traumatized, either physically or psychologically, the hypno-investigator should either refer the case to a psychologist or psychiatrist experienced in forensic hypnosis, or have a psychologist or psychiatrist sit in on the session(s).

Techniques for Revivification*

1. If the hypno-investigator decides that the case warrants a complete revivification and the subject has passed the suggested amnesia test, he should proceed in the following manner:

"Now that your body and your mind are completely relaxed we can successfully proceed to achieve what we both want most and that is the time regression, so that you can vividly re-experience the event that we decided upon. We are going to achieve this in the following manner. A short while ago, 'Nancy,' you were able to erase the numbers off of the blackboard as you counted backwards. As you erased each number it disappeared from your mind, and soon all of the numbers had disappeared from your mind so that your mind was a blank. We are now going to do something very similar, and as long as I speak to you, you will remain as deep as you are now and may even wish to go deeper, but no matter how deep you go you will always hear my voice. Now I want you to again imagine that same blackboard as best you can and you are standing in front of it as before. And again you see some numbers on that board, the numbers ___ back to ___. If you can see the numbers nod your head." *(Some subjects may have difficulty seeing the numbers as a result of the suggested amnesia, so you may have to reassert this suggestion until they can.)* "These numbers represent the years of your life from your present age back to the age to which you are going to return." *(Depending on the time span of the regression, you may have to use days of the week, or weeks, or months instead of years.)* "Now in a moment I am going to have you pick up the eraser again and as I call off the numbers, your ages, you will erase that number, that age, temporarily off the board and out of your mind. With each age that you erase off the board and out of your mind you will temporarily forget everything that happened from that age on, forgetting all those memories and experiences, so that by the time we

---

* The following verbalization is largely paraphrased from Myron Teitelbaum, *Hypnosis Induction Technics*, 1965. Courtesy of Charles C Thomas, Publisher, Springfield, Illinois.

reach __ years old, you will have forgotten everything that you learned and everything that happened to you after that age. As we count back you will feel yourself becoming younger and younger and smaller and smaller *(if applicable)* and your memory of prior years will increase. When you reach the age of __ you will find that you will be able to remember everything that occurred at the age of __ and you will be able to relive your life as you actually lived it then. You will feel as you felt at the age of __, you will think as you thought at the age of __, you will talk as you talked at the age of __, you will act as you acted at the age of __, in fact, you will be __ years old. When you arrive at the age of __ you will find yourself at *(the specific location of the regression event)*.

"I will accompany you on this trip. I will either be somebody who is present at the event, somebody you know and like to talk to, and you will still be able to hear my voice and to see me in that other person, or I may just be a voice in your mind.

"If for any reason you should lose contact with me all I'll have to do is touch your hand and you will immediately come back to where you can hear me. Also, any time I place my hand on your shoulder you will immediately go deeper. If for any reason you should be come concerned about anything just raise your left hand and reach out to me and we'll stop until we can resolve it. At any time you feel yourself coming up and you feel you need to go deeper, or you want to go deeper, just tell me. Do you understand?

"Everything that you relive at the age of __ you will have actually lived before. You are not to imagine or invent anything that did not occur. When you reach the age of __ you will describe to me out loud everything that is occurring as it actually happened.

"If I ask you to open your eyes, or you choose to open them, when you are __ years old, you will be able to do so, but the only thing you will see will be those things that actually occurred when you were __ years old. You will not awaken when you open your eyes nor will it affect your depth of trance in any way.

"After you have completed reliving the event that we agreed upon I will bring you back to your present age and then I will awaken you. During the time that you relive this event you will be completely unaware as to your present whereabouts and you will only know what is going on at that age, although you will always be able to hear my voice. You will also remain at least as deep as you are now as long as you are reliving this event. Do you understand?

"Now you're standing in front of that blackboard and you see those numbers, representing your ages, from __ back to __. Now, pick up the eraser and we're going to start going back. With each age I call out, you erase it off the blackboard and temporarily out of your mind, growing younger and younger. Alright, let's begin, __, erase if off the board and out of your mind, __, temporarily forgetting everything that happened from that age on, __, the memories of prior years increasing, __, getting younger and younger, __, getting smaller and smaller *(if applicable)*. . . . Now you are __ years old and you are at *(give specific location)*. Where are you, Nancy? Now look around and tell me what you see. What are you wearing? What are you doing?" *(Continue questioning the subject.)*

"That's good, Nancy, you've done very well, but now I want you to go **D–E–E–P, D–E–E–P, D–E–E–P.**" *(Deepen with the conditioned shoulder cue to break the subject's involvement in the regression.)* "Now I want you to again see yourself standing in front of that same blackboard with the number __ on it *(the regressed age)*. In a moment I am going to begin counting off some numbers, representing your ages, and they will reappear on the blackboard. As they do, all the memories and experiences that you temporarily put out of your mind will come back to you, all those experiences that you normally remember. With each age you will grow older and older and bigger and bigger *(if applicable)* until you are your actual present age and size. All right, now __, seeing that number, that age reappear, now __, getting older and bigger, now __, all those memories and experiences that you normally remember coming back." *(Continue up to the present age.)* "Now you are __ years old. It is *(specific time, date, and day of the week)* and you are at *(specific location)*. You've done very well, Nancy, but now in a moment I am going to awaken you by counting from one to five." *(Continue to waken the subject in the normal manner.)*

2. The above technique can be easily amended to use a visualized desk calendar if regressing only a few days or weeks. If regressing several months, a month wall calendar can be used. In either case, the subject is instructed to flip back through the calendar instead of erasing the numbers, ages, dates, days of the week, months, or years off of the blackboard. Similarly, if only regressing a number of hours, a visualized wall clock can be used effectively.

3. If the time span between the hypnotic session and the incident to be recalled is sufficiently short, such as a few hours or days, and given that the suggested amnesia was successful, you may opt to take an amended approach. This is essentially done by disorienting the subject as to time and place and transporting him directly back to the incident in the following manner: "Now that your mind is a blank, we can successfully proceed to what we both want most. Now I want you to extend this blankness, this amnesia to your present surroundings and orientation. I want you to forget all about where you are, about what time it is, and even what day it is, and we are soon going to go back in time, back to *(give specific time, date, location, day of the week)*, but, before we do, I want you to understand that when we do go back that you will have temporarily forgotten everything that happened to you after that time. When we reach that time you will remember and experience everything as it actually occurred and you will be able to tell me about it as I am going to accompany you on this trip and I will be either someone you know and like or just a voice in your mind. You are not to make up or invent anything; just describe to me everything that's happening, for you will be there reliving it. At the end of this experience I

will bring you back to the present and then awaken you, but while you are experiencing this you will always be able to hear my voice and talk to me. If you choose to open your eyes you will be able to do so without affecting your depth and you will see everything as it actually was. Also, if for any reason you should lose contact with me all I'll have to do is touch your hand, and you'll immediately come back to where you can hear me. If for any reason you should become concerned about anything, just raise your left hand and reach out to me and we'll stop until we can resolve it. Furthermore, as long as you are reliving this event you will remain at least as deep as you are now, but, if you need to go deeper just tell me. Do you understand?

"Now you are forgetting all about where you are, about what time it is, and even what day it is and we're going back to *(the hour or day before),* and *(the hour or day before that, etc.),* all the way to ___. You are there *(describe time, location, etc.).* Where are you? What is happening?"

4. As an alternative to number two above, particularly if the closed door visualization was used successfully, the regression instructions can be amended such that when the subject walks through the door he will find himself at the time and scene of the crime, i.e. "A little while ago I had you walk through that closed door into your favorite place. Now I want you to again imagine that you are standing in front of that same closed door. Can you see it? 'Yes.' Good. In a moment I am going to have you again open that door, but this time you will find on the other side the crime scene to which you want to return. Don't open the door yet, but listen to what I have to say now. When I have you open and step through that door you will be so immersed in that event that you will have temporarily forgotten everything that happened to you after that time. It will be as if you are stepping back into time so that you will remember and experience everything as it actually occurred. You will be able to tell me about it as I am going to accompany you on this trip. . . ." *(Continue with the appropriate suggestions from number two above.)* "Do you understand?"

"Now you are standing in front of that door and you're ready to go back in time. Now you place your hand on that doorknob and turn it and you swing the door open and on the other side you see the place of the crime, but just before it occurred. Do you see it? 'Yes.' Good. Now step through the door and into the scene. You are there and can now tell me everything that is happening."

Techniques for Hypermnesia

The techniques employed for hypermnesia are basically the same as for revivification; however, the subject is specifically informed that he will not relive prior events, only describe them without emotion. The purpose of the technique is to dissociate the emotional component, particularly if the experience was traumatic.

To induce hypermnesia, the operator regresses the subject to the decided upon event, but alters the regression suggestions such that the subject will find himself in a detached position from which he can unemotionally and objectively describe what is happening.

1. Inform the subject that when you regress him to the event in question he will assume the identity of a favorite news reporter and will be able to describe everything as it actually occurred. He will find himself standing on the sidelines. It is further suggested that he is to objectively, truthfully, and unemotionally report everything that is occurring. He must also be explicitly told that under no circumstances is he to identify with the actual victim or witness, but that he will always remain objective, detached, and unemotional. Truth in reporting should also be stressed.

2. A dissociation technique often used for painless childbirth is for the doctor to suggest to the hypnotized patient that she imagine and experience herself sitting in a chair across the room watching that woman who looks like her have a baby. In a similar fashion, the crime victim or witness is similarly told to dissociate by experiencing himself as separate and observing someone who looks like him go through the crime. Although very similar to the technique described above, this approach avoids the extraneous variable of having the subject assume another identity, which increases the likelihood of contamination. For example, if the subject was attacked and raped in the front seat of her car, the operator can dissociate her immediately before the attack by placing part of her in the back seat so she can objectify the situation. The operator must be certain, however, that he reunites the parts before waking. (For a specific verbalization of this technique, see the case transcript in Appendix 6.)

3. An effective technique for even greater dissociation is to regress the subject to the time of the crime event, but, instead of placing him at the scene, have him imagine he is sitting at home in his favorite chair in front of his television set (or at a movie theater if the crime took place at his home). Then inform the subject that very soon a special documentary film of the crime event in question will begin and that he will be able to vividly and accurately see and hear everything as it actually occurred. The subject is also informed that the program can be speeded up, slowed down, stopped, reversed, or even focused to show any person or object in greater detail. The subject is also explicitly told that he will only be watching someone who looks like him and that he will remain calm, relaxed, objective, and unemotional.

4. Amend the closed door revivification technique described above in such a manner as to take the subject to the door, open it, and view the crime event only, without becoming involved in it.

Last Ditch Recall Techniques

If the subject fails to recall a particular bit of information, such as a license number or name with the above techniques, proceed by using one of the following:

1. "Now I am going to talk to your subconscious mind. We know that everything we experience is recorded in our subconscious, but that most of it is unavailable consciously. If you truly saw the license number *(or heard*

the name, etc.) your subconscious mind will be able to give your conscious mind that information, and it will do so when I count up to three. When I reach three it will be as if the number *(name, etc.)* spontaneously comes to you. Alright, one, two, three! What is it?"

2. "Now I want you to imagine yourself standing in front of that blackboard again." *(Explain nature of subconscious as in number one above.)* "As you sit there and relax deeply, your subconscious will write the license number *(name, etc.)* on the board and you can call off the numbers *(letters)* as it does so."

3. "Now I want you to imagine in your mind's eye and to the best of your ability that there is a large closed book in your lap *(on the table in front of you).* Can you see it? 'Yes.' Good. As you open up this book you will see that all the pages are completely blank. I want you to begin to turn the pages in that book one by one, and on one of those pages, when your subconscious is ready, you will see a number *(name, etc.).* It will quite spontaneously and automatically appear before you on one of the pages."

4. Anesthetize the subject's dominant hand, give him a pad and pen, and induce automatic writing (see "Controls for Simulation and Lying" in Chapter 7 for a specific verbalization).

5. Less difficult than automatic writing is the production of a subconscious ideomotor response to answer yes or no questions. Dissociate the subject's hand by first producing glove anesthesia, then suggest that he will no longer be able to consciously control it, but that his subconscious will control it. Proceed to make a little pact with the subconscious that it will answer every question by lifting the forefinger for yes, the middle finger for no, and the ring finger for "I don't know." Before proceeding to ask questions of a yes or no variety, the operator should test the response by first asking simple questions to which he knows the answers, e.g. "Your name is Jane? You live at 618 Madison? You are a witness to this crime?"

6. Suggest sleep to the subject and then instruct him to dream in complete and accurate detail about the crime event, so that the dream itself will be an exact replica, but will only take a few seconds to experience.

7. Give the subject a posthypnotic suggestion that he will dream about the event and will be able to recall all the pertinent information and will wake up and write it down (or remember it in the morning and write it down.) Similarly, you can suggest that the number, name, etc. will spontaneously pop into his head when he least expects it over the next few days without consciously thinking about it.

8. Just as familiar sights, noises, and smells can trigger old memories, show the hypnotized victim or witness a picture of the crime scene.

Since most of these last ditch techniques appeal directly to the subject's subconscious, which receives and answers questions literally, the operator must make his instructions and suggestions very straightforward and clearly understandable.

Technique for Hypermnesia Type II

If the subject is unable to reach sufficient depth for time regression and the subsequent elicitation of hypermnesia or revivification even after repeated sessions, the hypno-investigator can attempt hypermnesia Type II, i.e. enhanced recall from a nonregressed state. Even if only a light trance has been reached, some subjects may still be able to recall some forgotten aspects or details of the crime, even though they obviously cannot regress to the actual incident. The basic difference between hypermnesia Type I or revivification Type I and hypermnesia Type II is that the emphasis is on tense. Whereas in the former the emphasis is clearly on the present tense, i.e. "What is happening now?," in the latter the emphasis is on the past tense, i.e. "What happened next?" To elicit hypermnesia Type II, the operator merely takes the subject as deep as possible, which may only be to a light trance, and simply instructs the subject to describe the crime event, i.e. "Now that you are as deeply relaxed as you can become, you might find it much easier to recall the event in question. What I now want you to do is to bring to mind that scene as clearly as you can and to begin to tell me about it. Tell me everything that you see as it actually happened. . . . What happened next. . . . ?"

Session Sequence

A common and natural concern of beginning hypno-investigators is to know just when to attempt hypermnesia or revivification with a victim or witness, i.e. do they try the very first session, the second session the same day, the second session on the following day, or just when. The major determining factor will be the susceptibility of the subject and subsequent hypnotic depth, but even with susceptible subjects the following sequence of sessions is most effective for inducing deep hypnosis, as well as for making the hypnotic experience and encounter a pleasurable and rewarding experience for both subject and operator.

FIRST SESSION: PREINDUCTION, INDUCTION OF CHOICE WITH SEVERAL DEEPENINGS, AWAKEN. The first session familiarizes the subject with hypnosis and his experience answers what questions and relieves what anxieties, fears, and misconceptions he still has, thereby reducing resistance and allowing for greater depth the second session. This session also gives the operator an indication of what type of subject the person is and through his postinduction quizzing he can tailor the second session to match the subject's individual response. Rapport is also increased as a result of the first session.

SECOND SESSION: INDUCTION AND DEEPENINGS OF CHOICE, TESTS AND CHALLENGES, AWAKEN. The operator may try a different induction and deepenings as well as those that worked well the first session. If the subject is responding adequately, the tests and challenges for respective depths may also be done. To help prepare the subject for these and to build his expectancy, the operator can mention just prior to the second session that he is going to show him some interesting things that can be done under hypnosis that will prove to him that he is in fact hypnotized. To further build expectancy and to subtlely commit the subject to increased depth, the operator can also say, "Well, are you ready to go real deep this time?"

THIRD SESSION: INDUCTION OF CHOICE OR BY A POSTHYPNOTIC CUE FOR RE-HYPNOTIZATION ESTABLISHED IN THE SECOND SESSION; TAILORED DEEPENINGS OF CHOICE; TESTS AND CHALLENGES; REGRESSION TO AN EARLIER VERIFIABLE PLEASANT EXPERIENCE; AWAKEN.

FOURTH SESSION: SAME AS THE THIRD SESSION EXCEPT FOR A DIRECT REGRESSION TO THE CRIME EVENT.

Obviously, this sequence of sessions represents an ideal situation; whereas, in actual practice it may be either considerably abridged or lengthened depending on the circumstances and the subject. For example, the third and fourth sessions can be consolidated in the interests of time, or the third session can be dispensed with altogether. With a susceptible subject the third and fourth sessions could be collapsed into the second session. With a highly susceptible subject the operator may feel confident enough to do everything the first session. On the other hand, if the subject responds relatively poorly, several additional sessions may be required to achieve the requisite depth.

Another consideration is the time element. Beginning operators often ask if the sessions should be done back to back on the same day or spread out over several days. The answer will depend largely on the time constraints of the operator as well as the subject. If both have a whole afternoon free, the sessions could be done back to back; if not, they can be scheduled over several days or even several weeks. In fact, sometimes a day or week is necessary between sittings for the subject's anxieties and reservations to dissipate sufficiently for hypnosis to be achieved. On the other hand, during the intervening time period the subject may build his resistance. In any case, it is important for the operator to ensure that enough time is set aside for the initial session(s) so that he or the subject will not feel rushed. A polygraph examiner will usually set aside a couple of hours if not an entire half day for one exam; the hypno-investigator should do the same.

DEHYPNOTIZATION OR WAKING

Dehypnotization or *waking* is generally the easiest and most routine part of any session, however, its importance should not be minimized. Once the operator has induced and deepened hypnosis, tested or challenged for depth, and elicited hypermnesia or revivification, he is ready to dehypnotize the subject.

Verbalization

"You've done very well, Janet; now I'm going to bring you out. In a few moments I am going to count from one to five and with each count you will gradually become more awake, so that when I reach five you will open your eyes and be wide awake, alert, refreshed and relaxed, and feeling good all over. You will also remember everything that occurred during this session."

(The operator praises the subject while making a smooth transition into the basic

waking instructions. Spontaneous posthypnotic amnesia is also insured against by a direct suggestion.)

"Tonight you will sleep very deep and profound and will awaken refreshed in the morning. You will also have very vivid, colorful, and pleasant dreams that you will remember in the morning."

(This posthypnotic suggestion is given to the subject for two reasons: (1) to give him a pleasant posthypnotic experience, and (2) as an indicator of depth, i.e. stimulation of dreams is listed as number 47 on the LeCron-Bordeaux scoring chart. Hence, if the operator does a subsequent session with the subject he can ask him about his dreaming the night of the first session. If he did indeed have vivid, colorful, and pleasant dreams that he remembered, this is indicative of a deep trance level, provided the subject does not normally dream in this fashion. This suggestion should only be given if the operator is reasonably certain that the subject was in a deep trance so as not to damage his credibility for future sessions by predicting something that will not happen.)

"The next time you are hypnotized you will go deeper, faster, and easier because you are now familiar with this experience, but you will only be able to be hypnotized when you want to and by a qualified person like myself, or in the event that you learn self-hypnosis."

(The operator gives another posthypnotic suggestion for increased depth and ease of hypnotization on the next session for which he provides a logical explanation. The operator then "places the seal," which prevents the subject from being hypnotized unless he wants to, and then only by a qualified person or by self-hypnosis. This also has the effect of allaying any conscious or subconscious fears the subject may have regarding spontaneously becoming rehypnotized or hypnotized against his will. Rapport is also increased due to this display of concern and professional care.)

"Coming up now, one, coming up a little more to two, coming more awake and beginning to move around a little, three, feeling more and more normal. Coming up a little more to four, moving around more now and feeling more alert and refreshed. Ready to come all the way up now to FIVE.

(Towards the end of the waking procedure the operator makes a transition to his normal waking voice and even increases the volume for the last sentence to help emphasize the fact that the subject is and should come awake.)

Precautions and Considerations

1. The operator may wish to give the subject a brief silent period of several minutes right before waking to let him enjoy the hypnotic experience on his own. Furthermore, some subjects will take a "plunge" once they know they are going to waken, i.e. they will quite suddenly let go and drop very deep. It seems that these subjects either feel safe in the realization that they are soon to come out and hence really let go for the experience, or

they enjoy it so much they want to get their money's worth before coming out. Whatever the reason, the operator should preface the silent period by saying, "In a moment I am going to give you (two) minutes of your own time just to enjoy this experience and to become very familiar and comfortable with it and you may even wish to let yourself go deeper. At the end of these (two) minutes I will speak to you again and then waken you. Alright, begin."

2. Praise the subject for his efforts, cooperation, and performance before waking him.

3. Be sure that all suggestions eliciting hypnotic phenomena have been erased or cancelled before waking. For example, if the suggested amnesia test was done, remove the amnesia before waking. If glove anesthesia is elicited, be sure to restore the feeling before waking. To cancel these suggestions, the operator may give appropriate countersuggestions either at the completion of the test, or preferably at the time of waking. Specifically, the operator can include in the waking instructions the exact countersuggestions, e.g. "When I reach five you will be able to easily remember all those numbers that you temporarily erased out of your mind."

4. Waken the subject slowly, and the deeper the hypnosis the slower he should be awakened. If the subject was very deep, additional suggestions of movement, straightening up, and deep breathing should be given between the counts.

5. The waking verbalization should be memorized essentially verbatim. As an alternative, some hypno-investigators have typed it out on a wallet-sized card to keep in their billfold along with their Miranda card.

Difficulties in Waking

The operator will rarely have any difficulty in dehypnotizing subjects. In a few instances, however, he may have to resort to additional techniques and suggestions.

Before discussing these techniques, the reader should be assured that there has never been a case reported of a subject not waking from hypnosis. Most, if not all, authorities on hypnosis will agree with Doctor Kroger who states that in several thousand subjects and lecture demonstrations, he *"has never had a patient who would not or could not come out of hypnosis"* (his italics).[67] Similarly, other well-known experts, Leslie LeCron and Jean Bordeaux, Ph.D., believe that "with almost everyone there is not the slightest difficulty in awakening, and the student hypnotist can dismiss any fear of encountering trouble."[68] Just the same, the hypno-investigator needs to be prepared for this eventuality. Resistance to dehypnotization generally takes one of several forms. Some subjects will literally refuse to waken. Other times a "subject appears to come out of the trance but remains in a dazed or semi-stuporous condition. . . . In other instances, the subject does not seem to become fully dehypnotized, but presently relapses into a hypnotic state."[69] The reasons for difficulties in waking are multiple and varied. Probably the most frequent reason for a subject frankly refusing to waken is due to a mistake in procedure made by the operator. In these instances, the operator has generally forgotten to cancel a suggestion. For example, subjects have been known to refuse to waken upon command because the operator forgot to restore the feeling in an anesthetized hand. In another instance, a beginning hypno-investigator could not waken an experienced subject because he had forgotten to include the seal. Once realizing and correcting his mistake, however, the subject awakened readily. Similarly, some subjects will resist dehypnotization if given a posthypnotic suggestion they do not wish to carry out. Other subjects will occasionally resist dehypnotization because the experience is literally so enjoyable and pleasurable that they quite naturally wish to prolong it. Still other subjects go so deep that they quite naturally find it difficult to waken fully without extra time.

Other resistances to dehypnotization are psychodynamic in nature and are generally pathological. The following are the most frequent ones:

1. An expression of hostility toward the operator.
2. A means of prolonging contact with the operator.
3. A need for dependency or passivity.
4. A means of controlling the operator.
5. A need for escape from reality and conflict.
6. As a test of the operator's "powers'" or ability to control him.
7. As a means of punishing the operator for making him do something he did not want to do or resented.

Techniques for Waking the Difficult Subject

The question remains of how to dehypnotize a subject who either frankly refuses to waken, does not waken fully, or relapses into hypnosis.

If a subject frankly refuses to waken, the best procedure seems to be to simply "ask him why he does not wake up. Most subjects are quite willing to explain why. If the subject is uncooperative you may have to request an answer more forcefully. Usually the answer tells the hypnotist what to do. If it does not, it is sometimes possible to get the subject to specifically tell you what to do to wake him up, by merely asking him about it."[70] The operator should also quickly review the session in his own mind to determine if he neglected to cancel a suggestion.

In the rare event that this procedure does not work, the operator can suggest to the subject that hypnosis will merge with true sleep and that he will waken when he is ready to. By this manner, most subjects will wake up in a few minutes and at the outside a couple of hours.

Weitzenhoffer states that an "excellent way to dehypnotize an intractable subject is simply to say to him in a final tone: 'Very well then, if you will not wake up I will just have to leave you as you are.' You then ignore the subject entirely and go on to other things."[71] Similarly, Elman states that he has had good success in waking the difficult subject by telling him "that if he didn't obey your instructions and rouse himself, he could never be hypnotized again."[72] Blowing on the subject's eyes and forehead can also be effective.

Subjects who appear not to be fully awake can usually be successfully dehypnotized by repeating the waking instructions in abbreviated form. At the count of five the operator can also snap his fingers or clap his hands close to the subject's face to help startle him awake.

Some subjects will spontaneously relapse into hypnosis shortly after waking. As the operator talks to the subject after waking, they will generally be obviously fixated on the operator's voice and will begin blinking heavily and gradually sink back into hypnosis. When this occurs the operator should repeat the waking suggestions. If this is ineffective in totally waking the subject, the operator may instruct him to close his eyes and to bring himself out when he is ready by counting to himself from one to five at his own pace.

To impress upon the subject the naturalness of difficulty in waking and to alleviate any concern he may have, the operator may preface a second attempt at waking by saying, "I know you enjoy it so much that you don't want to come out, but you can always return to it in the future."

If you know from experience that a subject wakens with difficulty, a natural sequence for dehypnotization is to have the subject walk back up the stairs if they were used as a deepening technique, while suggesting to the subject that he will come more awake with each step and be totally awake upon reaching the top.

If a subject does not waken readily, the operator should include the following posthypnotic suggestion in the waking instructions: "The next time you are hypnotized you will waken easily and completely when I count to five in the standard procedure as I did today."

A very rare subject may experience a negative aftereffect upon waking from hypnosis, such as a headache, slight dizziness or nausea, shivering, or confusion. Such reactions are generally the product of the subject attempting to resist a posthypnotic suggestion, or of a subconscious resistance to the induction itself.

To protect against this rare occurrence, the operator emphasizes the part of the waking suggestions where he says, " . . . be wide awake, alert, refreshed and relaxed, and feeling good all over." In the event that the subject still complains of a negative aftereffect, the operator should first talk with the subject for five or ten minutes to see if it spontaneously dissipates. If it does not, he should merely rehypnotize the subject with his permission and suggest the symptoms away, e.g. "When you waken this time you will find that your headache will be completely gone and you'll be feeling good all over."

POSTINDUCTION

The *postinduction* is the transition period between dehypnotization and dismissal of the subject. Once waking the subject, the operator should take a few minutes to talk to him to elicit the following information and to aid the transition to waking reality.

1. Quiz the subject after waking as to his hypnotic experience. Elicit feedback concerning the induction and deepenings used to determine what did and did not work well, so that you can tailor the next induction to suit his particular needs and likes. Also determine how the subject felt physically and mentally so that these feelings and sensations can be incorporated in the next session. Each subject reacts to the various inductions and deepenings differently and experiences the hypnotic state in a unique way. Hence, the more individual the session can be made, the greater the likelihood of success.

Such questioning serves a secondary purpose; it helps to focus the subject's awareness upon his personal experiences, which subtlely reinforces his feeling and realization that he was hypnotized. Another particularly useful question, which often helps to convince subjects that they were hypnotized, is to ask them what time it is. Often hypnosis is accompanied by a spontaneous time distortion in which the subject will be surprised to find that either so little or so much time has passed. Similarly, ask the subject what he thought of the challenges and obtrusive tests if performed. If you did the eye flinch and there was no response, ask the subject if he was aware that you touched his eyelash; many will be surprised that you did.

During this questioning period, the operator should also ask any other questions that come to mind regarding the subject's experience. By so doing he will gain new insights into the nature and variability of hypnosis. Don't be afraid to ask the subject how you did, what you did wrong, what you should have done, etc.

2. Besides asking questions, the operator is likely to get some questions in return, which he will have to be adequately prepared to answer. When subjects discover through experience that their expectations were incorrect, they often doubt that they were hypnotized. The following are some common posthypnotic responses:

- "I don't think I was hypnotized because I was aware of everything and heard everything."
- "You know, I really didn't feel any different. Are you sure I was hypnotized?"
- "I really felt I could have come out at any time."

Whatever the question, the operator should assure the subject that that is a normal and common response and then proceed to give a short discussion of the misconception upon which it is based.

3. Thank the subject for cooperating and compliment him on performing well. Tell him that he will do even better next time.

4. If the subject displayed some resistance, ask specific questions to try to determine the exact nature and source of the resistance. For example, if the subject's arm stops for a substantial length of time just before touching his leg in the arm drop, query him about this, e.g. "It seems that you really tried to keep your arm from touching your leg for a while. What were you thinking and how were you feeling at that time?" The elicited response will

give the operator an indication of the source of the subject's anxiety and resistance. Once determining this, the operator can adequately deal with it. For example, if the subject responds that he really felt himself going under, but was a little afraid of letting go completely, reassure him in the following manner: "I understand completely and, in fact, most subjects feel the same way at first, but now that you've experienced hypnosis, there's really nothing to be afraid of, is there?" The operator may then continue with a short discussion of the common misconceptions of hypnosis as a state of unconsciousness, domination by another's will, etc. while stressing its positive nature and uses.

5. Make sure the subject is totally awake. Have him stand up and move around, stretch, check his eye reactions, and walk him to the door or even outside.

6. Under no circumstances should the hypno-investigator and primary investigator discuss the case, offer opinions regarding what happened, who is suspect, etc., in the presence of the subject, either before or particularly after the session. Hypnosis has a tendency to perseverate anywhere from a few minutes to a few hours after dehypnotization. Hence, any suggestive discussion or comments in the presence of the subject gives defense experts an excellent point of attack and defense counsel a legitimate objection. The hypno-investigator should, however, complete an "Investigative Hypnosis Report/Hypnosis Session Evaluation" form (see Appendix 8) during the pre- and postinduction. The same care must be used in asking nonleading and nonsuggestive questions that is used during the hypnosis itself.

Dealing With Failure

Even though every session should be approached with the expectation of success, some will obviously be more successful than others, depending on such variables as: susceptibility of the subject, techniques used, skill of the operator, psychodynamics, subject-operator relationship, and environment. From the subject's point of view, his hypnotic experience may range from a literal amazement and profound satisfaction and enjoyment to a total sense of failure, disappointment, and even depression. The operator's experience of the session will vary as a function of the subject's experience. With highly susceptible subjects the operator will likely feel in complete control of the situation and intensely satisfied and even amazed with the way the subject is responding. With resistant subjects, the operator is likely to feel frustrated, disappointed, and even depressed, especially if he runs into a streak of unsusceptible subjects. With experience and a working familiarity with the dynamic and confusion methods, however, the operator can become very challenged by resistant subjects.

To help cope with the prospect of relatively unsuccessful sessions, the beginning operator should cultivate the perspective that *no* session is a failure. He should take to heart his preinduction assertion to the subject that, "Hypnosis always works, but the degree to which it works depends largely on you." In other words, the operator always does his best and goes to the limits of his technical proficiency during each session, and the rest depends upon such variables as the subject's susceptibility, motivation, expectation, psychodynamics, and defenses and resistances. These variables have been discussed at length in other sections, but there is an additional factor or variable that the operator must keep in mind — readiness. "The same person may be ready or not ready to be hypnotized, depending on many intervening factors. Each act of hypnosis requires a separate decision on the part of the subject that he wants to be hypnotized, or a continuing desire to be hypnotized. It will be found, even with experienced subjects, that if they are not in the mood to be hypnotized, there is no point in going further. In fact, it is best to concede to the new subject that if he does not wish to be hypnotized, he cannot be forced."[73]

With all these factors in mind, the beginning operator must realize that each session is unique; each subject will respond differently, which necessitates the operator adapting in accordance. Some subjects will respond rapidly while others just the reverse. Some will respond very well to one technique while others not at all. Any one particular subject may do very well one day, but poorly the next. The same subject may not respond to one induction, but go under rapidly with another. Any one session may speed up, slow down, come to a screeching halt, or reverse for any number of reasons. So as the beginning operator (and beginning subject for that matter) gains experience, it is important for him to realize that both he and the subject do the best they can during any particular session.

When met with a relatively unsuccessful session, there are some general rules and considerations to follow.

1. Never tell the subject that he is difficult to hypnotize or that he is a poor subject, as this will likely severely damage what expectancy and motivation he has. Instead, always motivate him for the next session by telling him that he did well, especially for the first time, and that he will go much deeper the next time as all subjects do.

2. Never blame the subject for not entering hypnosis: this will likely mobilize resistances and weaken the interpersonal relationship. If the operator suspects a lack of cooperation, however, he may tactfully and gently tell the subject that he needs to cooperate a little more next time. If the subject was obviously tense and resistant, the operator should explain its naturalness, i.e. "You seemed a little uptight, but that is very common and natural for the first time. Now that you're familiar with this experience I'm sure that you can really relax and let go next time. Don't you?"

3. The operator should never verbally blame himself or express doubt regarding his ability as this will undermine the subject's confidence in him. For example, instead of saying, "It was my fault as I should have known better than to use hand levitation," the operator should confidently remark, "You know, there are literally dozens of different techniques and combinations of techniques that work differently for different people, and it's largely a matter of trial and error to know which ones will work best, but

now I know just what will work best for you next time." Similarly, never admit that you prematurely tested, challenged, or attempted hypermnesia or revivification. For example, if a regression for revivification fails, say, "You are very close and I'm sure you can get it next time." The operator may even continue by explaining that he is relatively certain of this because the subject passed the suggested amnesia test which is indicative of a deep trance.

4. If the subject does not become hypnotized and the operator is at wits end, he should ask the subject why he does not experience hypnosis and quiz him regarding his feelings, sensations, thoughts and general experience. The subject will appreciate the concern and understanding and his reply will often give valuable clues as to his resistances, which can then be dealt with. Sometimes a subject will have placed certain limits upon his entering hypnosis. If this is the case, a straightforward "What can I do differently to help you into hypnosis" may suffice.

5. As a face-saver, the operator should explain that no one reaches his maximum depth the first session, but that it usually takes two or three sessions. He then continues to explain that hypnosis is a learning process and that with subsequent sessions people overcome their fears and learn to go deeper into hypnosis. The subject should never be told this in the preinduction.

6. If the subject remains resistant over three or more sessions, the operator can at that time explain some of the statistical parameters of hypnotic susceptibility to save face, i.e. "You've done pretty well, but quantitative studies have shown that approximately only 20 percent to 25 percent or one out of four or five people, can reach a deep level of hypnosis." The subject should never be told these statistics during the preinduction.

7. When doing a case-related session, the hypno-investigator should realize that even though sufficient depth for hypermnesia or revivification has been achieved, the victim or witness may not know anything of value or have witnessed what he thought he had.

8. Review, examine, and critique every session in light of strengths, weaknesses, and mistakes. The operator should ask himself such questions as the following: "What did I do right? What did I do wrong? Where could I have improved the session? What could I have done differently to adapt to this particular subject's response? Why was he resisting? How could I have circumvented or even used his defenses against him?"

9. There comes a time when dealing with a victim or witness that it is obvious that, in spite of the subject's and the operator's best efforts over a number of sessions, he is just not capable of a sufficient hypnotic depth to achieve even minimal enhanced recall. At this time, the operator is faced with the problem of gracefully terminating the contact with the subject. As a suggested verbalization, the operator may proceed as follows: "Well, 'Barbara,' although you have tried very hard, it seems that you are either just not ready at this time to go very deep, or you may not have the

necessary aptitude for a deep level of hypnosis. It seems that just as some people are born with a musical aptitude, others have an inherent aptitude for hypnosis while others don't. In fact, research on hypnotic susceptibility has shown that approximately 25 percent of normal adults can only reach a light stage of hypnosis even with repeated inductions. I know you want to remember this event as much as we do, but it's a fact of life that not all people are able to. So please don't feel bad about not being able to recall it." The operator may also explain the possibility of intervening psychodynamic variables with more sophisticated and intelligent subjects, which subtlely shifts possible responsibility for the failure to them.

10. If there is more than one hypno-investigator in the department, an alternative to number nine is to refer the victim or witness. It is possible that the psychodynamic interrelationship precludes hypnosis, whereas this might not be the case with another operator.

REFERENCES

1. Meares, Ainslie: *A System of Medical Hypnosis.* New York, Julian, 1960, p. 120.
2. Erickson, Milton H., Rossi, Ernest L., and Rossi, Sheila, I.: *Hypnotic Realities: The Induction of Clinical Hypnosis and Forms of Indirect Suggestion.* New York, Irvington, 1976, pp. 58-59.
3. Baudouin, Charles: *Suggestion and Auto Suggestion.* New York, Dodd Mead, 1922.
4. Gordon, David: *Therapeutic Metaphors.* Cupertino, Meta, 1978, p. 90.
5. Teitelbaum, Myron: *Hypnosis Induction Technics.* Springfield, Thomas, 1965, p. 20.
6. Meares, pp. 136-137.
7. Weitzenhoffer, André M.: *General Techniques of Hypnotism.* New York, Grune & Stratton, 1957, p. 233.
8. Erickson, Rossi, and Rossi, pp. 64-65.
9. Wolberg, Lewis R.: *Medical Hypnosis: The Principles of Hypnotherapy,* vol. I. New York, Grune & Stratton, 1948, p. 116.
10. Erickson, Milton H.: Deep hypnosis and its induction. In LeCron, Leslie M. (Ed.): *Experimental Hypnosis,* 2nd ed. New York, Citadel, 1968, pp. 98-99.
11. Erickson, Rossi, and Rossi, pp. 64, 65, 67.
12. Meares, p. 128.
13. Ibid., p. 129.
14. Christenson, James A.: Dynamics in hypnotic induction. In LeCron, Leslie M. (Ed.): *Experimental Hypnosis,* 2nd ed. New York, Citadel, 1968, p. 38.
15. Erickson, Milton H.: Deep hypnosis and its induction. In Haley, Jay (Ed.): *Advanced Techniques of Hypnosis and Therapy: Selected Papers of Milton H. Erickson, M.D.* New York, Grune & Stratton, 1967, p. 18.
16. Ibid., p. 20.
17. Watkins, John G.: *Hypnotherapy of War Neuroses.* New York, Ronald, 1949.
18. Gardner, Gail G.: Hypnosis with children. *International Journal of Clinical and Experimental Hypnosis, 22(1):*29, 1974.
19. Erickson, p. 19.
20. Jencks, Berta: Utilizing the phases of the breathing rhythm in hypnosis. In Frankel, F. H., and Zamansky, H. S. (Eds.): *Hypnosis at its Bicentennial.* New York, Plenum, 1978, p. 170.
21. Weitzenhoffer, p. 242.
22. Teitelbaum, p. 34.
23. Erickson, Rossi, and Rossi, pp. 307-309.
24. Teitelbaum, p. 58.
25. Young, P. C.: Hypnotic regression — fact or artifact? *Journal of Abnormal and Social Psychology, 35:*273-278, 1940.

26. Sarbin, T. R.: Mental changes in experimental regression. *Journal of Personality, 19:*221-228, 1950.

27. Orne, Martin T.: The mechanisms of hypnotic age regression: an experimental study. *Journal of Abnormal and Social Psychology, 46:*213-225, 1951.

28. Taylor, A.: The differentiation between true and hypnotic regression by figure drawings. Unpublished master's thesis, The College of the City of New York, 1950.

29. Mercer, M. and Gibson, R. W.: Rorschach content in hypnosis: chronological age level regression. *Journal of Clinical Psychology, 6:*352-358, 1950.

30. Bergman, M. S., Graham, H., and Leavitt, H. C.: Rorschach exploration of consecutive hypnotic chronological age level regression. *Psychosomatic Medicine, 9:*20-28, 1947.

31. Gakkebush, V. M.: The use of hypnotic inhibition to study the development of human personality. *The Johns Hopkins University Applied Physics Laboratory, Library Bulletin (Translation Series),* Report No. TG-230-T-153, 1960. Translation from *Sovremennaia Psikhonevrologiia, 7:*272-277, 1928.

32. Kline, M. V. and Haggerty, A. D.: An hypnotic experimental approach to the genesis of occupational interests and choice. III. Hypnotic age regression and the Thematic Apperception Test. A clinical case study in occupational identification. *International Journal of Clinical and Experimental Hypnosis, 1:*18-31, 1953.

33. Kline, M. V.: Hypnotic age regression and intelligence. *Journal of Genetic Psychology, 77:*129-132, 1950.

34. Gidro-Frank, L. and Bowersbuch, M. K.: A study of the plantar response in hypnotic age regression. *Journal of Nervous and Mental Disease, 107:*443-458, 1948.

35. True, R. M. and Stephenson, C. W.: Controlled experiments correlating electroencephalogram, pulse, and plantar reflexes with hypnotic age regression and induced emotional states. *Personality, 1:*252-263, 1951.

36. Lozanov, Georgi: *Suggestology and Outlines of Suggestopedy.* New York, Interface, 1978, pp. 141-147.

37. LeCron, Leslie M.: A study of age regression under hypnosis. In LeCron, Leslie M. (Ed.): *Experimental Hypnosis,* 2nd ed. New York, Citadel, 1968, p. 158.

38. Kline, M. V.: Childhood fears in relation to hypnotic age regression: a case report. *Journal of Genetic Psychology, 82:*137-142, 1953.

39. Wolberg, p. 45.

40. Cheek, David B.: Sequential head and shoulder movements appearing with age-regression in hypnosis to birth. *American Journal of Clinical Hypnosis, 16(4):*261-266, 1974.

41. Ford, L. F. and Yeager, C. L.: Changes in the electroencephalogram in subjects under hypnosis. *Diseases of the Nervous System, 9:*190-192, 1948.

42. Roberts, W. H. and Black, D.: Unpublished paper on a measured change in vision in a regressed myopic subject.

43. Moody, R. L.: Bodily changes during abreaction. *Lancet, 2:*934-935, 1946.

44. Kupper, H. I.: Psychic concomitants in wartime injuries. *Psychosomatic Medicine, 7:*15-21, 1945.

45. As, A.: The recovery of forgotten language knowledge through hypnotic age regression: A case report. *American Journal of Clinical Hypnosis, 5:*24-29, 1962.

46. LeCron, pp. 163-166.

47. Edmonston, William E.: An experimental investigation of hypnotic age-regression. *American Journal of Clinical Hypnosis, 3:*137, 1960.

48. Forrest, Derek, Stevens, Richard, and Dimond, Stuart: Hypnotic age regression: An experimental demonstration of functional ablation. *Irish Journal of Psychology, 2(2):*78-85, 1973.

49. True, R. M.: Experimental control in hypnotic age regression states. *Science, 110:*583-584, 1949.

50. Reiff, Robert and Scheerer, Martin: *Memory and Hypnotic Age Regression.* New York, International Universities Press, 1959, p. 191.

51. Wolberg, p. 42.

52. Cheek, David B.: Unconscious perception of meaningful sounds during surgical

anesthesia as revealed under hypnosis. *American Journal of Clinical Hypnosis, 1:*101, 1959.

53. Reiff and Scheerer, pp. 84-85.
54. Huse, Betty: Does the hypnotic trance favor the recall of faint memories? *Journal of Experimental Psychology, 13:*519-529, 1930.
55. White, R. W., Fox, G. F., and Harris, W. W.: Hypnotic hypermnesia for recently learned material. *Journal of Abnormal and Social Psychology, 35:*88-103, 1940.
56. McCranie, E. J. and Crasilneck, H. B.: The conditioned reflex in hypnotic age regression. *Journal of Clinical and Experimental Psychopathology, 16:*120-123, 1955.
57. LeCron, p. 167.
58. Wolberg, Lewis R.: *Hypnosis: Is It for You?* New York, Harcourt Brace Jovanovich, 1972, pp. 176-177.
59. Gebhard, J. W.: Hypnotic age-regression: a review. *American Journal of Clinical Hypnosis, 3:*159, 1961.
60. Stalnaker, J. M. and Riddle, E. E.: The effect of hypnosis on long-delayed recall. *Journal of General Psychology, 6:*429-440, 1932.
61. White, Fox, and Harris.
62. Rosenthal, B. G.: Hypnotic recall of material learned under anxiety- and non-anxiety-producing conditions. *Journal of Experimental Psychology, 34:*369-389, 1944.
63. Spiegel, H., Shor, J., and Fishman, S.: An hypnotic ablation technique for the study of personality development. *Psychosomatic Medicine, 7:*273-278, 1945.
64. Reiff and Scheerer, p. 186.
65. Cheek, "Unconscious Perception," p. 104.
66. Gibbons, Don: *Beyond Hypnosis: Explorations in Hyperempiria.* So. Orange, Power, 1973, pp. 40-41.
67. Kroger, William S.: *Clinical and Experimental Hypnosis.* Philadelphia, Lippincott, 1963, p. 101.
68. LeCron, Leslie M. and Bordeaux, Jean: *Hypnotism Today,* 1978 ed. No. Hollywood, Wilshire, 1978, p. 39.
69. Weitzenhoffer, p. 227.
70. Ibid., p. 228.
71. Ibid.
72. Elman, Dave: *Hypnotherapy.* Los Angeles, Westwood, 1964, p. 122.
73. Christenson, p. 38.

Chapter 5

PRACTICAL ASPECTS OF HYPNO-INVESTIGATION

CAPTAIN RICHARD K. KING, M.S.

ESTABLISHING A HYPNO-INVESTIGATION PROGRAM WITHIN A LAW ENFORCEMENT AGENCY

INVESTIGATIVE HYPNOSIS is a tool to aid the working detective. It is not a panacea for all investigations. Indeed, there are cases in which it serves no relevant purpose. On-site crime scene investigation still requires personal interviews, copious notetaking, photographs, sketches, measurements, recognizing-gathering-preserving-comparing of physical evidence, etc. Investigative hypnosis is just one additional scientific aid used to provide the working detective with additional information from victims and witnesses of crimes.

Law enforcement traditionally and justifiably moves very slowly before accepting new investigative tools. Modern police administrators, however, have now recognized the benefits of investigative hypnosis to the field investigator. Any law enforcement agency, large or small, can establish a research project to study and evaluate the merits of hypnosis as an investigative tool for themselves. The project should encompass an intense academic exercise, which will lend professional integrity to that agency and thereby gain the respect of the community it serves.

The research project may be structured as a three-phase model: (1) Training, (2) Supervised Application, and (3) Group Monitoring. These phases may be modified to apply to any size law enforcement agency whether the training involves one hypno-investigator or as many as twenty members of a large metropolitan police department.

PHASE I, TRAINING. A 30 to 40 hour training program should be composed of both lecture and laboratory or practice sessions. Recognized professional experts in the use of hypnosis should serve as instructors and guide and counsel the students during the time of the project. Suggested time length of the project will vary, but a minimum of six-months to a year will enhance its credibility. Due to a shortage of recognized authorities on hypnotism who are sensitive to the needs of law enforcement, courses of instruction and periodic seminars are conducted throughout the country to accommodate those investigators who do not have immediate access to these qualified resources. The lecture sessions should cover the topics included in this book. In the laboratory portion, the student group, under a controlled and guided setting, will be provided an opportunity to apply knowledge learned. The student group, using themselves and other volunteers as subjects, will be able to observe and experience hypnosis from the postion of both the operator and the subject. Each individual student will advance to Phase II only after he has reached a prescribed level of proficiency and expertise.

PHASE II, SUPERVISED APPLICATION. Advisors will be assigned to each student. An advisor may be a psychologist, a lay hypnotist, an experienced investigator trained in the use of hypnosis, or a medical doctor trained in the use of hypnosis. The important consideration is that the advisor be part of the training program and have an interest in hypnosis as an aid in the field of criminal investigation. For example, to use Doctor Jones, M.D., who specializes in pediatrics may seem impressive, but his contribution may be limited. A lay hypnotist, who has assisted with criminal investigations, may be a more competent instructor and advisor to the program. During this phase, the student, under the supervision of his advisors, will hypnotically induce hypermnesia and revivification in actual witnesses or victims in an effort to enhance their recall of events surrounding an investigation.

After each of these sessions, the student and his advisors will review and critique the methodology and results. Phase II will vary in length depending upon each student's level of competence and his faculty for learning and utilizing hypnosis at a professional level. Upon completion of Phase II, the student will be qualified as a professional hypno-investigator. At this time, departmental policies and procedures for the use of investigative hypnosis must be written and disseminated (see Appendix 9). A memo from the department head that states that the service is available and lists general guidelines for referral should also be disseminated.

PHASE III, GROUP MONITORING. The hypno-investigators will operate independently of their advisors. When possible, it should be the standard operating procedure that two qualified hypno-investigators be present at any time hypnosis is used in an effort to enhance victim or witness recall; one will be the actual operator, while the other will be the recorder and the evaluator. If this situation has to be modified because of budgetary constraints or the size of the law enforcement agency, which may employ only one hypno-investigator for all investigations, then a senior criminal investigator should be in attendance. After each session the operator and the evaluator will review and evaluate the methodology, techniques, and results. A written report will be made and submitted to the other members of the group. This documentation is important to maintain integrity in the project and will be available to serve as evidence in any subsequent judicial proceedings. Periodically, the entire group will meet with their advisors to review the group's progress, share in its experience, discuss mutual problems, evaluate their successes, and recommend whatever changes are deemed necessary.

The evaluation of the total project will be of crucial importance in assessing the project's effectiveness. From a management viewpoint, the determinative factor of project effectiveness will be its results in terms of man-hours expended equated to suspects arrested, crimes cleared and property recovered. The criminal investigator will judge the project in terms of how effective hypnosis is as an investigative tool. Therefore, exact and accurate documentation must be maintained.

TWO APPROACHES TO HYPNO-INVESTIGATION

Independent Clinicians v. Police Hypnotists

No innovative technique introduced to law enforcement has survived without controversy. The use of investigative hypnosis is no exception. The controversy is truly a matter of choice and interpretation, and it centers around two basic differing approaches to the use of hypnosis in criminal investigation.

One approach, usually endorsed by psychological and medical clinicians, is based on the premise that the hypno-investigator should be an independent and neutral psychological or medical professional to avoid the inherent risk of consciously or subconsciously leading and suggesting desired answers to an ultrasuggestible hypnotic subject by police hypnotists, who have prior information and preconceptions and a biased interest in the outcome of the case. To avoid this potential problem, whether real or imagined, outside clinicians with no law enforcement experience are utilized as hypno-investigators. To further ensure an unbiased neutrality, these clinicians are given no background information regarding the victim or witness, and only a general description of the case. In fact, when the clinician meets the subject referred by law enforcement, he often does not even know if he is dealing with the victim or witness. Theoretically, this approach and these precautions preclude the possibility of the clinician leading the subject or inadvertently planting ideas, and hence the resulting information is deemed to be more credible.

This approach, as developed and perfected by the Los Angeles County Sheriff's Office, even goes one step further to avoid unnecessary contact between the victim or witness and the clinician. The volunteer subject is introduced to hypnosis by listening to a tape recording of a psychologist as he explains a few highlights of "Hypnotic Investigation." Unfortunately, there is no tape prepared to answer the many questions a subject may have nor to allay all his fears and anxieties.

The philosophy of this technique has some validity. This approach theoretically circumvents possible challenges in court that police hypno-investigators may tend to guide the subject in response to desired answers. Such advocates overlook the most important safe-ty device and that is the necessity of corroborating all of the information before obtaining arrest or search warrants. The major weaknesses of such an approach, and this is readily admitted by the practitioners, is that a nonpolice hypnotist without information about the case will generally be able to obtain very little relevant information. It has been the author's experience that when hypnotic sessions are properly documented by electronic recording and/or videotape reproduction, there has been no evidence of any improper leading questions. The seasoned hypno-investigator has had years of experience developing techniques of interviewing. Regardless of what technique is used, if a case eventually is sent to court for adjudication and hypnosis becomes an issue, the defense counsel will certainly challenge the testimony of a witness obtained while under hypnosis. A trained hypno-investigator who documents his sessions with electronic recordings will successfully meet the challenge. In this author's experience in over several hundred hypno-investigations, only a handful of cases have ever gone to court on the issue of hypnosis, and in all of these its use was successfully defended.

Therefore, the second approach to hypno-investigation, as developed and perfected by the Los Angeles Police Department, involves trained police hypnotists who are provided copies of the reports and who have extensive interviews with the primary investigator on each case. Where deemed appropriate and necessary, the hypno-investigator will even view the crime scene. The purpose of this method is to permit the operator to gain insight about the incident and construct his interview session around the desired information that the primary investigator is seeking to help him solve the case. It makes sense to this author that a hypno-investigator with several years of experience, say in homicide investigation, will be more of an asset to the final outcome of a criminal case if he is aware of necessary background information. The necessity for objectivity, however, remains of paramount importance on behalf of the hypno-investigator.

A conflict of interest may arise in the situation where the primary investigator is also the operator. In such a case, the hypnotist could well be too close to the personalities involved in the investigation. His desire to seek a satisfactory conclusion to an investigation based on prior information obtained through his own extensive investigation may cause preconceived notions that could impede and even taint the final outcome of the case. Therefore, it would appear that in the interest of maintaining objective interviewing, an experienced police officer with a background in investigation and hypnosis, but not otherwise connected with a criminal case, is the best logical choice as a hypno-investigator.

THE HYPNO-INVESTIGATOR'S RELATIONSHIP WITH COMMAND OFFICERS

Command officers within most law enforcement agencies are generally classified as traditionalists, which often suggests inflexibility in management. Although the use of hypnosis in criminal investigation is not a new concept, the use of police officers as hypno-investigators is a modern concept.

Progressive police administrators are aware of the advantages and use of this investigative tool. Others are not. Command officers and others involved in the decision-making process should be approached with a realistic view of what hypnosis can offer their particular law enforcement agency. Be prepared to dispel the many myths and misconceptions of hypnosis with intelligent and simple explanations. For example, this author still receives calls from command officers who want to use hypnosis as a means of determining the veracity of a witness's testimony. Hypnosis, however, is not a truth-inducing technique per se because there are many cases of subjects lying while in hypnosis. Hypnosis is used in the field of law enforcement to aid witnesses and victims in memory enhancement. The testimony of a hypnotized subject must be corroborated by an independent investigation subsequent to the hypnosis session.

Most importantly, command officers should never be given false expectations. Like the use of fingerprints, polygraph, photography, and ballistics, the use of investigative hypnosis is an investigative tool that may reap tremendous profits by providing leads to the working detective, or it may not prove beneficial in a particular case.

One suggested method for approaching command officers with the idea of establishing a hypno-investigation program is to gain the support and backing of local medical practitioners who have some background in the field of hypnosis. Seek out the assistance of sympathetic persons in the medical profession because their input may be the deciding factor that will swing the weight toward adopting a program of investigative hypnosis. Be careful of quacks and other persons, however, who give their endorsement only for self-exploitation. They may wish to gain the support of the local police department for their own aggrandizement, although this is rare. Many persons in the medical professions are genuinely motivated as good citizens and will offer their services as a contribution to the community. Command officers are generally impressed with an endorsement from a highly respected source outside of their own element. Often local doctors, time permitting, will offer their services as consultants and advisors free of charge.

This is a major inducement to command officers who must operate with an austere budget.

Another suggested method is to have a command officer attend a seminar on investigative hypnosis: there he has endless resources available and may ask questions, participate in practice sessions, and learn first hand what benefit hypnosis may be as an investigative tool. Many a skeptic has been converted after a few days of training at a seminar.

Modern advertising agents would be quick to point out that successful use of hypnosis in a major criminal case would enhance the reputation of a chief of police or sheriff who instituted such a progressive program within his department. He would indeed be a man among his peers. Many fine reputations have been established by one significant case success, with the result that the chief or sheriff has been hailed as a genius.

THE HYPNO-INVESTIGATOR'S RELATIONSHIP WITH THE PRIMARY INVESTIGATOR

A hypno-investigator should not be the primary investigator in a criminal case. Such a situation could cause a conflict of interest, whether real or imagined. There may be exceptions to this situation, but any law enforcement agency should take the posture that the hypno-investigator is an auxiliary support unit for the case investigator. The ultimate responsibility for clearance of the case rests with the primary investigator and not the hypnotist. In small departments it is suggested that a hypno-investigator be shared with other local departments to maintain procedural integrity and quality control. This factor could be weighed in view of providing financial aid for the training of one hypno-investigator who will provide services to contributing agencies as needed. The less involved a hypno-investigator is with the outcome of a case the more objective he can be in his application of professional hypnotic techniques, as well as avoid or minimize likely defense objections.

Some basic problems do exist between the hypno-investigator and the primary investigator. This is particularly true of investigators who have never used hypnosis as a resource in their investigative process. As with command officers, the primary case investigator must be handled gingerly and tactfully to ensure his understanding, respect, and utilization of the hypno-in-

vestigator. The following are some general principles to follow when dealing with the primary case investigator:

EDUCATE THE PRIMARY INVESTIGATOR ABOUT HYPNOSIS. Dispel old tales and myths. Encourage him to ask questions, put him at ease, and do not laugh at his questions. Always remember that it is the hypno-investigator's responsibility to make sure the primary investigator understands hypnosis and hypno-investigation.

The operator needs to particularly educate the primary investigator on how to approach the victim or witness with the prospect of volunteering for hypnosis. The detective must first assess the case and the relation of the victim or witness to the actual crime event to determine if hypnosis may be of value. If he decides that it will, he should very matter-of-factly inform the subject that the department has a highly trained and skilled hypnotist on staff who has been very successful in aiding the recall of victims and witnesses. His speaking with an as yet unearned confidence and respect in the technique and operator will serve to motivate the subject and build the proper expectation.

The primary investigator, whether detective or patrolman, should never attempt to explain hypnosis to the victim or witness, but at the least sign of interest and willingness he should immediately call in the hypno-investigator or make an appointment. Generally, the less the referring officer says regarding hypnosis the better.

Similarly, the referring officer should never try to assess the person's susceptibility and to make his decision to refer or not to refer on that basis. His only criteria for referral should be whether or not he believes hypnosis may be of benefit, and, if uncertain, he should consult with the hypno-investigator. Whether or not to pursue the actual use of hypnosis with any particular victim or witness is the prerogative of the operator.

DO NOT BUILD UNREASONABLE EXPECTATIONS. Clearly define to the primary investigator what can be expected. Do not promise positive results. Although a subject may appear to be motivated, there may be resistance to the hypnotist or to hypnosis per se because of unknown psychological factors.

SHOW INTEREST IN THE CASE. Be sincere and convince the primary investigator that you will try to help him. Be honest. Experienced detectives can recognize a "con job." Lack of interest on the part of a hypno-investigator may end any confidence the detective has in him and spell doom for the whole program.

DO NOT CRITICIZE THE INVESTIGATIVE TECHNIQUES USED BY THE PRIMARY INVESTIGATOR. This may be hard to do. Experienced investigators should be selected and trained in the use of hypnosis primarily because of their extensive background in the field of investigation. It is only human to second-guess less experienced detectives. Law enforcement is a paramilitary experience and years of service, time-in-grade, and the seniority system still impact the profession. Nevertheless, the hypno-investigator must always remember that he is present to perform a support function, so tact is the key.

SHOW EMPATHY TO THE INVESTIGATOR. A good detective wants to solve his case as soon as possible. Sometimes he may want to "shortcut" the investigative process and use hypnosis as a primary resource before it would be prudent to do so. Even old timers, not experienced in investigative hypnosis, may panic and demand a hypnosis session when they have insufficient case background. The hypnotist may remind the investigator that sometimes, particularly in cases where a victim has suffered a severe traumatic experience, a period of time should elapse before the victim is asked to recount the unpleasant incident. There may be exceptions, however, such as in a kidnapping where time is of the essence. Conversely, hypnosis should not be used only as a last resort.

DISCUSS THE CASE WITH THE PRIMARY INVESTIGATOR. Read the original incident report and any follow-up reports available. The role of an investigative hypnotist cannot sever the years of experience that he has accumulated in investigation. Hypno-investigators are selected because of their expertise in the field of criminal investigation, and not necessarily because they will make good hypnotists. Discussion of the case with the primary investigator may give a new insight into what technique and approach may be best used.

MAKE THE PRIMARY INVESTIGATOR PART OF THE HYPNOSIS TEAM. Encourage him to submit questions and have him present at the hypnosis session. Solicit his ideas, encourage him to participate and make a follow-up interview, and learn the disposition of the case.

It is also important to ask the primary investigator what specific information he is seeking and give it priority. This will maximize the chances of a worthwhile session.

ALWAYS ASK THE PRIMARY INVESTIGATOR WHAT HE HAS TOLD THE SUBJECT ABOUT HYPNOSIS. This is a very important requirement. Some detectives unintentionally intimidate witnesses, and such a situation would result in little or no success in a hypnosis session. The hypnotist may therefore have to spend some time gaining the confidence of the subject.

The operator should also know exactly what the detective said about the nature of hypnosis and the upcoming session as he may have inadvertently given the subject some negative misconceptions with which the operator will have to deal.

Probably the most important consideration here is for the hypno-investigator to determine if the subject is a willing volunteer. If he has been coerced in any form by the primary investigator there is little reason for continuing unless the operator can transform him into a willing subject during the preinduction talk.

THE PRIMARY INVESTIGATOR MUST CORROBORATE ALL STATEMENTS MADE BY THE SUBJECT WHILE UNDER HYPNOSIS. Many important leads in a criminal investigation may be obtained from a subject while under hypnosis. The primary investigator, however, should be admonished that all information obtained under hypnosis must be corroborated because it has no prima facie evidential status. Hypnosis cannot solve criminal cases, but it may greatly assist the detective so that *he* can solve the case.

DOES THE PRIMARY INVESTIGATOR KNOW WHAT TYPE OF PERSON HE IS DEALING WITH? Use the experience and expertise of the investigator by having him evaluate the subject. Was the subject in a position to see what he claims? Is the subject mentally alert? Is the subject an emotionally stable person? All of this background information can be useful to the hypnotist and will give him insight into the subject he will be dealing with.

The hypno-investigator's relationship with the primary investigator can best be summed up as a team effort. The hypno-investigator must never look down upon the working detective because, as a hypnotist, he possesses skills that the detective does not have. Their efforts should both be directed towards the successful solution of a criminal investigation and personalities should not interfere with that common goal.

LOGISTICS AT THE SCENE

A witness or victim of a crime who volunteers for a hypnosis session is usually motivated to assist the police in solving the case. Oftentimes the hypnosis session may be an infringement on the personal time of the subject, so it is imperative that the hypnosis session be held at his convenience whenever possible.

Generally, hypnosis sessions are held at the local police station in the community where the subject resides. Though very few police buildings have a comfortable room that is both quiet and appropriately furnished, it is important that the subject feels welcome and at ease while in the station. Some persons feel ill at ease in a police building. This is particularly true of a subject who may have had a negative experience with the police in the past. The only contact some citizens have with law enforcement is when they receive a traffic citation, hardly a pleasant introduction. Some witnesses may have extensive prior police records and this "cooperative atmosphere" is difficult for them to adjust to quickly. Even law-abiding citizens will feel uneasy, anxious, and intimidated at a police station in the presence of uniformed police officers carrying guns, batons, and large flashlights.

When a hypnosis session is to be conducted at a police station, and a properly located, constructed, and equipped hypno-investigation room is not available, the following considerations are important (see "The Hypno-Investigation Room" in Chapter 2):

PRIVACY MUST EXIST. Most police stations are busily occupied by clerical staff typing and moving about. The police radio may serve as a constant source of interruption. Telephones ring constantly. Police officers starting their patrol vehicles and checking their special equipment, while essential, is often disturbing to a private conversation. Fortunately, most of these minor handicaps can be overcome by the use of a small private office or interview room with a closed door. Place a sign on the outside door large enough to be read by all which says, "HYPNOSIS SESSION IN PROGRESS. QUIET PLEASE."

NO TELEPHONE CALLS. It is desirable to obtain a room without a telephone. If an office has a telephone, either disconnect it or inform the desk officer that no telephone calls are to be accepted. Although experienced hypnotists can use the intruding sound of a ringing phone as a deepening technique during the induction, it is preferable not to have any interference if it can be avoided.

PROVIDE A COMFORTABLE CHAIR. Most police facilities intentionally avoid the use of comfortable chairs, with one notable exception; high ranking command officers may have a comfortable, high-backed swivel chair with armrests. If it is possible to borrow such a chair, do so. A soft reclining chair is ideal because the subject can adjust the angle to suit his preference. If such a chair is not available, at least a chair with arms should be included in the office furniture. If a subject cannot get comfortable in the chair provided, have a bed pillow on hand to provide additional back support. This will demonstrate personal consideration for the subject.

PROVIDE A BEVERAGE. The subject's throat may become dry before the hyp-

nosis session due to anxiety, and, after the session, the subject will definitely appreciate something to drink. While under hypnosis the subject's throat may also become dry and a glass of water is refreshingly welcome. If it appears that the subject's throat is becoming dry as evidenced by such signs as swallowing, do not hesitate to ask him if he would like a drink of water. As an alternative, the subject may be told to hallucinate taking a drink of fresh spring water or eating an orange. Attention to this minor detail will demonstrate concern for the welfare of the subject and help establish good rapport. Equally important is the hypnotist whose throat may become dry since he will be doing most of the talking during the session.

FEMALE CLOTHING. If the subject is female, she should be advised not to wear a short dress to the hypnosis session. As a subject relaxes she may slide down in the chair which results in her dress creeping-up her legs. This can be a serious distraction to the subject and a source of embarrassment for both subject and operator. As a result, she may not be able to totally concentrate. If a female subject is wearing a short dress, however, a quilt, blanket, coat, or sweater should be provided for her to cover her legs. This small act will serve to enhance the professional status of the hypno-investigator and encourage cooperation on behalf of the female subject.

RECORDING EQUIPMENT. Ideally, the hypno-investigation room should be equipped as described in "The Hypno-Investigation Room" in Chapter 2. Some people prefer not to be photographed while allowing themselves to be hypnotized, but a good hypno-investigator should be able to overcome such an objection by simply explaining the necessity and purpose of the procedure. The hypnosis session must be recorded to protect the subject against misquotes, to maintain the integrity of the hypno-investigator and his application of induction techniques, to serve as a possible source of lead information for the primary investigator and, finally, the recording may be a source of admissible evidence in court to refute claims by the defense that the subject was given leading questions with suggested answers.

The recording should begin as soon as the hypno-investigator begins a conversation with the subject. Immediate recording precludes any later criticism that the hypnotist led the subject or planted ideas for a desired answer prior to hypnosis. Such a recording may also be beneficial to the primary investigator if he misses an important statement early in the session. Sometimes a subject likes to hear the audio tape played after the session. This also gives the hyponotist an opportunity to inquire as to the moment the subject began to relax, when he felt he entered hypnosis, how he felt during this time, and other relevant data which may prove useful to the operator in future sessions.

SEATING ARRANGEMENTS. The comfortable seating position of the subject should be the first consideration. The hypno-investigator should sit off to the side of the subject. Never permit a table to separate the subject from the hypnotist. To do so would cause an impersonal relationship and may hamper the ability of the hypnotist to establish the rapport necessary with the subject. A table, however, can be an essential prop and should be used to hold the tape recorder, note pads, reports, beverages, an ash tray, tissues, etc.

The primary investigator should be present, but seated to the rear of the subject. If a child is the subject, a parent may wish to be present, but should also be seated out of the immediate sight of the subject to avoid distraction. Only those persons concerned with the investigation should be present in the room at the time of the hypnosis session. A carnival atmosphere should be avoided and the personal rights of the subject should be protected. Even if the subject says that he does not mind other spectators, they should not be allowed, as he may not be telling the truth. Furthermore, unnecessary persons in the room are additional factors with which the operator has to contend.

ROOM CLIMATE. Avoid a brightly lit room as most persons have difficulty closing their eyes in a bright room. It is a fact of human physiology that bright lights impede rapid eye closure. Lighting should therefore be dimmed or as subdued as possible. Some rooms may be equipped with a light dimmer, which will provide a very pleasant atmosphere and relaxing setting. If the room has drapes, they should be closed during the daylight hours.

Smoking should be prohibited in the room during a hypnosis session. Since the door will be closed there will be little outside ventilation. During the prehypnosis rapport session the subject may wish to smoke and this may help to relax him, but, during the session, neither the hypnotist nor others present should smoke in the presence of the subject. If the subject is a nonsmoker, the presence of cigarette smoke in the room may be offensive. Some persons are allergic to tobacco and this could be a source of distraction as well as an embarrassment to the hypno-investigator. Personal discipline in this matter is important.

USE PROMPTERS. Have a legal size tablet available on a nearby table listing the various inductions, deepenings, hypermnesia, and revivification instructions, etc. This is particularly good advice for the new hypno-investigator who may suddenly forget his line of patter or want to change to a different induction technique. Important information such as date, time, and location of the incident, vehicle descriptions, and other information that a hypnotist could not be expected to remember could be available on the table. Subjects interviewed by police officers are accustomed to seeing reports and writing materials present during the interview so do not be self-conscious about having notes present.

DRESS. The hypno-investigator should generally be in civilian dress as most people find it difficult to relax around a uniformed officer. There are exceptions, however. On occasion, the victim or witness may be an employee of a law enforcement agency, in which case the manner of dress will be unimportant. Some children, adolescents, and even adults who have a profound respect for police officers may react favorably to a uniformed operator.

LOCATION. For a variety of reasons, it may be necessary to conduct the hypnosis session at the home of the subject. Upon occasion this will be more convenient for the subject, while others will just not be able to relax in a police station. In these instances the subject is usually less anxious and feels more comfortable on his home ground. He may have a favorite chair he can relax in and provide a personal sanctuary away from other inquisitive members of the family. Small children should neither be seen nor heard during a hypnosis session unless one of them is the subject. Neighbors should be excluded to avoid unnecessary spectators. Always allow the subject to select the spot where he may be the most comfortable, even if it means lying on the floor in front of the fireplace. The convenience and comfort of the subject is the primary consideration. Some detectives do not like to interview witnesses on their "home turf" and prefer the sanctuary of the police station. This

type of witness, however, is strongly motivated to help the police, and consideration should be extended to the preference of the subject.

One final location should be discussed and that is the business office of the subject. In an effort to accommodate the subject, the hypno-investigator should acquiesce to the wishes of the primary investigator and go to the business location where the subject is employed. This is usually the least desirable of any location, however. Persons in a work environment feel constrained to do nothing but work-related tasks, which may preclude the subject from relaxing. A good hypnotist, however, should be able to largely overcome this problem.

In conclusion, hypnosis sessions conducted at a police facility provide the maximum control of the situation. When the hypno-investigator visits the home of the subject some control is surrendered, but a feeling of security and relaxation may outweigh the control factor. At a business office the stress of time constraints coupled with normal pressures of work generally interfere with a successful hypnosis session. Regardless of the location of the session, however, it is essential that the operator be assured that the subject, if employed, has permission from his superior to be absent from work. This is to insure the subject's undivided attention.

If the session is to be held at either the subject's residence or place of employment, the hypno-investigator will have to make the necessary arrangements for adequate electronic recording of the session.

PROBLEMS NEW HYPNO-INVESTIGATORS ENCOUNTER

The single greatest fault among new hypno-investigators is their lack of confidence in applying their newly acquired skills, which is easily understandable. A hypno-investigator may

forget a desired line of patter during an induction; he may become upset if the subject takes too long to close his eyes or if the subject begins to cry during the session. Sometimes a subject may appear to be in a good medium state of hypnosis and suddenly open his eyes. All of these things have happened to every practicing hypnotist and will continue to occur, but they are not fatal in themselves.

Some hypno-investigators may find it difficult to change their usual authoritarian role to that of a permissive listener. Others may find it difficult to suspend their normal tendency to interrogate their subjects before, during, and after hypnosis instead of passively and nonjudgmentally eliciting information. Analyzing and comparing witnesses' statements is the job of the primary investigator, not the hypno-investigator. Novice hypno-investigators often mistake subject resistance as a form of self-criticism. Actually, this is usually a lack of self-confidence on the part of the operator. Why are well known stage hypnotists so successful with members of a different audience every night? The answer is self-confidence, confidence that has been established through years of practice. Practice is the key. Once the hypno-investigator has learned basic skills of hypnosis, it is then necessary to practice a variety of induction procedures and techniques on a variety of subjects. A wise hypno-investigator will seek out less important criminal cases upon which he can build confidence and a good reputation. When a major case that attracts a lot of publicity comes along, he can confidently pursue the investigation and hopefully assist the primary investigator with a successful solution to the case. Hypnotic subjects are keenly sensitive to police officers who lack self-confidence and will react with suspicion towards them. A confident operator is easily recognized.

Another tendency for beginning operators is to try to hurry through the session and to talk too fast. Similarly, novice operators have the common assumption that they cannot freely converse with hypnotized subjects without bringing them out. Since this is untrue, the operator should feel free to ask his subject how he is feeling and what he is experiencing so that he can incorporate these in deepening techniques.

Peer pressure may be a form of anxiety to new hypno-investigators. Innocent kidding around the station by an officer's peers is harmless on the surface, but the lack of desired success in some major case may be an occasion for serious ignorant criticism. Once again, it is time to remind hypno-investigators not to promise any positive results on a given case. All witnesses are not good witnesses, just as all subjects for hypnosis are not good subjects, and any combination of one or both will not yield positive results.

This brings up another point and that is case referral, i.e. what cases should a hypno-investigator accept. Unfortunately, not all cases involving witnesses have the potential for utilizing hypnosis. It is incumbent upon the hypno-investigator to confer with the primary investigator to determine if the witness was present at the scene of the crime, if the witness perceived anything that may be of value to the investigation, and if the witness will be a willing subject for hypnosis. All too often witnesses are poor subjects, did not perceive anything of value, and do not want to be hypnotized.

These determinations should be mutually agreed upon between the hypno-investigator and the primary investigator. Considerations such as the health of the subject must be made prior to a hypnosis session. If a subject is under a doctor's care, permission should be first obtained before conducting hypnosis. If a subject is a victim of a vicious sexual assault, it may be prudent to wait for a period of time before conducting a hypnosis session. These problems will confront the new hypno-investigator, and he should discuss them with the primary investigator as the two form a team to work towards a successful solution of the case.

In summation, the new hypno-investigator should have a game plan established before he ever meets the subject. He should have several induction techniques available and some background or insight about his subject and the case. He must be able to modify his technique to fit the particular personality of the subject. He has to establish the team concept with the primary investigator. A hypno-investigator should not be aloof from other members in law enforcement. To set himself above others will only serve to alienate the very people he has been trained to serve.

USING HYPNOSIS WITH A COMPOSITE ARTIST

The use of hypnosis to enhance witnesses' memories has produced some startling look-alike sketches in major crimes. As a result, wanted suspects have been recognized, identified, and arrested through the efforts of a hypno-investigator and the artist.

Hypnosis sessions involving an artist demand very close teamwork. They must have a plan that will not confuse the witness, and the procedure to be followed should be explained to the subject at the beginning of the session. A suggested and field-tested plan is for the hypno-investigator to first establish rapport with the subject and answer any and all questions regarding the hypnosis. The artist is then introduced, and the subject works with him in the normal conscious state to provide as much information as he can to complete as accurate a composite as possible. When the subject can no longer give new input, he is then hypnotized. It should have already been explained to the subject that hypnosis is being induced to help him recall the exact likeness of the wanted suspect. While the subject is under hypnosis, he should be told to open his eyes, look at the sketch, and tell the artist to make whatever changes are necessary to make the composite more lifelike. It is very seldom that a subject will not suggest at least some minor alteration. Be careful, however, that the artist does not unduly influence the subject by suggesting changes that are not the sole idea of the witness.

These hypnosis sessions are usually very long because the subject is requested to open his eyes and make suggestions to the artist; the artist then asks questions of the subject; the subject closes his eys and enjoys the state of hypnosis while the artist makes the additional changes; and then the questioning continues. It is necessary to allow the artist to make the adjustments on his sketch before he solicits more detail. It would be advisable to have such an artist learn the basics of hypnosis. An artist who has no background in the field of hypnosis may ask too many questions too quickly and may confuse the subject. This situation is a variance from the norm because the hypno-investigator must give way to the artist as an interviewer because only he can ask the key questions that will supply the cosmetic features for the sketch.

In this situation, the hypno-investigator must exercise his role of a monitor not only to prohibit the artist from asking leading questions, but to recognize when the subject can no longer offer constructive input about the sketch. Because of the relationship that exists between the hypnotist and the subject, some witnesses will continue to alter a sketch just to please him. It is not unusual, however, for a subject to make some very significant, accurate, and detailed changes of a sketch while under hypnosis.

When the operator is ready to allow the artist to ask questions, he should forewarn the subject that a new voice will be heard and that it is perfectly all right to answer the questions by the artist. Most composite artists who work with hypno-investigators have learned the art of patience and will allow the subject ample time to make suggestions about the sketch. While the subject is under hypnosis, he should attain a reasonable state of satisfaction with the sketch before the session is terminated. Once the subject is dehypnotized, the artist should again ask the opinion of the subject and make the necessary changes to complete the sketch.

Occasionally, a hypnosis session with a composite artist may take two or more hours to complete. The hypno-investigator should therefore be alert to fatigue symptoms by the subject, i.e. signs of confusion, indifference, and over susceptibility to any suggestion by the artist to complete the sketch as soon as possible. In this event, a second hypnosis session may be in order.

To prolong the original session as long as possible, recognizing that most subjects will tend to come up to a lighter stage when asked questions at length by the artist or by reviewing the sketch with eyes open, the operator should suggest to the subject that he go to his favorite place and drift deeper during the periods when the artist embellishes on the sketch. The operator may also use some simple counting or breathing deepenings during these times if the subject appears to be coming up to lighter stages. Before asking the subject to open his eyes and look at the sketch, he must be told explicitly that he will be able to open his eyes without affecting his depth, i.e. "You will be able to open your eyes when I ask you and you will not wake up, but will remain as deep as you are now."

Some composite artists and detectives who frequently work with a hypno-investigator may become programmed to his induction techniques and find that they go under very easily during the hypnosis session. This does not have to be a problem as long as the operator suggests to the subject that he rest deeply for a while, and then goes over to the artist or detective and wakes him up when he needs him.

These same procedures should be utilized when using an identi-kit.

HOW TO CONDUCT HYPNOSIS WITH A RAPE VICTIM

The use of hypnosis in rape investigation has become one of the most successful and widely accepted approaches to the identification of the perpetrator as many victims block out the rapist's face. The hypno-investigator can play an important part in the investigating process with a warm, sensitive, and sympathetic approach to the victim.

If a hypno-investigator is requested by the primary investigator in a rape case, he should attempt to learn the present emotional status of the victim. In aggravated assault cases where the victim is sexually abused and seriously beaten, the advice of a medical doctor should be sought before using hypnosis. If a rape victim consents to the use of hypnosis, the operator should advise the subject that it will not be necessary to recall the details of the sexual abuse while under hypnosis. Such sordid facts are already included in the police report, and it will not be necessary to review them to the embarrassment of the victim. Even with this admonishment, some rape victims may wish to be explicit when describing the attack while under hypnosis. This is the exception rather than the rule as most subjects are greatly relieved that they do not have to relive the traumatic indignities they suffered.

If the operator is male, the victim should be asked if she would like to have a female present during the session. Although very rarely will they request the presence of a female, this demonstrates compassion. It is imperative for the operator to appear genuinely understanding and pensive, and he should assure the victim that her past sexual history cannot be brought out in court unless she does so herself.

During the hypnosis session it is advisable to have fresh tissue or a clean handkerchief close by because some victims will do everything from sobbing quietly to crying aloud and even shrieking at times. The hypno-investigator must remain calm and reassuring to the subject. He must support her and, if she cries, reassure her that it is all right to vent her emotions in this manner. Although police hypno-investigators are not therapists, there is a certain therapeutic effect of the hypnosis session and during the postinterview most rape victims will acknowledge a feeling of relief and satisfaction. Inexperienced hypno-investigators sometimes become alarmed when the subject demonstrates this lack of control, but it is at this time that he should place his hand on the subject's shoulder or hold her hand in a supportive fashion. The operator should forewarn the subject, however, that he is going to touch her. Such a movement unannounced may startle the subject, but when forewarned the gesture is always accepted as a warm and sensitive response.

Some rape subjects may take a long period before they enter hypnosis. This may be a reaction of distrust toward the hypno-investigator, and a second hypnosis session may be required. Also, if the subject gets too emotionally upset, the session may also have to be terminated and another one scheduled. The rape victim should never be rushed and the operator should always be permissive and go at her own speed. If the victim is hesitant, the hypno-investigator should not even attempt hypnosis.

Frequently, witnesses and victims will develop guilt feelings following an event in which they feel they should have done something, but did not. These subjects may resist hypnotic induction to avoid any unsatisfactory confrontation with these guilt feelings. Resistance is a reaction that rises automatically and not intentionally. Some hypno-investigators interpret resistance as a personal afront, whereas the subject is actually protecting himself from an awareness of his inner conflict. Such cases are frustrating to novice hypno-investigators because what appears to be a willing and supportive victim or witness to a crime is actually a resistant hypnotic subject.

The operator should never suggest that the subject is lying or challenge the story in any way. The duty of the primary investigator is to corroborate testimony by a follow-up investigation. If a subject is interviewed at home and that is also the location where the rape occurred, a neutral site may be offered for the hypnosis session, because the victim may feel uneasy at home.

Early in the hypnosis session the operator should give some words of absolution to the subject. Often there is a feeling of guilt on the part of the rape victim, and she should be told that she is still a good person, that what happened was beyond her control, and that she acted in the proper manner and did what any other female would do under similar conditions. It is imperative that the subject does not blame herself for the rape and that she understands the hypno-investigator does not hold her accountable for the sexual assault. It is also important for the operator to use permissive induction techniques and avoid any semblance of dominance that may abruptly end the session.

Very often an artist will be included in the hypnosis session to draw a composite sketch. Even though the subject is motivated to help the police identify her attacker, she may be unable or subconsciously unwilling to give the artist an accurate description of the suspect.

Under hypnosis this fear is often resolved, and the subject may give a very detailed description of the assailant.

Before waking the subject, several posthypnotic suggestions can be given the victim to help her deal with the trauma and guilt, however, the operator must make certain he does not invade the realm of the therapist. Specifically, the operator can suggest that she will feel better about herself with less pressure, stress, and guilt for having

recalled the incident and aided in the investigation. This is continually done by investigators at nonhypnotic levels so there is no reason why it should not be done under hypnosis.

This discussion clearly points out the empathy and understanding that the hypno-investigator must demonstrate to gain the confidence of a rape victim. Patience is a virtue that must be developed to be a successful hypno-investigator.

HOW TO CONDUCT HYPNOSIS WITH SEXUALLY ABUSED CHILDREN

Like the female adult rape victim, sexually abused children require a sensitive approach by a hypno-investigator when hypnosis is to be used to enhance memory recall. There are additional areas of concern, however, that a hypno-investigator must be aware of and always on guard. One of these is that children, especially preteenagers, are easy subjects to hypnotize because of a high degree of fantasy involvement. Children are so susceptible to suggestion that it may be difficult to separate fact from fiction. Since most children live in a semifantasy and enjoy telling stories, it is most important to corroborate all of their testimony given while under hypnosis.

During the prehypnosis discussion, the operator should question the child about the meaning of truth. Ask the child if he knows what a lie is and what will happen to him if he lies to his parents. Even though a subject can lie while in the hypnotic state, it is beneficial if the hypno-investigator knows if a child is discerning enough to understand the meaning of truth. The parents should be asked out of hearing range of the child if he usually tells the truth.

Children should be asked about their understanding of hypnosis if they are old enough to form an opinion. The child may have seen a stage hypnotist at school and has predicated an opinion

based upon that single performance. If a child is too young to understand the meaning of hypnosis, it may be better to omit that term from the conversation. A child may fully enter hypnosis without a formal comprehension of what is happening to him.

Child molestation victims should be encouraged to speak in terms that are familiar to them and to describe what the suspect did to them in their own childlike manner. Some sex crimes against children require specific intent and the child should be able to describe the sexual conduct of the suspect to the satisfaction of the primary investigator and the prosecuting attorney. It is important to know what the child calls the parts of his body and what glossary of terms he uses to describe sexual activity that allegedly occurred. A brief discussion with the parents beforehand about these matters will better equip the hypno-investigator so he can evaluate his subject.

The presence of uniform police officers in a police station may cause some anxiety on the part of the child. It may be desirable to conduct a brief tour of the police station and encourage the child to ask questions. Casual clothing should generally be worn by the hypno-investigator to alleviate any fear on the part of the child that the police officer may harm him.

The hypno-investigator should take

all the time necessary to gain the confidence of the child and convince him that hypnosis is a fun game and that he will enjoy the experience. To further relax the child and build rapport he should be allowed to play with the tape recorder and other equipment and even record a song on audio or a stunt on video. It is also often helpful to talk about a favorite TV show or movie.

With regards to the actual induction, eye fixation techniques should be avoided because young children cannot concentrate on any fixed object for very long. The conversational technique is usually considered the best induction method for children. The subject is literally talked into a state of relaxation by referring to some of the child's favorite fantasies, such as flying on a magic carpet, skin diving in beautiful clear water searching for lost treasure, or any pleasant fantasy that the child has revealed during the prehypnosis discussion. Visiting a favorite amusement site such as Disneyland or Sea World where the child has fond memories is also an excellent technique to use the imagination of the young subject. Unlike the adult, a child subject can be easily induced into hypnosis by using a gamelike approach. Children like to play games and one of the most popular techniques is the two-finger approach described in Chapter 4.

Prehypnosis Interview With the Child Victim

Some considerations that a hypno-investigator should have when dealing with the child victim is the child's developmental level and, in particular, the emotional perception of the sexual assault. The closeness of the child's relationship to the offender, e.g. natural or stepfather, the amount of secrecy surrounding the offense, as well as the degree of violence will all impact on the willingness of the child to cooperate. The child may fear the consequences of

reporting a sexual assault based upon the family support system. This influence could negate a successful hypnosis session as the victim may hold back important information.

Although the hypno-investigator must constantly be alert not to engage in hypnotherapy, he must empathize with the victim and be conscious of the needs of the child. A frank and thorough discussion with the parents out of the presence of the child will acquaint the hypno-investigator with the child's needs, fears, emotional stability, developmental level, etc. At this time the operator should also ask the parents what they have told the child about hypnosis.

Before the hypnosis session begins, the ground rules should be set with the parents and other family members present. First of all, the consent of both parents should be granted. If one objects to the use of hypnosis it should probably not be done, unless of course the objecting party is the suspect. Second, the parents or other siblings present should be seated out of the child's vision during the session. Third, do not give the parents the option of terminating the session if the child cries. The mere presence of the parents can make the child more secure, but he may also have a greater tendency to fabricate to impress them.

Hypnosis Session With the Child Victim

The more comfortable the setting the more information the child is likely to share with the hypno-investigator. Do not be distracted by the seeming inattention displayed by the child who will move, squirm, and explore. Physical movement does not preclude a medium state of hypnosis or even deeper, so that should not deter the operator from continuing with the interview.

The major obstacle in the use of hypnosis with children seems to rest more with the hypno-investigator than the child. As stated above, children squirm around and do not give the appearance of being hypnotized, hence, the operator often believes he has failed and does not attempt to illicit information from the subject. The more experience a hypno-investigator has working with children the easier he will come to recognize the random movements of the child as normal behavior under hypnosis.

The hypno-investigator should close the session by praising the child for his cooperation and congratulating him for being a good subject.

DEALING WITH THE PRESS

When first instituting an investigative hypnosis program in a law enforcement agency, the chief or sheriff must decide if he is going to announce the program's development, or if he is going to wait for the press to discover it. These two approaches may be referred to as the aggressive versus the defensive. Which approach to take will largely depend upon the particular bias of the local press and its reporters, as well as the sentiment of the community, i.e. pro- or anti-law enforcement.

Some administrators will quite naturally fear the likely controversy that an announcement of a hypnosis program is likely to foment. They should keep in mind, however, that they should never attempt to deliberately hide the program. As with most other matters, the best policy may be to give the press everything at a judicious time. If done in a spirit of, "Come in and see this fantastic new investigative tool we have developed for better law enforcement in the community," the press will be more likely to support the program.

On the other hand, the administrator should probably delay an announcement until the program is well underway or even completed to avoid premature criticism from the medical establishment and other groups that could kill the program before it starts. If the department head decides to try to keep the use of investigative hypnosis out of the press, he should probably have a release prepared just in case.

An advantage to informing the public about the program is that people knowing of its existence may be more willing to volunteer once victimized or becoming witnesses. Furthermore, if done properly, the professionalism and integrity of the law enforcement agency in the eyes of the community it serves may be enhanced.

Once the story is out, the department must make a concerted effort to give the press a realistic and accurate picture of just what hypnosis is and how it will be used. Either the hypnosis instructors or the hypno-investigators themselves must make certain that the common myths and misconceptions regarding hypnosis and its use by law enforcement are adequately neutralized to avoid headlines similar to the following actual ones: "Police to Trap Liars with Hypnosis Use," "Cops to Hypnotize Thugs," and "Eyes of Cops May Soon Lull Suspects Into Tell-Tale Talking." Probably one of the quickest and most effective means of assuring against this, besides thoroughly reviewing the program with the press, is to actually hypnotize the police reporter, if he will volunteer. There is nothing like personal experience to answer one's questions regarding hypnosis.

The use of hypnosis in criminal investigation frequently raises a high degree of interest when the press learns of its application in a local case. Information to be released in this instance should be channeled through the primary investigator to the press relations officer. If an agency is using investigative hypnosis as a tool for the first time in a major case, the hypno-investigator should be interviewed. His primary consideration is the protection of his subject who may be the victim or a primary witness whose name should never be released to the press. This duty is similar to the lawyer-client, doctor-patient, and newsman-source relationship that exists in our society. The integrity of the relationship must be maintained. The hypno-investigator should use the opportunity to explain some basic principles of hypnosis and dispel some of the current myths surrounding the hypnotic process. He should discuss, in general terms, some techniques and comment on the type of information elicited, but should avoid specific information about the case.

The most important issue in the discussion of dealing with the news media about investigative hypnosis is the absolute necessity of the hypno-investigator, or his designee, to control the press interview. There are two options. First, a prepared written statement can be made in the peace of a quiet room with the concurrence of the chief of police or sheriff. This prepared statement is then released or put on the wire for national distribution. Sounds simple? Not quite. Any good investigative reporter merely uses such a press release as a lever to initiate a personal interview with the principal actors. Thus, telephone interviews, person-to-person interviews, and third person interviews are all made in an effort to uncover some new piece of newsworthy information that will sell more newspapers and attract more television viewers.

Second, the hypno-investigator can grant a personal interview. Most police officers, however, considering their status as public servants, feel obligated to answer all questions put to them by a news reporter. They allow the reporter to control the interview and all too often reveal information that should not be made public prior to a criminal trial. Hypno-investigators should be aware that a polite, "decline to discuss that matter at this time," may serve to protect their witnesses and ultimately the outcome of their case. Unfortunately, some police officers even believe that they are compelled by law to tell the press everything about a criminal case, even though this is not true.

EXPERIENCES OF A HYPNO-INVESTIGATOR: CASE HISTORIES

The following case histories are offered for the purpose of identifying particular problems and providing possible solutions. These cases are an account of one hypno-investigator's efforts to assist the primary investigator toward the solution of a crime.

Case #1

Synopsis

A female, twenty-nine years of age, was kidnapped at gun point from her door step as she arrived home from work. She was driven to a remote area where she was robbed, raped twice, beaten by the suspect, and then returned to her home in the suspect's vehicle. The victim was able to give very little information about the description of the suspect because he wore a ski mask. The detectives requested a hypnosis session for the purpose of obtaining a description of the suspect vehicle.

Hypnosis Session

During hypnosis the subject had difficulty describing the vehicle because her knowledge was limited about various makes and models. The detectives were particularly interested in the vehicle since the suspect's M.O. had been identified in other crimes, but the vehicle description was not available.

When it became obvious that the subject could not verbally describe the interior or exterior of the vehicle because of her lack of technical knowledge, the hypno-investigator recalled that the subject was an art major in college. He asked the subject if she could sketch the interior and exterior of the suspect vehicle. She replied in the affirmative and was supplied with pencil and paper. The subject was told to open her eyes, although still in hypnosis, and to accurately sketch the vehicle and recall any unusual trademarks such as decals, racing stripes or any modifications on the vehicle. She sketched the inside and outside of the vehicle to such a close likeness that the detectives were able to recognize the year, make and model of the wanted vehicle. After the subject sketched the vehicle, she was provided with photographs of several vehicles. She easily selected a photo of a vehicle similar to the one she had sketched. Follow-up investigation resulted in the arrest of the rapist, and his vehicle was positively identified as being used in other robberies and rapes.

Conclusion

Hypno-investigators should take advantage of the talents and skills available through the subjects they are working with. In this case, the subject was an excellent artist and very capable of providing the desired information which led to the identification and arrest of the suspect. The hypno-investigator had only to recognize and use the talents of this subject who was eager to help with the investigation.

Case #2
Synopsis

A female, twenty-three years of age, was returning to her home via a freeway at approximately midnight. Her two-year-old daughter was asleep in the front seat as the woman took an off-ramp toward her country home. As she drove off the main freeway, the headlights of her vehicle caught the shape of a man as he walked from the roadside across the freeway. She slowed her vehicle to avoid the man as he crossed in front of her. She observed his dress and manner of walking, which she later described as a shuffle, and an unusual jacket he was wearing. The following day the body of a young woman was found off the road in a ditch at the same location the man was observed by the witness. The victim had been strangled and raped, and her partially clad body was dumped in the ditch. By coincidence, the witness knew the victim and had attended high school with her.

Hypnosis Session

The investigators were unable to obtain any information from the witness who claimed that she had a total blank about what the suspect looked like and what he was wearing. The subject originally agreed to be hypnotized, but upon arrival at the police station she changed her mind and declined. This turn of events was very frustrating to the case detectives because this was the only witness.

The hypno-investigator sensed that the witness was not against a hypnosis session per se, but was fearful of any consequences as the result of her testimony. After considerable time establishing rapport with the subject, the operator realized that her fear was for the safety of her child and herself. The subject conceded that the suspect may have seen her and would seek her out and harm her. This caused a great deal of anxiety on her behalf and she was unable to sufficiently relax and enter even a mild state of hypnosis. The hypno-investigator was able to explain to the subject that, because of the brightness of the headlights of her vehicle, the surrounding darkness of the area, and the speed with which the vehicle approached the suspect crossing the roadway, it would be impossible for him to look inside the car and see anyone, let alone recognize the driver. The hypno-investigator used analogous situations that the subject had experienced so she could come to recognize that there was little or no chance of anyone looking into headlights of an oncoming vehicle without experiencing some momentary blindness. Finally, the subject agreed to the logic of the explanation and was able to enter a satisfactory state of hypnosis. She was able to give a good description of the suspect and his clothing.

Conclusion

There may be a variety of psychological reasons that a subject may subconsciously resist hypnosis while at the same time wish to sincerely help the police. In this case, the hypno-investigator recognized the problem created in the mind of the subject and was able to remove the personal fear, which allowed her to enter hypnosis and assist the investigators.

Case #3

Synopsis

The subject was a sixteen-year-old boy who was riding his bike in the vicinity of a junior high school when he heard a woman scream in the vicinity of a classroom. A few seconds later he observed a male adult walk rapidly from a classroom, cross the street, enter a vehicle, and drive off. Investigation revealed that a female teacher had been stabbed to death while she was cleaning her room after school hours. The sixteen-year-old boy was the only witness who saw the suspect and his vehicle.

Hypnosis Session

While under hypnosis, the subject was able to give a very good description of the suspect but was unable to provide any information regarding the license plate on the vehicle. The subject, who was a high school dropout and a poor student, was asked by the hypno-investigator to visualize a blackboard covered with a dark velvet cloth. Upon suggestion from the hypnotist, the velvet cloth would be removed and the license number of the vehicle would be written on the blackboard. The cloth was removed from the imaginary blackboard and . . . nothing! Realizing that he had made a poor technique selection for recalling the license number, the hypno-investigator switched over to a suggestion that gave the subject a high-powered set of binoculars with which to focus on the vehicle as it sped away. By merely focusing the powerful lenses, the subject was able to provide the letters and one of the numbers of the plate, but most importantly, he was able to give the color combination of the license which revealed an out of state plate. This information, when corroborated by follow-up investigation, proved to be a significant clue in the case.

Conclusion

During the posthypnotic discussion with the subject it was learned that he was not only a poor student, but was frequently at odds with his teachers. So when the operator suggested that the subject watch a blackboard, similar to a classroom situation, he immediately closed his mind to any further suggestion that had anything to do with an academic setting. The hypno-investigator sensed that the subject was uncomfortable in the suggested setting so he quickly changed to an appealing gadget-oriented situation which gave the subject a powerful lens which he could manipulate to bring the license plate into view.

This particular subject, although only sixteen, was on probation for battery, auto theft, and robbery. His past three years had been spent in several foster homes, and he was a frequent runaway. The boy was street tough and his resistance to a hypnotic induction by a police officer was apparent after a short time. In this case the hypno-investigator had to abandon his usual pleasant and soft-spoken role and was forced to adopt an authoritarian style that commanded the subject to relax. In the application of hypno-investigation, then, the authoritative approach definitely has value and can be utilized with excellent results.

Case #4

Synopsis

A woman, thirty-five years of age, answered a knock on her screen door one summer evening. A man inquired about the price of a used car parked in front of her house. Before the woman could answer, her husband, who had also heard the knock on the door and responded from another room, took over the conversation. The woman then turned away and walked back to the kitchen. She had looked at the man through the screen door for approximately five seconds. While in the kitchen she heard three rapid gunshots and she ran to the front door and saw her husband lying on the floor. He was dead. The suspect was gone. There was no other witness.

Hypnosis Session

Three weeks after the murder, detectives still had no leads in the case, and the wife was unable to provide more than a general description of the suspect. A hypnosis session was arranged along with a composite artist. The subject was very quiet and appeared withdrawn. This was not unexpected due to the recent violent death of her husband. The hypno-investigator sensed the pending grief of the subject and assured her that under hypnosis she would be asked to relive only the few seconds that she actually observed the man standing in front of the screen door. She was assured that it would not be necessary to recount the gunshots and the death scene. This seemed to please her, and she readily agreed to hypnosis.

This case is a good example of the importance of a discussion with the detectives prior to meeting with the subject. The investigation had revealed that the subject never observed the suspect after she left him in the company of her husband. Hence, there was no reason to have the subject recall any portion of the incident beyond her brief encounter with the suspect at the front door.

A composite sketch was drawn utilizing the procedure outlined above in "Using Hypnosis with a Composite Artist." Upon completion of the sketch the subject was very pleased with the results and told the detectives that she would definitely recognize the man if she ever saw him again.

Conclusion

The homicide detectives had copies of the sketch made the following day. A narcotics officer noticed the sketch on a table in the squad room. He immediately recognized the sketch as a narcotics suspect that he had arrested a week previously, and the suspect was still in custody. A photo lineup was conducted and the witness identified the suspect. A lineup was conducted at the jail, and the witness positively identified the suspect. The artist did such an excellent job of recreating the sketch from information supplied by the hypnotized subject that it appeared to be a lifelike photograph of the suspect.

Case #5

Synopsis

A thirty-year-old female was attacked and raped in her beachfront apartment in the early morning hours. As a result of the attack she was unable to go to work for the next two weeks. According to the investigating detective, the victim had a very good public relations job with an airline company that required her to meet people daily and converse with them. After the attack the victim developed a speech impediment and stuttered constantly. Before the assault she was very articulate and had no speech impediment at all. The hypno-investigator, an artist, and the primary detective went to her apartment for the hypnosis session.

Hypnosis Session

The subject sat on a couch in her living room, and the hypno-investigator sat on her right. As the preinduction rapport session progressed the subject began to cry and almost became hysterical and sobbed loudly. The hypnotist suggested that a session could be conducted at a later date, but the subject almost as quickly regained control of herself. She then informed everyone present that this was the first time since the rape that she had permitted herself to cry. She felt tremendous psychological release that enabled her to enter hypnosis relatively easy. Due to the trauma that she had experienced, the operator allowed the subject to select a TV news reporter who she liked and assume a role similar to her and report the incident as it occurred. The subject was encouraged to omit the sexual assault portion of the story and only report on the description of the suspect and what he said to her. The subject was admonished to be as factual and objective as she could while reporting the assault.

During the induction, the subject was given an arm levitation suggestion. The arm rose steadily higher and higher and then suddenly stopped as the subject grimaced. The operator then returned the arm to her lap.

During the entire hypnosis session, the time spent working with the composite artist and the final interview with the operator, the subject never stuttered or stammered. She was calm and thorough and was very satisfied with the artist's completed sketch.

Conclusion

Two events occurred during this hypnosis session that the operator was unprepared for and had not previously experienced. First, the subject was most articulate while under hypnosis, and the speech impediment was not present during the session. However, upon return to the conscious state the subject began to stutter once again. The author had since conducted sessions with subjects who were paralyzed as the result of physical attacks and, while under hypnosis, would raise their paralyzed arms over their heads in a defensive motion while describing the brutal assaults on them by the assailants. Also, a subject who had a noticeable tic or twitch in his mouth when he spoke was normal and unimpaired by any such tic while under hypnosis. Upon coming out of hypnosis the tic returned as a constant reaction. Hypno-investigators should not be surprised when these seemingly minor miracles occur and should be aware that there are medical explanations for these experiences, but it is not within the area of expertise of a police-trained hypnotist to offer any opinion as to why these things occur. Rather, a hypno-investigator should consult with a local psychiatrist or psychologist for an explanation.

A second point of interest that aroused the curiosity of the operator was the pain caused by the arm levitation. Unknown to the operator, the subject's assailant had wrenched her shoulder during the struggle, and the entire area was still very tender and sore. The subject could raise her arm only to a level where it then became uncomfortable for her to proceed any further. It is always advisable during the preinduction to inquire of the subject, and this is particularly true of rape victims, if they sustained any physical injuries as a result of the attack. The hypno-investigator could then design his induction to avoid any physical discomfort to his subject.

Case #6

Synopsis

A female witness in her middle fifties observed what investigating officers believed to be the first account of a long sought rapist without his disguise. The suspect was being sought for over 100 rapes of women in their homes while their husbands were present. The M.O. of the rapist was to prowl the location while the victims were away. Upon their return he would enter the building wearing a ski mask, gloves, and armed with a large knife. He would capture the male, bind and gag him, and threaten to kill the woman if he made any attempt to free himself. The suspect would then take the woman into a hallway and rape her.

On the particular evening in question the witness was preparing for bed in her second story bedroom. Her husband was already asleep in the same room. The witness looked out of a small rectangular window and saw a man climb a fence which led into their backyard. Lighting of the area was supplied by a street lamp some 50 feet away. The witness observed the suspect take out a ski mask, pull it over his head and advance towards the house. The witness then opened a window and called out to the man who was by now fully concealed in the dark shadows. Upon hearing the voice of the woman the suspect hastily retreated over the fence and disappeared.

Hypnosis Session

The subject received a great deal of attention from the local police regarding the incident. She was told that she was probably the only witness who had ever seen the rape suspect without his mask. The hypno-investigator, along with a composite artist and three detectives, went to the home of the subject. The subject took the hypno-investigator to the location where she first observed the suspect. In this case the on-site location was important because it gave the hypno-investigator the opportunity to look out the window and caused him to consider several important questions.

While working with the artist, the hypnotized subject appeared very hesitant to commit herself to any specifics about the facial features of the suspect. This made it very difficult for the artist to compose a sketch of any significance and the subject seemed only too willing to let the artist draw what he thought the suspect might resemble. The subject had taken her eyeglasses off before the hypnosis session and put them on immediately afterward. The operator commented on this and the subject informed him that she had poor eyesight and had to wear her glasses full time.

Conclusion

This case clearly illustrates the benefit of training experienced detectives to be hypno-investigators as opposed to using the talents of exclusively medical and psychological professionals. When the subject stated that she always wore her eyeglasses the obvious question was asked of whether or not she had her glasses on that night she observed the suspect? The answer was no. When the hypno-investigator looked out of the bedroom window, he was able to determine that the subject would need exceptionally good eyesight to have seen what she reported. The fact that she did not have a good position as a vantage point and was not wearing her glasses made her description suspect. It was his opinion that the subject did not see the face of the suspect, and, due to limitations of her eyesight, she merely gave a general physical description of what she thought "the suspect should have looked like." This is a dangerous situation and good basic police work would have determined the limitations of the witness and avoided this embarrassing predicament.

Case #7

Synopsis

A well-known drug dealer and his girl friend were in bed during the early morning hours. The drug dealer had taken extensive means to install security systems around his apartment to avoid intruders. As the victim and his girl friend lay in bed, two men suddenly burst into the bedroom, one of them carrying a sawed-off shotgun. The victim was told not to move, but he reached for the nightstand where he kept a handgun. A single blast from the shotgun struck the victim in the head killing him instantly. The girl friend, fearing that she would be killed next, covered her face with a pillow and did not look at the suspects again. She was unable to describe the suspects due to the darkness of the room and the fact that she covered her head.

Another witness, located by detectives, had been walking across the street from the apartment when he observed a person lying on a second story ledge near an open window leading to the victim's apartment. The time was early in the morning and the dawn was just breaking. The witness watched the man on the ledge and saw him stand up and walk to an open window where he then observed a second suspect inside the apartment. The witness continued to observe both suspects although he walked approximately one-half block to a bus stop where he sat down. When first interviewed, the witness stated that it was too dark to identify either suspect and could only describe them as two black men. The witness agreed to hypnosis in an effort to enhance his recall about what he had observed.

Hypnosis Session

Although the subject agreed to hyp-

nosis he was very apprehensive and displayed an unusual amount of anxiety about being hypnotized. During the rapport session the hypno-investigator discovered the reason for the subject's anxiety. First, the subject was afraid that the operator was going to use drugs on him and, secondly, he was afraid that he would reveal past secrets about his personal life. Fortunately the hypno-investigator was able to dispel these common misconceptions about hypnosis and thereby gain the confidence of the subject.

While under hypnosis the subject was able to revisualize the entire incident. The subject gave a detailed description of both suspects including facial hair and described a previously unknown third suspect who was stationed as a lookout for the murder. The description given by the subject closely matched two former drug associates of the victim. The following day the detectives prepared two photo lineups containing photos of the two associates. The subject positively identified both suspects and arrest warrants were issued for the two men.

Conclusion

This case illustrates the importance of spending time during the rapport session to counter the myths that uninformed people still harbor. Although the experienced hypnotist has heard of all these myths on prior occasions he must never underestimate the influence of such tales on the prospective subject. A good hypno-investigator must be able to sense the psychological resistances which some subjects may offer subconsciously. Although police hypnotists are not trained as hypnotherapists or psychologists, they should be able to recognize anxiety in their subjects, inquire as to the reason, and attempt to put the subject at ease and establish personal confidence.

TESTIFYING IN COURT

Very few cases involving the use of hypnosis during the investigation will involve any testimony by the hypno-investigator. This author has used hypnosis in dozens of cases that have culminated in criminal trials, yet only two cases required testimony on behalf of the hypnotist. The necessity of qualifying the hypno-investigator as an expert and soliciting his testimony seems directly related to the information obtained while the subject was under hypnosis. If a defendant in a murder case was identified directly as the result of investigative hypnosis, the operator could anticipate court testimony if the case proceeded that far. In practical application, a hypno-investigator will not be called to testify in many cases. It is that rare instance, however, that may determine the fate of investigative hypnosis based upon the expert testimony of the hypnotist.

Total documentation of the hypnosis session is of paramount importance. Once a criminal case proceeds to the courtroom and the hypno-investigator is subpoenaed, it is too late to go back and document evidence. There can hardly be enough emphasis on preparation for a hypnosis session, i.e. videotaping, audio recording, notetaking, having it witnessed, postsession critique report, and any other procedure that will help lend credibility to the hypnosis process.

Upon receiving notice to appear in court, it is incumbent upon the hypno-investigator to contact the prosecuting attorney handling the case to prepare for court presentation. Because of the uniqueness involved in soliciting hypnotic testimony and the rareness of such court cases, most prosecuting attorneys have had no prior courtroom experience in this specialty. Therefore, the hypno-investigator must prepare his prosecutor and brief him on his qualifications as an expert witness. Every hypno-investigator who testifies in court must be prepared to be taken on voir dire examination, which is the preliminary examination by the court of one presented as a witness or juror, where his competency, interest, or expertise may be questioned by the opposition.

Establishing a Foundation on Voir Dire

To establish his competency as a qualified expert in the field of forensic hypnosis, a witness should be prepared to answer the following questions:

- "How long have you been using hypnosis in criminal investigation?"
- "How many persons have you hypnotized?"
- "How many hypnosis sessions have you participated in for the purpose of enhancing recall?"
- "What training have you received in the area of investigative hypnosis?"

The hypno-investigator should have a well rehearsed list of his qualifications as an investigator and as a hypnotist, which should include the following:

1. His time as a police officer and his time in an investigative assignment, special assignments, etc.

2. His educational background, including the number of hours expended in hypnosis training.

3. The names of instructors and their blue ribbon qualifications and degrees.

4. Follow-up training such as seminars and workshops. These will demonstrate the interest and dedication of the hypno-investigator in the pursuit of excellence.

5. Books and articles read on hypnosis and forensic hypnosis.

6. The number of hypnosis sessions observed, conducted, or participated in.

7. Memberships or offices held in professional organizations. These will give status to his background.

8. Independent research, articles published, past expert witness qualifications.

Ideally, all this information should be listed in a professionally typed expert witness vita or resumé.

It may be impressive if the prosecuting attorney select a few technical glossary terms and ask the witness to explain their meaning in terms of hypnosis application. This will demonstrate to the jury that the witness is in fact knowledgeable in the field.

Opposing counsel may ask such questions as "Doesn't a person have to be a doctor before he can practice hypnosis? Isn't it possible to suggest answers to hypnotized witnesses? Can you hypnotize people against their will? Is it possible to lie under hypnosis? Isn't it true that people can be forced to do things against their will under hypnosis?"

Court Presentation and Cross-Examination

After a hypno-investigator completes his testimony for the prosecution, he may reasonably expect to be thoroughly cross-examined by the defense. To protect himself as well as adequately prepare for court, the hypnotist should review and examine any audio and video tapes before he appears in court. The main thrust of any objection by the defense will be in the area of suggestion by the hypnotist.

Once a witness has been qualified as an expert, the emphasis will shift from a personal attack of his background to an endeavor to impeach his testimony by showing that information obtained was by hypnotic suggestion and not voluntarily rendered by the subject. For this reason, the hypno-investigator should intentionally avoid the term *suggestion* when describing the hypnosis session. The defense attorney will ask the hypno-investigator if he previously knew the subject, how did he know he

was hypnotized, how was the session conducted, who was present, can the tapes be identified, had anybody been arrested at the time of the hypnosis session and, if so, was the hypnotist aware of the arrest? If the answer was yes, then was a defense attorney present to cross-examine the subject and confront the witness? All of these questions and others will be part of the cross-examination so it is absolutely necessary for the hypno-investigator to do his homework before he goes to court.

As an expert witness, the hypno-investigator is subjected to a broader scope of cross-examination. By claiming to be an expert, the witness invites investigation into his field of expertise. Probably the best advice that can be given to a hypno-investigator on his court presentation is to not go beyond his field of expertise. Stay within that area of knowledge and experience that is familiar and do not attempt to impress the court by mentioning books that have not been read, experiments that have not been completed, written papers that were never actually published, and so on. Remember, everything that is said during the voir dire examination is subject to challenge by the defense attorney, so accuracy is a must. When asked, however, the expert witness may express his opinions. For example, when asked if hypnosis is a reliable process for memory enhancement, the witness should respond that it is.

Defense counsel will usually ask whether the information obtained by the hypno-investigator from the subject was true or false. There is no reliable way the hypnotist would be able to determine the accuracy of information he received until it was corroborated by the primary investigator. This is the answer that would best serve a question of that nature.

Frequently, defense attorneys fancy themselves as court jesters and seek to entertain the court at the cost of embarrassing the hypnotist. They will ask questions such as, "Can you make a witness fantasize that he is a very famous person in history, or that he is an animal?" They may attempt to show a correlation between stage hypnosis and investigative hypnosis in an effort to discredit the operator. They will ask the hypno-investigator if he believes that only a medical doctor or a psychologist should engage in the use of hypnosis. In answering all such questions, the hypno-investigator should be firm and testify only to his own personal knowledge. He should at all times remain professional and stay within the confined area of investigative hypnosis and never volunteer collateral information that may be in the field of medicine.

Chapter 6

CASE LAW ANALYSIS OF HYPNOTICALLY-RELATED EVIDENCE

DANIEL L. FALCON, J.D.

INTRODUCTION

THE PURPOSE of this section is to examine the treatment that courts of law have accorded hypnotically-related evidence. An examination of the earliest cases reveals that hypnosis was not readily accepted in the courtroom setting, but with advances in the state of the art, courts have been more willing to admit evidence about the hypnotic procedures, the effects of hypnosis on the subject and his testimony, and about the results of hypnosis.

It will be helpful to understand a few basic legal principles before proceeding. States are free to establish their own judicial systems, therefore court structures vary from state to state. There are generally a large number of locally based courts which handle small civil claims and/or minor criminal cases. Above these courts are usually some type of trial courts that handle the more serious criminal and civil cases. At the top of the system, there is usually a single state supreme court that hears both criminal and civil appeals.

A federal court system was established for disputes that arise between different states or residents of different states, or for disputes involving federal constitutional questions. In the federal system, the nation has been divided geographically into about ninety districts. Within each district, there is at least one district court, which is basically a trial court. Above the trial courts are the United States courts of appeals. Above these courts is The Supreme Court of the United States. Every court has some jurisdictional restrictions, which may include the amount of money involved in the dispute, the place where the action arose, or where the parties to the action reside. Therefore, a land dispute between two people who reside in the state of Montana may be properly taken before a district court within the state of Montana where the property exists, whereas a district court in Texas would not have jurisdiction to hear the issue between these two parties.

When a decision is rendered by a local court, there is often a procedure to appeal that decision to a higher court. Some decisions may be appealed through the court system a number of times. Once appealed to the highest state court, some decisions may then be appealed through the federal system, up to the United States Supreme Court. This usually happens if some federal constitutional question is involved. Once a decision is appealed to the appropriate higher court, that higher court generally will either affirm the decision of the lower court or reverse that decision.

Once one of the higher courts has made a decision on an issue, the Doctrine of Stare Decisis becomes important. This is a policy of courts to abide by precedent. Once the legal point has been decided, courts generally try to adhere to that holding in other cases with a similar factual basis. The main reason behind the Doctrine of Stare Decisis is the recognized need for uniformity in the application of laws.

Decisions by higher courts have a binding affect on all lower courts whose rulings the higher courts review. The courts of one state are not reviewed or appealed to the courts of another state. Naturally, lower courts will pay more attention to any higher court that has review power over it, whereas, if the higher court is from another jurisdiction and has no review power, then decisions from that higher court are not binding on the lower court. For example, in Montana, a city court decision is appealable to a state district court. That decision may be appealable to the state supreme court. This decision may then be appealed through the federal system. A ruling made by a state court in Nebraska is not binding on the city court in Montana. Therefore, as you examine the case law concerning hypnosis across the nation, remember that what may be admissible in one state, may not be admissible in another state.

Another point that must be remembered is that judges in most states have a great deal of discretion concerning the admissibility of evidence. Unless a judge has abused his discretion, a decision to allow or deny admission of evidence will not be reversed on appeal.

The following section is a chronological history of the case law concerning hypnotically-related evidence from state and federal courts. All cases cited are appellate decisions and can, at the least, be used as persuasive authority. A conscious effort has been made to avoid comments or criticisms of the rulings made concerning hypnotically-related evidence. This will allow the reader to form his own opinions as to the ramifications concerning the use of hypnosis in criminal and civil cases. A chronological sequence is used for this same reason, and in addition, will allow the reader to trace the changes in judicial acceptance and the reasons behind these changes.

After the examination of the case law, some special topics for safeguarding the admissibility of hypnotically-influenced testimony will be covered along with some other areas of concern for those who choose to use hypnosis as an aid in gathering evidence for presentation in the courtroom. In this section, references will be made to cases with a minimal amount of persuasive authority, such as trial court decisions, Canadian case law, and military court-martial cases. Some of the areas are addressed in other sections of this book, but this section is intended to add substance from a judicial perspective.

THE CASE LAW

The earliest reported case dealing with hypnosis is *People v. Worthington*.[1] This 1894 California case involved a defendant who was a young married woman. She developed an illicit relationship with a Mr. Baddeley and left her husband. In about ten days, Mr. Baddeley deserted her and she returned to her husband. Approximately five months later, the defendant's husband saw Mr. Baddeley in the street in front of their home. The husband gave the defendant a pistol and told her to protect herself and that if Mr. Baddeley

was to interfere with her, she was to kill him. That evening the defendant saw Mr. Baddeley on a wharf, she walked up to him and fired four shots, which caused his death. The defense was insanity and hypnosis. At trial, evidence concerning the effects of hypnosis was refused admission. The appellate court sustained this ruling with the following language: "The court ruled out the evidence and, I think, rightly. There was no evidence which tended to show that the defendant was subject to the disease, if it be such. Merely showing that she was told to kill the deceased and that she did it does not prove hypnotism, or, at least, does not tend to establish a defense to a charge of murder."[2]

In the 1897 case of *People v. Ebanks*,[3] the Supreme Court of Califonia ruled that testimony of an alleged hypnotist was properly excluded. The defendant, Joseph Ebanks, was convicted of first degree murder. The majority of the evidence against Ebanks was circumstantial. The defendant offered to qualify a Mr. Stevens as an expert hypnotist. Mr. Stevens's testimony would have been to the effect that he had hypnotized the defendant and that while hypnotized, he had made statements to Stevens concerning the incident. Mr. Stevens was willing to testify from this evidence that the defendant was not guilty and that he had denied his guilt while under hypnosis. The appellate court quoted the following language from the trial court: "The law of the United States does not recognize hypnotism. It would be an illegal defense and I can not admit it."[4]

The State of Indiana prosecuted George Parks for practicing medicine without a license in 1902.[5] In this case, Parks had advertised himself as a magnetic healer and styled himself as a "professor." He had not graduated from any medical school, and he had no license. He admitted practicing magnetic healing for several years when a patient came to him to be treated for a lame ankle. He diagnosed the case as rheumatism and gave treatment consisting of rubbing the afflicted parts. His remuneration was in the amount of one dollar. The court quoted extensively from J. G. McKendrick's article on "Animal Magnetism":

It is evident that animal magnetism or hypnotism is a peculiar physiological condition excited by perverted action of certain parts of the cerebral nervous organs, and that it is not caused by any occult force emanating from the operator. . . . It is also clear that the perverted condition of the nervous apparatus in hypnotism is of a serious character, and therefore that these experiments should not be performed by ignorant empirics for the sake of gain, or with the view of causing amusement. . . . Still, in the hands of skillful men, there is no reason why the proper employment of a method influencing the nervous system so powerfully as hypnotism should not be the means of relieving pain or of remedying disease.[6]

State v. Exum,[7] a 1905 North Carolina case, involved William Exum's appeal of his conviction for the murder of Guy Walston. There were three witnesses to the murder, one being the defendant's wife. Mrs. Exum testified during the trial. The state asked Mrs. Exum at trial whether she had ever been hypnotized by her husband. Mrs. Exum indicated she had been hypnotized three times. The court ruled as follows:

The prisoner testified to the effect that he had hypnotized his wife on three separate occasions, and as explained by him, it tended to show that he had influence over her to a greater extent than usually arise from the relationship between them. If this be correct, the evidence is competent as affecting her credibility, and if not, then we are unable to perceive how the prisoner's case was prejudiced by its admission.[8]

In *State v. Donovan*,[9] a 1905 Iowa Supreme Court case, the defendant, a married man, was charged with using flattery, lovemaking, and hypnosis to obtain control over an unmarried school teacher. The defendant's objection was to the qualifications of the two witnesses who were allowed to testify as experts concerning hypnosis. One was a superintendent of a mental hospital who had not made an extensive study of the subject, but who knew to a certain extent what modern authorities said on the subject. He had never practiced hypnotism, but had witnessed experiments by others. The second witness had studied hypnotism and had practiced its use, but had never attained any formal training in it. The witnesses testified that surgical operations may be performed on patients in a hypnotic state and that no pain would be felt. The court ruled that expert opinions may be based upon experience and it is in the discretion of the trial judge whether such evidence is to be admitted. In this case the court found that there was no evidence that the victim was under a "hypnotic spell" at the time the defendant first had intercourse with her. The court made one factual finding which, if only for purpose of historical significance, bears recognition. "Women are not all alike, and what might prove irresistible to one might arouse contempt only in another."[10]

In the 1930 case of *Louis v. State*,[11] the defendant was charged and convicted of the crime of robbery. The victim, Rosie Toney, testified that she had never met the defendant before and that he had hypnotized her. She also testified that she took her bank books from her home, traveled to the bank and entered unaccompanied by the defendant. She then withdrew her money, returned to the defendant, and handed her money over to him. The appellate court reversed and remanded the case on the grounds that the state had not proven an element of the offense of robbery, that being fear. The testimony showed that Toney was not scared or frightened at the time she parted with her money and, resorting to standard authorities, the court could not determine that fear was an element of hypnosis.

For damages suffered by reason of the seduction of his daughter, David Austin brought an action against Frank Barker in 1904.[12] The defendant had visited the daughter in her father's home on numerous occasions. The visits took place in a room that was separated by an ordinary door from another room in which the father and mother were usually present. Several weeks after the daughter gave birth, she was visited by an attorney who hypnotized her. At that time she remembered being hypnotized by the defendant during his visits. She also remembered writing down the dates of his visits in her diary which she was then able to produce. The appellate court ruled that for the plaintiff to rely on such a science or theory that is not generally known or understood, he is required to give some competent evidence tending to sustain the probabilities or at least the possibilities of what he had claimed.[13] The court rejected the evidence of the plaintiff that she had been hypnotized, reversed the verdict for the plaintiff, and granted the defendant a new trial.

In 1951, August Pusch was convicted of first degree murder for giving his former wife poison.[14] Doctor Burgess, who was formally trained in hypnosis and had practiced this profession for a number of years, had placed the defendant in a hypnotic trance and had asked him questions concerning the offense charged. The state had refused to attend the hypnotic examination by Doctor Burgess, even though they were provided with the opportunity. The questions and answers during the examination were recorded by wire recorder. These recordings, along with the testimony of Doctor Burgess, were offered for the purpose of ascertaining whether the defendant was telling the truth when he said under hypnosis that he was innocent of killing his wife. The defendant also contended that Doctor Burgess was able to establish the truthfulness of the answers given by the defendant in the hypnotic state due to his experience in hypnosis. The court ruled that there was no prior case authority for the admissibility of this type of evidence, and therefore the evidence was properly rejected. The court recognized that hypnosis may be used very effectively for investigation purposes, but like the polygraph test, it was not usable as evidence in court.

The chief issue raised by the defendant in the case of *People v. Leyra,*[15] was that his confessions were the result of the hypnotic influence of a physician called into the case by the district attorney. *Leyra* was a 1951 court of appeals case from the state of New York, in which the defendant was convicted of murdering his parents. After many long hours of questioning, the defendant was introduced to a physician who was a specialist in psychiatry and psychology. Although the physician unequivocally denied he had hypnotized the defendant, there was testimony from other psychiatrists that the various gestures the physician had used could be nothing but hypnotism. The defendant had confessed to the physician, to police officers, to his business partner, and then to state prosecutors. The highest state court reversed the conviction on the grounds that the first confession was obtained by coercion. At a second trial, only confessions obtained after the first confession were used. The defendant was convicted a second time. On a Writ of Certiorari, the United States Supreme Court found evidence from the record where the physician had the defendant open and close his eyes and as time went on the petitioner began to accept suggestions. The Supreme Court ruled as follows: "We hold that use of confessions extracted in such a manner from a lone defendant unprotected by counsel is not consistent with due process of law as required by our constitution."[16]

In 1959, an attorney, Harold D. Cornell, petitioned the Supreme Court of California by Writ of Mandamus to allow him to have his client examined by a hypnotist.[17] His client, Paul Le Claire Conrey, was in jail awaiting trial for murder. Cornell alleged that his client could not remember the events on the day in question because of intoxication or shock, and that he desired to have a skilled and experienced hypnotist attempt to induce memory recall.

The client had agreed to the procedure but the sheriff refused to allow it. The California Supreme Court in banc, i.e. the whole court, ruled that the client's constitutional right to counsel included the right of the client to be examined by an expert hypnotist.[18]

The defendant's sole defense, in *People v. Marsh,*[19] to a charge of escape was that his act was not voluntary because it was caused by a hypnotic suggestion given to him by a fellow inmate. In this 1959 California case, a psychiatrist, who was familiar with the principles of hypnosis and experienced in its use, testified at trial that a subject could be ordered to do simple acts and might not remember them, but that no one could be forced under hypnosis to perform an act which is contrary to his basic nature. The psychiatrist also testified that a hypnotist must have a forceful personality and that the best subjects are suggestible, weak, compliant, and peaceful. The psychiatrist also testified that the defendant in her opinion did not possess the qualities of an ideal subject. The court ruled that this testimony, as to the effects of hypnosis, was correctly admitted. The court also noted as follows: "The effects of hypnosis are not occurrances of such common knowledge and experience that men of ordinary education can form a conclusion concerning them as capably as an expert witness."[20]

The court went on to say "It does not appear that the court was in error in refusing to permit the defense to conduct a demonstration of hypnosis in the courtroom. The admission of such evidence is a matter for the discretion of the trial court. No abuse of discretion here appears."[21]

The defendant in *People v. Busch,*[22] was convicted of first degree murder, two counts of second degree murder, and assault with the intent to commit murder. His appeal, in 1961, was denied. The two issues raised on appeal involved the use of hypothetical questions asked of an expert and the refusal of proffered testimony of a physician. The physician had examined the defendant on thirteen separate occasions concerning his mental condition at the time of the killing. He used hypnosis as an analytical tool. His testimony was objected to on the grounds that hypnosis is not a sufficiently scientific means of exploring the state of mind and that the witness was not qualified in this field. The doctor was not a psychiatrist, and he began to specialize in hypnosis less than a year prior to this appearance as a witness in this case. He had never previously been qualified as an expert witness in a criminal case on the subject of a defendant's frame of mind, and he conceded he knew of no other experts who could by hypnosis determine a subject's state of mind at a certain time. The physician was allowed to testify as a medical doctor on the subject of the defendant's mental condition, but was not allowed to give an opinion based on any information obtained during hypnosis. The trial judge denied the admission of this evidence based on an improper foundation as to the reliability of hypnosis as an analytical tool and as to the qualifications of this particular witness. The appellate court ruled that he had not abused his discretion.

In 1962, Doctor Samuel H. Sheppard filed a Writ of Mandamus to compel the Chief of the Division of Corrections to permit him to subject himself to hypnosis or polygraph tests to determine his innocence. The defendant alleged he suffered from amnesia that was the result of injuries he sustained on the night of his wife's murder. The defendant was in the penitentiary after his conviction, at which time his attorney, F. Lee Bailey, argued that Sheppard's constitutional right to counsel included assistance by experts in exploring his mind. The court ruled as follows:

The right to counsel, so far as the constitutional mandate is concerned, extends only to the rights of representation by an attorney, it does not include the multitude of experts often employed in the preparation of criminal cases both by the state and by the accused. . . . The respondent in the instant case has control over the penal institution in this state. . . . As a part of the regulation thereof, it is within his discretion as to who shall have access to the prisoners. . . . [23]

Perhaps the most widely cited case involving the use of hypnosis has been *People v. Modesto.*[24] In this 1963 California case, the defendant was convicted of entering the home of Mr. and Mrs. Mack and killing their two daughters with a hammer. A psychiatrist had examined the defendant in a normal state and while he was in a hypnotic trance. The defendant had also been given neurological and electroencephalogram tests that were inconclusive. The defendant appealed the court's refusal to allow the psychiatrist to explain the use of hypnosis as an analytical tool, and the court's exclusion of the tape recording of the statements made by the defendant while under hypnosis. The psychiatrist at trial was allowed to testify as to the defendant's intent at the time he struck the girls, and she based her opinion on what the defendant told her during hypnosis and upon her psychiatric evaluation of him. She was allowed to use statements the defendant made while under hypnosis as part of the basis of her opinion, but not allowed to explain what those statements were. The court made the following rulings:

It was error, however, to exclude Doctor Zonnis' proffered explanation of hypnotic techniques as they are used in a psychiatric examination as a basis of her expert opinion. The evidence was clearly admissible for that purpose. (*People v. Brown*, 49 Cal. 2d 577, 585, 320 P.2d 5.) Although the tape recording of the defendant's statements while under hypnosis might properly have been excluded in the exercise of the trial court's discretion to weigh its probative value as part of the basis of the expert's opinion against the risk that the jury might improperly consider it as independent proof of the facts recited therein, the record shows that the trial court did not exercise this discretion, but erroneously concluded that *People v. Busch,* 56 Cal. 2d 868, 878, 16 Cal. Rptr. 898, 366 P.2d 314, required the exclusion of the evidence.[25]

The court went on to point out that in the Busch case the witness had not been qualified as an expert and that there was no showing that hypnosis was a reliable analytical tool. However, in the present case the defense had offered to prove that psychiatrists now have accepted and used hypnosis as an analytical tool in their profession. The appellate court ruled that the trial court should have exercised its discretion as to the admission of the recorded sessions. This evidence was not automatically excludable.

In 1965, the Oregon Supreme Court ruled that statements made by the defendant, which were tape recorded while under hypnosis, were self-serving and were not admissible to prove the truth of the matter asserted.[26] The defendant had been convicted of first degree murder of his wife. He had been treated by hypnosis to overcome an amnesic condition and the doctor felt that he had been successful in restoring the defendant's memory. Although the court permitted the doctor to testify as to what the defendant told him prior to the treatments on the basis that this was history that the doctor used as part of his diagnosis in treatment, the court excluded statements made by the defendant while under hypnosis. The tape recording of the defendant's statements were also denied admission into evidence. The defendant argued that the statements were permissible as a basis of the doctor's diagnosis, that the doctor's testimony as to what the defendant said and his manner in saying it while under hypnosis were also a basis for his

conclusion, and that the defendant was truly amnesic. The court ruled as follows:

The courts of both California and Washington have had occasion to pass on a similar question. Both have decided that where statements relied on by a physician as a basis for a diagnosis of mental condition are such that the jury would be confused as to whether it could consider the statement as independent proof of the facts recited, the witness may give the opinion but the statements of the patient may not be related to the jury. They held that it was a matter of discretion with the trial judge as to whether the danger of confusion on other important collateral issues outweighed the probative value of the evidence as part of the basis of the expert's opinion.[27]

The court also ruled that if the jury could get confused on other principle issues, the expert witness need not be allowed to give the entire basis for his opinion.[28]

An important case involving the use of hypnosis to refresh a witness's memory came out of the Court of Special Appeals of Maryland in 1968.[29] The defendant, James Harding, was in an automobile with two other people when he shot Mildred Coley and left her for dead beside the road. The victim was found the next day in a state of shock, approximately 2 to 3 miles from the spot where she had been shot. Upon initial questioning she told a state trooper that she had been raped and shot. At the hospital, while she was still in a state of shock, she identified, for an officer, a picture of Robert Lee Sanders as her attacker. Sanders was one of the passengers in the vehicle. Approximately a day later in an intensive care unit, the victim told officers that she remembered certain parts of what happened to her. She knew who had shot her and gave a complete description of the automobile.

A few weeks later, the victim was placed under hypnosis by a clinical psychologist and without prompting was able to recall the events that occurred after she was shot. The victim testified that she was not told what happened to her, but that while asleep it all came back to her and she was able to identify Harding as the person who shot her. Harding's first objection was that the psychologist had no formal training from any school of hypnotism and that he was not qualified to give the opinion rendered at trial. There was evidence that the psychologist was trained in hypnosis as a form of treatment. It was also shown that hypnosis is used as an analytical tool by psychologists and the medical profession, both as a form of therapy and as a means of assisting patients to recover lost memory. This psychologist had used hypnosis for the past four years under similar circumstances. Harding's first objection was denied. The defendant's second objection, that the victim had stated different stories and had acquired her present knowledge after being hypnotized was also overruled. The court ruled that this was a question of weight of the evidence, which the trier of fact must decide.

The psychologist had been allowed to testify in great detail as to the procedure he used during the hypnotic sessions. The doctor related that the witness was told to awaken and that she would recount the same things that she recounted under the state of reduced consciousness. When she was awakened she was able to recount what she remembered. The doctor went on to say that he did not make any suggestions during his sessions and did not allow a policeman to participate in anyway. He was also allowed to testify that in his opinion the information that resulted was reliable. The doctor's opinion was that some of the things the witness related could only be told by someone who was there. No witness was allowed to testify as to what they heard the witness say, either during or after hypnosis, and the trial judge gave the following precautionary instruction to the jury:

You have heard, during this trial, that portions of the testimony of the prosecution's witness, Mrs. Coley, was recalled by her as a result of her being placed under hypnosis. The phenomenon commonly known as hypnosis has been explained to you during this trial. I advise you to weight this testimony carefully. Do not place any greater weight on this portion of Mrs. Coley's testimony than on any other testimony that you have heard during this trial. Remember, you are the judges of the weight and the believability of all the evidence in this case.[30]

The court noted that the witness could recall by herself on the stand everything that she remembered by hypnosis and, in addition, the testimony of the operator verified that there were no improper suggestions made during the session. In addition, the trained and experienced psychologist gave his opinion that the witness's recollections were accurate. The court noted that modern medical science has now recognized the ability of hypnosis to restore the memory lost by painful events, even though some authorities feel that a person can fabricate facts while under hypnosis.

In the 1968 case of *People v. Hiser,*[31] the California Court of Appeals sustained the trial court's denial of proffered evidence of a psychiatrist's taped hypnotic interview of the defendant. The defendant had been subjected to sodium pentothal during the hypnotic interviews. The tapes of these interviews were offered to lay a foundation for the psychiatrist's opinion relating to the mental state of the defendant. The doctor was not prohibited from testifying as to his reasons for his opinion, but was prohibited from placing the tapes into evidence. The trial court's ruling was held to be a proper exercise of its discretion.

In *United States v. Miller,*[32] the defendant was granted a new trial on the grounds that it had not been disclosed to the defendant that hypnosis had been used on the government's principal witness prior to trial. One of the main concerns of the court was that the attorney on behalf of the state, who had examined the witness during the trial, was the operator who had administered hypnosis to the witness. The court examined the details of how the witness was put under hypnosis, the number of times the witness was hypnotized, and the possibility of suggestions during the session. The defendant put on three psychiatrists who were experts in hypnosis. They testified that the repetition used by the hypnotic operator had tended to imprint on the mind of the witness the answers that were desired. It was their opinion that after hypnosis the witness would always identify the defendant as the perpetrator of the events and would be immune from suggestions of the defense that he had picked the wrong man. The court held as follows:

Still, as the record stands, the hypnosis had arguably placed at least some obstacle in the way of one of the most valuable protections accorded Miller by the Sixth Amendment — the possibility that the sanctity of the oath and effective cross-examination might lead Caron to recant his identification or at least to admit doubt.[33]

In 1969, an appellate court in Illinois, in the case of *People v. Harper*,[34] was faced with the question of the admissibility of statements made while under the influence of "truth serum." Although the court was not faced with the admissibility of hypnotically-related evidence, the court expressed, in dictum, its view on the subject.

We see no reason to equate an examination under hypnosis and examination while under the influence of a drug having the effect of a so-called "truth serum" except to note that the scientific reliability of neither is sufficient to justify the use of test results of either in the serious business of criminal prosecution.[35]

Greenfield v. Virginia[36] was a 1974 case out of the Supreme Court of Virginia in which a psychiatrist was not allowed to enter into evidence that which he learned from the defendant while he was under hypnosis. The defendant was convicted of murdering Mary Frances by stabbing her with his pocket knife. The defendant claimed to have been using heroin and hallucinogenic drugs on the day of the murder. On appeal, the trial judge's ruling was upheld on the grounds that he had weighted the probative value of the defendant's statements under hypnosis as part of the expert's opinion against the risk that the jury would consider it as independent evidence of the facts.[37] The defendant also claimed error in that the trial court directed that he not undergo hypnosis during a recess of the trial. The court had been informed that the defendant had been put under hypnosis once during the recess without success in improving the defendant's memory. The court then ordered that the defendant not try it again. This ruling was also upheld on appeal.

In *Creamer v. State*,[38] a 1974 case, the defendant sought through discovery to get statements made by the prosecution's witness while in hypnosis. Debra Ann Kidd was the state's witness and she had been subjected to hypnotic sessions by Doctor Edward Hall, a psychologist. The State Supreme Court ruled that the hypnotic sessions did not taint Kidd's testimony. She had related to the Cobb County authorities the details and facts of the crime prior to meeting with Doctor Hall. Both Debra Kidd and Doctor Hall were extensively and thoroughly cross-examined. The purpose of hypnosis and the fact that Kidd had been subjected to it was fully explained to the jury. The court further ruled that since the statements that Kidd made during the hypnotic sessions were inadmissible, the defendant was not entitled to have them and this was not a denial under due process of the law or effective assistance of counsel.

The co-defendant of Creamer was George Herman Emmett, who was also convicted in 1974 of the murders of Mr. and Mrs. Matthew.[39] This defendant's cross-examination of Kidd was restricted and the State Supreme Court upheld the trial court's refusal of an in camera (in chambers) inspection of the tapes because of the psychologist-patient relationship.

In 1975, George Emmett and James Creamer filed appeals[40] that were consolidated in the United States District Court for the Northern District of Georgia. This federal court re-examined the facts and took the following position. Debra Ann Kidd, a self-admitted habitual and prolific user of amphetamines and former prostitute and shoplifter, provided testimony at the Emmett and Creamer trials. Her testimony was contrary in some respects to the physical evidence that existed and to the testimony of other witnesses. Kidd was taken to Doctor Hall primarily to enhance her memory and fill in gaps in her story through hypnosis. The psychologist was paid $3515 for his sessions with Kidd. The federal district court found that Hall had acted as a paid agent of the state as an investigative arm of the prosecution. Several of the sessions were viewed by other law enforcement officers. The court ruled that the therapeutic services rendered by Hall, if there were any, were merely incidental to the investigative mission. The court ruled that the district attorney's office and Hall were duty-bound under federal rules of evidence to produce the entire Hall file. The defendants were released from jail pending the state's desire to retry them within 120 days of the order.

William J. Pierce Jr. appealed his conviction of the murder of Peg Cuttino in 1974.[41] At the trial on the merits, the defendant called Robert Sauer, a hypnotist, who was to offer testimony that the defendant had been hypnotized. This was to aid Doctor Reid Johnson, a psychiatrist, who would later be called by the defendant to offer his opinion on the state of mind of the defendant. The trial court did not allow Sauer to testify as to the defendant's guilt or innocence. The appellate court upheld the trial court's ruling and went on to say "We have found no cases in which a court has upheld the admission or which has found it error to have excluded testimony of the results of hypnotic examination offered to prove the guilt or innocence of the accused."[42]

Civil litigation arose from a helicopter crash near Ketchikan, Alaska, in which two people were killed.[43] The sole survivor was Mr. Wyller. Four years after the crash, Mr. Wyller underwent several treatments involving hypnosis to improve his recollection of the events of the crash. The defendant moved to restrict Wyller's testimony to a previously given deposition or to require the hypnotist to establish the reliability of the process employed before Wyller's testimony would be admissible. A psychologist, trained in hypnosis, explained the procedure employed. The district court allowed Wyller to testify to his recollection both prior to and subsequent to his treatments. The court ruled that it was a matter of credibility and weight to be given the testimony which was for the jury to determine. The defendant in this action tested both the hypnotic procedure and the remembered facts through an extensive cross-examination of Wyller. Since the defendant had failed to properly object at trial, evidence concerning the contents of tape recordings made while Wyller was under hypnosis were properly admitted. The defendant also failed to offer a cautionary instruction on hypnosis at the close of the trial. The appellate court, however, believing that the instruction would have been proper under these circumstances ruled that the issue could not be raised on appeal because the proper objection had not been made at the trial.

On October 31, 1970, Karen Kline was killed in an automobile accident while she was driving her new Ford Pinto. Jacqueline Selby was a passenger in the vehicle, which was traveling about 50 to 60 m.p.h. down the highway when it suddenly turned and crashed into an embankment on the opposite side of the road. Kline's estate filed a civil action for damages against the Ford Motor Company.[44] Selby's memory was refreshed by the use of hypnosis, and the court ruled that since she was present and personally saw and heard the events at the time of the accident, and since she was testifying about her present recollection of the event, her testimony was admissible. The fact of hypnosis went to the credibility of her testimony and not to her competence as a witness.

In 1975, the Court of Criminal Appeals of Oklahoma struck down statements of the defendant, made during hypnosis, which were offered for the purpose of establishing the truth of those declarations.[45] The defendant, Ben Jones, had failed to appear for judgment and sentencing in the state court on August 27, 1973. His defense was that he fled not to avoid the hearing, but to avoid reprisals from people involved in a counterfeiting operation. He had provided information to the secret service concerning this operation. The court ruled that the evidence was offered to bolster the defendant's testimony and since a proper foundation and legally competent basis for such an expert opinion had not been established, the evidence was excluded. The court, at the same time, recognized the growing use of hypnosis in the following language: "We recognize that truth serum or hypnosis may be employed as an accepted analytical tool in psychological or psychiatric evaluation and diagnosis."[46]

Rodriguez v. State[47] is a case where the trial judge refused to allow the defendant's psychiatrist to testify to statements made by the defendant while under hypnosis, and barred the psychiatrist from testifying that the defendant had been placed under hypnosis. The only material issue at trial involved the defendant's sanity. The defendant offered testimony from Doctor Mutter to show the state of mind of the defendant at the time he did the shootings. The testimony was also offered as the basis of the doctor's opinion that the defendant was suffering from paranoid schizophrenia. The state objected on the grounds that the statements would be given undue credence by the jury and that statements made under hypnosis were inadmissible for the same reasons that statements made under truth drugs are inadmissible. The appellate court ruled that the judge had not abused his discretion in sustaining the state's objection. The court quoted this language:

Where the evidence is based solely upon scientific tests and experiments, it is essential that the reliability of the tests and the results thereof shall be recognized and accepted by scientists or that the demonstration shall have passed from a state of experimentation and uncertainty to that of a reasonable demonstrability.[48]

Shockey v. State[49] was a 1976 Florida District Court of Appeals case. Shockey and Kirsch were codefendants who were tried separately. The defendant and Kirsch were to drive the victim to a train station for a fee. The defendant claims that Kirsch began to struggle with the victim and told him to stop the car. Kirsch then began to stab the victim outside the car. The defendant claimed to be afraid of Kirsch and he admitted to helping him hide the body. Kirsch had been examined by Doctor Mutter through the use of hypnosis, subsequent to the conviction of Shockey. The defendant sought to have a new trial based on his understanding that Kirsch under hypnosis had completely absolved Shockey of any criminal liability. The appellate court examined Doctor Mutter's testimony, which had been made a part of the trial court records. It contained no material facts that were not presented a trial. The court denied the defendant's motion for a new trial.

On June 24, 1972, Barbara Kiser witnessed the execution-type murder of Linda Lingle and Wilma Norris. Five years later she was granted immunity from prosecution and at her request she was hypnotized in order to refresh her memory. The testimony was offered in the case of *State v. McQueen.*[50] The defense counsel had been given a tape of the hypnotic session the day before she testified. At trial, the defendant did not attack the procedure used nor the qualifications of the hypnotist. Nothing was put in the record as to whether the hypnotist was available for questioning or as to what happened during the hypnotic session. During the trial, the jury was fully advised that the witness had been hypnotized. On appeal in 1978, the defendant objected to the admission of the testimony of Barbara Kiser for the reason that it was the result of her hypnosis prior to trial. The court noted that there was nothing in the record to indicate the witness was under hypnosis during the trial. Kiser testified that as a result of her hypnosis she clearly remembered what she had seen and heard at the time the events took place. The court addressed the issue as follows:

The fact that the memory of the witness concerning events, distant in time, has been refreshed, prior to trial, as by the reading of documents or by conversation with another, does not render the witness incompetent to testify concerning his or her present recollection. The credibility of such testimony, in view of prior uncertainty on the part of the witness, is a matter for the jury's consideration. So it is when the witness has in the mean time, undergone some psychiatric or other medical treatment by which memory is said to have been refreshed or restored. So it is when the intervening experience has been hypnosis.[51]

The court took note that there was an abundance of corroborating evidence developed at trial. The court also quoted this language from the case of *Jewett v. United States.*[52]

It is quite immaterial by what means the memory is quickened; it may be a song, or a face, or a newspaper item, or a writing of some character. It is sufficient that by some mental operation, however mysterious, the memory is stimulated to recall the event, for when so set in motion it functions quite independently of the actuating cause.[53]

In June 1978, the Ninth Circuit Court of Appeals reaffirmed its decision in Kline, in the case of *United States v. Adams.*[54] Adams and another defendant had been convicted of conspiracy, assault with intent to rob, robbery, and murder. These charges stemmed from several attempts to rob postal employees. An eyewitness to the murder had been hypnotized before trial and the defendant objected to the admission of this evidence. The court addressed the issue as follows:

We are concerned however, that investigatory use of hypnosis on persons who may later be called upon to testify in court carries a dangerous potential for abuse. Great care must be exercised to insure that the statements after hypnosis are the product of the subjects' own recollections, rather than of recall tainted by suggestions received while under hypnosis.[55]

An interesting comment appears in one of the court's footnotes:

We think that, at a minimum complete stenographic records of interviews of hypnotized persons who later testify should be maintained. Only if the judge, jury and the opponent know who was present, questions that were asked, and the witness's responses can the matter be dealt with effectively. An audio or video recording of the interview would be helpful.[56]

In this case, an uncertified hypnotist had conducted the sessions. No record was made of who was present, the questions asked, or the answers given. Although the court did not approve of these methods, there were no objections made at trial. The court held that its ruling in Kline was equally applicable to criminal action.

In 1979, Thomas M. Colligan appealed his conviction for two robberies to the Court of Appeals, Third District, of the State of California.[57] Caroline Holmes, the victim of one of the robberies, had been hypnotized in an attempt to help her recall the entire license plate number of the car used in the robbery. She also gave a description of the robber during the session. Holmes made an in court identification of Colligan as the robber, which was objected to on the grounds that the possibility of suggestion by the hypnotist is so substantial that it must be assumed to be an unfair procedure. The defendant did not actually claim these were hypnotic suggestions. The court ruled: "We decline to hold that the use of hypnosis to help a witness remember a license number per se invalidates identification of a person seen and heard by that witness."[58]

This case is unique in that the hypnotist was a police officer. The court did not find that this fact tainted the evidence. The issue of his qualifications was not raised.

Conclusion

Hypnosis has been more readily accepted in the courtroom in recent years, largely because of a wider acceptance by the medical profession. Experts in psychiatry and psychology are now using hypnosis as an analytical tool in forming their opinions on the mental capacities of defendants in criminal cases. Hypnosis has been used to restore memories lost due to time or traumatic experiences. Courts, in admitting this type of evidence, have concerned themselves first with the reliability of the procedure. The more modern cases have now directed their attention to insuring the accuracy of the procedure. Any party trying to get hypnotic evidence admitted in a court of law needs to take steps to insure accuracy. These steps include using qualified personnel to perform the hypnosis, eliminating any possibility of undue suggestions, and preserving the procedure for review by the court or a party-opponent. The evidence then must be properly presented in the courtroom for legally accepted purposes. The next section will deal with procedures to insure accuracy and admissibility of hypnotic evidence.

SPECIAL TOPICS FOR SAFEGUARDING THE ADMISSIBILITY OF HYPNOTICALLY-INFLUENCED TESTIMONY

Any law enforcement personnel desiring to use hypnosis for investigation should first ask advice from competent counsel as to state and local requirements and restrictions on the use of hypnosis. In a number of states, hypnosis can only be performed by a qualified physician. In some states, hypnosis can only be used for medical purposes. Therefore, state and local laws should be examined before law enforcement officers invest time and money for training in hypnosis. A starting point from which to research this area is the *Handbook of Professional Hypnosis* by Arons and Bubeck, Chap. 5, "The Hypnotist and the Law."[59] Also see "Hypnotism and State Laws" by Romanoff.[60]

Once trained in hypnosis, however, there are some special areas of concern for safeguarding the admissibility of hypnotically-influenced testimony, with which the criminal justice professional should be familiar. We now turn to a discussion of these areas.

Selecting and Qualifying the Operator

In courts of law, the trier of fact is either a jury, consisting of the public at large, or a judge. The trier of fact is often called on to make decisions in highly technical and specialized areas. In order to assist the trier of fact, experts are allowed to testify concerning their expertise. Usually witnesses are only allowed to testify to facts within their own personal knowledge, whereas experts, in addition to this type of testimony, are usually allowed to offer opinions. These opinions should be based on facts that have already been proven, or can be proven. Not all jurisdictions have the same rules governing who can be an expert witness and what areas require expert testimony. Many jurisdictions have adopted, either totally or with minor differences, the Federal Rule of Evidence concerning expert testimony. Rule 702, of the Federal Rules of Evidence, reads as follows:

If scientific, technical or other specialized knowledge will assist the trier of fact to understand the evidence or to determine a fact in issue, a witness qualified as an expert by knowledge, skill, experience, training, or education, may testify thereto in the form of an opinion or otherwise.

As one can see under the federal rule, a witness does not have to have formal education to qualify as an expert. Case law from a number of jurisdictions is in accord with this position.[61] Therefore, if a law enforcement officer is properly qualified through education or experience, he can be an expert.[62] Hypnosis is recognized as a specialized area and testimony about this subject will have to come from a qualified expert.[63]

An expert must be able, from the witness stand, to get his point across to the trier of fact. If there is a choice as to which law enforcement officer is going to be selected and trained in hypnosis, some attention should be given to the officer's ability to communicate. He should be at ease in the courtroom, be able to speak fluently and plainly, and be able to get his point across, without making the jury or the judge feel that he is "talking down" to them.

There may be times when it would be preferable if the operator was an expert with extremely impressive credentials. In the courtroom, both parties may offer expert testimony. When this happens, the trier of fact often has to pick which expert he believes, since the testimony is usually conflicting. It is generally recognized that juries will favor experts who have a great deal of experience or impressive qualifications, over an expert who has a minimal amount of experience and qualifications. If most of a case is based on the testimony of one witness, and that witness required hypnosis to refresh his memory, then one must try to impress on the trier of fact both the validity and accuracy of hypnosis. To do this, an out of state witness, who has been to several special schools, who has lectured and perhaps authored a number of publications on the subject, will be more impressive than a local officer with minimal training and who has never testified in court. Therefore, where time and all other considerations allow, the attorney who will be presenting the case should be consulted on selecting the operator.

Naturally, the only way a law enforcement officer will get practice in testifying is if he is used in the courtroom. Therefore, the prosecuting attorney should use the law enforcement officer in minor cases at first, especially where there is a great deal of corroborating evidence. In this way, the officer gets experience and the judge is eased into acceptance of this "new type" of criminal investigation.

In a given case, perhaps the most overriding consideration in selecting an expert is the cost. Experts often charge rather large sums for their testimony. Naturally, the charge is dependent upon the time and work involved and the expertise of the witness. Cost can be greatly reduced by training law enforcement officers in the use of hypnosis.

One question that often arises is whether the operator should be the investigating officer. The investigating officer may have more knowledge about the case, but he may also be more involved in the case and therefore more likely to subconsciously use language or techniques that may be suggestive. To avoid this potential problem, the same procedure should be followed that is used when a witness is tested on the polygraph. The polygraph operator is usually not the investigating officer on the case; he is usually a neutral party who simply administers the test.[64]

For the same reasons, I would not advise the prosecutor or attorney involved in the case to function as the operator. Each prosecutor or attorney will have to decide for himself whether he should be formally trained in the use of hypnosis. Many attorneys feel it is very advantageous to know as much as possible about the subject they have to present in court. Others may feel that formal training will allow a party-opponent to accuse them of improperly using hypnosis on witnesses.

Suggestions for Setting and Technique

It has been suggested that to bring a witness into a law enforcement establishment for questioning may be suggestive. This is one factor that has been considered by courts in determining whether a witness was unduly influenced.[65] In order to help nullify this problem, the operator should wear civilian clothing, instead of a uniform. The room where the session takes place should be made to look like a business office. The operator may consider performing the session in a private home

as opposed to a police station. During the session it is desirable that as few people as possible be in the room. The purpose of this is to minimize the possibility of any improper suggestions during the session. If the session is witnessed by the primary investigator or other interested party, he should not ask questions directly of the subject unless knowledgeable and experienced in how to question hypnotized subjects. Generally, the third party should write out any questions and hand them to the hypno-investigator who will rephrase it and ask it. The third party should never converse with the operator during the session, even if in a whisper, as the form and content of the question or statement may be interpreted as suggestive. For example, the whole session could be invalidated if the primary investigator whispers to the operator, "Ask her about the green car."

In order to preserve the setting and to preserve the techniques and procedures used, it is desirable to videotape and tape record the sessions.[66] If a videotape can be used, the picture should focus on both the operator and the subject at the same time. The operator should be visible at all times to show that he is not influencing the witness by the use of hand gestures or facial expressions. A clock with a large face and hands should be displayed in the picture. The tape, when completed, can then be timed to show that there were no breaks. Naturally, the operator should have no contact with the subject outside of the hypnotic session. This means that from the time the operator first talks to the subject, everything should either be transcribed or recorded in some fashion. It follows that if there is more than one session, all sessions should be recorded in the same manner.

The induction technique will depend on the operator and the subject. It should have little effect on admissibility in the courtroom as long as the subject is truly hypnotized. During the session, the operator should test for trance level. This will allow the operator to verify his findings at a later date. For example, if a subject is asked to relive the event, the appropriate trance level must be reached. The trance level may be tested by a number of nonsimulatable tests such as the ammonia test.

The operator should also instruct the subject not to make up answers and not to fill in holes in his memory. This should be done prior to any questioning, but after the appropriate trance level has been reached. The use of this procedure should help quell the concern over fabricated answers.[67] It can be argued that during hypnosis, the subject, being more susceptible to suggestion, will accept this instruction, thereby eliminating the chance of fabricated answers.

It is necessary during the sessions for the operator to ask questions and to make statements. This is necessary to direct the subject's attention to the specific knowledge that is being sought. There are, however, some key points the operator should keep in mind when asking questions. The operator is trying to find out what the subject knows, so let him tell the story as much as possible. Remember, the less the operator talks, the less chance there is that he will suggest something that might influence the subject's testimony.

The operator should familiarize himself with the case well enough to know what type of information he is seeking from his subject. When a few specific points are sought, he should prepare his questions in advance, and rethink them a number of times so they are phrased in the least suggestive manner. Ideally, the operator should try to build on what the subject has already said by using facts he has already given you to form new questions.

One suggestion that should be made to the subject is that when he awakens he will remember everything that hap-

pened during the session and especially everything he told the operator. Remember that hypnosis has been accepted in the courtroom mainly for the purpose of refreshing a subject's memory. If the subject can't remember what he said during the session, it is highly unlikely that the results of the session will ever be accepted in the courtroom. Where there is the chance that remembering the particular information sought will cause distress to the subject, it would be wise to consult a psychologist or psychiatrist trained in hypnosis, and get his approval first for the procedures.

The operator should demonstrate that the subject, at the end of the session, has been brought back to his normal waking state. This procedure takes on added importance if the session takes place close to the time the subject testifies in court. This will help overcome objections that the witness was under the effects of hypnosis while testifying. This problem can also be minimized by holding the session long before the witness has to testify.

Disclosure of the Use of Hypnosis

There is little doubt that party-opponents should be informed about the use of hypnosis on witnesses. In *United States v. Miller,*[68] the appellate court granted the defendant a new trial on the grounds of nondisclosure. The fact that the prosecution's chief witness had been hypnotized was not made known to defense counsel prior to trial. In this case, the witness had been hypnotized about a year before the trial by one of the prosecuting attorneys.

The Ninth Circuit Court of Appeals, in *United States v. Adams,*[69] also stressed the necessity of informing the judge, the jury, and the opponent about hypnosis. The court also stressed the necessity to provide complete records of the sessions.

The reasoning in these cases is in line with authority holding that the fact that a witness was hypnotized goes to the credibility of the testimony but does not make the testimony inadmissible per se.[70] In military courts the fact that a witness has been hypnotized may directly affect admissibility,[71] at least as to statements made during or after hypnosis, or to conclusions based on the sessions.[72]

In making the decision as to whether to use hypnosis on a witness, some consideration should be given to what will happen if the witness does not respond to the sessions or only partially responds. Will that allow the opponent another means to attack the witness's credibility? It may be wise to have some "negative evidence" testimony at time of trial, i.e. it may be desirable to have an expert explain the reasons why the witness, even with the help of hypnosis, cannot recall every detail. For example the witness may not have been in a position to see or hear the desired information, or is not sufficiently susceptible to hypnosis.

Stipulation as a Means of Admissibility

A stipulation is basically a contract between the parties to an action. The parties may wish to save time and money, therefore they will agree that the trier of fact may consider the stipulated material, without the necessity of presenting the actual evidence. Stipulations mainly concern facts or rules of evidence, and should not violate sound public policy or abate a third party's interest.[73] Although the parties become bound by the stipulation in the absence of some extraordinary circumstances,[74] problems may arise when the stipulation does not meet the approval of the presiding judge. For example, in a history on the admissibility of stipulations concerning polygraphs,[75] the author points out that there are two general lines of authority that courts have taken.[76] Some

courts will not admit the results of polygraphs even with a stipulation because the results are too experimental. This argument could also be applied to hypnosis. Other courts admit the results pursuant to stipulation because the parties should be bound by their agreements. As of this writing, this author has found no cases wherein the results of hypnosis have been admitted in the courtroom pursuant to a stipulation.

Should the situation arise where the parties to an action desire to stipulate to the admission of hypnotic evidence, a review of the above cited A.L.R. annotation on polygraph stipulations may be helpful. The drafter of a stipulation should take into consideration the following points.[77] The stipulation should be addressed to the admissibility in court of the test results subject to the discretion of the judge. Both parties should be allowed to cross-examine the operator respecting his qualifications and training and the conditions under which the test or tests were administered. The subject and counsel for both parties should sign the stipulation. An instruction similar to the one given in *Harding v. State* may be appropriate.[78]

Hypnosis in the Courtroom

The use of hypnosis at or near the time of trial has met with limited success. Generally, the admission of this type of evidence is in the judge's discretion.[79] In *Greenfield v. Virginia,*[80] the defendant was hypnotized to improve his memory during a recess of the trial. The defendant's memory did not improve. The judge ordered that the defendant not be hypnotized again. This ruling was upheld on appeal.

In the unreported case of *State v. Nebb,*[81] the defendant in a first degree murder case was hypnotized by a psychiatrist qualified in hypnosis. The defendant was hypnotized in the courtroom. The jury had been removed. After the defendant related his story, but before the judge had to rule on the admissibility of the evidence, the prosecutor agreed to reduce the charges. The court never ruled on admissibility.

In the Canadian case of *Regina v. Pitt*,[82] the court allowed a defendant, who claimed to have amnesia, to be hypnotized in the courtroom while the jury was present. The defendant did not offer testimony while hypnotized. She was given a posthypnotic suggestion to awaken and to remember all the critical facts. After she was awakened, she offered testimony from the witness stand.

This does not appear to be a recommended procedure. The defendant's attorney did not know exactly what his client would remember. In this case the defendant may have felt that she had little to lose. In the United States, this procedure would make it difficult for an attorney to advise his client on whether to testify. Furthermore, the

prosecution can not properly analyze the procedure used on such short notice. New facts that come out may not be verifiable on such short notice.

As has been pointed out in other sections of this book, some subjects may require several hypnotic sessions before they can achieve a state where their memory can be refreshed. It is doubtful that many judges will allow prolonged recesses of the trial to allow for numerous sessions, since the trial is the time for presenting the evidence, not for preparing it.

A well prepared attorney will want to know everything about his case long before he has to go to trial. This will allow him to plan and prepare an effective presentation. It also helps avoid unpleasant surprises. It would appear that there is little need to use hypnosis in the courtroom, since the procedure used in the Regina case can be accomplished before trial.

Conclusion

The above topics and comments are those of one attorney who has researched hypnosis and the law. Since judicial interpretations and legal opinions are often a matter of individual

perspective, the interested reader is encouraged to review the analyses of other authors who have similarly researched the law.[83-97]

REFERENCES

1. People v. Worthington, 105 Cal. 167, 38 P.689 (1894).
2. *Id.* at 172.
3. People v. Ebanks, 117 Cal. 652, 49 P.1049 (1897).
4. *Id.* at 1053.
5. Parks v. State, 159 Ind. 211, 64 N.E. 862 (1902).
6. *Id.* at 868.
7. State v. Exum, 138 N.C. 599, 50 S.E. 283 (1905).
8. *Id.* at 286.
9. State v. Donovan, 128 Iowa 44, 102 N.W. 791 (1905).
10. *Id.* at 792.
11. Louis v. State, 8 Div. 256, 180 S. 904 (1930).
12. Austin v. Barker, 85 N.Y.S. 30, 119 N.Y. Sup. Ct. 465 (1904).
13. *Id.* at 467.
14. State v. Pusch, 77 N.D. 860, 46 N.W.2d 508 (1951).
15. People v. Leyra, 302 N.Y. 353, 98 N.E.2d 553 (1951).
16. Leyra v. Denno, 347 U.S. 556, 561, 98 Led 948, 952, 74 S. Ct. 716 (1954); Reh. den. 348 U.S. 851, 99 Led 671, 75 S. Ct. 18.
17. Cornell v. Superior Court of San Diego County, 52 Cal.2d 99, 338 P.2d 447, 72 A.L.R.2d 1116 (1959); Cited approvingly in In Re Ketchel, 68 Cal.2d 397, 66 Cal.Rptr. 881, 438 P.2d 625, 627 (1968).
18. *Id.* at 1120.
19. People v. Marsh, 170 Cal. App.2d 284, 338 P.2d 495 (1959).
20. *Id.* at 497.

21. *Id.* at 498.
22. People v. Busch, 56 Cal.2d 868, 16 Cal. Rptr. 898, 366 P.2d 314 (1961).
23. State v. Koblentz, 174 Ohio 120, 121, 187 N.E.2d 40, 41 (1962); Cert. den. 373 U.S. 911, 10 Le.2d 413, 83 S. Ct. 1301.
24. People v. Modesto, 59 Cal.2d 722, 31 Cal. Rptr. 225, 382 P.2d 33, disapproved on other grounds People v. Morse, 60 Cal.2d 631, 36 Cal. Rptr. 201, 388 P.2d 33, 12 A.L.R.3d 810, Later app. on other grounds 62 Cal.2d 436, 42 Cal. Rptr. 417, 398 P.2d 753; Later app. on other grounds 66 Cal.2d 695, 59 Cal. Rptr. 124, 427 P.2d 788, cert. denied 389 U.S. 1009, 19 Led 2d 608 88 S. Ct. 574; disapproved on other grounds Maine v. Superior Ct. of Mendocino County, 68 Cal. 2d 375, 66 Cal. Rptr. 724, 438 P.2d 372, ovrld on other grounds People v. Sedeno, 10 Cal. 3rd 703, 112 Cal. Rptr. 1, 518 P.2d 913.
25. 382 P.2d 39.
26. State v. Harris, 241 Or. 224, 405 P.2d 492 (1965).
27. *Id.* at 499.
28. *Id.* at 500.
29. Harding v. State, 5 Md. App. 230, 246 A.2d 302 (1968); Cert. den. 395 U.S. 949, 23 Led 2d 468, 89 S. Ct. 2030.
30. *Id.* at 310.
31. People v. Hiser, 267 Cal. App. 2d 47, 72 Cal. Rptr. 906 (1968), 41 A.L.R. 3d 1353.
32. U.S. v. Miller, 411 F.2d 825 (2nd Cir. 1969).
33. *Id.* at 832.
34. People v. Harper, 111 Ill. App. 2d 204, 250 N.E. 2d 5 (1969).
35. *Id.* at 7.
36. Greenfield v. Virginia, 214 Va. 710, 204 S.E. 2d 414 (1974).
37. Greenfield v. Robinson (D.C. Va.) 413 F. Supp. 1113 (1976).
38. Creamer v. State, 232 Ga. 136, 205 S.E. 2d 240 (1974).
39. Emmett v. State, 232 Ga. 110, 205 S.E. 2d 231 (1974).
40. Emmett v. Ricketts, 397 F. Supp. 1025 (1975).
41. State v. Pierce, 263 S.C. 23, 207 S.E. 2d 414 (1974).

42. *Id.* at 418.
43. Wyller v. Fairchild, 503 F.2d 506 (9th Cir. 1974).
44. Kline v. Ford Motor Co., 523 F.2d 1067 (9th Cir. 1975).
45. Jones v. State (Okla. crim.) 542 P.2d 1316 (1975).
46. *Id.* at 1328.
47. Rodriguez v. State (Fla. App.) 327 So. 2d 903 (1976).
48. *Id.* at 904.
49. Shockey v. State (Fla. App.) 338 So. 2d 33 (1976).
50. State v. McQueen, 295 N.C. 96, 244 S.E. 2d 414 (1978).
51. *Id.* at 427.
52. Jewett v. United States, 15 F.2d 955 (9th Cir. 1926).
53. State v. McQueen, 295 N.C. 96, 244 S.E. 2d 429 (1978).
54. U.S. v. Adams, 581 F.2d 193 (9th Cir. 1978).
55. *Id.* at 198.
56. *Id.* at 199.
57. People v. Colligan, 154 Cal. Rptr. 389, 91 Cal. App. 3d 846 (1979).
58. *Id.* at 391.
59. Arons, Harry and Bubeck, M. F. H.: *Handbook of Professional Hypnosis.* So. Orange, Power, 1971, pp. 30-46.
60. Romanoff, Robert A.: Hypnotism and state laws. *Hypnosis Quarterly, 22(3):*22-27, 1979.
61. State v. Donovan, 128 Iowa 44, 102 N.W. 791 (1905).
62. People v. Colligan, 154 Cal. Rptr. 391, 91 Cal. App. 3d 846 (1979).
63. *Id.* at 286.
64. A number of courts have suggested that the operator not be connected with the case. *See* State v. White, 26 Cr. L. 2168 11/21/79; U.S. v. Miller, 411 F.2d 825 (1969).
65. People v. Leyra, 302 N.Y. 353, 98 N.E.2d 553, 558 (1951); U.S. v. Andrews, General Court-Martial No. 74-14 (N.E. Jud. Cir., Navy-Marine Corps. Judiciary, Phila., Pa., Oct. 6, 1975).
66. U.S. v. Adams, 581 F.2d 193, 199 (1978), see footnote 12. *See also* State v. White, 26 Cr. L. 2168, 11/21/79.
67. Admissibility of Hypnotic Evidence, 92 A.L.R. 3d 442, 451 (1979).

68. United States v. Miller, 411 F.2d 825 (2nd Cir. 1969). In State v. Exum, 138 N.C. 599, 50 S.E. 283 (1905), the court ruled that the fact the defendant had hypnotized his wife (a witness) was relevant as to her credibility.

69. U.S. v. Adams, 581 F.2d 193, 199, (1978) footnote 12.

70. U.S. v. Adams, 581 F.2d 193, 198 (9th Cir. 1978), Kline v. Ford Motor Co., Inc., 523 F.2d 1067, 1069 (9th Cir. 1975); Wyller v. Fairchild Hiller Corp., 503 F.2d 506, 509 (9th Cir. 1974); State v. Jorgenson, 492 P.2d 312, 315 (Ore. App. 1971).

71. U.S. v. White-G.C.M. (First Jud. Cir., Army Trial Judiciary, Ft. Monmouth, N.J. Sept. 19, 1974. Here the military judge ruled that according to the Manual for Court-Martial para. 142e (1969) this kind of testimony is not allowed. Generally, hypnotic testimony has not been accepted in Military Courts. *See, e.g.,* United States v. Andrews G.C.M. No. 75-14 (N.E. Jud. Cir., Navy-Marine Corps Judiciary, Phila., Pa., Oct. 6, 1975); United States v. Walker, G.C.M. No. 25-74 (N.E. Jud. Cir., Navy-Marine Corps Judiciary, Phila., Pa., Oct. 24, 1974); United States v. Barr, G.C.M. No. 25-74 (N.E. Jud. Cir., Navy-Marine Corps Judiciary, Phila., Pa., Oct. 24, 1974).

72. Manual for Courts-Martial, para. 142e (1969).

73. 9 J. Wigmore, Evidence Sec. 2592 at 591 (3rd Ed.); 1 J. Wigmore, Evidence Sec. 7 (a) at 213-14 (3rd Ed.).

74. 1 J. Wigmore, Evidence Sec. 7 (a) at 213-14 (3rd Ed.).

75. Admissibility of Lie Detector Test Taken upon Stipulation That the Result Will be Admissible in Evidence, 53 A.L.R. 3rd 1005.

76. *Id.* at 1008.

77. *See, e.g.,* State v. Valdez, 91 Ariz. 274, 371 P. 2d 894 (1962).

78. Harding v. State, 5 Md. App. 230, 246 P.2d 302, 1968; cert. den. 395 U.S. 949, 23 Led 2d 468, 89 S. Ct. 2030.

79. People v. Marsh, 170 Cal. App.2d 284, 338 P.2d 495, 498 (1959).

80. Greenfield v. Virginia, 214 Va. 710, 204 S.E. 2d 414 (1974).

81. State v. Nebb, No. 39 540 Ohio C.P. Franklin Co., May 28 (1962); *See also,* State of Oregon v. B.G. No. 95066, where the jury was removed, this case is examined in *The American Journal of Clinical Hypnosis, 19(3):*163, 1977.

82. Regina v. Pitt, 68 D.L.P. 2d 1513, 1968, noted in 15 McGill L.J. 189 (1969).

83. Comment, *Hypno-induced statements: Safeguards for admissibility,* Law & Social Order 99 (1970).

84. Herman, The Use of Hypno-induced Statements in Criminal Cases, 25 Ohio St. L.J.1 (1964); Annot., 41 A.L.R. 3d 1369 (1973).

85. Dilloff, *The Admissibility of Hypnotically Influenced Testimony,* 4 Ohio North L. Rev. 1 (1977).

86. Ladd, *Legal Aspects of Hypnotism,* 11 Yale L.J. 173 (1902).

87. Levy, *Hypnosis and the Law,* 41 Chi. B. Rec. 243 (1960).

88. Levy, *Hypnosis and Legal Immutability,* 46 J. Crim. L. C. & P. S. 333 (1955).

89. Teitelbaum, *Admissibility of Hypnotically Adduced Evidence and the Arthur Nebb Case,* 8 St. Louis U.L.J. 205 (1963).

90. Teitelbaum, *Personal Injury Law and Hypnotism,* 1963 Med. Trial Tech. Q. 95.

91. Comment, *Hypnotism as a Criminal Defense,* 6 Calif. West. L. Rev. 303 (1970).

92. Note, *Hypnotism and the Law,* 14 Vand. L. Rev. 1509 (1961).

93. Note, *Hypnotism, Suggestibility, and the Law,* 31 Neb. L. Rev. 575 (1952).

94. Note, *Hypnosis as an Evidentiary Tool,* S. Utah L. R. 79 (1962).

95. Spector and Foster, *Admissibility of Hypnotic Statements: Is the Law of Evidence Susceptible?* 38 Ohio St. L. J. 567 (1977).

96. Sarno, *Admissibility of Hypnotic Evidence at Criminal Trial,* 92 A.L.R. 3d 442 (1979).

97. Bryan, W. J.: *Legal Aspects of Hypnosis.* Springfield, Thomas, 1959.

CASE LAW ANALYSIS OF
HYPNOTICALLY–RELATED EVIDENCE

INTRODUCTION

SINCE THE WRITING of Chapter 6, "Case Law Analysis of Hypnotically-Related Evidence" in 1981, there has been a great deal of case law generated on this topic. In fact, a computer search from 1981–1995 revealed 507 cases that were heard in which the issue of "hypnotically-influenced testimony" was on trial. In spite of all this case law, the admissibility in court of information obtained through the use of hypnotically-refreshed memory is still hotly debated and has not been resolved by the United States Supreme Court. The primary issues that are subject to debate can be classified under two general headings: (1) reliability of hypnosis as a means of enhancing memory, and (2) the admissibility of hypnotically-enhanced testimony as an evidentiary question and point of law. We will deal with each of these in turn.

RELIABILITY OF HYPNOSIS

Although hypnosis in criminal and civil investigations has proven to be a valuable tool for eliciting new and important information, science cannot guarantee the accuracy and reliability of such information. This is not a constitutional concern in investigation, but is crucial in a trial. Defense experts have convinced many courts that there are several problems inherent in the use of hypnosis, all centering around the reliability issue.

Suggestibility

Adverse experts maintain that hypnotized subjects are generally highly susceptible to suggestion; therefore a hypnotist can consciously, or even unconsciously, lead the subject to a desired answer through suggestive questions. It has been clearly demonstrated in experimental studies that the beliefs and prejudices of an experimenter can, in spite of careful controls, influence the behavior of experimental subjects.[1] This problem is believed to be compounded when a subject is under hypnosis. Although inappropriate explicit suggestions can be controlled, the hypnotized subject is susceptible to nonverbal and implicit cues, is sensitive to the expectations of the hypnotist and investigator, and wants to please those in authority who have stressed the importance of remembering certain events, any of which may prejudice the information recalled.

Proponents present the argument that a hypnotic state is not necessarily synonymous with hypersuggestibility and that "there is a scientific consensus that suggestibility plays a relatively small role in hypnotic processes."[2] In fact, they maintain that suggestibility is ubiquitous in normal waking life and doesn't require hypnosis to function. They argue that people are suggestible to varying degrees with or without hypnosis[3] and think that defense experts largely overvalue the suggestibility factor. To support their argument, proponents cite studies that failed to verify the contention that hypnotized subjects are more influenced by suggestion than unhypnotized subjects.[4]

Confabulation

Adverse experts stress that hypnotized subjects can knowingly or unknowingly fill in gaps in their memory with erroneous "remembrances." Hypnotized individuals may fill in memory gaps in an attempt to reconstruct a past occurrence and the hypnotically-enhanced memory is likely to be a "mosaic of (1) appropriate actual events, (2) entirely irrelevant actual events, (3) pure fantasy, and (4) fantasized details supplied to make a logical whole."[5] It is difficult, if not impossible, for the hypnotist or subject to distinguish truthful remembrances from fantasized ones.

Proponents counter this argument with studies that clearly show the unreliability of eyewitness testimony from nonhypnotized witnesses, who experience many of the same alleged recall problems as hypnotized subjects.[6,7,8] They cite studies that have shown that hypnotized subjects do not confabulate more than nonhypnotized subjects.[9,10,11] "Evidence on the whole has been against, rather than in support of, the hypothesis that hypnosis generally created inherent distortion in memory reports."[12] This camp argues, therefore, that the legal question is not one of *admissibility* (as many courts have held), but one of *credibility* of the testimony. "The important legal issue is not whether the recall is truthful, per se, but whether the recall is based upon what the witness actually saw or experienced, as opposed to suggestion."[13] Any testimony, either from hypnotized or nonhypnotized witnesses, does not legally have to be totally accurate, but only have probative value in order to be admissible.[14] Furthermore, it has been the experience of Dr. Martin Reiser, a pioneer in the special field of investigative and forensic hypnosis, that confabulation does not routinely occur. This assertion was based on some 700 hypno-investigations of the Los Angeles Police Department over a 10-year period.[15]

Memory Hardening

The contention is made that after hypnosis, a subject will tend to be more certain about memories or facts recalled prior to hypnosis; in other words, their memory becomes "hardened" or "cemented" as a result of the hypnotic experience. Furthermore, it is argued that this memory hardening may render a witness impervious to cross-examination, and the witness may testify to the false "memory" with complete confidence, hence misleading the trier of fact (the jury). This is due to "posthypnotic source amnesia," a phenomenon in which the subject retains memories created under hypnosis, but is unaware that the memory was acquired under hypnosis.

This position is rebutted by experts who cite studies that failed to find a difference between confidence ratings of hypnotized versus nonhypnotized subjects.[16] Furthermore, research shows that in investigative hypnosis the hypnotized witnesses were generally able to differentiate what they remembered before, during, and after the hypnosis interview. They did not become absolutely certain of their recall and did not develop hardening of their perceptions.[17]

Fabrication

All experts concede that hypnosis is not a guarantee of truthfulness. In fact, it has been established in the laboratory that hypnotized subjects can feign hypnosis and willfully withhold information or lie under hypnosis, an experimental finding that adverse experts stress.[18] Unfortunately, conventional wisdom holds that hypnosis is a method of uncovering the truth. Hence, a concern is expressed that jurors will tend to place an unwarranted credence on hypnotically-generated testimony.

Proponents stress that hypnosis is not a truth detection technique, but is only an interview technique which cannot guarantee accuracy anymore than any other interviewing technique.

Factual accuracy of testimony is not an inflexible requirement for admissibility. Psychologists concur in their estimation that eyewitness testimony is often factually inaccurate and unreliable, being riddled with fantasy, prejudice, misperception, and biased. Yet such testimony is routinely admitted for jurors' consideration because it is insulated to some degree from the dangers of ambiguity, erroneous recall, flawed perception, and prevarication by the enforcement of procedural safeguards, such as the opportunity for cross-examination.[19]

In *State v. Hurd,*[20] the Supreme Court of New Jersey

did not demand, as a precondition of admissibility, that hypnosis be generally accepted as a means of reviving truthful or historically accurate recall. . . . The purpose of using hypnosis is not to obtain truth, as a polygraph or "truth serum" is supposed to do. Instead, hypnosis is employed as a means of overcoming amnesia and restoring the memory of a witness. . . . In light of this purpose, hypnosis can be considered reasonably reliable if it is able to yield recollections as accurate as those of an ordinary witness, which likewise are often historically inaccurate. . . . If it is conducted properly and used only in appropriate

cases, hypnosis is generally accepted as a reasonably reliable method of restoring a person's memory. Consequently, hypnotically-induced testimony may be admissible if the proponent of the testimony can demonstrate that the use of hypnosis in the particular case was a reasonably reliable means of restoring memory comparable to normal recall in its accuracy.[21]

Memory Distortion

The claim is presented to courts by adverse experts that hypnotized witnesses lose their ability to discriminate between prehypnotic, hypnotic, and posthypnotic memories.

Proponents point out that this is merely a matter of conjecture not supported by research as there are no convincing evidence or studies to support this contention. In fact, a survey of the literature revealed that the information reported by hypnotized witnesses was more complete and internally consistent with no increase in erroneous information when compared to nonhypnotized controls.[22] They further stress that it is the experience of working hypno-investigators that hypnotized witnesses can in fact distinguish between prehypnosis recall and recall generated during hypnosis.[23]

Conclusion

It is of paramount importance that any counsel seeking admissibility of hypnotically-refreshed memory in a court of law educate himself or herself on these issues (as they are surely to surface), and find one or more friendly experts to give supporting testimony. It is recommended that they contact the **International Society for Investigative and Forensic Hypnosis** for a list of experts and supporting materials. Although the objectionable issues enumerated above seem formidable obstacles, they can be successfully countered with well credentialled experts. Excellent resource papers that will put all these issues in their proper perspective (and de-intimidate counsel faced with surmounting them) are *Police Use of Investigative Hypnosis: Scientism, Ethics, and Power Games*[24] and *Investigative Hypnosis*[25] both by Dr. Martin Reiser, Director of Behavioral Science Services (ret.), Los Angeles Police Department.

In my experience, theorists, such as Orne, are patently incorrect in asserting that eyewitness identification under hypnosis is less reliable than non-hypnotic recall. Hard data collected at the Los Angeles Police Department and other jurisdictions indicate a generally high corroboration rate of significant crime-related details. This assumes that the sessions are properly conducted by trained investigative hypnosis persons using relevant cuing techniques.

In dozens of investigative hypnosis cases which I have personally conducted and in numerous others where I have consulted as an expert witness, the Los Angeles Police Department records clearly indicate that hypnotized witnesses were able to discriminate what they knew before, during, and after hypnosis. They did not develop the hardening of perceptions as asserted by critics and did not become unshakeably certain of their recall after the hypnosis experience. . . .

By presenting inaccurate and biased accounts of the current state of research and knowledge in the area of memory, the opponents to the police use of investigative hypnosis have utilized scientism under the guise of science in courtrooms, in the media, and at "scientific" conferences.[26]

ADMISSIBILITY OF HYPNOTICALLY-ENHANCED TESTIMONY

Understandably, many courts are reluctant to admit such testimony in the absence of scientifically established reliability, and they differ in how they deal with this problem. Originally, evidence influenced by hypnosis was regarded as inadmissible, and courts tended to follow the first precedent set in *People v. Ebanks*[27] in 1897, in which the California Supreme Court affirmed the exclusion of hypnotically-influenced testimony stating, "The law of the United States does not recognize hypnotism."[28] "Today, however, most courts recognize hypnosis as a potentially useful evidentiary tool, absolute exclusion of which would result in the loss of valuable evidence. Accordingly, most courts will admit the testimony of an individual whose recollection has been refreshed by hypnosis."[29] Yet, some courts hold that all hypnotically-influenced testimony should be excluded carte blanche, whereas others hold just the opposite, while others hold that witnesses should only be allowed to testify to their prehypnosis memories, while

others argue for admissibility with procedural safeguards, or insist that each case be evaluated on a case-by-case basis. We will look at each of these positions in turn.

Per se Inadmissible

Some courts simply exclude the introduction of hypnotically-enhanced testimony altogether. This is generally done under the *Frye* test, or the "general scientific acceptance test," which holds that there must be a consensus of the relevant scientific community before a new scientific technique can be admitted as evidence.[30] In other words, the scientific technique must be developed to an extent experts in the particular field believe is accurate. Evidence failing to meet the *Frye* standard is inadmissible unless stipulated to by all parties. A typical case is *People v. Shirley,*[31] an influential California Supreme Court case that arrived at a per se ruling against hypnotically-enhanced testimony. This ruling is unique in that the court not only disallowed admission of hypnotically-enhanced testimony, but excluded the witness from testifying at all regarding the facts of the case.

"The *Frye* test has frequently faced challenges from those who argue that it is inappropriate to apply it in the context of hypnosis because *Frye* refers to the admissibility of expert testimony, whereas here the concern is with the hypnotically refreshed testimony of a witness."[32] For instance, in *State v. Brown*,[33] the court refused to apply the *Frye* test since *Frye* is concerned with expert opinion generated from a scientific technique rather than the admissibility of eyewitness testimony. Therefore, the *Frye* test may not be applicable to hypnotically-enhanced testimony. Many "courts that have considered this argument have found it unpersuasive, and consequently, *Frye* now stands for a much broader principle than the original case opinion."[34]

Hence, courts following the *Frye* standard will not admit hypnotically-enhanced testimony until hypnosis is established as a generally accepted scientific technique. Some courts that take the *Frye* standard to an extreme and disallow a witness who has been hypnotized from testifying at all, i.e., even to their prehypnotic recollections. Other jurisdictions take a less drastic position and allow testimony to facts remembered prior to hypnosis, but not to any facts remembered during hypnosis.

The *Frye* test underwent a serious challenge in a landmark case, *Rock v. Arkansas*,[35] in which the United States Supreme Court held that a per se rule excluding hypnotically-refreshed testimony infringes on a criminal defendant's right to testify on his own behalf and is therefore unconstitutional.[32]

In the majority opinion, Justice Blackmun touched upon the possibility of reducing the dangers of contamination through the use of

safeguards, as well as through such traditional methods of evaluating testimony as corroborating evidence, cross-examination, expert testimony and cautionary instructions. Although the majority opinion did not advocate the use of this procedure as a forensic tool, the recognition of these prophylactics suggests that a per se exclusion of posthypnosis testimony is unwarranted. Rather, the Court seems to lean toward a case by case evaluation of hypnosis—including those cases involving the use of hypnosis by the prosecution—until the area is more clearly defined.

Rock's four dissenters concluded that the Constitution does not mandate an ad hoc approach to determining the admissibility of hypnotically refreshed testimony. Rather, according to the dissenters, lower courts should be given great deference in determining their own standards of admissibility.[36]

In the absence of a Constitutional issue, then, the Court is not likely to commit to any per se rule of admissibility or inadmissibility. And although *Rock* is specific to a criminal defendant, it is expected that the ruling will be persuasive authority for including victims and witnesses as well, and could apply to the prosecution's use of hypnosis as well as the defense's use. If prohibition of hypnotically-enhanced testimony by the defendant violates his constitutional right to testify on his own behalf, doesn't that mean that the Constitution is violated if *other* witnesses (whether defense *or* prosecution) are prohibited from presenting hypnotically-induced testimony? Judge Sawaya of the County Court of Marion County, Florida, thinks so: "After all, the Court has said the rules of procedure and evidence in criminal cases are 'designed to assure both fairness and reliability in the ascertainment of guilt and innocence.' *Chamber v. Mississippi*, 93 S. Ct. 1038, 1049 (1973). If the playing field is to be level, shouldn't both sides be able to use Dr. Mesmer's art?"[37]

More recently, the *Frye* test was essentially reversed by the United States Supreme Court in *Daubert v. Merrell Dow Pharmaceuticals Inc.,*[38] when it held that the legislatively-enacted Federal Rules of Evidence have superseded it. As noted by Paul Kincade, president of the **International Society for Investigative & Forensic Hypnosis:**

The rules state that all evidence is relevant and it is the responsibility of the trier of fact to determine its credibility and reliability. The high court took special note of Rule 702, which says, "If scientific, technical, or other specialized knowledge will assist the trier of fact to understand the evidence or to determine a fact in issue, a witness qualified as an expert by knowledge, skill, experience, training, or education, may testify thereto in the form of an opinion or otherwise." The justices also noted that nothing in the text of Rule 702 establishes "general acceptance" as an absolute prerequisite to admissibility, nor was there any clear indication that Rule 702, or the Rules as a whole, were intended to incorporate a general acceptance standard. Although the court's ruling pertains to federal courts, it is expected it will soon become precedent for state courts.[39]

Some courts have deemed hypnotically-induced testimony inadmissible on sixth amendment concerns. The Arizona Supreme Court, in *State v. Mena,* questioned the effectiveness of cross-examination of a witness who had been hypnotized previously.[37]

The witness will assimilate the hypnotically-adduced memory as his or her own, and often become convinced of the accuracy of the memory. The sixth amendment provides the accused with the right to be confronted with the witnesses against him in all criminal prosecutions, and the clause is applicable to the states through the fourteenth amendment. The right to confrontation includes the right of cross-examination. If the previously hypnotized witness cannot be effectively cross-examined, the accused is denied his or her sixth amendment rights. The witness' memory may

have been altered by hypnosis to the extent any cross-examination will be unable to reach the witness' initial observations at the time the original event occurred.[38]

As a result, the Arizona Supreme Court wrote, "In order to ensure against the dangers of hypnosis, therefore, this Court will consider testimony from witnesses who have been questioned under hypnosis regarding the subject of their offered testimony to be inadmissible in criminal trials from the time of the hypnotic session forward."[39]

Relevant Annotated Case Law

State v. Mack, 292 N.W.2d 764 (Minn. 1980). To allow the jury to rely on the testimony of a previously hypnotized witness, the court would be allowing the jury to rely on the ability of hypnosis to accurately refresh recollections. Applying the *Frye* test, hypnotically-enhanced testimony was excluded since it has not been established to be scientifically reliable.

State v. Conley, 6 Kan. App. 2d 280, 627 P.2d 1174 (1981). Required general scientific recognition of the efficacy of hypnosis to produce truthful statements before admission of hypnotically-generated evidence.

Tardi v. Henry, 212 Ill. App. 3d 1027, 1036–37, 571 N.E. 2d 1020, 1025–26 (App. Ct. 1991). Held that hypnotically-induced testimony should be inadmissible because the scientific community generally finds such recall inaccurate.

State v. Grimmett, 459 N.W.2d 515, 517 (Minn. Ct. App. 1990). Held that a witness in a criminal proceeding is not permitted to testify to what he remembered under hypnosis.

State v. Blackman, 826 S.W.2d 76, 79 (Mo. Ct. App. 1992). Didn't allow previously hypnotized witness to testify despite use of procedural safeguards.

Commonwealth v. Reed, 400 Pa. Super. 207, 226, 583 A.2d 459, 468 (Super. Ct. 1990). Disallowed testimony elicited from a defendant under hypnosis because it did not meet the *Frye* test for admissibility.

State v. Pierce, 263 S.C. 23, 207 S.E.2d 414, 418 (1974). Held that the results of a hypnotic examination are not admissible for the truth of the matter asserted.

State v. Tuttle, 780 P.2d 1203, 1211 (Utah 1989). Held that testimony enhanced from hypnosis is unreliable and therefore inadmissible under Utah Rule of Evidence 702, *cert. denied,* 494 U.S. 1018 (1990).

Archie v. Commonwealth, 14 Va. App. 684, 692, 420 S.E.2d 718, 723 (Ct. App. 1992). Held that hypnotic evidence is unreliable because a person under hypnosis can invent statements and is subject to heightened suggestibility.

State v. Hurd, 86 N.J. 550, 432 A.2d 98 (1981). Held that hypnotically enhanced-memory should be inadmissible in a criminal trial. The court placed the burden of proof upon the state to show by clear and convincing evidence the hypnotically-induced recollections were reliable, and therefore admissible. The state did not meet this burden.

State v. LaMountain, 125 Ariz. 547, 611 P.2d 551 (1980). Held a witness who has been hypnotized should not be allowed to testify when the testimony may have been produced by that hypnosis.

Per se Admissible

Some courts freely admit hypnotically-enhanced testimony on the grounds that hypnosis affects credibility, but not admissibility. In this approach, courts regard hypnotically-enhanced testimony as they do any other testimony which is subject to cross-examination and the testimony of experts to help the trier of fact determine its reliability and accuracy. In essence, the question is not one of admissi-bility of the evidence, but one of credibility of the witness, and the trier of fact is believed responsible enough to weigh the reliability of hypnotically-refreshed testimony. The Ninth Circuit Court of Appeals in *United States v. Adams,* [43] affirmed this position, and also disputed the contention that a defendant's sixth amendment rights are jeopardized by the use of hypnosis.

A typical case is *State v. Brown* [44] in which the North Dakota Supreme Court examined the issue of whether " . . . a witness whose memory has been previously enhanced through the use of hypnosis may testify in a criminal trial in North Dakota." [45] The court allowed a crime victim's testimony, ruling that hypnotically-enhanced testimony is a matter of credibility and not an issue of admissibility. [46] The court reasoned that hypnosis is only one of many factors that may stimulate a witness's memory (e.g., just as a document, newspaper article, photograph, or other tangible exhibit might), that skillful cross-examination enables the trier of fact to evaluate the credibility of the testimony, and that a witness who had undergone hypnosis should be treated like any other witnesses.

Relevant Annotated Case Law

Harding v. State, 5 Md. App. 230, 246 A.2d 302 (Ct. Spec. App. 1968), *cert. denied,* 395 U.S. 949 (1969), *overruled* by Collins v. State, 447 A.2d 1272 (Md. Ct. Spec. App. 1982). Testimony of a witness whose memory had been restored by hypnosis was allowed.

Beck v. Norris, 801 F.2d 242, 244 (6th Cir. 1986). Held that the "State of Tennessee allows the admission of testimony by witnesses who have been previously hypnotized."

State v. Pollit, 205 Conn. 61, 81, 530 A.2d 155, 165 (1987). Held that "a witness who has previously been hypnotized is competent to testify at trial where that testimony is consistent with his prehypnotic recollection."

Odem v. State, 483 N.W.2d 17, 20 (Iowa Ct. App. 1992). Held that posthypnotic testimony is admissible when the post hypnotic testimony is substantially the same as the statements made by the witness prior to being hypnotized.

State v. Armstrong, 110 Wis.2d 555, 329 N.W.2d 386, 389, *cert. denied,* 461 U.S. 946 (1983). Held that hypnosis, if not impermissibly suggestive, may be used to refresh recollection of a witness.

Prime v. State, 767 P.2d 149, 153 (Wyo. 1989). Held that a witness who has been hypnotized is not incompetent to testify.

Pearson v. State, 441 N.E.2d 468, 473 (Ind. 1982). Held that hypnosis affects the weight of a witness's testimony and does not result in a per se disqualification.

Chapman v. State, 638 P.2d 1280, 1284 (Wyo. 1982). Held that an attack on credibility of a previously hypnotized witness is the proper method to evaluate the testimony.

Admissibility with Procedural Safeguards

Some jurisdictions allow the introduction of testimony refreshed by hypnosis if certain procedural safeguards are followed to help insure reliability during the hypnosis session. These safeguards are deemed necessary to mitigate the potential problems cited earlier of suggestibility, confabulation, memory hardening, truthfulness, and memory distortion. Such guidelines generally call for, at a minimum, a qualified professional (usually a health professional) trained in hypnosis and independent of either the prosecution, defense, or investigator; the subject should be thoroughly interviewed before the induction of hypnosis and all facts recorded; and a permanent audio or videotape (preferable) record of all contacts between hypnotist and subject should be made.

A noted case is *State v. Hurd*[47] in which the New Jersey Supreme Court adopted procedural safeguards recommended by a psychiatrist who was an expert witness for the defense. The intent of the guidelines was to provide for an adequate level of reliability (by preventing undue suggestions) and recording of the hypnotic procedure for subsequent review.

There is general agreement of all parties that procedural safeguards are important. The bone of contention is the specific safeguards themselves. For instance, whereas the *Hurd* court adopted a safeguard requiring that the hypnosis be conducted by a psychologist or psychiatrist experienced in the use of hypnosis, critics (including the authors) argue that this is a totally inappropriate and indefensible requirement (see pp. 12–14).

Relevant Annotated Case Law

State v. Butterworth, 246 Kan. 541, 552–55, 792 P.2d 1049, 1057–58 (1990). Held that hypnotically-refreshed testimony may be received in evidence if substantial safeguards are met.

State v. Woodfin, 539 So.2d 645, 649 (La. Ct. App. 1989). Adopted the procedural safeguards set forth in *Hurd* in order to minimize the dangers of unreliability in using hypnosis.

House v. State, 445 So.2d 815, 827 (Miss. 1984). Held that certain guidelines must be complied with and that the probative value of the hypnotically-refreshed memory must outweigh the prejudicial impact on the accused before a jury can hear testimony from a previously hypnotized witness.

State v. King, 84 Or. App. 165, 175–77, 733 P.2d 472, 479–80 (Ct. App. 1987). Held that statutory guidelines must be followed in obtaining testimony from a witness under hypnosis.

State v. Boykin, 432 N.W.2d 60, 67 (S.D. 1988). Allowed posthypnotic testimony because procedural safeguards were followed.

State v. Yapp, 45 Wash. App. 601, 603–04, 726 P.2d 1003, 1005 (Ct. App. 1986). Held that witness may testify to prehypnosis memory if procedural safeguards are followed.

Admissibility of Prehypnosis Memory Only

A number of courts have taken the position that posthypnotic testimony is inherently unreliable, but that does not disqualify the witness from testifying to recollections prior to the hypnosis. A typical case is *Collins v. Superior Court*[48] in which the court held that a "witness will be permitted to testify with regard to those matters which he or she was able to recall and relate prior to hypnosis."[49] Similarly, in *State v. Palmer*,[50] the court held that hypnosis does not render a witness incompetent, but will permit him to testify to those matters that he recalled prior to hypnosis. The United States Supreme Court denied certiorari and thereby let the lower court's ruling stand.

As a practical procedural matter, courts have recognized the necessity for an accurate and full record of the witness's prehypnotic memory. In the absence of such, "there is no reliable way to determine after hypnosis what the witness knew at the earlier time." In a later case, the Arizona Supreme Court held: "We adhere to our holding in *Collins II* that posthypnotic testimony must have been demonstrably recalled and recorded prior to hypnosis in order to be admissible."[52] Similarly, Michigan requires "clear and convincing evidence that the testimony being offered was based on facts recalled and related prior to hypnosis."[53]

Relevant Annotated Case Law

Contreras v. State, 718 P.2d 129, 139 (Alaska 1986). Held that a previously hypnotized witness may testify only as to facts that he related before the hypnotic session.

Neely v. Sherill, 165 Ariz. 508, 512, 799 P.2d 849, 853 (1990). Held that testimony must be recalled and recorded prior to hypnosis in order to be admissible.

People v. Clark, 3 Cal. 4th 41, 150, 833 P.2d 561, 622, 10 Cal. Rptr. 2d 554, 615 (1992), *cert. denied* 113 S. Ct. 1604 (1993). Allowed witness's testimony about events that predated or were not discussed in the hypnotic session.

Elliotte v. State, 515 A.2d 677, 681 (Del. 1986). Held that hypnosis does not render a witness incompetent to testify to events recalled prior to being hypnotized.

Stokes v. State, 548 So.2d 188, 196 (Fla. 1989). Held that a witness who has been hypnotized may testify only to those statements made before the hypnotic session provided that those sessions are properly recorded.

Walraven v. State, 255 Ga. 276, 282, 336 S.E.2d 798, 803 (1985). Held that a witness may testify to statements made prior to hypnosis or events occurring after hypnosis.

State v. Moreno, 68 Haw. 233, 236, 709 P.2d 103, 105 (1985). Held that a witness may testify to matters recollected by that witness prior to hypnosis.

State v. Iwakiri, 106 Idaho 618, 653, 682 P.2d 571, 606 (1984). Held that a witness cannot testify to those matters "remembered" under hypnosis.

Calhoun v. State, 297 Md. 563, 577, 468 A.2d 45, 51. Held that witnesses should be able to testify to statements made prior to hypnosis.

Commonwealth v. Kater, 412 Mass. 800,

802, 592 N.E.2d 1328, 1329 (1992). Held that the admissibility of a witness's testimony depends on separating pre-hypnotic memory from posthypnotic memory.

People v. Schreiner, 77 N.Y.2d 733, 739 n.2, 573 N.E.2d 552, 555 n.2, 570 N.Y.S.2d 464, 467 n.2 (1991). Held that, if the hypnotic process was not suggestive, a witness's pre-hypnotic recollection may be admissible.

State v. Annadale, 329 N.C. 557, 570, 406 S.E.2d 837, 845 (1991). Held that a witness may testify to facts he related before the hypnotic session.

Robinson v. State, 677 P.2d 1080, 1085 (Okla. Crim. App.), *cert. denied*, 467 U.S. 1246 (1984). Not allowing a witness to make an in-court identification following hypnosis when no identification had been made prior to hypnosis.

People v. Guerra, 690 P.2d 635 (Cal. 1984). Held that "prehypnotic testimony at preliminary hearing is admissible in lieu of witness' testimony at trial as to events that were subject of subsequent hypnotic session . . . " Hypnotically-induced testimony is inadmissible since the "use of hypnosis to restore or improve memory of potential witness is not accepted as reliable procedure by consensus of relevant scientific community."

Admissibility on a Case-by-Case Basis

A few courts have taken yet a fifth approach to the question of admitting hypnotically-influenced testimony—to rule on admissibility on a case-by-case basis balancing the possible prejudicial effect with the probative value. For example, in an effort to determine the reliability of hypnotically-influenced testimony, an Ohio court in *State v. Johnston*[54] held a pretrial hearing to apply a "totality of circumstances" test. In *State v. Iwakiri*,[55] the court held that trial courts must make an individualized inquiry into each case

to determine whether the trial testimony of a witness who has been hypnotized will be sufficiently reliable to qualify for admission.

In ruling on the admissibility of post-hypnotic testimony, the court in *People v. Romero*[56] gave some guidelines of things to consider under the "totality of circumstances" standard.

. . . , trial court should consider totality of the circumstances bearing on the issue of reliability, including level of training of the hypnotist; hypnotist's independence from law enforcement investigators or the defense; any information given or known by the hypnotist concerning the case prior to the session; existence of written or recorded account of the facts as the witness remembers them prior to undergoing hypnosis; creation and recording of all contacts between hypnotist and witness; presence of persons other than hypnotist and witness during the session; location of the session, appropriateness of induction and memory retrieval techniques; appropriateness of using hypnosis for the kind of memory loss involved; and existence of evidence to corroborate the hypnotically enhanced testimony.[57]

Relevant Annotated Case Law

McQueen v. Garrison, 814 F.2d 951, 958 (4th Cir.), *cert. denied*, 484 U.S. 944 (1987). Held that a court must conduct a balanced inquiry to determine if a witness's memory was distorted by the hypnosis.

Chamblee v. State, 527 So.2d 173, 177 (Ala. Crim. App. 1988). Held that the admissibility of hypnotically-induced testimony is to be weighed on a case-by-case basis.

People v. Romero, 745 P.2d 1003, 1005, 1016 (Colo. 1987). Rejected previous rule of per se inadmissibility and ruled that "trial courts must make individualized inquiry in each case to determine whether trial testimony of witness who has been hypnotized will be sufficiently reliable to qualify for admission."

State v. Armstrong, 329 N.W.2d 386 (1983). Held that hypnotically-refreshed testimony was neither excluded per se or automatically admissible. The court mandated a case-by-case evaluation with the burden of proof to demonstrate admissibility and the absence of undue suggestiveness resting upon the side that wishes to introduce the hypnotically-refreshed testimony.

Zani v. State, 767 S.W.2d 825, 835–38 (Tex. Crim. App. 1989). Must consider hypersuggestibility, loss of critical judgment, confabulation, and memory cementing in admissibility of hypnotically-induced testimony.

Summary

To help evaluate the current status of the admissibility of hypnotically-influenced testimony and to provide the reader with a quick reference list of the dominant precedent (as of this writing) in their jurisdiction, the following list is offered.

Supreme Court

Rock v. Arkansas, 107 S. Ct. 2704 (1987). Held that a per se rule excluding hypnotically-induced testimony by a criminal defendant infringes on his constitutional right to testify in his own behalf. Daubert v. Merrell Dow Pharmaceuticals, 113 S. Ct. 2786 (1993). Held that "general acceptance" (the Frye Rule) is not a necessary precondition to the admissibility of scientific evidence under the Federal Rules of Evidence, but the Rules of Evidence (especially Rule 702) do assign to the trial judge the task of ensuring that an expert's testimony both rests on a reliable foundation and is relevant to the task at hand.

Federal Courts

Circuit	Status	Precedent
1st Circuit	Admissible	Clay v. Vose, 771 F.2d 1 (1985)
2nd Circuit	Admissible	United States v. Miller, 411 F.2d 825 (1969)
3rd Circuit	No controlling rule	
4th Circuit	Admissible	McQueen v. Garrison, 814 F.2d 951 (1987)
5th Circuit	Admissible	Wicker v. McCotter, 783 F.2d 487 (1986) United States v. Valdez, 722 F.2d 1196 (1984)
6th Circuit	Admissible w/safeguards	Beck v. Norris, 801 F.2d 242 (1986)
7th Circuit	Admissible	United States v. Kimberlin, 805 F.2d 210 (1986)
8th Circuit	Admissible w/safeguards	Sprynczynatyk v. General Motors, 771 F.2d 1112 (1985)
9th Circuit	Admissible	United States v. Awkard, 597 F.2d 667 (1979)

State Courts

State	Status	Precedent
Alabama	Prehypnosis only	Prewitt v. State, 460 So.2d 296 (Ala. Crim. App. 1984)

Alaska	Prehypnosis only	Contreras v. State, 718 P.2d 129 (1986)
Arizona	Prehypnosis only	State ex rel. Collins v. Superior Court, 644 P.2d 1269 (1982)
		State v. McMurtrey, 664 P.2d 637 (1983)
		State v. Rodriguez, 1700 P.2d 855 (Ariz. App. 1984)
		State v. Superior Court, 690 P.2d 94 (1984)
		State v. Poland, 698 P.2d 183 (1985)
Arkansas	Prehypnosis only	Rock v. State, 708 S.W.2d 78 (1986), vacated and remanded 107 S. CT. 2704 (1987)
California	Prehypnosis only	Cal. Evidence Code sec. 795 (West 1984)
Colorado	Admissible w/safeguards	People v. Romero, 745 P.2d 1003 (1987)
Connecticut	Admissible	State v. Pollitt, 530 A.2d 155 (1987)
Delaware	Per se inadmissible	State v. Davis, 490 A.2d 601 (Del. Super. 1985)
DC	No controlling rule	
Florida	Prehypnosis only	Bundy v. State, 471 So.2d 9 (1985)
Georgia	Prehypnosis only	Walraven v. State, 336 S.E.2d 798 (1985)
Hawaii	Prehypnosis only	State v. Moreno, 709 P.2d 103 (1985)
Idaho	Admissible w/safeguards	State v. Iwakiri, 682 P.2d 571 (1984)
		State v. Bainbridge, 698 P.2d 335 (1984)
		State v. Joblin, 689 P.2d 767 (1984)
Illinois	Prehypnosis only	People v. Wilson, 506 N.E.2d 571 (1987)
		People v. Smrekar, 385 N.E.2d 848 (Ill. App. 4 Dist. 1979)
		People v. Byas, 453 N.E.2d 1141 (Ill. App. 3 Dist. 1983)
		People v. Cohoon, 457 N.E.2d 998 (Ill. App. 5 Dist. 1983)
		People v. Zayas, 510 N.E.2d 1125 (Ill. App. 1 Dist. 1987)
Indiana	Prehypnosis only	Strong v. State, 435 N.E.2d 969 (1982)
		Peterson v. State, 448 N.E.2d 673 (1983)
		Gentry v. State, 471 N.E.2d 263 (1984)
		Rowley v. State, 483 N.E.2d 1078 (1985)
Iowa	Prehypnosis only	State v. Seager, 341 N.W.2d 420 (1983)
		State v. Groscost, 355 N.W.2d 32 (1984)
Kansas	Prehypnosis only	State v. Conley, 627 P.2d 1174 (Kan. App. 1981)
		State v. Haislip, 701 P.2d 909 (1985)
Kentucky	Admissible	Rowland v. Com., 901 S.W.2d 871 (1995)
Louisiana	Admissible	State v. Wren, 425 So.2d 756 (1983)

		State v. Goutro, 444 So.2d 615 (1984)
		State v. Porretto, 468 So.2d 1142 (1985)
		State v. White, 498 So.2d 1100 (1986)
Maine	No controlling rule	
Maryland	Prehypnosis only	State v. Collins, 464 A.2d 1028 (Md. App. 1983)
		McCoy v. State, 484 A.2d 624 (1984)
		Calhoun v. State, 468 A.2d 45 (1983)
Massachusetts	Prehypnosis only	Commonwealth v. Kater, 447 N.E.2d 1190 (1983)
Michigan	Prehypnosis only	People v. Hangsleben, 273 N.W.2d 539 (Mich. App. 1978)
		People v. Gonzales, 329 N.W.2d 743 (1982)
		as modified 336 N.W.2d 751 (1983)
		People v. Nixon, 364 N.W.2d 593 (1984)
		People v. Centers, 377 N.W.2d 4 (1985)
		People v. McIntosh, 376 N.W.2d 653 (1985)
		People v. Reese, 385 N.W.2d 722 (Mich. App. 1986)
Minnesota	Prehypnosis only	State v. Mack, 292 N.W.2d 764 (1980)
		State v. Koehler, 312 N.W.2d 108 (1981)
		State v. Blanchard, 315 N.W.2d 427 (1982)
		Rodriquez v. State, 345 N.W.2d 781 (Minn. App. 1984)
		Matter of J.R.D., 342 N.W.2d 162 (Minn. App. 1984)
		State v. Ture, 353 N.W.2d 502 (1984)
Mississippi	Admissible w/safeguards	House v. State, 445 So.2d 815 (1984)
Missouri	Admissible w/safeguards	State v. Greer, 609 S.W.2d 423 (Mo. App. 1980)
		State v. Little, 674 S.W.2d 541 (1984)
Montana	No controlling rule	
Nebraska	Prehypnosis only	State v. Patterson, 331 N.W.2d 500 (1983)
		State v. Levering, 331 N.W.2d 505 (1983)
		State v. Palmer, 313 N.W.2d 648 (1981)
Nevada	No controlling rule	
New Hampshire	No controlling rule	
New Jersey	Admissible w/safeguards	State v. Hurd, 432 A.2d 86 (1981)
New Mexico	Admissible w/safeguards	State v. Beachum, 643 P2d 246 (N.M. App. 1982)

		State v. Hutchinson, 661 P.2d 1315 (1983)
		State v. Clark, 722 P.2d 685 (N.M. App. 1986)
New York	Prehypnosis only	People v. Hughes, 453 N.E.2d 484 (N.Y. App. 1983)
North Carolina	Prehypnosis only	State v. Peoples, 319 S.E.2d 177 (1984)
North Dakota	Admissible	State v. Pusch, 46 N.W.2d 508 (1950)
		State v. Brown, 337 N.W.2d 138 (1983)
Ohio	Prehypnosis only	State v. Maurer, 473 N.E.2d 768 (1984)
		State v. Weston, 475 N.E.2d 805 (Ohio App. 1984)
Oklahoma	Prehypnosis only	Jones v. State, 542 P.2d 1316 (Okla. Cr. App. 1975)
		Robison v. State, 677 P.2d 1080 (Okla. Cr. App. 1984)
		Harmon v. State, 700 P.2d 212 (Okla. Cr. App. 1985)
		Standridge v. State, 701 P.2d 761 (Okla. Cr. App. 1985)
		Stafford v. State, 731 P.2d 1372 (Okla. Cr. App. 1987)
Oregon	Admissible	State v. Jorgensen, 492 P.2d 312 (Or. App. 1971)
		State v. King, 733 P.2d 472 (Or. App. 1987)
		Or. Rev. Stat. sec. 136.675 (1984)
Pennsylvania	Prehypnosis only	Commonwealth v. Nazarovitch, 436 A.2d 170 (1981)
		Commonwealth v. Taylor, 439 A.2d 805 (Pa. Super. 1982)
		Commonwealth v. Smoyer, 476 A.2d 1304 (1984)
Rhode Island	No controlling rule	
South Carolina	No controlling rule	
South Dakota	No controlling rule	
Tennessee	Admissible w/safeguards	State v. Glebock, 616 S.W.2d 897 (Tenn. Cr. App. 1981)
Texas	Admissible	Zani v. State, 679 S.W.2d 144 (Tex. App. 6 Dist. 1984)
		Walters v. State, 680 S.W.2d 60 (Tex. App. 7 Dist. 1984)
		Vester v. State, 713 S.W.2d 920 (Tex. Cr. App. 1986)

Utah	Prehypnosis only	State v. Tuttle, No. 20068 (Utah April 12, 1989) (Lexus, Utah library, Utah file)
Vermont	No controlling rule	
Virginia	Prehypnosis only	Greenfield v. Commonwealth, 204 S.E.2d 414 (1974)
		Hopkins v. Commonwealth, 337 S.E.2d 264 (1985)
Washington	Prehypnosis only	State v. Martin, 684 P.2d 651 (1984)
		State v. Coe, 684 P.2d 668 (1984)
		State v. Laureano, 682 P.2d 889 (1984)
		State v. Yapp, 726 P.2d 1003 (Wash. App. 1986)
West Virginia	No controlling rule	
Wisconsin	Admissible w/safeguards	State v. Armstrong, 329 N.W.2d 386 (1982)
Wyoming	Admissible	Chapman v. State, 638 P.2d 1280 (1982)
		Gee v. State, 662 P.2d 103 (1983)
		Pote v. State, 695 P.2d 617 (1985)
		Haselhuhn v. State, 727 P.2d 280 (1986)

Totals

Inadmissible—1 state
Admissible—7 states
Admissible w/safeguards—8 states
Prehypnosis only—25 states
No controlling rule—10 states

Without question, the least controversial use of hypnosis in criminal and civil investigations is as a means of obtaining new and independent corroborative evidence. And the safest witness to submit to hypnotic memory enhancement is one who is unlikely to testify in court (e.g., a "throw away witness"), hence avoiding the issue of admissibility. If, however, pretrial hypnosis is to be used on a prospective trial witness to enhance memory, counsel is advised to thoroughly research the status of its admissibility in their jurisdiction and be willing and prepared to argue for its acceptance. This chapter is offered as a starting point to that end.

Conclusions

The working hypno-investigator, the counsel who ultimately must seek admission of hypnotically-influenced testimony in court, and the courts themselves, all have one thing in common—they recognize the potential benefits of hypnosis as an investigative tool. Where they differ is on the question of admissibility. As we have seen, courts in the various jurisdictions in the United States, both state and federal, have taken several different approaches regarding the admissibility of evidence derived from hypnosis. A thorough knowledge of the dominant position in one's jurisdiction is crucial as to know how best to use hypnosis in a criminal or civil case, and how best to introduce it in court (if at all).

The uncertainty about whether or not previously hypnotized witnesses should be allowed to testify stems from the uncertainty about the effect of hypnosis on memory. Hypnosis may well aid in recovering important information during an investigation which can help to solve crimes, but adverse expert witnesses caution courts that hypnotized witnesses may (1) be led incorrectly to a desired answer through suggestive questioning, (2) fill in gaps in their memory with erroneous "remembrances," (3) "harden" their memory as a result of hypnotic recall, which may render a witness impervious to cross-examination and unduly impress a jury with his confident testimony, (4) unduly influence a jury due to the conventional belief that hypnosis is a guarantee of truthfulness, and (5) lose their ability to discriminate between prehypnotic, hypnotic, and posthypnotic memories. These contentions have been persuasively (and rightfully, we think) countered by Dr. Martin Reiser.[58,59,60] Unfortunately, as Dr. Reiser lucidly points out, courts have been unduly influenced by adverse expert witnesses who should not even be qualified as expert witnesses because they are *not* trained in investigative hypnosis, nor do they have any measurable degree of experience in the field.

Recommendations for the Future

Based on a careful review of the case law, the testimony of expert witnesses on both sides of the issues, the compounded years of experience of many working hypno-investigators in this developing specialty, and the recommendations set forth in this book (see "Why Should Law Enforcement Officers be Trained in Hypnosis," p. 10; "Two Approaches to Hypno-Investigation," p. 194; and "Special Topics for Safeguarding the Admissibility of Hypnotically-Influenced Testi-

mony," p. 232), the authors would predict, hope, and lobby for "admissibility with procedural safeguards." Experience and research have clearly shown that hypnosis is too valuable of a memory-enhancement tool to be discarded, and the authors believe that law enforcement and criminal justice personnel should actively work towards a more universal acceptance by the courts. One of the best ways to do this is to ensure that all hypno-investigations are done according to sound procedural safeguards. In their absence, the risk runs high that an improperly conducted hypno-investigation could lead to an unduly restrictive precedent, even by the U.S. Supreme Court. Therefore, we would highly encourage any counsel faced with seeking admissibility of hypnotically-influenced testimony to actively prepare their argument and petition the court for "admissibility with procedural safeguards." Yet, we would restate the safeguards currently used by most courts as set forth by Orne in *Hurd*[61] in the following manner:

(1) The hypnotic session should be conducted by a criminal justice professional trained in investigative and forensic hypnosis. In the absence of such, the hypnotic session should be conducted by a mental health professional specifically trained in investigative and forensic hypnosis. The hypno-investigator should meet the minimum training requirements of the **International Society for Investigative and Forensic Hypnosis.**

(2) The qualified professional conducting the hypnotic session should not be the primary case investigator, but may inform himself or herself of the details of the case to aid in conducting a focused and effective interview.

(3) Before induction of hypnosis, the hypno-investigator should obtain from the subject a detailed description of the facts as the subject remembers them, care-

fully avoiding adding any new elements to the witness's description of the events.

(4) The hypno-investigator should have no unrecorded contact with the subject outside of the hypnosis session. All contacts between the hypnotist and the subject should be electronically recorded (audiotaping is sufficient but videotaping is preferable) to verify that the witness was not unduly influenced by leading questions.

(5) Only the hypno-investigator, the subject, a parent or guardian if the subject is a minor, and a primary investigator should be present. Parties other than the hypno-investigator and subject should remain silent and only communicate with the hypno-investigator via written notes.

Any jurisdiction faced with the prospect of introducing hypnotically-influenced testimony in a court of law is highly encouraged to contact the **International Society for Investigative and Forensic Hypnosis** for support services and information.

REFERENCES

1. Rosenthal, R.: *Experimenter Effects in Behavioral Research.* New York, Appleton-Century-Crofts, 1966.
2. Reiser, M.: Investigative Hypnosis. In Raskin, D. (Ed.): *Psychological Methods in Criminal Investigation and Evidence,* New York, Springer, 1989, p. 159.
3. Kroger, W.: *Clinical and Experimental Hypnosis,* 2nd ed. Philadelphia, Lippincott, 1977.
4. Ready, D. J.: The effects of hypnosis and guided memory on eyewitness recall and suggestibility. Unpublished doctoral dissertation, Florida State University, 1986.
5. Diamond, *Inherent Problems in the Use of Pretrial Hypnosis on a Prospective Witness,* 68 Calif. L. Rev. 313, 314 (1980).
6. Loftus, E.: *Eyewitness Testimony.* Cambridge, Harvard University Press, 1979.
7. Buckhout, R.: Eyewitness testimony. *Scientific American,* 231, 23–31, 1974.
8. Yarmey, D.: *Eyewitness Testimony.* New York, Free Press, 1979.
9. Rainer, D.: Eyewitness testimony: Does hypnosis enhance accuracy, distortion and confidence? Unpublished doctoral dissertation, University of Wyoming, Cheyenne, 1983.
10. Griffin, G.: Hypnosis: Toward a logical approach in using hypnosis in law enforcement. *Journal of Police Science and Administration, 8,* 385–389, 1980.
11. Relinger, H.: Are courts restricting hyp-

notherapy? Current status of forensic hypnosis. Presented at the American Psychological Association Convention, Anaheim, CA, August 26, 1983.
12. Sheehan, P.: Confidence, memory and hypnosis. In Pettinati, H. (Ed.): *Hypnosis and Memory,* New York, Guilford Press, 1988, p. 99.
13. Commonwealth v. Colihan, Suffolk County, Mass. Superior Court #030301, Feb. 20, 1981.
14. Spector and Foster, *Admissibility of hypnotic statements: Is the law of evidence susceptible?* Ohio State University Law Journal, *38,* 567 (1978).
15. Reiser, M.: Police Use of Investigative Hypnosis: Scientism, Ethics, and Power Games. *American Journal of Forensic Psychology,* Vol. II, No. 3, pp. 115–143, 1984.
16. Sanders, G., Gansler, D., & Riesman, S.: *The effect of hypnosis in eyewitness testimony and reactions to cross-examination.* State University of New York, Albany, 1987.
17. Reiser, M.: Some current issues in investigative hypnosis. *International Journal of Investigative and Forensic Hypnosis, 8,* 41–56, 1985.
18. Orne, M.: The Use and Misuse of Hypnosis in Court. *The International Journal of Clinical and Experimental Hypnosis.* Vol. XXVII, No. 4, 311–341, 1979.
18. State v. Hurd, 86 N.J. 525, 432 A.2d 86 (1981).

19. Spector & Foster, p. 567.

20. State v. Hurd.

21. *Id.* at 92.

22. Geiselman, R., & Machlovitz, H.: Hypnosis memory recall: Implications for forensic use. *American Journal of Forensic Psychology, 5(1),* 37–47, 1987.

23. Reiser, 1985.

24. Reiser, 1984.

25. Reiser, 1989.

26. Reiser, 1984, pp. 69–70.

27. People v. Eubanks, 117 Cal. 652, 665, 49 P. 1049 (1987).

28. *Id.* at 1053.

29. Bailey and Shapiro, *Hypnosis: Should Hypnotically Induced Testimony be Excluded?* Washburn Law Journal, Vol. 21, p. 607, 1987.

30. Frye v. United States, 293 F. 1013 (D.C. Cir. 1923).

31. People v. Shirley, 31 Cal. 3rd 18 (CA, 1982).

32. Morris, R.: The Admissibility of Evidence Derived from Hypnosis and Polygraphy. In Raskin, D. (Ed.): *Psychological Methods in Criminal Investigation and Evidence.* New York, Springer, 1989, p. 337.

33. State v. Brown, 337 N.W.2d 138 (N.D. 1983).

34. Morris, p. 337.

35. Rock v. Arkansas, 483 U.S. 44, 107 S.Ct. 2704, 97 L. Ed. 2d 37 (1987).

36. Rozzano, *The Use of Hypnosis in Criminal Trials: The Black Letter of the Black Art.* Loyola of Los Angeles Law Review, Vol. 21:581, p. 704, 1988.

37. Sawaya, T.: From the Bench: Hypnotic Testimony. *Litigation,* Vol. 15, Number 4, Summer 1989, p. 66.

38. Daubert v. Merrell Dow Pharmaceuticals, 113 S.Ct. 2786, (1993).

39. Kincade, P. *A Hypnotist's Casebook,* privately printed, 1993, p. 111.

40. State v. Mena, 128 Ariz. 226, 624 P.2d 1274 (1981).

41. Bailey and Shapiro, *Hypnosis: Should Hypnotically Induced Testimony be Excluded?* Washburn Law Journal, Vol. 21, pp. 619–620, 1987.

42. State v. Mena, 128 Ariz. 228–29, 624 P.2d 1276–77 (1981).

43. United States v. Adams, 581 F.2d 193, 199 (9th Cir. 1978).

44. State v. Brown.

45. *Id.* at 138.

46. Ibid.

47. State v. Hurd.

48. State ex rel. Collins v. Superior Court (Collins II), 132 Ariz. at 209, 644 P.2d.

49. *Id.* at 1295.

50. State v. Palmer, 224 Neb. 282, 298, 399 N.W.2d 706, 719 (1986), *cert. denied,* 484 U.S. 872 (1987).

51. Giannelli, *Forensic Science: Hypnotic Evidence.* Criminal Law Bulletin, p. 268, 1993.

52. State ex rel. Neely v. Sherrill, 165 Ariz. 508, 513, 799 P.2d 849, 854 (1990).

53. People v. Lee, 434 Mich. 59, 84–85, 450 N.W.2d 883, 895 (1990), *cert. denied,* 111 S.211 (1990).

54. State v. Johnston, 39 Ohio St. 3d 48, 64, 529 N.E.2d 898, 905 (1988).

55. State v. Iwakiri, 106 Idaho 618, 625–626, 682 P.2d 571, 578–579 (1984).

56. People v. Romero, 745 P.2d 1003, (Colo. 1987).

57. *Id.* at 1005.

58. Reiser, 1984, pp. 115–143.

59. Reiser, M.: Some Current Issues in Investigative Hypnosis. Presented at the UCLA Symposium on Legal Psychology, Los Angeles, March 9, 1985.

60. Reiser, M.: Investigative Hypnosis. In Raskin, D., (Ed.): *Psychological Methods in Criminal Investigation and Evidence.* New York, Springer, 1989.

61. State v. Hurd.

Chapter 7

SPECIAL PROBLEMS AND TOPICS IN
FORENSIC HYPNOSIS

THE CORPSE IN THE LABORATORY
THE POSSIBLE ANTISOCIAL AND CRIMINAL USE OF HYPNOSIS

Since the time of the Mesmerists, a question has plagued the minds of laymen and professionals alike — Can a person with a noncriminal mentality be forced to commit self-injurious, immoral, antisocial, or criminal acts under hypnosis? As is the case with most aspects of hypnosis, the experts have aligned themselves on both sides of the issue; there are those who emphatically deny the possibility and those who claim just the opposite, and both base their respective opinions on "conclusive" research experiments.

It is important for the forensic hypnotist to have a basic understanding and knowledge of this question for several reasons. First, any individual or department utilizing investigative hypnosis will inevitably be confronted with the predominant cultural misconception that hypnosis can be used for illegitimate ends, whether to force confessions out of unwilling defendants or suspects, extract fabricated incriminating evidence out of witnesses, cause innocent and hapless hypnotic subjects to do one's bidding by committing crimes, or to hypnotize people against their will. Second, there is the additional popular misconception that hypnotized people are under the control of the hypnotist and lose their basic moral and ethical standards and sensibilities and therefore cannot consciously resist his suggestions. The individual hypnoinvestigator or department will need to know how to realistically address these misconceptions whether talking to a potential subject, the media, department personnel, the public, or defense counsel when on the witness stand. Third, it is important for the forensic hypnotist to know what the possibility and probability is of the criminal element using hypnosis for criminal purposes.

To this end, the authors will review some of the major studies; illustrate some of the methodological problems in researching this question; derive a realistic assessment of the possibility and probability of forcing people to commit immoral, self-injurious, antisocial, or criminal acts under hypnosis; discuss the legal ramifications and problem of culpability; assess the possibility of hypnotizing people against their will or without consent; critique the belief that these possibilities warrant the legislation of hypnosis; and examine the possibility of beating the polygraph with hypnosis.

The Evidence: Laboratory Experiments and Criminal Cases

The hypnosis literature, particularly the older works of the nineteenth century, is replete with case reports of alleged rapes, seductions, immoral acts, murders and other crimes committed with the aid of hypnosis. In 1889, in Paris, a man was sentenced to death on the testimony of his lover. She said that he hypnotized her to lure the victim to her apartment and to put a rope around his neck so her lover could strangle him. In 1897, a Swiss doctor was sentenced to five years in jail after being found guilty of hypnotizing and then seducing eleven women.[1] Much later, in the first half of the twentieth century, an amateur hypnotist in Denmark was found guilty and sentenced to life in prison for inducing an individual to commit murder under hypnosis, and the subject received a two-year sentence on the basis of temporary insanity.[2] Some years later, also in Denmark, a man was convicted as an accomplice to a bank robbery for giving the defendant a posthypnotic suggestion to rob a bank, which he did.[3] In 1948, in the United States, a man was convicted on the charge that he raped a woman that he had hypnotized against her will.[4]

As a result of these and other crimes alleged to have been committed under hypnosis or as the result of a posthypnotic suggestion, the predominant cultural belief that a hypnotic subject is under the total domination of the will of the hypnotist was reinforced. Serious workers in the field wished to counter this negative and unfounded belief that hindered the positive and beneficial utilization of hypnosis. As a result, they promulgated the belief that hypnotic subjects will not do anything against their will, nor can they be made to behave immorally or criminally, if not so predisposed during the waking state. Such early writers as Bramwell asserted that a hypnotic subject could adequately defend himself against immoral suggestions by becoming alert, and, in fact, that hypnosis actually increased the person's moral sense.[5] Similarly, Hollander stated that "even a person in the hypnotic state will refuse to perform any act which is contrary to his or her natural disposition. But both normal and hypnotized people will readily accept any notion for which their own nature has already prepared them."[6] Schilder, after an extensive review of the literature and based on his

own extensive experience, concludes:

> If a profoundly hypnotized person is asked to perform an act that is unreasonable, an act in contradiction with his total will, his total personality, the following may happen: In spite of his profound hypnosis, the hypnotized man may refuse to obey . . . or awake from his hypnosis if the demand of the hypnotizer as well as the total situation are no longer in accord with his other ego ideals.[7]

Most of the above opinions are based on clinical experience, personal bias, theoretical positions, and limited informal and poorly controlled experimental studies. Based on these same variables, one would certainly find other early authorities who derived the opposite conclusions.

In one of the earliest, provocative, and most often referred to studies conducted in an attempt to empirically examine this problem under carefully controlled laboratory conditions was conducted by Rowland, in 1939. The purpose of his experiment was to determine the extent to which deeply hypnotized persons will subject themselves to unreasonably dangerous situations and will perform acts unreasonably dangerous to the welfare of others. To test the commonly held notion that hypnotized subjects will *not* violate their own good judgment with respect to doing possible harm either to themselves or others, Rowland designed a two-part experiment.

In the first part, designed to determine if hypnotized subjects would expose themselves to unreasonably dangerous situations, four somnambulistic subjects were asked to pick up a live large diamondback rattlesnake placed in a cage behind invisible glass. During the experiment the snake was poked with a wire to force him to coil ready to strike and to rattle loudly enough to be clearly heard.

The first two hypnotized subjects were individually told by the experimenter to go over to the box, reach in, and pick up a piece of coiled rope in it. The first subject promptly did so and was surprised to hit the glass with her hand. The second subject walked to the box, saw the snake, and awoke from trance. (Rowland notes that he was unsure beforehand of the depth of this subject.)

The second pair of hypnotized subjects were individually told by Rowland to go over to the box and pick up the dangerous rattlesnake. Both subjects readily complied and even explored the glass for an opening.

In the second part of the experiment, designed to determine if hypnotized subjects would perform acts unreasonably dangerous to others, Rowland redesigned the apparatus such that an experimenter's face would appear behind the invisible glass. Another pair of hypnotized subjects were individually told to throw very dangerous sulphuric acid on the experimenter which would "scar the skin and put out the eyes." For realism, the experimenter dipped a strip of zinc into the acid which resulted in a strong fuming reaction.

The first subject, although reluctant, threw the acid at the experimenter with additional prompting and seemed very disturbed at having done so. The second subject forcefully threw the acid at the experimenter.

Quite naturally, Rowland concludes that "persons in deep hypnosis will allow themselves to be exposed to unreasonably dangerous situations," and that they will also "perform acts unreasonably dangerous to others."[8]

Several years later, the results of this study were replicated in a similar experiment in which hypnotized subjects readily handled snakes believed to be dangerous water moccasins, and threw what they believed to be nitric acid on research assistants. "The results show that seven of the eight subjects would enter into a situation which unhypno-

tized observers shrank from, the subjects carrying out suggestions to handle snakes and throw nitric acid under conditions from which they themselves recoiled in the waking state."[9]

Another equally convincing and often cited series of case studies was conducted by Watkins, in 1947. In the first case study, Watkins set out to determine if, under hypnosis, some people can be made to unconsciously divulge information for which they had a strong prior motivation not to divulge. To examine this possibility, Watkins individually hypnotized nine different military men who were experimental volunteers. Each subject was given "confidential" information by a superior officer and ordered not to divulge it. Some were even offered a monetary reward for not divulging the information. Under hypnosis, each subject willingly told the confidential information.

In a similar instance, an Army WAC volunteer began to willingly divulge secret information in front of an audience of 200 people before being stopped by a high-ranking officer in the interest of military secrecy.

In another case study, Watkins wished to determine if, under deep hypnosis, hallucinations could be created in some subjects that would cause them to commit criminal acts, even murder. To test this proposition, Watkins hypnotized a private with a very good military record in the presence of a lieutenant colonel. Under hypnosis, the private was told, "In a minute you will slowly open your eyes. In front of you, you will see a dirty Jap soldier. He has a bayonet, and is going to kill you unless you kill him first. You will have to strangle him with your bare hands." Upon opening his eyes, the private crept cautiously forward and then lunged at the lieutenant colonel, knocking him against the wall and strangling him with both hands. It took three others present to break the private's grip and to pull him from the officer.

In a similar instance, Watkins initiated a murderous attack by a 21-year-old lieutenant upon a brother officer and friend. Unknown to the experimenter, the subject possessed a pocket knife which he pulled out and opened as he lunged at the "dirty Jap." "Only the quick intercession of witnesses and an upward wrist parry by his officer friend (the Jap soldier) prevented a serious stabbing."[10]

Other seemingly positive experimental results which support the possibility of inducing hypnotic subjects to commit antisocial or criminal acts were found by Wells and Brenman. Wells was able to cause a hypnotic subject to steal money posthypnotically, and this finding was supported by Brenman who succeeded in inducing theft with three female students. Wells concludes that the fact must be "recognized that even so extreme a phenomenon as real crime against the will of the fully forewarned subject can be produced" by hypnosis.[11] Similarly, Brenman concurs with Wells when she concludes that antisocial and self-injurious "acts can be induced even when contrary to the subject's personal wishes or his moral nature."[12]

Conclusive evidence? Not at all! Other equally well-recognized authorities have reached the opposite conclusion on the basis of empirical studies.

In 1939, the same year as Rowland's celebrated study, Erickson published a comprehensive study which summarized several years of work in which he attempted by both direct and indirect suggestion to get hypnotized subjects to carry out self-injurious, antisocial, and criminal acts. His research methodology consisted of seizing upon any favorable opportunity or situation in a clinical setting to suggest some form of objectionable behavior be carried out by hypnotized subjects. In so doing, he utilized approximately fifty subjects who were all "well trained to accept any type of suggestion and to develop profound somnambulistic trances, as well as complete amnesias for all trance experiences."[13] Erickson also made every effort to avoid the subjects perceiving the situation as experimental, to make each suggested act and situation seem absolutely realistic, and purposefully avoided suggesting acts of an extreme nature, but instead employed relatively minor acts that were less apt to be rejected outright. In all instances he made every effort to induce either an actual or approximate performance of the suggested act, even going to the extreme of using elaborate techniques of suggestion to allow for the particular subject's personality in the more complicated and difficult experiments.

In every instance of hypnotically suggested self-injurious, antisocial, or criminal behavior, Erickson met with failure. In fact, it was found that subjects were more resistant to carrying out the suggested acts during hypnosis than in the waking state. Erickson summarizes his findings in the following manner:

The findings disclosed consistently the failure of all experimental measures to induce hypnotic subjects, in response to hypnotic suggestion, to perform acts of an objectionable character, even though many of the suggested acts were acceptable to them under circumstances of waking consciousness. Instead of blind, submissive, automatic, unthinking obedience and acquiescence to the hypnotist and the acceptance of carefully given suggestions and commands, the subjects demonstrated a full capacity and ability for self-protection, ready and complete understanding with critical judgment, avoidance, evasion, or complete rejection of commands, resentment and objection to instrumentalization by the hypnotist, and for aggression and retaliation, direct and immediate, against the hypnotist for his objectionable suggestions and commands. In addition, many demonstrated a full capacity to take over control of the hypnotic situation and actually did so by compelling the experimenter to make amends for his unacceptable suggestions. . . .

Hence, the conclusion warranted by these experimental findings is that hypnosis cannot be misused to induce hypnotized persons to commit actual wrongful acts either against themselves or others, and that the only serious risk encountered in such attempts is incurred by the hypnotists in the form of condemnation, rejection and exposure.[14]

As early as 1903, Bramwell conducted a number of experiments in which he suggested to his best somnambulists to either steal someone else's watch or to put arsenic into another's tea. When consistently met with refusal, Bramwell concluded that his somnambulists "refused to carry out suggestions in hypnosis, which they would have rejected in the waking state."[15]

After examining this issue, Wolberg similarly concluded that "it is quite unlikely . . . that any person could be induced to do anything in a trance or posthypnotically as a result of suggestion, that he would not do with adequate persuasion in the waking state."[16] To support his position, Wolberg offers an interesting case history:

While doing experimental work with hypnosis, I suggested to a somnambulistic subject in a trance that he would open his eyes and conspire with me in a crime. I informed him that two lumps of sugar in a bowl, which I marked with a pencil, contained a deadly poison. He was to select them and place them in the cup of tea served to a doctor friend whom I expected shortly. This doctor was an evil fellow who had perfected a virus with which he planned to kill a number of people. It was best to get him out of the way before it was too late. I asked the subject if he would cooperate with me in getting rid of the man. While no one would find out that the man had been killed, the subject would, if it were ever known, be hailed as a benefactor. The subject readily agreed to cooperate with me. On signal the supposed victim entered the room and the three of us started a conversation. The subject, it was

noted, was very irritated with the doctor and made biting sarcastic remarks about people who put on a front. I suggested that we have tea, and the subject volunteered to make it. I noticed that he carefully put the marked lumps into the victim's tea and passed the cup to him. The doctor drank the tea, without effect of course. I then called the subject to one side and mentioned there was probably some mistake, that we had not given the doctor a large enough dose of cyanide. Thereupon I gave him two capsules from a box marked "Potassium cyanide" and asked him to put these in the next cup of tea. He immediately awoke from the trance. So long as he was playing a role, he was willing to follow suggestions. He knew very well that the lumps of sugar were not really cyanide. However, the possibility that there might be cyanide in the capsules brought him out of the trance.[17]

Wolberg concludes by saying that, "experimental work with artificially induced dissociated states, in which a suggested criminal personality alternated or operated in conjunction with the usual personality, has convinced me that the patient, even though he is a potential criminal, is capable of inhibiting any impulses he conceives to be wrong."[18]

After reviewing all the above and other experimental studies and case histories, Orne concludes that

no evidence is available to indicate that hypnosis increases the behavioral control of the hypnotist over that already present prior to its induction. Certainly, the popular view which holds that hypnosis is able to exert a unique form of control over the hypnotized individual, which can compel him to carry out otherwise repugnant actions, must be rejected.[19]

In reference to the documented cases of hypnotically-induced criminal behavior, Orne concludes that the criminal behavior could have been performed without the utilization of hypnosis and that "an explanation which purports to account for such behavior by singling out one aspect of the relationship — i.e. hypnosis — must be viewed with skepticism."[20] Similarly, in specific reference to two documented cases of hypnotically induced criminal behavior, Barber concludes that, "If 'hypnosis' played a role in these cases, this role may have consisted in reinforcing and extending a delusional system . . . , and in providing the subject with a rationale for justifying his behavior to himself and to others."[21]

After reviewing the literature with specific reference to documented cases of antisocial, immoral, and criminal acts committed under hypnosis, Conn concludes that, when studied, they "are revealed as flimsy rationalizations to provide criminals with alibis."[22] After a comprehensive review of the experimental research, Conn similarly concludes that hypnosis cannot be utilized to produce definitive antisocial acts and that it cannot be considered "a cause" or an external "force" capable of producing antisocial or criminal behavior, but instead "it is a form of adaptation . . . , an alibi, a neurotic compromise and a rationalized, regressive, masochistic maneuver, whose goal is to obtain the gratification of unacceptable wishes and to avoid superego condemnation."[23] Similarly, in discussing a reported hypno-induced crime, Orne concludes that "the role that hypnosis plays is to disguise for the subject his own motivation and to create a situation which allows the subject to, at some level, disclaim responsibility for his actions."[24]

In specific reference to the reported cases of criminal behavior involving hypnosis, Kline concludes that

there is enough evidence to suggest a degree of psychopathology in the hypnotist or a degree of readiness to act upon repressed impulses of a damaging, self-destructive, or sadistic nature on the part of the subject. In reviewing both the experimental and clinical literature, it would seem that the element most responsible for the effectiveness of hypnotic manipulations is to be found within the personality dynamics of both the hypnotist and the subject.[25]

In discussing three therapy cases of successful immoral transgressions by medical and psychological professionals upon hypnotic subjects, Kline concludes that "transgressive or antisocial behavior cannot be viewed within the construct of hypnosis alone."[26] Instead it must be viewed within the "nature, intensity, and dimension of the hypnotic relationship."[27] After conducting psychotherapy with a fifty-six-year-old physician who utilized hypnosis and the hypnotic relationship to manipulate patients sexually, a twenty-six-year-old psychology graduate student who utilized hypnosis to homosexually abuse children, and a thirty-six-year-old gynecologist who achieved a sense of gratification and omnipotence in deeply hypnotizing women, Kline concludes that

The production of transgressive behavior within a personal-social context can be enhanced by hypnosis as well as by other motivational or perceptually altering devices. There are certain factors which appear significant in connection with the effective utilization of hypnosis in this respect. One is the personality of the hypnotist, his commitment to the goal involved without emotional ambivalence and perhaps without question, and a degree of confidence in his ability to organize and direct the type of behavior desired. Second is the subject's ability to be readily and easily hypnotized within a relationship that is designed to promote transgressive behavior. Third is the intensity and frequency of the utilization of hypnosis. Thus, the relationship between hypnotist and subject may incorporate strong transference feelings and the activation of a tie to the hypnotist that represents the revivification of a neurotically desired, dependent, compliant, and erotically satisfying relationship.[28]

Although hypnosis was a positive factor in producing the transgressive behavior in the above cases, Kline believes that "it is not unlikely that such manipulative behavior could also be accomplished *without* the use of hypnosis. . . ."[29]

The Controversy

The controversy between the two opposing camps has been long and at times heated. It has waged openly in the public forum as well as on silent pages of professional journals and books. Those researchers who successfully induced self-injurious, antisocial, or criminal behavior in subjects under hypnosis accuse those who were unable to of utilizing "meager methodology," "incomplete techniques," insufficiently susceptible subjects, or having a negative operator-attitude. On the other hand, the authorities who were unable to induce such hypnotic behavior accuse those who did of not sufficiently isolating other experimental variables that could account fully for their findings, such as the definitely important subject-hypnotist relationship of trust, confidence, and even friendship; the experimental laboratory situation which legitimizes the subject's extreme behavior; subconscious and latent antisocial or criminal tendencies; the subject's belief that there were hidden protective measures taken; the subject's confidence that the experimenter subconsciously conveyed to the subject that he was supposed to carry out the requested act; the subject's faith in the integrity and prestige of the sponsoring academic institution and experimenter; utilization of hypnotically-induced perceptual distortions; selecting only the most highly hypnotizable subjects who are trained to carry out experimental suggestions; and the subject's expectation that the experimenter would necessarily assume responsibility for any negative consequences of the suggested acts.

If these seemingly divergent findings are to be reconciled, the essential question of why some researchers were able to elicit self-injurious, antisocial, or criminal behavior while others were not must be answered. In an attempt to seek a resolution to this controversy,

Weitzenhoffer carefully examined the representative studies of both sides and shrewdly discerned that both points of view are correct because they differ substantially in at least two respects: "(a) the form and contents of the suggestions used and (b) the interpretation placed upon such expressions as 'criminal act,' and 'antisocial act.' "[30] In addition to these two critical differences is the experimental setting. Each of these differences will be discussed individually below.

It becomes obvious when reading the various studies that those in which self-injurious, antisocial, or criminal behavior was successfully elicited for the most part made considerable use of hallucinations, illusions, delusions, and amnesias for the event. This was done to reconstruct the actual antisocial or criminal event, such that it was in line with the subjects' usual moral and ethic standards. For example, Watkins induced a hallucination in the young soldiers such that they were attacking a "dirty Jap" and not a superior officer, hence the act was transposed from a serious court-martial offense into a necessary and even commendable act of self-defense.

On the other hand, Erickson, who achieved only negative findings, used almost entirely direct suggestions without making any attempt to reconcile the requested act through the use of hallucinations and other hypnotic phenomena with the subjects' own sensibilities. For example, if Erickson were to attempt to replicate the previous case study he would suggest directly to the hypnotized subject that he open his eyes and kill his superior officer.

Next is the crucial matter of the different definitions and interpretations placed upon the terms "criminal act" and "antisocial act." The experimenters who successfully elicited criminal and antisocial acts under hypnosis will generally agree with Young, who adamantly maintains that the subject does not have to willfully or even consciously perform an act for it to be antisocial or criminal, and that "what the subject *thinks* he is doing is immaterial."[31] All that matters is that the act was indeed committed and is judged to be antisocial or criminal by objective observers who themselves are not hypnotized. Similarly, Brenman regards any act to be antisocial or criminal, even if moral conflict is eliminated by inducing hallucinations, delusions, and amnesias, if a court of law renders the usual verdict of "guilty but not responsible by virtue of mental disease." Brenman does not maintain that these subjects are "responsible," but that they are in fact "guilty."

In leading the opposition, Erickson just as adamantly maintains that for an act to be antisocial or criminal there must be *the unescapable fact of the subject's own participation in an undesirable performance directed either against himself or against others*" (his italics).[32] In other words, for an act to be antisocial or criminal, there has to be a full knowledge of the act and an intent by the subject. The moment a subject loses the conscious realization that he is engaging in an actual antisocial or criminal act, whether because of hallucinations, delusions, or amnesias, the act is no longer antisocial or criminal.

Probably the most important, but often overlooked, variable differentiating the positive and negative results obtained by various researchers are a multitude of factors that comprise the experimental setting. In 1939, when Erickson published his much acclaimed study, he openly criticized Rowland's equally lauded study for not giving sufficient attention "to the highly important factors of trust and confidence in the experimenter, the subject's probable realization of the actual use of concealed protective measures, and the general tendency . . . for subjects to look upon any hypnotic situation as essentially an experimental procedure,

particularly so in any formal laboratory setting."[33] It is for this reason that Erickson made every effort to avoid a formal laboratory setting and to use informal realistic situations for the inducement of antisocial or criminal behavior. It can be surmised that it is for this very reason that Erickson was unsuccessful in his experiment whereas Rowland and others readily elicited antisocial and criminal behavior in their laboratories.

The full importance of the experimental laboratory setting upon subject behavior was not adequately appreciated until the works of Orne,[34-36] Rosenthal,[37, 38] and Rosenthal and Fode.[39] These studies explicitly demonstrated that both the subject and the experimenter subconsciously influence the outcome of any given experiment. "The subject takes an active role in interpreting the nature of the investigation and makes implicit assumptions about the hypotheses being investigated which influence his performance in the experimental situation."[40] In other words, the experimental subject will behave in such a manner as to confirm his understanding of the purpose and desired results of the experiment. Similarly, the expectations of the experimenter, even though never overtly or knowingly communicated to the subject, nevertheless influence the subject's behavior such that it tends to confirm the expectations of the experimenter. In other words, two different experimenters with two different hypotheses may conduct the same experiment, but each will derive results congruent with his original hypotheses.

In a similar vein, Estabrooks cautions repeatedly that operator-attitude is very important and must not be overlooked. He stresses "the uncanny ability which a good subject has in reading the wishes and intentions of the operator."[41] In reference to Sidis,[42] he states that "the subject will resist a suggestion if he has the least idea that the operator does not fully expect him to comply."[43] Conversely, a subject will usually gladly carry out a suggestion if it is in fact expected of him. (The reader should reflect for a moment on the importance of genuinely believing in time regression.)

Orne and Evans conclusively demonstrate that implicit cues in any experimental situation are of crucial importance:

A subject is aware of certain realities imposed by the experimental situation. It is as clear to a subject as it is to any scientist that no reputable investigator can risk injuring a subject during the course of an experiment. A subject knows that an experimenter will outline in advance any possible specific and deliberate danger which could be associated with his actual participation in a study. Consequently, any requested behavior which appears to a subject to be dangerous at face value may be reinterpreted in the context of a laboratory situation. In spite of the apparent objective danger of a task it may nonetheless be perceived to be harmless because the subject realizes that necessary precautions will be taken to avoid possible injury to him. If an apparently dangerous task is requested of a subject during an experiment the subject's compliance, or refusal, may depend on whether he perceives that he is expected, or is not expected, to carry out the task.[44]

In essence, the mere "fact that the experimenter makes such a request inevitably communicates that — regardless of appearances — it is safe for the subject to comply."[45]

The behavioral extremes to which experimental subjects will go was demonstrated in a dramatic experiment that caused an international sensation and even resulted in a television movie. In 1965, at Yale University, Milgram designed and conducted an elaborate experiment to examine the following question: "If an experimenter tells a subject to hurt another person, under what conditions will the subject go along with this instruction, and under

what conditions will he refuse to obey."[46] The experimental procedure used to examine this question is described by Milgram as follows:

The focus of the study concerns the amount of electric shock a subject is willing to administer to another person when ordered by an experimenter to give the "victim" increasingly more severe punishment. The act of administering shock is set in the context of a learning experiment, ostensibly designed to study the effect of punishment on memory. Aside from the experimenter, one naive subject and one accomplice perform in each session. On arrival each subject is paid $4.50. After a general talk by the experimenter, telling how little scientists know about the effect of punishment on memory, subjects are informed that one member of the pair will serve as teacher and one as learner. A rigged drawing is held so that the naive subject is always the teacher, and the accomplice becomes the learner. The learner is taken to an adjacent room and strapped into an "electric chair."

The naive subject is told that it is his task to teach the learner a list of paired associates, to test him on the list, and to administer punishment whenever the learner errs in the test. Punishment takes the form of electric shock, delivered to the learner by means of a shock generator controlled by the naive subject. The teacher is instructed to increase the intensity of electric shock one step on the generator on each error. The learner, according to plan, provides many wrong answers, so that before long the naive subject must give him the strongest shock on the generator. Increases in shock level are met by increasingly insistent demands from the learner that the experiment be stopped because of the growing discomfort to him. However, in clear terms the experimenter orders the teacher to continue with the procedure in disregard of the learner's protests. . . .

For the purpose of delivering shock, a simulated shock generator is used, with 30 clearly marked voltage levels that range from 15 to 450 volts (and each activated by one of 30 individual lever switches set in a horizontal line). The naive subject is given a sample shock of 45 volts to convince him of the authenticity of the instrument. The generator bears verbal designations that range from "Slight Shock" to "Danger: Severe Shock."

The responses of the victim are standardized on tape, and each protest is coordinated to a particular voltage level on the shock generator. Starting with 75 volts the learner begins to grunt and moan. At 150 volts he demands to be let out of the experiment. At 180 volts he cries out that he can no longer stand the pain. At 300 volts he refuses to provide any more answers to the memory test, insisting that he is no longer a participant in the experiment and must be freed. In response to this last tactic, the experimenter instructs the naive subject to treat the absence of an answer as equivalent to a wrong answer, and to follow the usual shock procedure. The experimenter reinforces his demand with the statement: "You have no other choice, you must go on!" (This imperative is used whenever the naive subject tries to break off the experiment.) If the subject refuses to give the next higher level of shock, the experiment is considered at an end.[47]

That the experiment seemed real to the naive subjects seems to be beyond question. With few exceptions the shocks were perceived as real, extremely painful, and even dangerous. The "victims" would shout in desperation at 300 volts, violently scream at 315 volts, and shriek in agony every time a shock was administered up to 450 volts. The naive subjects for the most part displayed reactions of tension and emotional strain which increased in proportion to each successive shock given. The subjects sweated, trembled, stuttered, bit their lips, groaned, and some were even on the verge of nervous collapse and expressed grave concern about the victim. Furthermore, upon termination of the experiment, many of the subjects "heaved sighs of relief, mopped their brows, rubbed their fingers over their eyes, or nervously fumbled cigarettes. Some shook their heads, apparently in regret."[48]

When fourteen Yale senior psychology majors were asked to predict how many out of one hundred experimental subjects would continue ad-

ministering the shocks up to the maximum of 450 volts, their estimates ranged from zero to three subjects.[49] Similarly, when forty psychiatrists were asked to estimate the rate of compliance, they responded that approximately one tenth of 1 percent would administer the maximum.[50]

In actuality, in spite of severe emotional conflict and even outright disapproval and denouncement of the experiment, 65 percent of the naive subjects went all the way to administering the 450 volts to their paired "learners!" "With numbing regularity good people were seen to knuckle under the demands of authority and perform actions that were callous and severe. Men who are in everyday life responsible and decent were seduced by the trappings of authority, by the control of their perceptions, and by the uncritical acceptance of the experimenter's definition of the situation, into performing harsh acts."[51] Even when told that the "learner" had a bad heart and who complained of chest pains at the higher voltages before passing out, the subjects still pressed on.

Although Milgram offers a fairly detailed analysis of the inherent variables in the experimental situation that compel compliance, they will not be belabored here. The above study was described at length only as an illustration of the unsurmountable problem of deciding the issue of the hypnotic production of self-injurious, antisocial, or criminal behavior in an experimental context.

In an attempt to determine just how important the experimental context is in relation to the hypnotic production of self-injurious, antisocial, or criminal behavior, Orne and Evans designed an experiment that would answer the following question: "does the degree of social and behavioral control under hypnosis exceed that which is legitimized by the special social and behavioral control implicit in the experimental situation?"[52] In other words, is hypnosis and not some other factor or set of factors already existing in the experimental situation the critical variable?

To answer this question it is necessary to determine if experimental hypnotic subjects can be compelled to carry out self-injurious, antisocial, or criminal behavior that nonhypnotized control subjects will not carry out under the exact same conditions. If both groups of subjects carry out the requested behavior, it would be unfounded to conclude, as Rowland and Young did, that hypnosis was the crucial variable in causing the subjects' behavior. "Rather, the behavior of both groups could be interpreted more parsimoniously as an appropriate response to the existing cues in the experimental situation,"[53] in which the subjects perceived the requested behavior as being reasonable, legitimate, and somehow meaningful and safe within the experimental context.

To examine this proposition, Orne and Evans replicated in exact detail the procedures outlined by Young. The results obtained agreed with both Rowland's and Young's in that five of six deeply hypnotized subjects attempted to grasp the snake, remove a coin from a dish of fuming nitric acid, and throw the acid at an assistant. Under the identical situation, however, six out of six nonhypnotized subjects instructed to simulate hypnosis also carried out the tasks! Furthermore, recognizing that simulators may be more likely to comply with the suggested behavior due to special motivations of their own, a normal control group of six waking subjects was used to test the actual range of implicit social and behavioral control inherent in the experimental situation. The same requested behaviors were achieved to varying degrees depending upon the amount of pressure applied to the subjects, "indicating that the tasks are within the broad range of activities which are perceived as legitimized by the nature of the situation: they were requests made by experimenters, viewed by subjects as responsible scientists, in the context of a psychological experiment."[54] In fact, the compliance of the waking controls was only slightly inferior to the performance of either the hypnotized or simulating subjects.

Conclusions

From the above and other laboratory studies, Orne rightly concludes that "it has become clear that it is all but meaningless to test whether subjects will or will not carry out antisocial or destructive behaviors in a context that is perceived as experimental by the subject."[55] These studies also demonstrate how easy it is to reach unwarranted conclusions. The reader might consider for a moment what the conclusion of the Milgram study would have been if only hypnotized subjects had been used with either no or insufficient simulation and waking control groups. Undoubtedly, the mistakenly "obvious" conclusion would have been that hypnosis is a causal agent in the production of dangerous antisocial behavior. It would be interesting and informative if this study were replicated with hypnotized subjects. The authors would surmise that a similar if not greater percentage of the subjects would go to the maximum, but the emotional conflict would most likely be less due to the protective alibi of hypnosis that legitimizes the behavior; it is the subject's awareness that he is hypnotized that serves to rationalize and legitimize his otherwise unacceptable and extreme behavior.

So the question remains: Can hypnosis cause self-injurious, antisocial, or criminal behavior? As Estabrooks concludes, "No one knows the answer for the question is unanswerable without the actual commission of a criminal act."[56] In other words, without a corpse in the laboratory, it is impossible to tell. For obvious reasons, no reputable scientist can possibly jeopardize his career, tarnish the reputation of the institution with which he is professionally affiliated, or cause injury to an experimental subject, so the question will likely remain unanswered. Even in the eventuality of a corpse in the laboratory, no one would be able to say for certain that it was caused by hypnosis because the other crucial variables described above may be responsible, unless of course a simulator and waking control subject were also used, but then there may be three corpses in the laboratory!

In light of the above research, it seems safe to conclude that it has yet to be shown that hypnosis and hypnotic suggestion alone possess an inherent compulsive power by which otherwise unwilling individuals can be forced to commit self-injurious, antisocial, or criminal acts. (Clinicians reading this should consider for a moment how difficult it is using hypnosis to get a client to do something he *consciously wants* to do, such as stopping smoking and losing weight.) Even "those who agree that it is possible to commit a crime under hypnosis, and have conducted experimental studies, are unanimous in their conclusions that hypnosis is not an essential and sufficient antecedent to crime."[57]

An obvious question has probably crossed the reader's mind: Could not the experimental situation be misused by an unscrupulous operator to carry out a crime? This question has been answered by Orne who

does not deny the possibility that an unscrupulous individual might utilize the pretext of an experimental situation to cause individuals to behave in desired self-destructive or antisocial ways. That such a perversion of the experimental situation is possible can-

not be doubted, but its consequences should be conceptualized as the result of trickery, no different from any other kind of deceptive maneuver designed to cause individuals to behave in a desired way by misrepresentation.[58]

In reference to his own unsuccessful nonlaboratory setting experiments, Erickson similarly concludes that had they

been conducted as obviously experimental investigations, it is entirely possible that the subjects would have given realistic performances in such protected situations, but under those conditions, the outcome would not have been a function of the hypnosis itself but of the general situation. In that type of setting, one might deceive a subject into performing some objectionable act, but the deception would not be dependent upon the hypnosis. Rather, it would depend upon entirely different factors. . . . [59]

As an illustration of this possibility, the reader may ponder an actual occurrence that resulted from a mistake in technique during Young's study. In one instance, an experimental subject was mistakenly given real nitric acid, instead of the look-alike methylene blue solution, which he threw on the experimenter. Only the immediate application of first aid prevented scarring.[60]

The following is another related question that has probably occurred to the reader: Could not a criminally inclined hypnotist utilize such hypnotic phenomena as induced hallucinations, artifically created neurotic complexes, transidentification with another individual, and amnesia to sufficiently distort a subject's perception and reality to the point where he may commit a criminal act in what is perceived to be self-defense, e.g. Watkins's soldier attacking the "dirty Jap"? Many authorities believe this to be possible and would agree with Wells when he states:

If a criminal hypnotist were actually trying to force a subject to commit a real crime, e.g., a murder, the hypnotist, if he wished to use the art of hypnosis to the full, would certainly try to prevent any moral conflict in the subject by producing hallucinations, illusions, and delusions. . . . The hypnotist would try to produce amnesia in the subject, not only for everything said to him in the hypnotic trance in which the crime had been elaborated, but also for the fact that he had ever been a hypnotic subject. The hypnotist would then try to implant a post-hypnotic inhibition which would prevent anyone else from ever being able to hypnotize him.[61]

In response to this question and these tactics, Orne believes that "careful evaluations of these situations invariably suggests that the distortions of perception or memory serve more to rationalize and legitimize the behavior than to act as causal factors."[62] The reader is reminded of Hilgard's hidden observer, Watkins's ego states, and the experiments involving functional sensory alterations, e.g. functional deafness and negative hallucinations, in which at some level of awareness the subject still perceives and functions normally. The subject made functionally deaf to the point of not flinching when a gunshot goes off behind his head, the subject walking around the negatively hallucinated chair, and the unconscious surgery patient remembering operating room conversation in a regressed state all indicate that the hypnotic subject is still nevertheless aware at some level of consciousness and can consequently call a halt to any hypnotically suggested behavior if it deviates sufficiently from his moral and ethical standards. An often cited historical anecdote was reported by Janet, in 1889, when he readily commanded a hypnotized subject to perform "murder" by stabbing with a rubber knife and poisoning with powdered sugar before the French Academy at the famous Salpêtrière Hospital. When asked to undress, however, she refused to cooperate and quickly woke up.[63] Another case in point is Wolberg's

hypnotized subject who willfully "poisoned" until the stakes became too high. Wolberg appropriately concludes that "people in the trance state easily sense when they are being used for experimental purposes. They will play a role with great sincerity, and, where they have faith in the hypnotist's integrity, will expose themselves to presumably dangerous situations. There is, nevertheless, a limit to how far they will go."[64]

This review of the research and literature seems to weigh in favor of the position that hypnosis is not a necessary condition in the production of self-injurious, antisocial, or criminal behavior, but only plays an ancillary role as one variable among many. In fact, there are writers who maintain that hypnosis would serve as an actual obstacle to the production of such behavior. Erickson's experiments showed that hypnosis could easily constitute an actual obstacle to deception due to the fact that his experimental subjects invariably scrutinized every suggestion carefully. The self-reports of his experimental subjects indicated that they believed, based upon their experience of attempted forced antisocial behavior under hypnosis, that they were less apt to be deceived under hypnosis than in the waking state because the hypnotic trance and interrelationship constitutes an actual protection in itself by precluding the dangers of overconfidence likely to exist in the waking state.

This same position is supported by Arons, who concluded after decades of working with crime victims, witnesses, suspects, and defendants:

In everyday suggestibility, the subject, being unaware that he is in an unduly responsive condition, may succumb to suggestion that is inimical to his well-being. But in the concentrated hypnotic state, in which he is aware of the vulnerable position he occupies, he automatically sets up a "guard" against possibly harmful suggestion. Something inside of him (whether it be in the conscious, subconscious or superconscious sphere is a matter of opinion) assumes the function of a sort of "guardian angel," keeping a part of his mind alert against suggestion which may run counter to his normal pattern of behavior. Thus I maintain that a hypnotized person is actually safer from harm than one who is influenced by the myriad suggestions with which he is constantly bombarded every day of his life.[65]

LeCron reached a similar conclusion after a long career as a hypnotherapist, researcher, and author:

The subject is not an automaton when he is in a deep hypnotic state, nor is he unconscious. He thinks and is rational, though he may be hallucinated and deluded. In considering antisocial actions provoked under hypnosis, it is quite likely, if the hypnotist's purpose is criminal, that the subject would analyze and detect his nefarious purpose and would refuse to accept suggestions, despite the subject-hypnotist relationship. Furthermore, even with the most devious and best of techniques, the hypnotist will not find it easy to overcome the censorship of the subject's superego. . . . Deceit may be easier, at times, under hypnosis, but certainly most of us can be deceived more or less readily, and hypnosis is not a requisite. The newspaper columns and court actions show that deceit is common and "suckers" are plentiful. The unhypnotized person can be led to commit objectionable and criminal acts by deceit and delusion with no necessity for hypnosis.[66]

It should be obvious by now that even if it is possible to produce self-injurious, antisocial, or criminal behavior by hypnosis (which is a doubtful proposition) it should be remembered that "hypnosis is so difficult, and the opportunities for criminals to learn the art and to use it in criminal ways are so slight, that little is to be feared in a practical way. . . ."[67] After all, in the last forty five years, the number of reported criminal cases involving the use of hypnosis can be counted on one hand, and an analysis of these shows that hypnosis was not a crucial variable. LeCron summarizes that "it is likely that not more than one

person out of fifty or even 100 is a sufficiently good one to be in any danger whatsoever of being victimized by a hypnotic Fagin."[68] "The fact is that it is not at all likely for any prospective hypnotic subject to ever encounter a villainous hypnotist possessed of the requisite skill."[69] Furthermore, it is hardly conceivable that any hypnotist would go to the extreme of fabricating an experimental situation, finding a sufficiently susceptible subject, developing the relationship of trust, designing the techniques, etc., as there is no guarantee that he will avoid detection. "Any hypnotist intelligent enough to work out the intricate techniques necessary successfully to accomplish his purpose is more likely to pass up a procedure so doubtful of results and so full of danger for himself and to resort to his own efforts in carrying out his projected crime, knowing there would be less chance of apprehension."[70]

The Legal Question

It was noted in the above discussion that the conflicting results are largely a result of the different perspectives and definitions of *antisocial*. According to one viewpoint "an act, to be antisocial, need not be willfully so or even consciously so. It is enough if it is antisocial only . . . in its actual or potential *effects* upon the actor or others. In fact, the criterion of danger or immorality must be the judgment of observers who themselves are not hypnotized, rather than the subjective appraisal of the situation by the hypnotized subject."[71] The opposing viewpoint holds that for an act to be antisocial, the suggested act must become an accomplished fact and the subject must know that the act is antisocial or criminal. This conflict is largely academic as, in the final analysis, it is a matter to be resolved by the courts.

From a legal standpoint, *antisocial* must first be distinguished from *crim-*

inal, as an antisocial act may or may not be criminal, whereas all criminal acts are antisocial. If an act is to be criminal it first must be so defined by statute. If a person is to be convicted of a crime, it must be proven that there was first an act that violated a statute, and, second, that the defendant had the requisite intent. As regards hypnotically-induced criminal behavior, assuming for the moment that it is possible, there remains the nagging legal question of culpability. It is obvious that the unscrupulous hypnotist would be held culpable as an accomplice, but what of the subject who actually carried out the criminal act? That the act was committed is a given fact, but the question becomes: Did he have the requisite intent? In other words, did he knowingly, negligently, or purposely commit the act?[72]

To illustrate the complexity of the problem, Watkins offers the following example: "a subject who was told directly, while under hypnosis to kill his best friend would certainly be engaging in criminal activity if he followed the instructions. Would it, however, be deemed antisocial if he carried out an aggressive assault under the hypnotically-induced misperception that he was protecting himself from the attack of an enemy soldier?"[73] Obviously, the act would be antisocial, but the legal question is whether or not the perpetrator would be criminally culpable. In other words, would he be found to be not guilty by reason of mental disease or defect, or, if standing trial, would he be convicted of deliberate homicide, mitigated deliberate homicide, negligent homicide, or acquitted?[74]

In a trial in which defense counsel claims the defendant did not have the requisite intent due to the fact that he was acting under the influence of hypnotic suggestion, expert witness testimony would have to be introduced and the jury convinced that, depending on the exact nature of the case, either the defendant was unable to resist the compulsive power of the hypnotic suggestion, or was somehow made to misperceive the true nature of the event. In either case it would have to be shown that it is possible to get someone to do something under hypnosis that he would not do in the waking state. In other words, defense counsel will have to prove that hypnosis was a crucial variable. The mere fact hypnosis was used necessitates that it be determined if it caused the defendant to commit the crime. If it can be established by the defense that he would not have done it without hypnosis, then he did not have the requisite intent.

On the other hand, if the prosecution can enter expert testimony and convince the jury that hypnotic suggestions can be effectively resisted and that it is not possible for a subject to be sufficiently deluded through various hypnotic techniques to the point of committing real crime, then the subject would have had the requisite intent. Essentially, the prosecution would have to prove that the defendant was actually in control and made a conscious decision to commit the crime for him to be culpable.

Trial experience teaches that in such a case where a jury is left to decide the fact of conflicting expert testimony, they will probably convict the subject because it is not being held that he did not commit the act, but that he did not know what he was doing while doing it; hence it is freely admitted that he did it. On the other hand, mere existence of the hypnotic variable, the greater the reasonable doubt; hence, the more likely the jury will be to acquit.

The definitions of *mental disease or defect* and *diminished mental capacity* varies a great deal from state to state, e.g. some say that an irresistable impulse is enough to eliminate one's normal controls. Depending upon this definition, the beliefs of a trial judge, and the information he has before him, it is conceivable that a criminal case involving hypnotically-induced behavior may never reach trial because the defendant will be found incompetent to stand trial. Such a ruling would be a dangerous and disconcerting precedent, to say the least, especially if it became common knowledge among street-wise felons who know how to play the psychiatric game of affixing personal responsibility on psychiatric labels, categories, classifications, and states of mind. If ever confronted with such a case, a wise trial court would follow the lead of the Denmark court in the case reviewed by Reiter, which sidestepped the issue of hypnosis as a causal factor and focused upon such variables as the following: the interpersonal relationship between hypnotist and subject, the defendant's criminal record, and the mental status of both hypnotist and subject.

Hypnosis Against One's Will or Unknowingly?

The weight of the above evidence indicates that hypnosis is not a causal or crucial variable in the production of antisocial and criminal behavior. In those instances in which such behavior was hypnotically elicited, it was determined that other variables inherent in the experimental situation were responsible. An examination of the possibility of inducing hypnosis against a person's will reaches the same conclusion.

Wells, Brenman, and Watkins[75] have all reported cases of inducing hypnosis in subjects in spite of active opposition. In each case, however, the subject had been previously hypnotized by the experimenter who was a respected professional in an academic experimental setting. Just as important were the demand characteristics of the experiments. Orne has shown that experimental subjects often perceive the true purpose of an experiment and unwittingly try to make it work, hence supporting the experimenter's hypothesis.[76] In these experiments, the subjects were instructed to resist hypnosis to prove that they could not. It is probable, then, that the subjects had two levels of motivation: first, to overtly resist the experimenter as requested and, second, to cooperate to fill the experimenter's more fundamental expectation and hypothesis.[77] The latter motivation is often at a subconscious level for both experimenter and subject; the experimenter does not expect the subject to be able to resist and the subject knows this. In reference to one of the above studies, Erickson described the same problem in the following manner: "One writer on hypnosis naively . . . asked subjects to resist going into trance in an effort to demonstrate that they could not resist hypnotic suggestion. The subjects cooperatively and willingly proved that they could readily accept suggestions to prove that they could not."[78]

Although there are no reported cases of inducing hypnosis in unwilling subjects in nonexperimental settings, the authors submit that this would be impossible in an interrogation setting for the following reasons. First, the interpersonal relationship of trust and respect would not exist. Second, the demand characteristics of the experimental setting would not be present. Third, the interests and aims of both interrogator and subject would be at odds. Fourth, the stakes would be much higher and the subject would be more highly motivated to resist. Furthermore, assuming for a moment that a police hypnotist, for example, could hypnotize an unwilling suspect, there is little chance of that person being forced to say anything against his self-interest, and he may even fake hypnosis or lie.

In fact, the only formal study on the use of hypnosis in interrogation showed that only 23 percent of twenty-six hypnotized subjects could be forced to reveal a number told to be kept secret, in spite of the fact that it was done in a nonthreatening experimental situation.[79] Since no control group was used, no comparison was made of the effectiveness of a good interrogator in revealing the same information with the same subjects in the awake state.

A corollary issue is the possibility of hypnotizing a person unknowingly. There are two basic ways in which this is alleged to be able to be done: (1) by inducing hypnosis while the subject is asleep and (2) by the use of disguised induction techniques.

In a review of the available literature and studies conducted on the first proposition, Orne concludes that "no reliable evidence exists that hypnosis can be induced directly from sleep in an unaware subject. . . ."[80]

The hypnotic literature is filled with references to disguised induction techniques which are so designed to prevent the subject from consciously knowing that he is being hypnotized. All such techniques depend on a legitimate (or what is believed to be a legitimate) therapeutic or medical situation. In a review of the literature, Orne concludes by stating the following:

In all the instances cited it must be emphasized that although the subject does not explicitly consent to enter hypnosis, a relationship of trust and confidence exists in which the subject has reason to expect help from the hypnotist. Furthermore, the hypnotist is an individual of high reputation and high prestige and there is some legitimacy in the subject's expectations. Standard medical practice includes many maneuvers by the physician which are essentially meaningless rituals to the average patient, and to which the patient complies without hesitation because it is assumed by him that this will eventually benefit him. These situations, despite their outward similarity, differ greatly from those where trance induction is attempted by a stranger, without the subject's knowledge or consent.[81]

The Possible Criminal Uses of Hypnosis

Many authors have speculated on ways in which the criminally-oriented hypnotist may utilize hypnosis to further his personal designs. These authors give detailed examples and protocols for eliciting various criminal acts secure in the belief that their hypnotic production is entirely feasible. It is maintained by these authors that otherwise unwilling or unsuspecting individuals can be made to commit criminal acts and that the hypnotist can avoid detection by utilizing such hypnotic phenomena and techniques as the following: inducing hallucinations, delusions, illusions, or transidentifications with other personalities to align the subject's perception of the requested act with his own moral and ethical standards; creating artificial neurotic conflicts, split personalities, and compulsions; erasing memories and substituting fabricated ones; manipulating the intense interpersonal hypnotic relationship of trust, confidence, and prestige; suggesting amnesia for the hypnotic suggestions, the criminal act, and even the hypnosis itself; and placing a seal such that no one else will be able to hypnotize the subject. Murder, check forgery, forcing a person to change his will, inducing false confessions, creating false alibis and witnesses, international espionage, industrial espionage, unduly influencing businessmen to sign unfavorable contracts, obtaining secret formulas, sexual manipulation, creating human time bombs, framing innocent people, and creating super spies and double-agents are only a few of the alleged uses to which hypnosis can be put.

Since the actual production of such

behavior was seriously questioned by the evidence presented in the above discussion, and recognizing the extremely rare or nonexistent incidence of such occurrences, and further recognizing the hypothetical nature of the offered protocols and examples, the interested reader is referred to Teitelbaum and Estrabrooks for an elaboration on the above and other possibilities. For an excellent critique of these possibilities, see Orne.[82]

Does the Possibility of the Antisocial and Criminal Use of Hypnosis Warrant Legislation?

Several authors, among them Watkins, Wolberg, and Wells, draw the unwarranted inference that the remote possibility of the production of antisocial or criminal behavior necessitates the regulation by law of the practice of hypnosis. Watkins believes "that the practice of hypnosis [should] be regulated by law and restricted to the professional treatment office, the research laboratory, or the professional advanced classroom and practiced only by those legally and ethically prepared to assume the necessary responsibility."[83] Wolberg similarly states that "the fact that criminally inclined persons may, under the protective alibi of a trance, seize the occasion to act out their criminal drives, is one reason why hypnotic practice should be made illegal among unqualified lay practitioners."[84] And likewise, Wells holds that hypnosis should be "reserved for its proper uses, of instruction, research, and therapy, in the hands of properly qualified psychologists or physicians."[85]

Given the negligible possibility of hypnotically producing antisocial and criminal behavior, this seems to be a rather drastic and unwarranted conclusion. Respectable scientists, of which the above three qualify, are generally extremely careful about drawing conclusions based on insufficient hard data. They seem to have further forgotten the fact that such an unscrupulous operator would not escape criminal prosecution if caught, of which there is a high likelihood.

The implicit assumptions in the statements of these professionals are that laymen are not "legally and ethically prepared to assume the necessary responsibility," and that they are not only unqualified but incapable of becoming qualified without formal medical or psychological training resulting in a terminal degree. These professionals should consider for a moment that many of their medical and psychological peers have been trained in hypnosis by laymen. Furthermore, the authors can think of no group, whether professional or lay, who is more prepared and mandated by law to assume the legal and ethical responsibility of practicing hypnosis than are law enforcement officers. Ironically enough, it is the medical and psychological professional who has the best opportunity to abuse hypnosis and the hypnotic relationship by manipulating his patients within the walls of his private practice and behind the protective barrier of doctor-patient confidentiality.

Another implicit assumption in the above statements is that medical and psychological professionals are competent to practice hypnosis by virtue of their training. First of all, most medical professionals, with the one exception of psychiatrists, receive no training in psychology in medical school. Second, the assumption that psychiatrists and psychologists who have been trained in psychology and psychotherapy are competent by virtue of that training has been seriously questioned over the past few decades.

In a comprehensive examination of the existing studies as well as their own years of experience and experimentation with the effectiveness of graduate training in psychology, a team of psychologists concludes "that in graduate school something very deleterious happens to the functioning of graduate students . . . " and that while *"there are no training programs which have demonstrated their efficacy in terms of a translation to client benefits, there is a suggestion that on those dimensions related to constructive client change or gain, the trainees deteriorate in functioning"* (their italics). To make matters worse, *"there is a direct suggestion that the professional teachers, counselors, and therapists involved never again achieve the level of functioning on the relevant therapeutic process variables that they had on entering graduate school"* (their italics.[86]

The cultural stereotype of counselors and psychotherapists is also supported by these researchers' findings:

If counselors and psychotherapists functioned in real life the way most of them do in the therapeutic hour, they would be patients. The professional helpers to whom we turn because human sustenance is not available in the general environment are themselves functioning at ineffectual levels of those dimensions related to constructive change or gain. Beyond their counseling and psychotherapy, their distorted perceptions and communications lead to the deterioration of their own significant human relationships. They find the same lack of personal fulfillment in their daily living that their clients do. Perhaps most important, they cannot allow the clients to find more in life than they themselves have found.[87]

If functioning at an inadequate level personally and suffering further deterioration during graduate training were not enough, the very effectiveness of counseling and psychotherapy has been seriously questioned. After reviewing the major studies,[88-92] Carkhuff and Berenson conclude that *"troubled people, both children and adults, are as likely to be rehabilitated if they are left alone as if they are treated in professional counseling and psychotherapy"* (their italics).[93]

The point of this critique is to demonstrate that by mere virtue of having the parchment in hand for having gone through the ritual of graduate training does by no means guarantee that the holder is a competent psychologist or psychiatrist. The above critique holds equally true for medical schools' effect on their trainees' ability to deal personably with patients. This critique is not intended to mean, however, that there are not competent clinicians around, but only that they are scarce and that those of them who argue that they are the only ones capable of handling and practicing hypnosis by virtue of their training are to be seriously doubted.

Those who maintain that the practice of hypnosis should be regulated by law and restricted to the use of medical and psychological professionals do not seem to realize that an unscrupulous operator plotting a felony with hypnosis will hardly be concerned if his utilization of hypnosis is against the law. Ironically, such an offense would most likely only be a misdemeanor anyway. Furthermore, the mere fact that anyone can learn hypnosis by going to a public library and reading a few books would require, if this law were to be strictly enforced, that those books be taken off the shelves.

For some excellent comments regarding the impossibility of legislating the use of hypnosis as well as the economic motives of the medical community, the reader is referred back to former Judge Dewey Kelley's remarks in Chapter 1.

In conclusion, the authors urge those professionals who support the legislation of hypnosis to resume their strictly scientific purpose of discovery and truth.

Hypnotism may be a very dangerous thing in the hands of the unscrupulous, but so is the airplane, the rifle, the disease germ. Science wishes to know the facts. Once discovered, these truths are handed over to the public. If that public uses the airplane to drop bombs, rather than to carry passengers, the scientist is not responsible. So with hypnotism. The psychologist seeks to unearth the truth. This is his problem. The use to which his discoveries may be put is something else.[94]

That a technique is misused is no argument against its use.[95]

Beating the Polygraph with Hypnosis?

Several authors believe that hypnosis can be used in several different ways to beat the polygraph. First, a guilty party can learn to control his various physiological stress signs through either hetero- or self-hypnosis so that he can consciously lie during a polygraph examination with no stress reaction. Second, a guilty party may through either hetero- or self-hypnosis give a posthypnotic suggestion for complete amnesia for the crime itself, the rationale being: no guilt, no stress.

It is a well-established fact that hypnotic suggestion can dramatically influence what are normally believed to be autonomic responses, so it is natural to assume that this control can be used to influence the polygraph. Although an important question from a criminal justice perspective, there has been only one reported experimental investigation of voluntarily controlling physiological responses through self-hypnosis. A possible reason is that the remote likelihood of the criminal element attempting this type of sophisticated deception does not warrant time consuming and expensive experimental studies. As part of a larger study, seven subjects were trained in autohypnosis to voluntarily control their arousal level for one month. When compared with a control group in their ability to deceive an experienced polygraph examiner in identifying which number, letter, or color the subjects selected in a series of card tests, the hypnosis group was able to deceive the examiner and remain undetected at a statistically significant level over the

control group.[96] These laboratory results, however, cannot be extrapolated to field conditions.

The more likely approach that a guilty party would take is to induce hypnosis and give a posthypnotic suggestion for complete amnesia for the crime itself. In so doing it is believed that induced amnesia will alleviate guilt and anxiety in a guilty subject. There have been two reported studies examining this possibility, but, unfortunately, they reached opposite conclusions.

In 1961, Germann used the polygraph to test for deception with respect to selected names, places, and playing cards in five somnambulistic hypnotic subjects. Examinations were conducted in deep trance with amnesia suggested for the selected information, and later by posthypnotic suggestion for amnesia. In eight out of a total of fifteen examinations, "a significant response indicating deception was immediately detected by the examiner. In several examinations, abnormal patterns were evaluated by the examiner as indicative of excessive emotion, yet were deemed somewhat inconclusive as indicative of either truthfulness or deception." Germann concludes that "amnesia induced hypnotically may not be able to surreptitiously defeat the process."[97] It should be noted, however, that there seemed to be some influence due to the fact that seven out of fifteen were inconclusive, which is not a good percentage for polygraph; one or two at most should have been inconclusive, unless of course the laboratory and make-believe nature of the deception is responsible, i.e. lying for names, places, and playing cards. One can only guess what the results would have been if they were real crimes where more was at stake, and the guilt indices would likely be much higher.

In another study, three somnambulistic subjects were instructed to enter an empty office and take either a $1, or

$5, or a $20 bill from a desk drawer. Each subject was then hypnotized, and amnesia and an absence of guilt were suggested for the act. Another group of three somnambulistic subjects were only told under hypnosis that they had stolen one of the bills and that they would feel considerably guilty about it. These subjects were instructed to deny their guilt.

A polygraph expert, who only knew that some of the students were guilty of taking one of the three bills and that hypnosis had been used in some manner, examined each subject to determine who had taken money and which denomination of bill.

The results showed the following:

The polygraph expert was completely misled by the three students who, under hypnosis, had been led to believe that they had stolen the money. He not only conclusively stated that they had taken the money, but also indicated which bill each student was hypnotized to believe he had taken.

Of the three students who had actually taken the money, the technician was unable to state conclusively whether or not they were guilty of the act. When pressured for a response, however, he indicated that they probably had taken the money, although in all three instances he was not certain enough to be able to present this evidence in court. When questioned as to which of the three bills each student might have taken, the polygraph expert was correct in only one of the three cases. He was therefore partially misled by the hypnotic approach since he could not state conclusively that the students were guilty. However, he was obviously not completely deceived since he did not see them as innocent either.[98]

Although the above two studies are suggestive, they cannot be considered conclusive for several reasons: (1) neither simulation or waking control groups were used, (2) the experimental populations were too small, and (3) the experimental nature of the studies invokes serious questions in and of itself. The authors would speculate that a guilty party may attempt to utilize hypnosis to mask his guilt on the polygraph by inducing self-hypnosis with a conditioned cue at the time of the examination, and using a variety of powerful imagery to dramatically alter his physiological processes, resulting in a highly erratic tracing. For example, a guilty party well versed in self-hypnosis may alternately visualize favorite physical activities such as skiing down a freezing mountain, basking in the warm sun, sleeping, racing, etc. Such an effort, however, is unlikely to get a person very far when stacked against a qualified polygraph examiner. It would be immediately apparent to the examiner that the subject was deliberately attempting to alter the tracings, which in itself is an indicator of deception. The examiner would simply proceed to deal with it in the same manner as he does with others who attempt to thwart the process by other means, e.g. deliberately moving, pressing down on a tack in one's shoe, hyperventilating, taking drugs beforehand, etc. In essence, the examiner stops the test and calls the subject's bluff. Furthermore, if a stipulation has been signed before the test, the examiner may testify in court that although the tracings were inconclusive, it is his judgment that the defendant's behavior was indicative of an attempt at deception. In conclusion, then, hypnosis used in this manner is likely to get the guilty party nowhere.

The problem remains of how a polygraph examiner would detect the possible use of hypnosis by an examinee. An examiner may suspect that his subject is under hypnosis for several reasons: (1) outward observable signs of hypnosis (see Chapter 3), (2) a sudden and dramatic behavioral change, (3) erratic tracings, (4) pre- or postexamination indications of guilt but no such indications during the exam, and (5) background information on the subject indicating an interest in or exposure to hypnosis. If the examiner does suspect that hypnosis may somehow be involved, the authors recommend that he do what he knows best — test. Through properly phrased questions the examiner should be able to discover if and how hypnosis is involved.

THE NATURE OF MEMORY

Memory is undoubtedly one of the most important, but least understood, faculties of the human psyche. In spite of the fact that it has probably been the object of more study and research than any other psychological function, it remains a mystery as to exactly how it works, i.e. how memories are stored and retrieved. To summarize the theories of research on memory could easily be a life's work and would fill volumes. A quick trip to any library will show the reader that there are stacks of books on the subject, let alone the numerous scientific periodicals bulging with extensive research papers.

From a practical standpoint, it is important that the hypno-investigator have a basic understanding of memory as it will influence the way in which he conducts a hypno-investigation and especially the way in which he questions hypnotized subjects. In order for the hypno-investigator to understand and work with memory more effectively, the authors have reviewed the most recent research concerning the brain and its capacity for memory and retrieval, and factors that influence memory. For ease of understanding a complex topic, the information will be presented in a question and answer format.

What Is Memory?

Memory refers specifically to the *content* or storehouse of past feelings, images, thoughts, and experiences within one's mind, as well as to the *process* of bringing to mind, recalling, or reviving those past feelings, images, thoughts, and experiences. In other words, *memory* refers not only to the capacity for storing information, but also as the ability to remember or bring to mind some of that information.

How Are Memories Stored?

Since the time of Plato in the fourth century BC, it has been commonly believed that the mind is a *tabula rasa* or blank slate upon which a man's experience is written. In some mysterious way, everything a person experiences, thinks, or feels is literally imprinted on the brain, and, depending on which school of thought you belong, this imprint is believed to remain in its perfect original form, wither away with time, or become covered up and destroyed with subsequent imprints. According to the former belief, the process of forgetting is due to the momentary inability to find the correct associations which lead to it. Hence, the memory is never permanently lost or erased, but just not presently available. According to the latter belief, the process of forgetting is due to an actual permanent change in the imprint.

With the advent of modern techniques of brain surgery and biochemical analysis, the actual physical search began for the imprint, known as the engram or trace, which was believed to be a permanent change in the protoplasm or tissue caused by some stimulation. Basically, each specific memory was believed to have a specific engram; all the brain surgeon had to do was to find the unit of changed protoplasm and he would know where and how information was stored in the brain. It was hypnothesized that engrams or traces generally took the form of new connections or pathways between the neurons.

After decades of searching and thousands of brain operations, such noted neurosurgeons as Karl Lashley and Wilder Penfield finally abandoned the search for the engram. They conclude that memories are in fact not stored in specific localized neuronal alterations, but are instead distributed throughout the brain. Doctor Lashley, for instance,

trained rats to run mazes and then removed various parts of their brains. But whichever part he removed, he could not remove the memory; by removing successively larger and larger chunks he could only impair the memory to a greater degree. From this he developed two theories: the theory of 'mass action,' which stated that the intensity of recall depended upon the mass of the brain left intact; and the theory of 'equipotentiality,' which held that the memory was distributed evenly throughout the brain.[99]

Other research that supports the idea of equipotentiality is the biochemical study of memory transfer from one living organism to another. It has been found that chemical extracts from the brains of trained rats and monkeys will transfer the memory of the learned behavior directly to nontrained rats and monkeys when injected into their brains.[100, 101] In other experiments it was discovered that specific brain chemicals — synthesized proteins — were produced during new learning. When this chemical was synthetically manufactured by chemists and injected into the brains of normal rats, it produced the same behavior.[102] Furthermore, when this same chemical was injected into goldfish the same behavior was exhibited (avoidance of the dark),[103] which suggests that there may be universal interspecies chemicals for every type of learned behavior.

Probably the most exciting development in theories of memory storage has been the recent application of the photographic process of holography to the process of memory. Basically, holography involves a process of splitting a laser beam in two by a half-silvered mirror in such a way that one beam is reflected off of the object to be photographed to a photographic plate, where it intersects with the other beam

projected directly to the plate. The intersection of the two beams causes an interference wave pattern that is recorded on the photographic plate and is called a hologram. When developed, the hologram bares no relationship to the object photographed, but looks like a series of overlapping wave patterns. When the procedure is in essence reversed, a three-dimensional image of the object appears where the original object was. The image is not reflected off of a surface but is suspended in space and can be viewed from any angle.

An interesting property of holograms is that the entire image can be reconstructed from any section of the plate, no matter how small. However, clarity and detail of the three-dimensional image decreases in direct proportion to the smallness of the section. In other words, "each small part of the hologram contains information from the entire original image and therefore can reproduce it."[104] For this reason, holograms are very resistant to damage. Interestingly, it has also been discovered that "several images can be superimposed on a single plate on successive exposures, and each image can be recovered without being affected by other images."[105] In other words, each superimposed image can be reconstructed from any piece of the plate. Due to this fact the storage capacity for information on holograms is phenomenal.

Brain researchers have theorized that memory is a holographic process and that "the arrival of impulses at neuronal junctions . . . from at least two sources . . . would [converge and] produce interference patterns."[106]

What is the Brain's Storage Capacity?

"Some ten billion *bits* . . . of information have been usefully stored holographically in a cubic centimeter."[107] If the human memory is indeed a holographic process as many authorities now believe, the following computation can be made from this fact:

The human brain is fifteen hundred times as large, and the proteins involved are much smaller than the silver grains in photographic film. Human memory capacity is probably several thousand times greater still. It can probably store something on the order of a quadrillion (1,000,000,000,000,000) bits of information. If all this were given over to memory, the brain would have the ability to record a thousand new bits of information per second for every second from birth onward and still have only used a fraction of its memory potential after seventy-five years. [75 (years) × 365 (days) × 24 (hours) × 60 (minutes) × 60 (seconds) × 1,000 (bits per second) = 2,365,200,000,000.][108]

It seems reasonable to conclude that the storage capacity of the human brain is probably limitless.

How are Memories Retrieved?

There are two basic types or categories of theories for memory retrieval. The first type, commonly considered *static* theories, generally maintain that the process of remembering involves finding the proper associative connections or bonds that lead to an exact copy of the original information, even though some hold this copy may fade or blur with the ravages of time.

The second type, commonly considered *dynamic* theories, generally maintain that the process of remembering involves the reconstruction of the original event. "Remembering is not the re-excitation of innumerable, fixed, lifeless and fragmentary traces . . . ," but instead is actually an imaginative reconstruction.[109] Memory is believed to be a selective process that is largely dependent upon the developmental stage of the individual, his personality organization, and the environmental context. Memory is therefore not a static and unchangeable entity, but can undergo changes over time and, more importantly, is largely dependent upon the present psychological and environmental context of the person.

What Types of Memory are There?

When one thinks of memory, he usually considers it to be a unitary phenomenon, and does not consider that there are actually many different types.

The mind has a memory for products of its own subjective experience such as thoughts, dreams, fantasies, and ideas, as well as a memory for the objectively experienced world. The five senses are the conduits of objective experience to the brain, and as such, there is a memory for each, which varies greatly among different people. The strongest form of sensory memory for most people is visual. People also have an auditory, olfactory, tactile, and gustatory memory to varying degrees.

People also have a cognitive memory for facts and meaning. They also have a psychophysical memory for learned skills. Each person is also born with a certain instinctive memory for such responses as breathing and nursing. Some psychologists believe that there is also a genetically encoded memory of collective human history and past lives.

How Good Can Waking Memory Be?

The ability to recall past events from a waking state varies tremendously. The reader will undoubtedly know those with seemingly very poor memories and those with excellent memories. In any law enforcement agency, there are those officers who are walking encyclopedias of vehicle descriptions, license numbers, types and locations of offenses, and names. Then there are those who have difficulty remembering the name of someone they arrested even the day before. There are also those who seem to have good memory for faces and poor memory for names, while others are just the opposite.

The upper limits of waking recall has long been of interest to psychologists, and, in their search, they have reached a rather startling conclusion: for some people it is virtually limitless. Consider the following examples:

1. A professor of mathematics at the University of Edinburgh in Scotland, the late A. C. Aitken, could easily remember, forward and backward, the first thousand decimal places of the value of pi. He also had verbatim recall of lists of words from memory tests from twenty-seven years earlier.[110]

2. A nineteenth century American, Daniel McCartney, could give the cube roots of numbers up to millions almost instantly, even though he couldn't read or write. At fifty-four years of age he could still immediately recall what he had done every day of his life since childhood including what he had eaten for breakfast, lunch, and supper, as well as give the exact weather conditions on any specific date.[111]

3. A ninety-six-year-old man memorized fifty three-digit numbers shouted out to him by an audience.[112]

Visual memory, which is believed to be the strongest in most people, has been exhaustively studied by psychologists. Of particular interest for the investigator is the accuracy of visual memory. In 1965, Nickerson tested fifty-six subjects for their ability to recognize and distinguish old photos (photos previously seen) from new photos (photos not previously seen). The subjects were shown a series of 200 black and white photographs followed immediately by an additional 400 photographs of which 200 were repeats of the original 200. Each subject was allowed to look at each photo for five seconds and was instructed to point out the ones that were duplicates as they were shown. The average performance level in distinguishing the duplicate photos was 95 percent.[113]

In a similar experiment, subjects correctly identified the duplicate pictures out of a series of 612 shown for six seconds each, 98.5 percent of the time.[114]

In another study, thirteen subjects were shown 2,560 photographic slides at ten second intervals over several days.

One hour after a subject had seen the last of the slides he was shown 280 pairs of pictures. One member of each pair was a picture from the series the subject had already seen. The other was from a similar set, but it had never been shown to the subject. When the subjects were asked to say which of the two pictures they had seen before, 85 to 95 percent of their choices were correct. Surprisingly, subjects whose endurance had been pressed did as well as subjects who had followed a more leisurely viewing schedule. In another version of the experiment the high scores were maintained even when the pictures were shown as their mirror image during the identification sessions, so that the right-hand side became the left-hand side.[115]

The experimenter commented that this experiment "suggests that recognition of pictures is essentially perfect. The results would probably have been the same if we had used 25,000 pictures instead of 2,500."[116]

In yet another study in Canada, in 1973, six subjects were shown 1,000 vivid pictures (slides with definitely interesting subject matter) at five seconds per slide. Two days later the subjects were shown 100 pairs of slides, each with one old photo (one seen before) and one new photo (one not seen before). The average score was 99.6 percent correct, which corresponds to a retention of 992 photos out of the one thousand. Extrapolating these results, it is estimated that the subjects would recognize 986,300 pictures out of one million. To make the test more difficult, subjects were shown 100 normal pictures at two seconds per picture. Two days later they were shown a sequential series of thirty-two new pictures with a single old one from the original one hundred. Each picture was shown for five seconds, and each subject had to answer yes or no to indicate if they had seen it before, which is obviously more difficult than forced pair comparisons. The subjects average was still a high 92 percent correct. From this data the experimenter extrapolated that one second of memory scanning time allows the subject to search for 51,180 pictures. The obvious conclusion was that "the capacity of recognition memory for pictures is almost limitless."[117]

A fascinating visual memory ability possessed by a minority of people is known as "eidetic imagery," which has been defined as "the ability to retain an accurate, detailed visual image of a complex scene or pattern."[118] Eidetic imagery is different from ordinary memory imagery in that it is an exact copy of the original thing perceived. If a person with eidetic imagery is asked to look attentively at an object, regardless of whether it be of two or three dimensions, this person actually sees the object again, with eyes either open or closed, whereas the ordinary memory image would be more hazy, incomplete, and unstable.

Although often confused with photographic memory, eidetic imagery differs from both ordinary and photographic memory in the following ways:

1. It is generally superior in clearness and richness of detail.
2. It is generally more accurate in its reproduction of detail.
3. Its coloration is generally more brilliant and accurate.
4. It is more flexible in that it can be viewed from different angles.
5. It is subject to voluntary recall after the lapse of considerable time, i.e. days, weeks, and even months.[119]

The vividness and accurateness of eidetic images is dramatically illustrated in several experiments. When

Allport examined a number of children with eidetic imagery (known as eidetikers) he was surprised to find that they

were able to spell out correctly, or almost correctly, from their image the German word *Gartenwirthschaft,* which was for them quite meaningless. The exposure of 35 seconds was not sufficient to permit a "learning" of the word, especially since the picture itself was filled with incident and detail of lively interest which the child had likewise to describe. The essential features of the picture were described with more fluency, to be sure; but upon being pressed to "observe" their image more closely each child was able, often to his own surprise, to "see" the small letters over the door. Three of my 30 *Eidetiker* spelled the word correctly; 7 had not more than two errors; and only 5 failed to give at least five letters correctly. In all cases the letters were given with equal accuracy, whether read from left to right or from right to left. I do not argue that foreign words have no interest for the child, but simply wish to point out that such detail is extraneous and relatively meaningless, and is not retained by virtue of any inherent structuration or organization with the remaining content.[120]

Similarly, a team of researchers reported that their eidetikers retained enough detail in their eidetic images after briefly looking at a picture with ten Indians, that they would actually count the number of feathers worn by each.[121] In yet another study, one eidetic boy correctly counted the sixteen stripes in a cat's tail.[122]

In a case study of a twenty-three-year-old female teacher and artist at Harvard University, it was determined that her

eidetic ability is remarkable, for she can hallucinate at will a beard on a beardless man, leaves on a barren tree, or a page of poetry in a known foreign language which she can copy from bottom line to the top line as fast as her hand can write. These visions can often obscure a real object. Thus the chin on a beardless man may disappear beneath the hallucinated beard.[123]

This same subject could look at a million dot stereogram and four hours later superimpose the eidetic image over another random-dot stereogram and clearly distinguish the emergent figure (the stereograms were preselected to form an image when overlayed).[124]

Interestingly, another study showed that some adults who do not display eidetic imagery in the waking state, do so when regressed to the age of seven. In the regressed state they are able to superimpose the eidetic image of one random-dot stereogram over another so that the concealed image will appear.[125]

Depending on the population, i.e. age, nationality, level and type of education, etc., Jaensch found that the frequency of eidetikers ranged from virtual absence up to 90 percent.[126] As the ability is much more frequent among children than adults, it is generally believed that it is an inherent and normal ability with which most people are born, but through lack of use and an educational system that does not stress visual and imagery ability, most people slowly lose it. Once considered a rare and unique ability, one present authority on the subject has "shown that the eidetic is a truly universal phenomenon; it is not restricted to people having a particular gift or talent in the perceptual area, and it is possible for each person to have experiences which can be reproduced in this eidetic way."[127]

This same authority, Doctor Akhter Ahsen, has developed a comprehensive form of psychotherapy utilizing eidetic imagery, which he believes to be a natural potential for most people. Ahsen's extensive clinical experience has shown that "the eidetic . . . catches the total experience in all its original authenticity. . . . Through the eidetic we can experience the same moment all over again and can do so repeatedly. The stream of experience does leave a remarkable and repeatable record in the living cells of the brain."[128] Ahsen has

found that eidetic images of experience can be retrieved years later.

It should be stressed that eidetics are not just visual, but involve the other senses as well. Any given person may have an auditory eidetic and be able to remember, for example, the exact wording of a conversation for life. Another person may have an olfactory or tactile eidetic and be able to call to mind an exact smell, taste, or texture. Similarly, emotionally charged eidetics are also accompanied by the original affect.

The importance and relevance of eidetic imagery to the hypno-investigator is the striking similarities between the eidetic image and the visual images experienced during hypnotic hypermnesia and revivification. In fact, some writers have postulated that they are actually the same phenomenon. Ahsen reports that his "findings show that . . . forgotten memories or the unconscious parts of the mind are not truly forgotten but are always available through the eidetic images."[129]

How Good Can Memory Under Hypnosis Be?

The genuineness of hypermnesia and revivification have already been discussed, but consider the following additional examples:

1. A bricklayer was hypnotized and asked to describe a special brick wall that he had worked on ten years previously in which distinctive bricks were used on a neo-Gothic building. Under hypnosis he was able to describe the exact shapes, colors, anomalies, and locations of numerous bricks, all of which were later corroborated perfectly by the experimenter, even though he had laid two thousand bricks a day.[130]

2. A nineteen-year-old Finnish girl was regressed to a time preceding birth whereupon she assumed the personality of a thirteenth century English girl named Dorothy. During the regression

"Dorothy" sang a song in modernized medieval English which she did not know, nor, once awakened, did she have any recollection of ever having heard the words or the melody of the song. When subsequently rehypnotized and regressed to the age of thirteen, she remembered taking a book, by chance, titled *Musiikin vaiheet (The Phases of Music)*, from a library shelf. She did not read the book, merely flipped through the pages. During the regression she could remember the names of the book's two authors and exactly where the song appeared. The experimenters concluded that "the recording of a song from a book by merely turning over the leaves of the book at the age of 13, is an outstanding example of how very detailed information can be stored in our brain without any idea whatever of it in the conscious mind, and how it can be retrieved in deep hypnosis."[131]

Are Only Those Stimuli Consciously Attended to Stored in Memory?

A popular conception held by psychologists and neurologists is that only those stimuli that receive conscious attention produce physiological correlates in the brain. Other psychologists and neurologists have reached just the opposite conclusion based on such case studies as cited above. Cobb, a neurologist, maintains that "experiments with hypnosis prove that even in one's most alert moments innumerable stimuli do not get conscious attention, but many of these stimuli outside the field of attention are taken in and remembered."[132] Similarly, Gerard, a neurophysiologist, asserts that "the initial impression need not have entered awareness in order to be retained and recalled."[133] As with some of the examples above, Gerard refers to the findings under hypnosis for support of his belief. For example, he cites the case of

a bricklayer who "described correctly every bump and grain on the top surface of a brick he had laid in a wall twenty years before."[134] On the basis of such findings he concludes "that consciousness in the normal sense is neither necessary for retention of an impression nor for recall. He also calls into question the assumption that experience-traces are really irrevocably expunged and favors the possibility that reproduction may be at fault when traces appear to be lost."[135]

Given the evidence cited throughout this book, it seems relatively safe to conclude that the answer to the above question is a resounding no.

Are Exact Copy Memories Stored Permanently in the Brain?

Evidence for this proposition has already been presented, but work with the electronic stimulation of the brain has been particularly revealing.

During over one thousand brain operations between 1936 and 1960, Wilder Penfield, a neurosurgeon at the Montreal Neurological Institute, experimented with the application of small electric currents using fine electrodes to patients' temporal cortexes. Since there are no pain receptors in the brain, the surgery patients were fully conscious at all times and were asked to report what they experienced at the application of the electrodes. The patients consistently reported a wealth of vivid remembrances in minute detail that progressed in time and unfolded in more detail with repeated application of the electrode. The patients reported that they were not merely remembering these past events, but actually were reliving them in all their original authenticity, including appropriate affect, sounds, smells, and even touches. Penfield offers this conclusion:

The great body of current experience seems to be forgotten by an individual but is not lost, for the little strips of record that the electrode activates reproduce experiences that are clear and accurate in every detail. . . . A continuous strip of current experience is converted into a subconscious record and one might well say that it forms a neuronal basis of what has been called the subconscious mind.[136]

In discussing Penfield's findings, Ahsen states that he

argued that without conscious knowledge or effort such strips [of time] are being recorded constantly by our eye, taking close up and distant shots. . . . These high fidelity single image frames, as in a cinematographic film, catch every nuance in split-second miniatures and preserve them for later recall. When released again in consciousness, these frames reenact the whole experience to the most minute detail for the consideration of the individual.[137]

Given the evidence cited throughout this book, it seems relatively safe to conclude that the answer to the above question is a resounding yes. Memory is perfect, but recall usually isn't.

What Are Some Factors That Influence Memory?

Memory retention and recall, which are actually two different phenomena (a memory may be retained but unable to be recalled), were originally believed to be a function of the number of repetitions or trials and the reinforcement given for each repetition. In later research it was determined that memory retention and recall is greatly affected by the meaningfulness of the material learned; the more meaningful the experience, the greater the likelihood of retention and recall. For example, if lists of nonsense syllables are memorized, approximately 56 percent of them will be forgotten within one hour, 65 percent after nine hours, and 80 percent after one month.[138] In testing memory of a picture or scene, it was found that 10 percent was forgotten immediately, 14 percent forgotten in 5 days, 18 percent after 15 days, and 22 percent after 45 days.[139] If the material is meaningful, however, the same person may remember it intact for life.

In addition to the meaningfulness of the material learned, it was also discovered that the principle of association was very important, which states: "If two states of consciousness have been experienced together, when one of them enters consciousness the other tends to follow (the concept of contiguity), and of two objects having characteristics in common, the sight of one arouses the recall of the other (the concept of similarity)."[140] Various factors influence association, among them being frequency, recency, intensity, and attraction. We tend to remember what we observe, experience, or think of frequently; the more recent the experience, the easier it is to remember it; the more vivid, distinct, or extraordinary the thing observed, experienced, or thought, the easier it is to recall clearly; and lastly, memory is best for those things liked, next for those things disliked, and least for those things to which we are indifferent.

Waking recall will also be largely dependent upon the degree of attention given the object, i.e. only noticed in passing or carefully scrutinized. The sheer volume of stimuli and the rapidity with which they are experienced will also affect retention and recall. Other variables, such as the degree of fatigue at the time, and level of distraction, will also greatly affect the degree and accuracy of voluntary recall.

Other important factors that influence memory are the environmental and psychological (cognitive-emotional) context in which something was learned and subsequently recalled. The more similar the context the greater the chance of recall. Consider for a moment your own experience. We all know how memories of long forgotten events will often flood back when a familiar place is revisited. Many of you know, when angry with your spouse, how long forgotten grudges, arguements, and irritations will spontaneously come to mind. Others have experienced an alcohol-induced amnesia for the events of a party, only for them to return at the next alcohol-induced state. Clinical observations have shown that "alcoholics frequently reported hiding liquor or money while drinking with no recall of the event until intoxicated again."[141]

This phenomenon has received a great deal of theoretical and experimental attention recently, and has been referred to as the "state-bound" nature of experience. Basically, the theory states that an experience that takes place in either a hypo- or hyper-aroused state of consciousness is bound to that level of arousal. Therefore, unless that level of arousal is reactivated, the individual will have only partial recall or even total amnesia for the original experience.

As evidence for this theory, there are several studies in which it was shown that subjects who memorized nonsense syllables while drunk had better recall of the material at a later time when drunk than when sober.[142, 143] Other researchers have confirmed this finding with amphetamine and barbiturate-induced states. Evidently, then, there is a certain degree of amnesia between the two different states of consciousness as there is no direct and continuous communication and transfer of knowledge and experience from one to the other. In order to recall the material learned while drunk, for instance, the arousal level at the time of learning must be reactivated or reinstated. Theoretically, cerebral "data processing is a function of the level of arousal," hence, in order to key into that data processed at any specific level, the "particular spatio-temporal neuronal-synaptic firing pattern that prevailed during the initial experience" must be re-presented.[144] In other words, the memory retrieval of a particular data content is dependent on reinstating "the specific rate of data processing which prevailed during the initial experience. . . . The phenomenon of stateboundness implies, then, that retrieval of the data content of a particular experience is optimal only at that specific rate of data processing which corresponds to the level of arousal prevailing during the initial experience."[145] The degree of disparity between the levels of arousal, then, will determine the degree of awareness and transfer between them; if the disparity is great enough there may be total amnesia.

This theory is often used to explain the hypnotic phenomenon of spontaneous amnesia of some deeply hypnotized subjects upon waking, as well as the partial amnesia of excitable eyewitnesses. In the same vein, Fischer believes that "an analogous amnesia may follow a violent act of crime, and a criminal thus sincerely deny an act he cannot recall."[146]

The amnesia resulting from the discontinuity between different states of arousal explains why Sirhan Sirhan, murderer of Robert Kennedy, "had no recollection of shooting Kennedy," and why hypnosis could clear up many details of the assassination. In our interpretation, psychiatrist Bernard L. Diamond . . . hypnotically induced in Sirhan on several occasions that state of . . . hyperarousal during which the murder was committed. Only in this state could Sirhan re-experience and re-enact the murder. The amnesia between this state and the normal waking state of interrogation was so complete that Sirhan denied having been hypnotized, and "would say that the tape recordings made by Diamond during each session were fake or that the psychiatrist had a handwriting expert fake his writing."[147]

Fischer believes that state-bound experiences can be recollected or re-experienced either by inducing the level of hypo- or hyperarousal associated with the state-bound experience, or by presenting some associated symbol of the context of the experience, such as an image, melody, or taste. As is obvious from the above example, the value of hypnotic regression lies in its power to reinstate the necessary arousal level for complete recall. Its importance particularly for amnesic victims of violent crimes is self-evident.

Hypnosis is not a requirement for eliciting state-bound experiences, but drugs, familiar sensory stimulation, images, or environment may also serve as the requisite triggers as the following examples well illustrate:

A young man complaining of unpleasant "flashbacks" from a previous LSD experience remembered on questioning that they seemed to occur each time he took some pills prescribed for him (in the emergency room of a university hospital) "to drain his sinuses." The tablets were soon identified as amphetamine, which apparently *produced the level of arousal* necessary for recall of his previous (state-bound) drug experience.[148]

Juan Luis Vives wrote in 1538, "When I was a boy in Valencia, I was ill of a fever; while my taste was deranged I ate cherries; for many years afterwards, whenever I tasted the fruit I not only recalled the fever, but also seemed to experience it again."[149]

[N.B., a college volunteer,] was repeatedly exposed to the hallucinogenic drug psilocybin. Later on, a hypnotically induced drug experience was substituted for the psilocybin experience. The hypnotic induction placed the subject in a peaceful beach scene with waves lapping at the seashore. Our experiments had to be interrupted after two such sessions, since N.B. left for a Florida vacation. Upon her return, she reported to us the surprising event which happened to her while walking down to the beach for the first time: when gazing at the seashore the whole scene suddenly 'blacked-out,' and instead 'her old' beach returned — the beach of the hypnotically induced psilocybin experience. Just as Sirhan's state-bound experience may have been evoked by hypnotically inducing the appropriate level of arousal and/or by presenting symbols of its experiential content, our ... college-girl's hypnotically induced experience could be recalled (and re-lived) by exposure to an aspect of ordinary reality which represented the hypnotic experience.[150]

The theory of state-bounded experience seems to support, and in several ways is an extension of, Reiff's and Scheerer's conclusions reached after a meticulous analysis of memory and hypnotic age regression, who support

the possibility that memory-trace systems may be revived in their original form after long periods. We suggested that one of the most favorable conditions for this resuscitation is hypnotic ablation of the present, conscious ego organization, and the suggested reinstatement of the cognitive-emotional matrix, i.e., the ego stratum prevalent at the pertinent age period.... There are two possibilities as to how we may conceptualize the revival of trace systems in terms of earlier functional schemata and ego apparatuses: first the trace systems have remained preserved in unaltered form but forgotten, not being accessible to normal consciousness. Being buried under layers of subsequent experiences and their corresponding trace systems, the layer belonging to the former ego stratum has to be somehow "reached" by the suggested method. A second possibility would be that the fate of the individual trace may have undergone some change over time ... ; that through the method of hypnotic ablation and gradual age regression to the former ego-environment organization, the layer of the original trace systems is reached. A reconstitution of the original traces may thus be accomplished — in spite of its change over time — when a phenomenally similar environment and ego stratum can be induced.[151]

Why Do People Often Forget?

Any criminal justice professional is constantly plagued by the incompetent memories of victims and witnesses. The following are probably the most frustrating and common phrases heard during interviews: "I can't remember exactly," and "I forget." If, as seen above, memory can be so good, why is it that people often forget things? Some common factors influencing forgetting follow.

REPRESSION. According to psychoanalytic theory, the psychological defense mechanism of repression is responsible for most forgetting. When confronted with a psychologically painful, anxiety-producing, traumatic, or ego-threatening experience, a person will often subconsciously and purposefully repress that experience out of conscious awareness to shield himself from conflict. Consider the rape victim who blocks out her assailant's face and remarks, "I don't want to see him."

DETERIORATION. As mentioned above, some theorists believe that memory traces organically decay over time. As also seen above, however, this is probably not the case. Critics of this theory point to the phenomenon of reminiscence, which is the spontaneous improvement of recall over time after learning, i.e. research has often shown that recall for learned material is better a day after instead of immediately after the learning.

BRAIN DAMAGE. Memories of perceived events of victims who suffered brain damage as a result of traumatic crimes can change due to such malfunctions as neural misfiring. Hence, accurate memories may be lost forever. The holographic theory of memory questions this proposition, however.

INTERFERENCE. According to Gestalt psychology, "forgetting is a matter of disturbing interaction rather than of a deterioration which each trace undergoes independently."[152] In other words, forgetting occurs when the proper association leading to a specific trace is interfered with. As support for this theory, the Gestaltists point to the experimental results that have shown that the more similar the material learned the more difficult it is to recall, and the more dissimilar the easier to recall, indicating that similar associations tend to interfere with recall.

CONTEXT. The different psychological and environmental context at the time of recall is an important factor in forgetting. Put the individual back into the context in which the sought after material was originally learned or experienced, e.g. returning the victim to the scene of the crime either physically or hypnotically, and the appropriate context may serve as the necessary association or cue for retrieval.

ACUTE TRAUMA. Any acute traumatic experience may so startle or terrorize an individual that, as a psychological defense mechanism, he may mentally retreat and block out objective reality. Although similar to repression, this particular reaction to acute trauma seems to be more of a natural psychophysiological response when literally overwhelmed by a negative experience. Consider for a moment the individual who literally freezes in fear, often being totally oblivious to what's happening. Most experienced police officers have seen such cases, and they know all too well how anxiety experienced at the time of a crime often clouds the witness's or victim's memory. Psychologists have determined that emotional trauma surrounding an event tends to produce amnesia for that event, and experience has taught that hypnosis facilitates the lifting of the amnesia.

In conclusion, there are many factors that may converge at any particular time to cause forgetting. The reader should realize that forgetting is not a pathological process, but is actually a natural process in the mind, for if we remembered everything at the same time, our minds would become utterly confused.

How Variable Are People's Perceptions?

We have examined some reasons why people may forget, but what is particularly disconcerting to the investigator and prosecutor is the often abundant conflicting testimonial evidence offered by honest, sincere, and credible witnesses who claim their memories to be clear and accurate. There are several ways to explain the discrepancies. Any given witness may have (1) remembered accurately what he originally misperceived, or (2) he may misremember what he originally perceived. In this section we will deal with the first alternative while saving the second for the following section.

Any two witnesses to the same event will undoubtedly and unfailingly observe it differently, yet each may insist that he is right and the other wrong. In all likelihood both are right in some respects, but wrong in others. In any event, what is subjectively true to the witness may in fact be objectively false due to faulty or defective perception. Perception is not a fixed or static ability that all people have to the same degree, but it is highly variable and fluid. Consider the following:

VISION. Witnesses to crimes will testify predominantly to what they saw, but many people have any number of a variety of visual defects, such as farsightedness, nearsightedness, colorblindness (one man out of twenty-five, one woman out of 200), or other medical conditions interfering with accurate visual perception.

VISUAL ACUITY. Different levels and types of illumination as well as drastic and sudden changes in light intensity affect visual acuity.

VISUAL ATTENTIVENESS. It is often more amazing what witnesses did not see than what they did see. In one experiment, one hundred Harvard students were asked to observe every act of a professor during a certain time interval. With his left hand the professor held up a spinning color wheel while he performed six distinct acts with his right hand, such as removing a cigarette from a case and snapping the lid shut. Eighteen of the students *only* saw

him holding the spinning wheel.[153]

VISUAL JUDGMENTS. Witnesses will generally tend to judge the physical dimensions of any object in relation to its surroundings. A man of medium height standing among relatively short women will appear tall, and a room full of people will look smaller than an empty room. Estimates of an object held at arm's length in front of subjects, which was large enough to cover the full moon, ranged from the size of a pea (correct) to the size of a carriage wheel.[154] When asked to estimate the number of black squares on a card containing fifty, subjects estimates ranged from twenty-five to 200, and for a card containing only twenty squares, estimates varied from ten to seventy.[155]

AUDITORY PERCEPTION. A sound that is heard either directly in front, overhead, or behind cannot easily be located by the sound alone, and estimations of the distance of sounds are unreliable unless very familiar and distinctly heard. When subjects were asked to describe the sound of an unseen tuning fork, the descriptions compared it to a bell, a lion's growl, and a steam whistle. It was also said to be clear, rumbling, sharp, and whistling.[156]

TIME JUDGMENTS. As personal experience attests, people tend to overestimate the length of slow or idle periods and underestimate busy and engrossing intervals. In one study, estimates of a given ten second interval varied from one-half to sixty seconds and from one-half to fifteen seconds for a three second period.[157]

SPEED JUDGMENTS. Estimates of the speed of moving objects will vary greatly depending on the distance of the object from the observer, the angle and direction of travel of the object in relation to the observer, the size and noise level of the object, and the experience and general knowledge that the observer has about the object. In a test administered to a group of Air Force personnel who were told in advance that they were to estimate the speed of an automobile, estimates ranged from ten to fifty miles per hour. The car was actually traveling at twelve miles per hour.[158]

Once an event is perceived, whether correctly or incorrectly, the witness must report what he observed. Depending upon his level of articulation and the adequacy of his language, the report may be only a partial and even misleading statement of the real experience.

Why Do People Misremember?

Particularly disconcerting to the trial lawyer is the all too obvious and frequent changes in witnesses' memories over time. All too often a crucial witness will have a substantially different conception of the crime by the time of the trial, and who may even be quite baffled when confronted with his original signed statement, even insisting that it must be in error.

That there are sometimes drastic changes in witnesses' memories cannot be denied. In 1974, a man in California was erroneously convicted on the basis of the testimony of seven witnesses who identified him as the robber of a bank. In another case in 1973, seventeen witnesses identified a man who was erroneously charged with shooting a police officer; it later turned out that he was not even in the vicinity of the crime.[159] In New York City in October, 1974, a nineteen-year-old high school honor student was indicted for robbery in the first degree after being positively identified by the victim. At approximately the same time, a seventeen-year-old college freshman in New York City was positively identified by three rape victims and held on $60,000 bail. Both defendants were later cleared when a third man confessed to the crimes.[160]

Experimental studies have also demonstrated the fallibility of the eyewitness. A simulated purse-snatching was staged before sixty-four witnesses. Forty-eight of the witnesses attempted to identify the suspect from two videotaped lineups, one with and one without the suspect. Only 13.5 percent made a positive identification while the remainder either chose the wrong man, made no identification, or impeached themselves by picking two men.[161]

In a similar experiment, 141 college students witnessed a dramatic staged assault on a professor. Seven weeks later the witnesses were asked to identify the assailant from a six photo layout. Of the witnesses, 60 percent, including the attacked professor, identified the wrong man, and another 25 percent picked a man who was only a bystander at the scene.[162]

It is quite obvious from these criminal cases and experiments that something drastic happened to the witnesses' memories after the original event, unless, of course, it was misperceived originally. From the material discussed above on forgetting, it can be inferred that memory may similarly change as a result of psychodynamic defense mechanisms within one's own personality, faulty reconstruction, or interference and misassociations. Two additional factors not yet mentioned are imagination and suggestion.

Obviously, peoples' retention and voluntary recall decreases for the bulk of what they experience in direct proportion to the time interval. Also, the greater the time interval, the greater the possibility of influence from the imagination. When called upon to recall an event poorly remembered, there is the possibility that "imagination retouches the details; where this is done unconsciously, therefore honestly, we are apt to recall what we *think* should have normally occurred, or, if personally involved, what we *wish* had occurred, or what, from suggestions now half-forgotten, we *believe* occurred."[163] This all too frequent "filling-in" of memory happens insidiously, below the person's conscious level of awareness, and, hence, the sketched-in details are incorporated and believed to be one's own.

The predominant factors affecting imagination are bias, mood, motives, prejudice, belief, personality, and opinion. We easily and willingly believe what we wish to be true or expect to be true.

We tend to recall what we want to recall, especially when we are uncertain of the true facts. Bias may be the deciding factor in filling the gaps in memory, as when the owner of the car which, left running, has injured someone, recalls positively that he stopped the car, cut off the switch, set the brakes, etc. Personal interest facilitates the recall of the desired and congenial, represses the unwanted and distasteful. Our system of cross-examination assumes, correctly, that bias of prejudice and sympathy are valuable allies and dangerous opponents. Unconscious bias is more dangerous than conscious bias. In every witness there is "an empire of subconscious loyalties," likes and dislikes, preferences and hatreds, some conscious, others unconscious, but all entering into and affecting what we perceive, how we perceive it, and, most important of all, how we recall it.[164]

Unfortunately, it is not uncommon for an honest and sincere witness to confuse his recollection of what actually occurred with what he has persuaded himself to have happened.

It has been written that "imagination and suggestion co-operating will rewrite the perceptual truth until it is unrecognizable."[165] The power of hypnotic suggestion has been well demonstrated in this book, but the reader must realize that everyone reacts continuously to a myriad of suggestions in their daily lives, usually at a subconscious level. Modern advertising quite literally subconsciously programs each and every one of us. It should not be assumed that these waking suggestions are less powerful than hypnotic suggestions, because in many instances they are actually stronger in that they usually operate below our level of conscious awareness, hence beyond conscious control.

It is this form of subtle waking suggestion that often manipulates and alters a witness's conception of the event witnessed. Suggestions from the press, acquaintances, and interviewing law enforcement officers or attorneys, can all quite easily and inadvertently alter the person's memory, which he may unknowingly incorporate as his own at a later date.

Experienced trial lawyers are often masters of suggestion, even if unknowingly, and can subtlely influence a jury as well as a witness. Consider the following extreme example:

At the Luetgert trial in Chicago shortly before the turn of the century, a thirteen year old girl, in giving evidence for the prosecution, stated that she had seen Luetgert and his wife go up a lane near the factory on the night of the murder. In cross-examination she said that her former statements were untrue, that she was at home all evening, and had been paid by the police to give false evidence. After the lawyer for the defense had taken his seat in glory, and the child had a chance to think over the admissions she had made under the bulldozing suggestions of the defense's lawyer, the judge turned *quietly* to her and asked if she had actually seen Mr. and Mrs. Luetgert on that eventful evening. Her reply was, "Yes, sir; I did."[166]

Although the modern court has recognized the importance and necessity of controlling undue suggestion, trial lawyers still well realize the usefulness of deliberately making suggestive statements and asking leading questions, knowing full well that their impact will be realized upon the minds of the jury and witness before adverse counsel can object and the judge rule it improper.

Can Interviewers Inadvertently Alter Witnesses' Memories?

It is obvious that trial lawyers may deliberately attempt to influence witnesses through suggestive statements and leading questions, but it begs to be asked: Can investigators inadvertently alter or influence the memory of a witness during an interview?

All of the above factors influencing misremembering are quite beyond the control of the investigator, with the single exception of suggestion. Since any investigator is searching for the truth, it is essential that he have a basic understanding of his role as a suggester. Due to the hypersuggestibility of the hypnotized subject, this is especially important for the hypno-investigator.

Even though law enforcement officers spend a great deal of time and have years of experience in interviewing crime victims and witnesses, few of them have even considered the influence of the form of the interview upon the completeness and accuracy of the information received. Most quite innocently assume that they will eventually and accurately extract what information the person has regardless of the way in which it is done. In other words, even if two different investigators were to interview the same witness, both would gain the same information. Research into this very assumption has clearly shown that this is definitely not always the case.

The results of experimental studies indicate the following:

1. The most accurate testimonial evidence is obtained by narrative with supplemental questioning.[167] "Forced memory (answers to questions) is less accurate than natural recall (free narration)," but direct questioning covers a much greater range and brings out more information than the narrative, although there is a corresponding loss in accuracy due to "forcing" the memory.[168] In a review of the literature, Whipple found that the narrative, which is a free account, either oral or written, given without comment, question, or suggestion from the interviewer is approximately 90 percent correct, while the deposition (replies to prearranged questions) was approximately 75 percent accurate. The length of the narrative, however, was found to be often 50 percent greater.[169] Another study showed that narratives of a witnessed event were 23 percent complete and 94 percent accurate, while direct examinations were 31 percent complete and 83 percent accurate.[170] In summary, it seems that if the narrative is supplemented with direct questioning after the fact, the interviewer gains the advantages and avoids the disadvantages of both types of interviews.

2. The number of errors in unsworn testimony is nearly twice as great as in sworn testimony, but the error in sworn testimony still remains as high as 10 percent.[171]

3. Leading or suggestive questions very noticeably decrease the accuracy of experimental witnesses, especially for children. In a comparison of different types of questions, it was found that there is a 26 percent error for indifferent, 38 percent error for moderately suggestive, and 61 percent error for strongly suggestive questions with children.[172]

4. The assertiveness and positiveness of a witness's belief in the accuracy of his testimony is no guarantee or evidence of its truthfulness. "In exploring the level of confidence of witnesses, our data clash with the widely held respect in the legal establishment for expressions of certainty by a witness, e.g. 'I'll never forget his face.' In the present study, as well as in our other research efforts, we have found no evidence to support this assertion. Correlations between confidence and recall accuracy have generally been low and non-significant."[173]

5. When a witness

is called upon to make his report several times, the effect of this repetition is complex, for (1) it tends in part to establish in mind the items reported, whether they be true or false, and (2) it tends also to induce some departure in the later reports, because these are based more upon the memory of the verbal statements of the earlier reports than upon the original experience itself, i.e., the later reports undergo distortion on account of the flexibility of verbal expression.[174]

6. The form of questions asked subsequent to a witnessed event can cause an erroneous reconstruction in one's memory of that event. In one study, groups of graduate students were shown a film of an automobile accident and then asked specific questions about events that did and did not actually occur. For example, half of the subjects were asked, "Did you see *a* broken headlight?" The other half were asked, "Did you see *the* broken headlight?" A total of six such questions were asked each student, three of which pertained to items in the film and the other three to items not present. The results showed that whether an item was acutally present or not in the film, subjects interviewed with *a* were over twice as likely to respond "I don't know," while subjects interviewed with *the* tended to commit themselves to either a yes or no answer. When questioned about items not actually present in the film, students asked *the* questions gave false yes answers twice as often (15 percent of the time) as those asked *a* questions (7 percent of the time).[175]

7. Quantitative adjectives or adverbs in a question can affect a subject's estimation of a measurement, e.g. height, distance, weight, speed, etc. A group of forty-six college students was asked to make as accurate a numerical guess as possible about the size of an object in an experiment designed to study the accuracy of guessing measurements. The students were then presented with an item to measure and asked one of two questions, such as "How high was the building?" or "How low was the building?" The questioning was arranged such that half of the stu-

dents were asked the first question and half the second question. "Presumably, the former question should presuppose nothing about the degree of height of the building, while the latter sentence, with the marked adjective *low,* should necessarily presuppose that the building is low. . . ." The hypothesis being tested is that the marked adjective will skew the subject's response toward the direction indicated by the adjective. Out of a list of thirty-two items, twenty-three of the differences were in the predicted direction. For example, when asked, "How tall was the basketball player?" or "How short was the basketball player?" subjects guessed on the average that he was 79 and 69 inches, respectively. When asked, "How long was the movie?" the subjects' average estimate was 130 minutes, but only 100 minutes when asked, "How short was the movie?"[176]

When subjects questioned about their hypnotic experiences were asked, "Did you experience the hypnotic state as basically *similar* to the waking state?" Eighty-three percent responded yes.[177] If the question is changed to "Did you experience the hypnotic state as basically *different* from the waking state?" 64 percent of the same people responded yes. In other words, what a subject says about this hypnotic experience depends largely on how the question is worded.[178]

8. The wording of questions asked immediately after an event can influence the answers to different questions asked at some later time. In other words, questions asked about an event shortly after it occurs may distort the witness's memory for the event. In a series of four experiments, subjects were asked questions that contained true and false presuppositions about events witnessed on films to determine if the presupposition contained in the original question influenced the subjects response to the same question at a

later date. For example, if asked, "How fast was Car A going when it ran the stop sign?" would these subjects be more likely to respond that there was a stop sign when later asked than those not asked the original question? The results support the hypothesis that the wording of a presupposition into a question, even though the presupposition is true, "can influence the answer to a subsequent question concerning the presupposition itself . . . in the direction of conforming with the supplied information."[179]

Similarly, when a false presupposition about a numerical fact is worded into an original question, responses to a later question can be affected about the quantitative fact. Even when nonexistent objects are assumed to exist in a previous question, witnesses tend to report the existence of the object in later reports.[180]

This study indicates that witnesses may incorporate within their original experience or conception of an event some external information inadvertently provided subsequent to the event through questions containing true or false presuppositions.

9. Questions asked at the time of a witnessed event can influence the answer in the direction of the verbs used in the question, as well as to cause a biased reconstruction of the event under later questioning. In two experiments reported by Loftus and Palmer,

subjects viewed films of automobile accidents and then answered questions about events occurring in the films. The question, "About how fast were the cars going when they smashed into each other?" elicited higher estimates of speed than questions which used the verbs *collided, bumped, contacted,* or *hit* in place of *smashed.* On a retest one week later, those subjects who received the verb *smashed* were more likely to say "yes" to the question, "Did you see any broken glass?" even though broken glass was not present in the film.[181]

Loftus concludes by saying

that when we experience an event, we do not simply file a memory, then on some later occasion retrieve it and read off what we've stored. Rather, at the time of recall or recognition, we reconstruct the event, using information from many sources. These include both the original perception of the event and inferences drawn later, after the fact. Over a period of time, information from these sources may integrate, so that a witness becomes unable to say how he knows a specific detail. He has only a single, unified memory.[182]

CONCLUSIONS. The obvious conclusion from these studies is that extreme care must be used when interviewing victims and witnesses, regardless of whether the person is in the waking state or hypnosis. It is interesting to note that the critics of forensic hypnosis claim that, due to the hypersuggestibility of the hypnotized person, it is easy to inadvertently alter the memory of victims or witnesses to crimes during trance and that that person may awaken convinced of the truth and accuracy of the created memory. These critics further maintain that it is just as easy to create a convincing "eyewitness" and that "it is virtually impossible to say when or if the information you have obtained is true or confabulated — unless it can be substantiated by independent evidence."[183] From the above studies and case histories, it is obvious that this criticism holds equally true for nonhypnotized witnesses as well. Hypnosis should not be singled out as the culprit when faulty interview techniques, imagination, interference and misassociations, reconstruction, and defense mechanisms are actually responsible. It does not take hypnosis to create an eyewitness. In fact, one of the greatest sources of misconvictions is due to eyewitnesses.

The critics of forensic hypnosis also make the unrealistic assertion that hypno-induced testimony should not be admitted in court because there is no guarantee of truth. This argument is ludicrous because courts do not require that testimony be truthful before it can be admitted. All that is required is that the witness tell to the best of his knowledge what he believes to have happened and to be true. The normal procedure is to allow a witness to testify to the best of his ability, and any extraneous variables, such as undue suggestion by an interviewer, that may have influenced that testimony can be considered by the jury for the purpose of deciding whether or not to believe the witness. Such extraneous variables are not normally used for the purpose of preventing the witness from testifying. Since statements made under hypnosis are really no different than any other statements, they ought to be treated by the same rules of law. The testimony of the hypnotized witness ought to be admitted and the fact of hypnosis and the possibility of suggestion is considered by the jury to decide if the witness should be believed. It is an unrealistic requirement that hypno-induced statements must be true before admitting them. Even insisting on a high level of reliability is unreasonable because it has been repeatedly demonstrated that eyewitness accounts are frequently unreliable, yet they are readily admissible. The bottom line for hypno-induced testimony is that expert witnesses can testify as to the probable reliability of the testimony in any particular case, and, if the experts disagree, the jury decides which expert to believe. Furthermore, since hypnosis is a mental science, like psychiatry, and complete reliability is not a prerequisite for psychiatric testimony, it should not be a prerequisite for hypno-induced testimony.

Even though most experts agree that hypnotic subjects can misremember, fantasize, or lie to suit their purposes, most experts also seem to believe that they are less likely to do so under hyp-

nosis than in the awake state. Furthermore, investigators deal with this problem daily at nonhypnotic levels, so this is no justification for indicting hypnosis. In the authors' experience, the fear of suggesting what isn't true to hypnotized subjects is greatly overrated. Hypnotic subjects are often depicted by the critics of forensic hypnosis as believing of any and all explicit and implicit suggestions. On numerous occasions, the authors have attempted to suggest answers to regressed practice subjects, but always without success. On all occasions they have outright rejected what is not true. The experience of many clinicians who work with amnesia patients has also been that they cannot suggest what is not true.

The critics often point to the conviction of John Philip Quaglino for the 1975 murder of his estranged wife as an argument against the use of hypnosis by law enforcement. Quaglino was convicted largely on the hypno-induced testimony of a key prosecution witness. The authors find it curious that these critics will object to such cases on the criticism that inadvertent hypnotic suggestions may have created an eyewitness, but they say nothing about the criminal cases cited above where there was no shortage of nonhypnotized eyewitnesses. They also seem to neglect the fact that it is the very system of cross-examination and requirement for collaborative evidence that is designed to protect against this possibility.

Probably the most powerful tool for altering the memories of witnesses is the press. Von Schrenck cites a triple murder case where eighteen witnesses gave testimony under oath that was subsequently proved false. It was determined that the false testimony was due to the many newspaper accounts of the crime.[184] Experimental studies have also shown the influence of the press upon potential witnesses. In one study the data showed "that groups of college students who have not been subjected to the errors of a newspaper report are consistently more accurate in their answers to specific questions which deal with the facts distorted than are other groups of college students who have, perhaps unwittingly, formed contradictory habits through the medium of the newspaper."[185] This problem is another argument for the hypnotic regression of witnesses.

The authors maintain that inadvertently altering a witness's memory during a properly conducted hypnosis interview is less apt to occur than in the waking state for two basic reasons: (1) the hypno-investigator is well aware of the hypersuggestibility of his subjects and hence is extremely careful in phrasing his questions, much more so than the primary investigator and attorneys and (2) by regressing the witness or victim to the crime event he neutralizes, bypasses, or obviates any memory alteration or contamination subsequent to the event (which is another argument in support of time regression).

What Are Some Guidelines for Interviewing Hypnotized Victims and Witnesses?

From the above discussion and other material in this book, several conclusions and guidelines for questioning hypnotized victims and witnesses can be formulated.

1. Prior to the induction, the hypno-investigator should not interrogate the subject regarding any inconsistencies or discrepancies in his recollection of the crime event. He should seek only the necessary details of the victim's or witness's recollection of the crime which are needed for the regression and were not present in the reports.

2. During hypermnesia or revivification the hypno-investigator should first attempt to elicit a free flowing uninterrupted narrative of the entire event,

e.g. "Tell me everything that occurs now as it's happening" or, "Tell me more."

3. At the completion of the narration, the operator may at that time ask specific nonsuggestive, nonaccusatory, or nonleading questions regarding specific aspects of the event. He must make all questions neutral and drop no hints. For example, if the operator has been told by the primary investigator that a gun was most likely involved but the subject failed to say anything about it during the narrative, he should ask, "Is there a weapon of any kind involved?" and not, "Do you see the gun?"

4. The hypno-investigator must dispense with all his value judgments and opinions regarding the case. He must also separate out the primary investigator's opinions and biases from the facts. To do otherwise will make nonsuggestive and nonleading questioning difficult.

5. No comments of any sort should be exchanged by the hypno-investigator and primary investigator. The primary investigator should preferably write out any additional questions that come to mind during the session and let the operator phrase them properly and ask them. If allowed to speak, the primary investigator should only do so at the permission of the operator, and a signal should be arranged between them so the detective can be stopped instantly. If the session is videotaped, there should be as little movement as possible and nothing should be done that can be interpreted as suggestive.

6. If the subject is shown a photo line-up of mugshots, they should all be viewed at once and never singly. The subject's first impression will be the best; if he has to think, little or nothing has been gained.

7. Build up to the event in question. Ask questions all around the desired information and lead up to it. This tends to build the subject's involvement and keeps him from thinking too hard

about the forgotten information.

8. Do not push the subject or he may fantasize to please you. It is a good idea to intermittently say some of the following phrases as precautionary measures, particularly if the subject seems to be trying too hard: (1) "You are not here to please me; just tell me what you can remember," (2) "If you can't see it, just tell me. Don't try too hard," (3) "We are only interested in what actually happened."

9. Don't ask the witness or victim what he couldn't have seen or heard. Similarly, tell the subject that he can respond, "I don't know."

The following are some additional precautions and considerations in formulating questions:

a. Keep questions short, i.e. less than twenty words.

b. Initially, avoid yes or no questions.

c. Avoid multiple choice answers.

d. Avoid asking any leading questions. A leading question is one that is so worded that it is not neutral, i.e. it suggests to the witness, by its form or content, what the answer should be, leads him to the desired answer, or indicates the questioner's point of view.

e. Avoid loaded words or phrases, i.e. one that is emotionally colored and suggests an automatic feeling of approval or disapproval, such as creep, boss, socialist, faggot. The use of such loaded words runs the risk of the subject reacting to it and what it connotes instead of the actual question.

f. Avoid asking embarrassing questions.[186]

ADDITIONAL USES OF FORENSIC HYPNOSIS

Although the obvious and primary use of hypnosis in criminal and civil investigations is to enhance the memory of volunteer victims and witnesses, there are many additional ways in which it can be effectively utilized, some of which are briefly discussed below.

SELF-HYPNOSIS INSTRUCTION FOR DEPARTMENTAL PERSONNEL. Law enforcement agencies are all too familiar with the problem of job-related stress and the problems it engenders. Some agencies, such as the Department of Public Safety in Oklahoma City, are instructing all new recruits in self-hypnosis and stress management as a preventative health measure. Other departments instruct patrol teams in group self-hypnosis so the officers can relax after shift. Dispatchers, detectives, and other special divisions can benefit equally from self-hypnosis.

PREPARING OFFICERS FOR TRIAL. Any experienced police officer has experienced the frustrating and embarrassing situation of receiving a subpoena to testify on a two-year-old case for which he has little or no recollection. In such instances, a departmental hypno-investigator can refresh the officer's memory of the incident for trial and give posthypnotic suggestions for calm and relaxation while on the witness stand.

REVIEWING CRIME SCENES WITH INVESTIGATORS. One detective will search a crime scene and miss important evidence, while another detective of equal expertise will immediately spot it on a walk-through. In other instances, investigators will have a different recollection of a crime scene on an old case, and there are insufficient photos to reconcile the difference. In either instance, hypnosis could be of value in refreshing their memories and researching the crime scene in their minds.

HYPNOSIS AS AN AID TO THE POLYGRAPH. In considering hypnosis as an aid to the polygraph, there are basically two potential areas of application. First is the use of hypnosis and posthypnotic suggestion to render otherwise unexaminable persons examinable. Polygraph examiners are often faced with suspects who are so nervous that the resulting tracings are erratic and inconclusive, so the question of whether or not hypnosis can be used to relax the person immediately comes to mind. Arons reports a case in which a murder suspect was exonerated on the basis of hypnotically suggested relaxation during his polygraph examination. The first examination was inconclusive due to excessive nervousness, so Arons hypnotized the suspect and gave him posthypnotic suggestions to relax and be free from nervousness or agitation during a subsequent exam, which later showed veracity.[187] Similarly, one law enforcement agency used the progressive relaxation form of indirect hypnosis on twenty-eight paternity cases. "In twenty-one of these cases, the subjects were rendered examinable by the polygraph as a result of the relaxation produced with this technique," and it also "was definitely helpful to the polygraph examiners in indicating veracity or deception."[188]

A second area of application is utilizing hypnotic suggestion to reinforce polygraph technique by exaggerating the physiological stress reactions. In one study, experimental hypnotic subjects were instructed to lie with respect to names, places, and playing cards during a polygraph examination. As a part of the study, subjects were hypnotized and first told under hypnosis and then posthypnotically, that they would respond to any attempt at deception in one of the following manners: would be unable to speak, make a tight fist, or clench their jaws tightly. The results indicated that fourteen out of fifteen examinations showed a very exaggerated response to deception. The fifteenth trial was inconclusive.[189]

If hypnosis were to be used in this manner, which is a sensitive legal and ethical question, the hypnotic suggestions given for an exaggerated response to deception could be more subtle than the ones used in the above study. For example, a simple posthypnotic suggestion that the subject would feel relaxed and calm during the exam, but would have intense feelings of guilt and anxiety at the telling of an untruth may suffice, although a conditioned involuntary movement is more effective (see "Controls for Simulation and Lying").[190] This technique could be utilized with volunteer examinees whose tracings on a first examination are inconclusive.

DETECTING MALINGERERS. With the advent of large personal injury settlements in torts, the old problem of malingering victims has become more frequent. An often overlooked tool for the detection of malingering is hypnosis.

Dorcus cites a case in which a hospitalized paraplegic confined to a wheelchair for seven years moved his legs easily under hypnosis. Subsequent unobtrusive observation found him walking in his hospital room.[191]

In instances where malingering is suspected, the hypnosis should be done by a psychologist or psychiatrist and not a lay hypno-investigator because the alleged malingerer may have a legitimate psychosomatic or psychophysiologic ailment or a conversion hysteria.

DETERMINING THE STATE OF MIND OF A DEFENDANT. A defendant has a legal right to a private hypno-examination to assist in his defense. As such, hypnosis is often used by consulting defense psychologists and psychiatrists to help determine the state of mind of the defendant, i.e. did he have the requisite intent at the time of the crime and/or is he mentally competent to stand trial?

REHABILITATION. A potentially beneficial use of individual and group hypnosis would be as a rehabilitative method in any penal institution, juvenile or adult probation office, group homes, halfway houses, etc. This should also only be conducted by licensed doctors or by lay practitioners under the supervision of a doctor.

VERIFYING VERBAL CONTRACTS. Many civil cases arise from disputes over verbal contracts with each party having a different recollection. A possible out-of-court settlement would be for both parties to undergo hypnosis to enhance their memories while agreeing to adhere to the results. Since hypnosis is not a truth establishing procedure, however, this potential use is fraught with problems.

HYPNOSIS AS A THREAT. Much as law enforcement officers will use the threat of polygraph to turn an uncredible victim, witness, or defendant, the threat of hypnosis can serve the same function. The threat is only implied since no one can be legally forced to submit to either polygraph or hypnosis, but some people do not know this, and the ones who do, realize that a denial can be interpreted as an implicit admission of guilt. Just as a few guilty persons will risk the polygraph if they can avoid it, few will risk hypnosis due to the pervasive misconception that people cannot lie under hypnosis.

If hypnosis is to ever be used in this way, the threat must be subtle and only implied. For example, a primary investigator should never say in frustration, "Okay then, we'll call in our department hypnotist and he'll get the truth out of you." Rather, he should say,

"Would you mind submitting to hypnosis?" Furthermore, this should probably never be done with defendants as if it stimulated a confession, it may be thrown out of court on a Fifth Amendment question. Its potential area of application is particularly with crime victims and witnesses suspected of being dishonest.

VERIFYING UFO, BIGFOOT, AND OTHER SIGHTINGS. Although a debate rages among the authorities on the veracity of such sightings and even the usefulness of hypnosis as a tool for sorting out fact from fantasy, it remains an interesting prospect for investigating sightings.[192]

ASSISTING A DEFENDANT IN HIS DEFENSE. Occasionally, lay hypno-investigators will assist a defendant in the preparation of his defense at his request and with permission of his defense counsel. This is usually done in cases where the defendant is amnesic, or has difficulty remembering pertinent information that could corroborate his alibi. Just as law enforcement generally makes available its polygraph service to defense counsel, there is little reason that they should not do likewise with their hypno-investigation service. This can prove beneficial in the long run, particularly if the use of hypnosis resulted in vindicating an innocent defendant. In this event, defense counsel would be much less likely to seriously object to its use in a court challenge.

CONTROLS FOR SIMULATION AND LYING

Although simulation and lying are two different potential problems associated with hypnosis, they are closely related and will be discussed together.

Many experts in hypnosis believe that it is impossible to tell if subjects are feigning hypnosis or lying. They maintain that just as simulators can convincingly deceive even experienced onlookers, so can subjects convincingly

lie under hypnosis and that there are no reliable means of detecting simulation and lying. The authors believe that both these assertions are not only false, but that an operator can easily reliably test for both simulation and lying given he knows the proper techniques.

The reader may ask why a victim, witness, or even a defendant would volunteer for hypnosis and then simulate and/or lie. The answer is that they will for the very same reasons that they will consent to and then lie during a standard police interview or polygraph examination. Although probably 99 percent of volunteer subjects will do so in legitimate good faith, the hypno-investigator should still examine every subject's motive for volunteering to undergo a hypno-examination. Consider the motives of the following victim, witness, and defendant:

1. The rape victim who was actually a willing participant, but who alleges rape due to intense feelings of guilt.
2. The witness who has an ulterior motive of providing an alibi for his friend, the accused.
3. The defendant who feigns amnesia, but volunteers to undergo hypnosis at the request of his defense counsel.

The reader may also ask why he would ever need to test for simulation and lying. The overriding reason will be to assess the reliability of the information provided by an uncredible subject. Recognizing that the hypno-investigator's basic objective is to obtain complete and accurate information for the primary investigator, he will want to be relatively certain that he is not going to waste the primary investigator's valuable time running down misinformation. Hence, if the subject passes tests for simulation and lying, the information obtained will be more credible. An ancillary reason for testing for simulation is to determine if in fact the subject is hypnotized, and, if not, the operator can take the necessary and appropriate measures.

An often overlooked, but important reason for testing for simulation and lying is to facilitate and maximize the chances of the hypno-investigation withstanding a court challenge. When hypno-induced evidence and testimony is at issue in a case, the videotapes of the hypnosis session(s) will likely be examined in scrupulous detail by defense psychologists or psychiatrists. It is very easy to discredit the testimony of an expert witness hypno-investigator on the basis of not adequately determining hypnotic depth, simulation, and reliability of the information obtained.

When to test for simulation and/or lying will be an individual decision the hypno-investigator will have to make depending on several factors, including the following: (1) the subject's motivation, (2) visible signs of simulation, (3) the nature of the information provided, i.e. the operator may suspect it to be fabricated, (4) the reason for the session, e.g. to obtain a better description of a rapist from his victim versus establishing an alibi for an alleged amnesic defendant, and (5) the likelihood of the case going to court on the issue of hypno-induced evidence. Chances are that unless a hypno-investigator does sessions for defense counsel with their defendants, he may never have a need for testing for simulation and particularly lying.

Ammonia Test for Simulation

According to the LeCron-Bordeaux depth scale, olfactory illusions are indicative of a medium trance. An excellent method of testing for simulation, as well as a test for hypnotic depth, is the ammonia test. Several alternative, but equally effective, versions are presented below. In any approach it is recommended that the ammonia be diluted with water to approximately a 50 percent solution to avoid unnecessarily impinging upon and insulting the subject's nasal tissue.

Test #1

In this simple direct approach, the operator is prepared with a small opaque cologne or aftershave bottle filled with the ammonia/water solution. During the preinduction, he casually brings it out in sight of the subject while remarking, "I might show you some interesting things that can be done with your sense of smell under hypnosis."

During the session, when the operator is ready to test either for a medium trance level or simulation, he simply tells the subject to take a deep whiff of the bottle of aftershave or cologne as he holds it under his nose, i.e. "You remember that bottle of aftershave I showed you? Well I want you to take a deep whiff of it now as I hold it under your nose."

This approach is best used if relatively certain of success. The problem remains, however, of how to recover if it fails and without the subject feeling that you have tricked him. This is easier to do than one would suspect as it is the subject that was trying to deceive you, unless of course the operator prematurely tests a genuine subject. In either case, the operator should resort to a simple explanation. For example "You'll remember, Rick, that at the outset I told you that I might show you some interesting things that can be done with your sense of smell under hypnosis. Well, if you were deep enough you actually would have hallucinated the smell of the aftershave and would not have smelled the ammonia at all, so you obviously aren't deep enough." If the subject was simulating he will realize that he has been discovered which is likely to enhance his confidence that you know what you are doing, as well as to increase his subsequent cooperation. The operator is saved embarrassment because the egg is on the subject's face. If the subject was honestly cooperating and the operator prematurely tested, the explanation should be adequate to alleviate any negative influence. In either case, the operator knows that he has to back up and deepen the subject further or discuss his resistance if deemed necessary.

To recover further, the operator can continue in the following manner: "Okay, Rick, you weren't quite able to hallucinate the aftershave; so let's do one more deepening technique. Then I'll show you something else interesting with your sense of smell that I'm sure you'll be able to do." (The operator deepens further and then proceeds to anesthetize the subject's sense of smell and "test" with the capped bottle as in test number 3.)

Test #2

When the operator is ready to either test for a medium level trance or simulation, have the subject imagine to the best of his ability his favorite fragrance. This is determined during the preinduction by a question on the Preinduction Questionnaire or, if not done, by simply asking the subject at the time of the test. Give him some time to conjure up the fragrance as best he can while helping him with appropriate suggestions. For example, if the subject's favorite fragrance is that of a rose, describe the rose to him visually, tactilely, and olfactorily as follows: "Now you picture a brilliant red rose in your mind's eye and you cup that rose in your hands. You can feel its soft velvety petals. Now you lift it up to your nose and take a deep inhale, smelling it as if it were actually real." If the subject is sufficiently deep he will quite obviously enjoy the smell of it. At this point, the operator brings out a small bottle of ammonia/water solution that he had concealed and tells the subject to take another deep whiff of the rose as he holds the bottle under his nose.

This approach should be used if the operator is less certain of success, as it takes more time and direct suggestion to elicit the subject's hallucinated fragrance. Furthermore, there is the built-in safety check of the observable degree of involvement in the hallucinated fragrance. The likelihood of the test succeeding is positively correlated with the degree of involvement in the hallucinated fragrance. Hence, if the involvement is minimal, the operator may choose to deepen additionally before testing. If the test fails, recover in the same manner as in the above approach.

Test #3

Be prepared with two bottles, one of aftershave or cologne and one of ammonia/water solution. During the preinduction talk, casually bring out the real bottle in sight of the subject as in the above approach. When ready to test for the medium level or simulation, have the subject smell the real aftershave or cologne. Proceed to tell him that a good test of a medium level of hypnosis is to be able to anesthetize his sense of smell so that he cannot smell anything. Continue by giving suggestions to this effect, e.g. "As I count from one to five your sense of smell will steadily decrease, as if it were becoming numb to the point where you won't be able to smell anything. You might think of those times when you've had a cold and your nose was all stuffed up and you couldn't smell anything. One, . . . " Once reaching five, hold up the capped bottle while telling the subject to take a deep whiff and ask him what he smells. When he says that he smells nothing, praise him by saying that he is doing very well. This will increase his suggestibility and conviction that he is hypnotized, hence helping him to go deeper while preparing him for the next step. Continue by telling the subject that you are going to demonstrate to him another interesting phenomenon that will show him how much control he has over his body and senses in hypnosis. Restore his sense of smell by reversing the previous suggestions. Ask him now to imagine his favorite fragrance, and once it is thoroughly fixed in his mind's eye tell him that again you will have him smell the aftershave, but instead of the aftershave he will smell his favorite fragrance. When he's ready, hold up the capped ammonia/water bottle and have him take a whiff and ask him what

he smells. If he smells nothing, you know he is not sufficiently deep so you have to back up and do more deepenings, eventually retesting. If he smells his favorite fragrance he is either simulating or truly hypnotized. To determined which is the case, tell the subject to take another deep whiff as you uncap the bottle and hold it directly under his nose. If he does not recoil, but actually still enjoys the smell of his fragrance of choice, the test was successful and you can be sure that he is not simulating. If he recoils from the ammonia, recover in the same manner as in test number 1.

Hallucination Test for Simulation

A drawback of the ammonia test is that, although indicative of a medium level trance, it does not guarantee a deep trance. Hence, a subject may pass the test and still simulate a regression. A highly reliable test for simulation was described by Orne that requires a somnambulistic level of hypnosis, and hence is a reliable predictor of a genuine regression. The test capitalizes on the hypnotic phenomenon of trance logic described in Chapter 3.

When the subject is believed to be in a deep trance, he is instructed to open his eyes and look at a third party in the room who has been seated in full view of the subject. The primary investigator can serve as the third party. The subject is then told to close his eyes, at which point the third party silently moves behind the subject out of his line of sight. The subject is then told to open his eyes and that he will see a hallucinated image of the third party in the chair. Upon opening his eyes and accepting the hallucination as real, the operator tells him to turn around and then asks, "Who is that behind you?" Orne found that genuinely hypnotized subjects would almost invariably look at the third party, then quickly turn back to look at the empty chair and back again. The subjects stated they saw two images of the same person, and, when asked, they said that it must be a trick or that mirrors were responsible.

The simulating subjects, on the other hand, for the most part "either refused to see anyone behind them, or claimed that they could not recognize the person. Occasionally, they admitted recognizing the associate behind them and then claimed that the hallucination had vanished."[193] The hypnotized subjects could readily accept the illogical presence of a double image, whereas the simulators, who know that this is impossible and not logical, will usually deny the existence of one of the images.

A Test for Lying

The operator should usually decide before the session if it will be necessary to test for lying for any of the reasons mentioned previously. If so, during the preinduction, he should have the subject write down a number between one and ten on a small piece of paper out of the sight of the operator, which the subject then folds and puts in his pocket. The operator merely explains that he may show him something interesting or play a little game with him later.

After the operator has elicited either hypermnesia or revivification, he proceeds in the following manner: "You've done very well, Rick, but now I'm going to bring you back to the present location, date, and time, but as I do you will remain as deep as you are now. *(The operator progresses the subject up to the present in the usual manner.)* Now we're going to do something else that's kind of interesting. I'm going to demonstrate to you how you can actually make parts of your body completely numb and also how it can work entirely automatically, so that you cannot consciously control it. Now, with eyes still closed, focus your attention on the left hand. Now imagine that hand becoming numb. In fact, the longer you concentrate on that

numb feeling the more numb it gets. To help you, think of how it felt when your hands have been so cold in the past that they were actually numb and stiff, and you could hardly bend the fingers. Or, you know how it feels when you sometimes sleep on an arm wrong and when you wake up it is completely numb and asleep so that you can't control it. Well, it's that same feeling or nonfeeling developing in the left hand now. I can help you in this by lightly stroking the hand, and, each time I do, more and more feeling temporarily goes out of that hand. *(Begin gently stroking the hand.)* It's as if I am pushing the feeling right out, and it's getting more and more numb, so numb that it's as if the hand is no longer yours, as if it's just attached or even not attached. Is it numb yet? 'Yes.' Okay, that's good. *(If the subject responds no, continue with more suggestions to induce glove anesthesia. An additional deepening technique or two may also be necessary if the subject came up to a lighter trance after the regression, or is simulating. If the subject responds that it is numb, test for the degree of numbness by sticking a safety pin or needle under the fingernail on his index finger and observe for any flinch either in the finger itself or in a facial response. To know how far in to push the pin, the operator should practice this on himself. The depth of the pin can easily be observed under the fingernail. This technique is an effective test for glove anesthesia, which can be done as an indicator of a medium level trance in place of or in conjunction with other medium level tests and challenges.)*

"That's good, 'Rick,' you're doing very well. Now I'm going to show you something kind of magical that you can do with that numb hand. I'm going to pick up that hand and move it over here and rub this spot in the middle of the right forearm with the left index finger. Now you'll notice that as I do this, that numbness in the left hand will make that small spot on the right forearm also numb. It's as if the numbness is transferring, but now both the left hand and that spot on the right forearm are numb. *(Return the left hand to his leg or the arm of the chair.)* Now 'Rick,' what I'm going to do is gently poke the right forearm with a pin, and I want you to tell me when you can feel the pinprick. *(The operator gently pricks the skin on various places on the forearm to which the subject responds yes. The operator then intermittently pricks the anesthetized spot to which the subject will generally respond no if truly hypnotized. If he is simulating he will generally be silent. This seemingly paradoxical reaction is based on the fact that truly hypnotized and anesthetized subjects do not feel pain but still generally feel pressure. Therefore, when pricked with a pin they will not feel any pain, but just a dull pressure to which they will either respond, "No, I didn't feel that," or will display a quizzical facial expression like they are uncertain if they did or did not actually feel it. A simulator, on the other hand, in an attempt to fool the operator, does not know this and will merely say nothing and betray no signs of feeling the pinprick in the erroneous belief that if truly anesthetized he would not feel anything.)*

"Now we're going to do something else that's just as interesting, but this is something that your subconscious mind does and your conscious mind has absolutely no control over it. Now what's going to happen is that I'm going to say your name and when I do the left index finger, even though it is completely numb, will immediately jerk up. You will find that you won't be able to control this response because it will be automatic. In effect, it is your subconscious I am talking to and it will make the left index finger jerk up as soon as I say your name, even though you can't feel the left hand. Now, I'll say your name and the left index finger will automatically and spontaneously jerk up. *(Proceed to say his name and repeat several times until the reflex is spontaneous and distinct.)* That's good, Rick, you see, it's working. *(To convince himself as well*

as the subject that the reflex is thoroughly conditioned, the operator may even challenge him to stop it.)

"Now in a moment I am going to awaken you by counting from 'one' to 'three' at which point you will open your eyes and be wide awake, but before I do I want you to understand that all I'll have to do is to put my hand on your right shoulder and press down and you will immediately and automatically go back under hypnosis, but even deeper than you are now. Do you understand? *(He nods.)* Before I bring you out I want you to know that the left index finger will continue to jerk up automatically everytime I say your name as well as at the telling of an untruth, and we're going to play a little game. In other words, whenever you tell an untruth your subconscious mind will automatically move that finger. Also, when I awaken you, you will remember everything except the automatic response in the left index finger that will continue to work spontaneously and below conscious awareness even though you will be awake. When I bring you out, the left hand will still be numb, but you won't pay any attention to it and it won't concern you. Do you understand? *(He nods.)* Alright, coming up now, 'one,' 'two,' 'three,' AWAKE! How do you feel, Rick? *(The left forefinger should jerk up.)* Say, do you remember that number I had you write down before we began? Well, I'm going to try to guess that number. What I'm going to do is call off each number from one to ten and ask you if that is the one. At each number, however, I want you to respond no. In other words, don't tell me what the number is, okay? Alright, let's begin. Is it number one?" *(Continue calling off each number while you casually watch for the conditioned reflex. When the subject responds no to his number of choice the finger should jerk up. Once you determine the number, however, continue on up to ten and then tell him which number. At this point, if successful, the operator, primary investigator, or attorney can ask whatever questions they believe the subject may be lying on. At the termination of the additional questioning, the operator then rehypnotizes the subject with the posthypnotic cue and erases the conditioned reflex, the anesthesia in both the left hand and right forearm, and the rehypnotization cue. He then wakens the subject by the standard means.)*

Automatic Writing as a Test for Lying

As in the above approach, the operator anesthetizes the subject's hand and tests for simulation with the pinprick test, both under the fingernail and with the "magic" spot on the forearm. The subject is then handed a pen and pad and told that the hand will be the mouthpiece of the subconscious and that it will respond spontaneously and automatically when asked a question. The subject is further told that he will not be consciously aware of what the hand is writing nor can he consciously control it. Finally, the operator instructs the subconscious that he or another present is going to ask some questions and that it will write out the truth of the matter. At this point the operator, or others present, can ask questions of the subject while he remains hypnotized.

As an alternative approach, the operator may induce fractionation and suggest amnesia for the automatic writing suggestions. He then wakens the subject and asks questions.

Considerations

1. The glove anesthesia component of the test for lying is also a test for simulation, although it is not as foolproof as the ammonia test. Glove anesthesia as a test for simulation suffers from several weaknesses: (a) the pain threshold varies greatly among individuals, (b) it is only a medium level test, hence a subject may successfully produce glove anesthesia, yet simulate the more important regression, (c) the location of pain receptors varies among individuals, and (d) some subjects may exhibit an avoidance reflex in the anticipation of pain even though they are sufficiently anesthetized. Although the first two weaknesses pertain to the glove anesthesia test as outlined above, the latter two do not pertain because of the particularly sensitive area (under the fingernail) and since it is unannounced.

2. Although relatively accurate and consistent, the pinprick test for simulation and deception may not work with all subjects, as very deeply hypnotized subjects with complete anesthesia may not even feel pressure.

SELF-HYPNOSIS

One may rightfully ask why a book on forensic hypnosis has a section on self-hypnosis. Consider the following reasons:

1. Many officers who learn investigative hypnosis are also interested in self-hypnosis, whether to ease job-related tension and anxiety, for personal development and improvement, or a host of other reasons.
2. Many subjects in the practice pool will want to learn self-hypnosis. Some doctors may disapprove of a lay hypno-investigator teaching self-hypnosis, but the authors think this objection is unfounded for the following reasons: (a) any person can easily learn self-hypnosis by reading any one of a multitude of books on the subject that are readily available at any bookstore or library, so why not learn from a trained hypnotist? (b) some of the practice subjects will

attempt self-hypnosis on their own without guidance, so it is best that those interested receive formal instruction, and (c) it is safe and legal.

3. It often helps in recruiting practice subjects to offer instruction in self-hypnosis at the end of the course.

4. Teaching self-hypnosis to departmental personnel for such things as stress management is a viable alternative use.

Unfortunately, space does not allow for a detailed exposition of self-hypnosis. By this point, however, the operator can easily adapt the techniques he has learned for self-hypnosis, because it differs in no essential way from heterohypnosis. The subject merely hypnotizes himself by following the same induction, deepening, and waking techniques in this book. In essence, he silently talks himself into a hypnotic state. The interested reader can find a wealth of sources on self-hypnosis in any bookstore or library. There are some general concerns and important guidelines that the hypno-investigator should be aware of before teaching anyone self-hypnosis.

If a subject from the practice pool requests to be instructed in self-hypnosis, the hypno-investigator, if he chooses to so instruct the person, should realize that he assumes the responsibility to thoroughly and properly instruct the subject in self-hypnosis techniques, which he will easily be able to do with his working knowledge of hypnosis. Before agreeing to instruct a subject in self-hypnosis, the hypno-investigator should assess the person's motives and maturity. If the person is stable and mature and wishes to use self-hypnosis in an intelligent and sensible manner and there are no apparent contraindications, then by all means the person should be taught. If, on the other hand, the subject has proven to be immature, somewhat hys-

terical or neurotic, and wishes to use self-hypnosis for therapeutic reasons, a frank discussion and refusal may be called for. The authors agree with Weitzenhoffer's admonition that " the indiscriminate training in self-hypnosis of disturbed individuals as a form of therapy must be strongly condemned."[194] Those persons who are taught self-hypnosis should be cautioned not to try to treat any illness, whether physical or mental, without the knowledge, consent, and advice of their doctor. For instance, it only takes good common sense for a person practicing self-hypnosis to know if his abdominal pain is appendicitis or tension.

If the hypno-investigator is approached by a department member who wishes to use self-hypnosis in a job-related capacity, e.g. to wind down after shift, he should be first screened on the basis of his answers to the Preinduction Questionnaire and any signs of contraindication. If the operator determines he is a suitable candidate, he should hypnotize him several times first before instructing him in self-hypnosis. This will determine which techniques are best for that individual and will give him a model to follow. It will also aid him in going much deeper as his initial resistances will break down and he will be comfortable with the experience.

Whenever a subject is taught self-hypnosis, it is essential that he first attempt it in the presence of the operator. This is to insure that he can successfully induce, deepen, and most importantly, terminate self-hypnosis. Furthermore, most subjects will be very skeptical about whether or not self-hypnosis will be effective with them or may be afraid of not awakening. The initial supervised session will resolve these types of fears and reservations.

Any subject interested in self-hypnosis should be encouraged to survey the literature and read a few good books on the subject. In this way he can learn how to develop his own positive and effective self-suggestions for per-sonal improvement and development. Instruction in self-therapy is the responsibility of the subject and not the hypno-investigator.

REFERENCES

1. Ellenberger, H. F.: *The Discovery of the Unconscious: The History and Evaluation of Dynamic Psychiatry.* New York, Basic, 1970.

2. Estabrooks, G. H.: *Hypnotism.* New York, Dutton, 1957.

3. Reiter, P. J.: *Antisocial or Criminal Acts and Hypnosis: A Case Study.* Springfield, Thomas, 1958.

4. Associated Press, Martinez, California, April 1, 1948.

5. Bramwell, J. M.: *Hypnotism: Its History, Practice and Theory.* London, Grant Richards, 1903.

6. Hollander, B.: *Psychology of Misconduct, Vice and Crime.* New York, Macmillan, 1923, p. 40.

7. Schilder, Paul: Hypnosis. *Nervous and Mental Disease Monograph Series, 46:*33.

8. Rowland, Loyd W.: Will hypnotized persons try to harm themselves or others? *Journal of Abnormal and Social Psychology, 34:*117, 1939.

9. Young, Paul C.: Antisocial uses of hypnosis. In LeCron, Leslie M. (Ed.): *Experimental Hypnosis,* 2nd ed. New York, Citadel, 1968, p. 405.

10. Watkins, John G.: Antisocial compulsions induced under hypnotic trance. *Journal of Abnormal and Social Psychology, 42:*258, 1947.

11. Wells, Raymond W.: Experiments in the hypnotic production of crime. *The Journal of Psychology, 11:*100-101, 1941.

12. Brenman, Margaret: Experiments in the hypnotic production of anti-social and self-injurious behavior. *Psychiatry, 5:*60, 1942.

13. Erickson, Milton H.: An experimental investigation of the possible anti-social use of hypnosis. *Psychiatry, 2:*393, 1939.

14. Ibid., p. 414.

15. Bramwell, p. 323.

16. Wolberg, Lewis R.: *Medical Hypnosis: The Principles of Hypnotherapy.* New York, Grune & Stratton, 1948, vol. I, p. 414.

17. Ibid., pp. 414-415.

18. Ibid., p. 415.

19. Orne, Martin T.: Can a hypnotized subject be compelled to carry out otherwise unacceptable behavior? *International Journal of Clinical and Experimental Hypnosis, 20(2):*101, 1972.

20. Orne, Martin T.: Review of P. J. Reiter, *Antisocial or Criminal Acts and Hypnosis: A Case Study. International Journal of Clinical and Experimental Hypnosis, 8:*133, 1960.

21. Barber, T. X.: Antisocial and criminal acts induced by "hypnosis": a review of experimental and clinical findings. *Archives of General Psychiatry, 5:*311, 1961.

22. Conn, Jacob H.: Is hypnosis really dangerous? *International Journal of Clinical and Experimental Hypnosis, 20:*62, 1972.

23. Ibid., p. 61.

24. Orne, Review of P. J. Reiter, pp. 133-134.

25. Kline, Milton V.: The production of antisocial behavior through hypnosis: New clinical data. *International Journal of Clinical and Experimental Hypnosis, 20(2):*80-81, 1972.

26. Ibid., p. 82.

27. Ibid., p. 93.

28. Ibid., pp. 84-85.

29. Ibid., p. 84.

30. Weitzenhoffer, André M.: The production of antisocial acts under hypnosis. *Journal of Abnormal and Social Psychology, 44:*420, 1949.

31. Young, p. 399.

32. Erickson, p. 393.

33. Erickson, p. 392.

34. Orne, Martin T.: The nature of hypnosis: artifact and essence. *Journal of Abnormal and Social Psychology, 58:*277-299, 1959.

35. Orne, Martin T.: Antisocial behavior

and hypnosis: Problems of control and validation in empirical studies. In Estabrooks, G. H. (Ed.): *Hypnosis: Current Problems.* New York, Harper & Row, 1962.

36. Orne, Martin T.: On the social psychology of the psychological experiment: with particular reference to demand characteristics and their implications. *American Psychologist, 17:*776-783, 1962.

37. Rosenthal, Robert: Experimenter outcome-orientation and the results of the psychological experiment. *Psychological Bulletin, 61:*405-412, 1964.

38. Rosenthal, Robert: *Experimenter Effects in Behavioral Research.* New York, Appleton-Century-Crofts, 1966.

39. Rosenthal, R., and Fode, K. L.: Psychology of the scientist: V. Three experiments in experimenter bias. *Psychological Reports, 12:*491-511, 1963.

40. Orne, Martin T., and Evans, Frederick J.: Social control in the psychological experiment: Antisocial behavior and hypnosis. *Journal of Personality and Social Psychology, 1(3):*189, 1965.

41. Estabrooks, p. 186.

42. Sidis, B.: *The Psychology of Suggestion.* New York, Appleton, 1910.

43. Estabrooks, pp. 84-85.

44. Orne and Evans, p. 191.

45. Orne, "Can a hypnotized subject," p. 104.

46. Milgram, Stanley: Some conditions of obedience and disobedience to authority. *Human Relations, 18:*57, 1965.

47. Ibid., pp. 59-60.

48. Milgram, Stanley: Behavioral study of obedience. *Journal of Abnormal and Social Psychology, 67:*376, 1963.

49. Ibid., p. 375.

50. Milgram, "Some conditions," p. 72.

51. Ibid., p. 74.

52. Orne and Evans, p. 191.

53. Ibid., p. 192.

54. Ibid., p. 199.

55. Orne, "Can a hypnotized subject," p. 104.

56. Estabrooks, p. 186.

57. Conn, p. 69.

58. Orne, "Can a hypnotized subject," p. 105.

59. Erickson, p. 414.

60. Young, p. 405.

61. Wells, p. 67.

62. Orne, "Can a hypnotized subject," p. 110.

63. Janet, P.: *Psychological Healing.* New York, Macmillan, 1925.

64. Wolberg, p. 414.

65. Arons, Harry: *Hypnosis in Criminal Investigation.* So. Orange, Power, 1977, p. 20.

66. LeCron, Leslie M.: Editor's note to Antisocial uses of hypnosis. In LeCron, Leslie M. (Ed.): *Experimental Hypnosis,* 2nd ed. New York, Citadel, 1968, p. 373.

67. Wells, p. 100.

68. LeCron, p. 372.

69. Ibid., p. 374.

70. Ibid., p. 375.

71. Young, p. 376.

72. Revised Montana Codes of 1947.

73. Watkins, John G.: Antisocial behavior under hypnosis: Possible or impossible? *International Journal of Clinical and Experimental Hypnosis, 20(2):*96, 1972.

74. Revised Montana Codes of 1947.

75. Watkins, John G.: A case of hypnotic trance induced in a resistant subject in spite of active opposition. *British Journal of Medical Hypnotism, 2:*26-31, 1941.

76. Orne, "The nature of hypnosis," p. 277-299.

77. Orne, Martin T.: The potential uses of hypnosis in interrogation. In Biderman, A. D. and Zimmer, H. (Eds.): *The Manipulation of Human Behavior.* New York, Wiley, 1961, pp. 169-215.

78. Erickson, Milton H.: Deep hypnosis and its induction. In Haley, Jay (Ed.): *Advanced Techniques of Hypnosis and Therapy: Selected Papers of Milton H. Erickson, M.D.* New York, Grune & Stratton, 1967, p. 20.

79. Field, P. B., and Dworkin, S. F.: Strategies of hypnotic interrogation. *The Journal of Psychology, 67:*47-58, 1967.

80. Orne, "The potential uses of hypnosis," p. 179.

81. Ibid., pp. 176-177.

82. Ibid., pp. 169-215.

83. Watkins, "A case of hypnotic trance," p. 27.

84. Wolberg, p. 415.

85. Wells, p. 100.

86. Carkhuff, Robert R. and Berenson, Bernard G.: *Beyond Counseling and Therapy*. New York, Holt, Rinehart & Winston, 1967, pp. 10, 13-14, 10-11.

87. Ibid., pp. 11-12.

88. Eysenck, H. J.: The effects of psychotherapy: An evaluation. *Journal of Consulting Psychology, 16:*319-324, 1952.

89. Eysenck, H. J.: The effects of psychotherapy. In Eysenck, H. J. (Ed.): *The Handbook of Abnormal Psychology*. New York, Basic, 1960.

90. Eysenck, H. J.: The effects of psychotherapy. *International Journal of Psychotherapy, 1:*99-178, 1965.

91. Levitt, E. E.: The results of psychotherapy with children. *Journal of Consulting Psychology, 21:*189-196, 1957.

92. Levitt, E. E.: Psychotherapy with children: A further evaluation. *Behaviour Research and Therapy, 1:*45-51, 1963.

93. Carkhuff and Berenson, p. 13.

94. Estabrooks, p. 40.

95. Marcuse, F. L.: Anti-social behavior and hypnosis. *International Journal of Clinical and Experimental Hypnosis, 1:*18, 1953.

96. Corcoran, J. F. T., Lewis, M. D., and Garver, R. B.: Biofeedback-conditioned galvanic skin response and hypnotic suppression of arousal: A pilot study of relation to deception. *Polygraph, 7(2):*113-122, 1978.

97. Germann, A. C.: Hypnosis as related to the scientific detection of deception by polygraph examination: A pilot study. *International Journal of Clinical and Experimental Hypnosis, 9:*309-311.

98. Weinstein, E., and Abrams, S., and Gibbons, D.: The validity of the polygraph with hypnotically induced repression and guilt. *American Journal of Psychiatry, 126(8):*1160, 1970.

99. Russell, Peter: *The Brain Book*. New York, Hawthorn, 1979, p. 154.

100. McConnell, J. V., Shigehisha, T., and Salive, H.: Attempts to transfer approach and avoidance responses by RNA injection in rats. *Journal of Biological Psychology, 10(2):*32-50.

101. Ungar, G.: Chemical transfer of learning; Its stimulus specificity. *Federation Proceedings, Federation of American Societies for Experimental Biology, 25:*109.

102. Ungar, G., Galvan L., and Clark, R. H.: Chemical transfer of learned fear. *Nature, 217:*1259-1261.

103. Ferguson, Marilyn: *The Brain Revolution*. New York, Bantam, 1973, p. 291.

104. Pribram, Karl H.: *Languages of the Brain: Experimental Paradoxes and Principles in Neuropsychology*. Monterey, Brooks/Cole, 1971, p. 150.

105. Leith, E. N., and Upatnicks, J.: Photography by laser. *Scientific American, 212:*31, 1965.

106. Pribram, p. 152.

107. Ibid., p. 150.

108. Russell, p. 157.

109. Barlett, M. A.: *Remembering*. London, Cambridge, 1932, p. 213.

110. Baddeley, A. D.: *The Psychology of Memory*. New York, Harper & Row, 1976, pp. 365-367.

111. Creighton, J. H.: A prodigy of memory. *Knowledge, 11:*275.

112. Bower, Gordon H.: Memory freaks I have known. *Psychology Today*, October, 1973, p. 65.

113. Nickerson, Raymond S.: Short-term memory for complex meaningful visual configurations: A demonstration of capacity. *Canadian Journal of Psychology, 19(2):*155-160, 1965.

114. Shepard, Roger N.: Recognition memory for words, sentences, and pictures. *Journal of Verbal Learning and Verbal Behavior, 6:*156-163, 1967.

115. Haber, Ralph N.: How we remember what we see. *Scientific American, 222:*104, 1970.

116. Ibid., p. 105.

117. Standing, Lionel: Learning 10,000 pictures. *Quarterly Journal of Ex-*

*perimental Psychology, 25:*207-222, 1973.

118. Landauer, T. K.: *Psychology: A Brief Review.* New York, McGraw-Hill, 1972, pp. 6-7.
119. Allport, G. W.: Eidetic imagery. *British Journal of Psychology, 15:*119, 1924.
120. Ibid., p. 109.
121. Haber, R. N. and Haber, R. B.: Eidetic imagery: I. Frequency. *Perceptual and Motor Skills, 19:*136, 1964.
122. Leask, J., Haber, R. N., and Haber, R. B.: Eidetic imagery in children: II. Longitudinal and experimental results. *Psychonomic Monograph Supplements, 3(3, Whole No. 35),* 1969.
123. Stromeyer, C. F., and Psotka, J.: The detailed texture of eidetic images. *Nature, 225:*347, 1970.
124. Ibid., p. 349.
125. *Science News, 108:*168.
126. Jaensch, E. R.: *Eidetic Imagery.* Trans. by Oscar Oeser. New York, Harcourt Brace, 1930.
127. *Glascow Journal of Psychology,* Book Review, *Eidetic Parents Test and Analysis, 12:*16, 1974.
128. Ahsen, Akhter: *Psycheye: Self-Analytic Consciousness.* New York, Brandon, 1977, p. 50.
129. Ibid., pp. 103-104.
130. Pfeiffer, John: *The Human Brain.* London, Gollanz, 1955, p. 84.
131. Kampman, Reima and Hirvenoja, Reijo: Dynamic relation of the secondary personality induced by hypnosis to the present personality. In Frankel, F. H. and Zamansky, H. S. (Eds.): *Hypnosis At Its Bicentennial,* New York, Plenum, 1978, p. 187.
132. Cobb, S.: *Foundations of Neuropsychiatry.* Baltimore, Williams & Wilkins, 1958, p. 117.
133. Gerard, R. W.: What is memory? *Scientific American, 189:*118, 1953.
134. Ibid.
135. Reiff and Scheerer, p. 233.
136. Penfield, Wilder: Studies of cerebral cortex of man — a review and interpretation. In Delafresnaye, J. F. (Ed.): *Brain Mechanisms and Consciousness.* Springfield, Thomas, 1954, p. 303.

137. Ahsen, p. 50.
138. Ebbinghaus, Hermann: *Memory.* Trans. by D. H. Ruyer and C. E. Bussenius, New York, Teachers College Press, 1913.
139. Dallenbach, K. M.: The relation of memory error to time interval. *Psychological Review, 20:*323-335, 1913.
140. Gardner, Dillard S.: The perception and memory of witnesses. *Cornell Law Quarterly, 18:*392, 1933.
141. Goodwin, D. W., Powell, B., Bremer, D., Heine, H., and Stern J.: Alcohol and recall: State-dependent effects in man. *Science, 163:*1359, 1969.
142. Ibid., pp. 1358-1360.
143. Fischer, Roland: A cartography of ecstatic and meditative states. *Science, 174:*897-904, 1971.
144. Fischer, Roland: On flashback and hypnotic recall. *International Journal of Clinical and Experimental Hypnosis, 25(4):*222-223, 1977.
145. Fischer, Roland and Landon, G. M.: On the arousal state-dependent recall of 'subconscious' experience: Stateboundness. *British Journal of Psychiatry, 120:*163, 1972.
146. Fischer, Roland: Cartography of inner space. *Altered States of Consciousness: Current Views and Research Problems,* Washington, D.C., Drug Abuse Council, 1975, p. 5.
147. Ibid.
148. Ibid., p. 3.
149. Vives, J. L.: Quoted by G. Zilboorg in *A History of Medical Psychology,* New York, Norton, 1941, p. 192.
150. Fischer and Landon, p. 163.
151. Reiff and Scheerer, pp. 230-231.
152. Köhler, W.: *Dynamics in Psychology.* New York, Liveright, 1940, p. 37.
153. Münsterberg, Hugo: *On the Witness Stand: Essays on Psychology and Crime.* New York, McClure, 1908, p. 29.
154. Ibid., p. 27.
155. Ibid., p. 20.
156. Ibid., p. 24.
157. Ibid., p. 22.
158. Marshall, J.: *Law and Psychology in Conflict.* New York, Anchor, 1969, p. 23.

159. Loftus, Elizabeth F.: Reconstructing memory: The incredible eyewitness. *Psychology Today, 8:*117, 1974.
160. *New York Times*, 11 January 1974.
161. Buckhout, R. et al.: Determinants of eyewitness performance on a lineup. *Bulletin of the Psychonomic Society, 4(3):*191-192, 1974.
162. Buckhout, R., Figueroa, D., and Huff, E.: Psychology and the eyewitness. *American Journal of Criminal Law,* May 1973.
163. Gardner, pp. 400-401.
164. Ibid., p. 406.
165. Ibid., p. 402.
166. Teitelbaum, Myron: *Hypnosis Induction Technics.* Springfield, Thomas, 1965, p. 144.
167. Cady, H. M.: On the psychology of testimony. *American Journal of Psychology, 35:*110, 1924.
168. Gardner, p. 404.
169. Whipple, G. M.: The observer as reporter: A survey of the 'psychology of testimony.' *Psychological Bulletin, 6(5):*153-169, 1909.
170. Marston, W. M.: Studies in testimony. *Journal of Criminal Law and Criminology, 15:*1-31, 1924.
171. Whipple, p. 162.
172. Ibid., p. 165.
173. Buckhout et. al., p. 192.
174. Whipple, pp. 166-167.
175. Loftus, Elizabeth F. and Zanni, Guido: Eyewitness testimony: The influence of the wording of a question. *Bulletin of the Psychonomic Society, 5(1):*86-88, 1975.
176. Harris, Richard J.: Answering questions containing marked and unmarked adjectives and adverbs. *Journal of Experimental Psychology, 97(3):*399-401, 1973.
177. Barber, T. X., Dalal, A. S., and Calverley, D. S.: The subjective reports of hypnotic subjects. *American Journal of Clinical Hynosis, 11:*74-88. 1968.
178. Barber, T. X. and Calverley, D. S.: Multi-dimensional analysis of "hypnotic" behavior. *Journal of Abnormal Psychology, 74:*209-220, 1969.
179. Loftus, Elizabeth F.: Leading questions and the eyewitness report. *Cognitive Psychology, 7:*564, 1975.
180. Ibid., pp. 565-569.
181. Loftus, Elizabeth F., and Palmer, John C.: Reconstruction of automobile destruction: An example of the interaction between language and memory. *Journal of Verbal Learning and Verbal Behavior, 13:*585, 1974.
182. Loftus, "Reconstructing memory," p. 118.
183. Monrose, Renee: Justice with glazed eyes: The growing use of hypnotism in law enforcement. *Juris Doctor, 8(8):*56, 1978.
184. Von Schrenck: The medico-forensic aspects of suggestion. *Archiv für Criminal-Anthropologie und Criminalistik,* August 1900.
185. Bird, Charles: The influence of the press upon the accuracy of report. *Journal of Abnormal and Social Psychology, 22:*129, 1927.
186. Oppenheim, A. M.: *Questionnaire Design and Attitude Measurement.* New York, Basic, 1966.
187. Arons, pp. 149-151.
188. Ibid., pp. xvi-xvii.
189. Germann, p. 310.
190. Field and Dworkin, p. 53.
191. Dorcus, R. M.: *Hypnosis and Its Therapeutic Applications.* New York, McGraw-Hill, 1956.
192. Hendry, Allan: UFO update. *Omni,* July 1979, p. 32.
193. Orne, "The nature of hypnosis," p. 296.
194. Weitzenhoffer, André M.: *General Techniques of Hypnotism.* New York, Grune & Stratton, 1957, p. 319.

APPENDICES

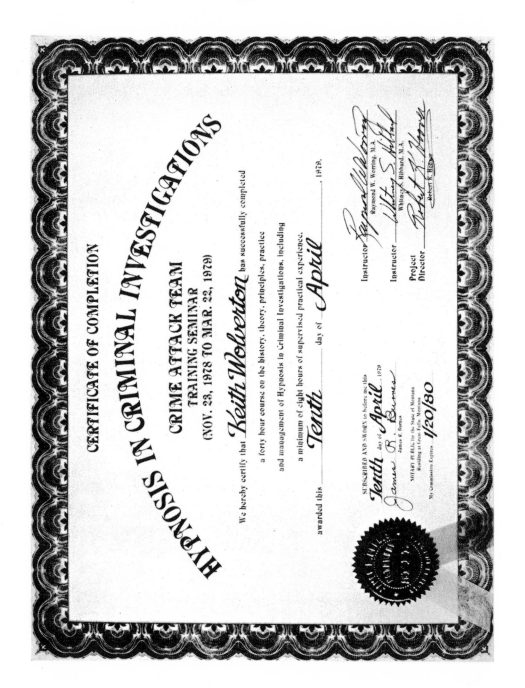

SCOPE OF CERTIFICATION

THE PURPOSE of this certificate is to document the fact that the designee on said certificate satisfactorily completed the described course, which was taught at the request of the participating departments for their professional utilization.

The designee received instruction and training in the following hypnotic techniques:

Inductions	Deepenings	Elicited Hypnotic Phenomena
Eye Fixation	Counting	Eye Catalepsy
Eye Blink	Breathing	Arm Catalepsy
Arm Drop	Rapid Arm Drop	Suggested Amnesia
Hand Levitation	Silent Periods	Time Regression:
Postural Sway	Descending Stairs	Hypermnesia
Dynamic Method	Closed Door	Revivification
Confusion Technic	Talking	
	Progressive Anesthesia	
	Visualization	
	Self-Reporting Scale	
	Fractionation	

This document is not a certificate to authorize the practice of hypnosis, but merely a record of course completion. The designee's utilization of hypnosis within his/her respective department is contingent upon authorization by the department head.

The instructors and project director take no responsibility for the performance of the practitioner designated on this certificate.

DEFINITIONS OF HYPNOSIS

THERE ARE PROBABLY as many definitions of hypnosis as there are hypnotists. What follows are some of the better known definitions of some of the better known hypnotists.

- Hypnosis is "a state of intensified attention and receptiveness and an increased responsiveness to an idea or to a set of ideas." (Erickson, Milton H.: Hypnosis in painful terminal illness. *American Journal of Clinical Hypnosis, 1:*117, 1958.)
- Hypnosis is basically a "regression to the primitive mode of mental functioning in which ideas are accepted uncritically by the primitive process of suggestion." (Meares, Ainslie: The atavistic theory of hypnosis in relation to yoga and pseudo trance states. *Proceedings of the Third World Congress of Psychiatry,* Montreal, *1:*712-714, 1961.)
- "Psychophysiologically, the hypnotic trance may be defined as a controlled dissociated state." (West, L. J.: Psychophysiology of hypnosis. *Journal of the American Medical Association, 172:*672-675, 1960.)
- "Hypnosis is a condition or state of selective hypersuggestibility. . . . " (Weitzenhoffer, André M.: *General Techniques of Hypnotism.* New York, Grune & Stratton, 1957, p. 32.)
- Hypnosis is "the control of thought and action through suggestion." (LeCron, Leslie M. and Bordeaux, Jean: *Hypnotism Today,* 1978 ed. No. Hollywood, Wilshire, 1978, p. 139.)
- "Hypnosis is a subtle perceptual alteration involving a capacity for attentive, responsive concentration which is inherent in the person and which can be *tapped* by the examiner." (Spiegel, Herbert and Spiegel, David: *Trance and Treatment: Clinical Uses of Hypnosis.* New York, Basic, 1978, p. 39.)
- "Hypnosis is a state of mind in which the critical faculty of the human is bypassed, and selective thinking established." (Elman, Dave: *Hypnotherapy.* Los Angeles, Westwood, 1964, p. 26.)

MAJOR THEORIES AND THEIR WEAKNESSES

PHYSIOLOGICAL THEORIES

THIS GROUP OF THEORIES maintains that hypnosis is the result of a physiological change within the cerebral cortex, most predominantly a selective inhibition of certain brain centers. Emphasis and responsibility is upon the hypnotist for inducing the state of hypnosis, i.e., his person, will, mind and special ability to affect the behavior and experiences of his subject.

1. *Type of Theory.* Somnambulism and Sleep.
   Proponent. Marquis de Puységur.
   Basic Elements. Hypnosis is maintained to be a form of sleep.
   Weaknesses. Physiological tests prove that hypnosis is not a state of sleep. (For specifics, see misconception #1 in "Misconceptions: What Hypnosis Is Not" in Chapter 2.)
   Present Status. Obsolete.

2. *Type of Theory.* Conditioned Reflex.
   Proponents. Pavlov, Eysenck.
   Basic Elements. Hypnosis is a conditioned response due to monotonous stimuli partially inhibiting the cerebral hemispheres.
   Weaknesses. This theory does not explain rapid inductions of naive subjects resulting in deep trance, nor does it account for certain hypnotic phenomena such as hypermnesia, revivification, or posthypnotic hallucinations.
   Present Status. Widely accepted in Russia, but has few serious supporters in the United States. It may be of future interest, however, when technological advances make more accurate and discrete measurements of cerebral functioning.

3. *Type of Theory.* A Form of Hysteria.
   Proponent. Charcot.
   Basic Elements. Hypnosis, like hysteria, is the result of a disease process in the central nervous system. Hypnosis, therefore, is basically a pathological state and certain individuals are constitutionally predisposed.
   Weaknesses. Almost any normal person can be hypnotized if sufficiently motivated. No organic substrate for either hypnosis or hysteria has been discovered.
   Present Status. Obsolete.

PSYCHOLOGICAL THEORIES

This group of theories tend to emphasize psychological processes and mechanisms, both intrapersonal and interpersonal, while they de-emphasize physiological factors and changes. These theories largely sprang from the observation and realization of the importance of the subject's responsivity and inner processes.

1. *Type of Theory.* A State of Hypersuggestibility.
Proponents. Hull, Braid, Liebeault, Bernheim.
Basic Elements. Hypnosis is induced by the incremental response to ever increasingly difficult suggestions. Once induced, hypersuggestibility is the single most marked characteristic of hypnosis.
Weaknesses. This theory is descriptive, not explanatory, i.e., it gives no explanation as to what causes the increased suggestibility. Furthermore, it is inherently only partially true because some deeply hypnotized subjects will respond poorly or not at all to suggestion.
Present Status. Commonly accepted and believed to be true.

2. *Type of Theory.* Psychoanalytic.
Proponents. Ferenczi.
Basic Elements. Hypnosis is believed to be a state of regression to a childlike state that is caused by the subject entering into an intense trans-ference relationship in which he transposes and behaves toward the hyp-notist as a domineering parental figure.
Weaknesses. This theory does not explain hypnosis by mechanical aids such as the hypnodisc or metronome, nor does it explain self-hypnosis.
Present Status. Popular among psyhoanalytically-oriented hypnotists

3. *Type of Theory.* Goal-Directed Striving.
Proponent. White.
Elements. Hypnosis is a meaningful goal-directed striving in which the goal is to behave like a hypnotized person as this is continually defined by the operator and understood by the subject.
Weaknesses. This theory, as the psychoanalytic theory, does not explain mechanical inductions. Furthermore, it does not explain the occurrence of spontaneous regressions, anesthesia, amnesia, hallucinations, or involun-tary contraction of pupils to a hallucinated light.
Present Status. Widely accepted as partially true.

4. *Type of Theory.* Role-Playing.
Proponent. Sarbin.
Basic Elements. The subject acts the role of what he believes a hypno-tized person to be.
Weaknesses. This theory does not explain some physiological responses such as the control of pain, or long-term carrying out of posthypnotic suggestions.
Present Status. Of current research interest.

5. *Type of Theory.* Dissociation.
Proponents. Janet, Prince.
Basic Elements. Hypnosis is a state in which the subconscious is func-tionally independent from the conscious mind. Under hypnosis, the sub-

conscious is dissociated or split off from the dominant personality and can act independently upon the direction of the hypnotist's suggestions.

Weaknesses. A complete dissociation would necessarily result in a posthypnotic amnesia, a loss of ability to think during trance, and the blocking of conscious awareness during trance. Research and clinical experience, however, have shown that very few subjects are amnesic posthypnotically, that they can actively think during trance, and are generally very aware during hypnosis. Furthermore, the dissociation theory does not account for how a subject in self-hypnosis can direct his own activities and experience.

Present Status. Of interest, but has few serious adherents.

6. *Type of Theory.* Interpersonal Relationship.
Proponent. Barber.
Basic Elements. Hypnosis is primarily and essentially an interpersonal relationship between the subject and operator in which the subject (a) is selectively attuned to the words of the operator, (b) accepts the words of the operator as literally true, and (c) is cognitively prepared and motivated to carry out the operator's suggestions. Hypnosis is not discontinuously different from ordinary waking consciousness.

Weaknesses. Fails to explain self-hypnosis and hypnosis by mechanical aids as well as some deep trance phenomena such as control of pain.

Present Status. Widely accepted as partially true.

7. *Type of Theory.* Atavistic.
Proponent. Meares.
Basic Elements. Hypnosis is a regression to an archaic or primitive mode of mental functioning in which behavior is motivated and ideas accepted by the process of suggestion.

Weaknesses. This theory cannot explain commonly reported hypnotic experiences of a transpersonal, mystical, or states of heightened and expanded awareness and consciousness.

Present Status. Popular and widely accepted.

8. *Type of Theory.* Altered State of Consciousness.
Proponents. Hilgard, Tart.
Basic Elements. Hypnosis is a sufficiently recognizable deviation from the normal waking consciousness. As such, it is an altered state of consciousness characterized by certain primary features.

Weaknesses. This theory is not scientifically verifiable, but is largely based on the subjective experiences and reports of subjects.

Present Status. Most popular.

9. *Type of Theory.* Manipulation of Ego Cathexis.
Proponents. Watkins.
Basic Elements. Hypnosis is the process of withdrawing ego cathexis ("self" energy) from mental contents until they become un-egotized (de-energized) and subject to more basic mental processes, such as is found in the child.

Weaknesses. This theory rests on the hypothetical existence of an ego energy that may or may not exist, but which cannot be proven either way.

Present Status. Not widely known or subscribed to, but of growing interest.

10. *Type of Theory.* Ideomotor Action/Heteroaction/Dissociation of Awareness.

Proponent. Weitzenhoffer.

Basic Elements. The induction of hypnosis consists in the activation and enhancement of the above three processes. Weitzenhoffer defines these processes in the following manner:

Ideomotor Action — "the tendency of thoughts or ideas to be automatically translated, reflex-like, into specific patterns of muscular activity."

Heteroaction — "when an individual is made to respond to a number of suggestions, a progressively increasing tendency for him to respond to other suggestions arises." Hence, there is "generalization of suggestibility."

Dissociation of Awareness — "a selective constriction of awareness which excludes all but the hypnotist as a source of stimulation."

(Weitzenhoffer, André M.: *General Techniques of Hypnotism.* New York, Grune & Stratton, 1957, pp. 35-38.)

Weaknesses. Does not seem to adequately explain very rapid or instantaneous inductions. It also does not adequately account for age regression and the lifting of repressions.

Present Status. Fairly well-known and accepted.

In conclusion, there are several important historical lessons to be learned from this survey. First, it becomes apparent that the various theories of hypnosis are largely the product of the state of the art of science, religion, and philosophy at any particular time. Secondly, as in the case of Charcot, it reveals "that a scientist of the most impeccable credentials, using tightly controlled methods of observation, can commit the grossest errors of observation." (Sheehan, W., and Perry, C. W.: *Methodologies of Hypnosis: A Critical Appraisal of Contemporary Paradigms of Hypnosis.* Hillsdale, Erlbaum, 1976, p. 39.) Just as the science of present day has uncovered many errors in the theories of the past, so the science of the future will uncover the errors of the present day theories. Current knowledge of the human mind and body is insufficient to provide a comprehensive scientific psychophysiological explanation of hypnosis.

Appendix 4

SUGGESTIBILITY TESTS

Imagined Weight

THE SUBJECT is asked to stand with his arms outstretched in front of him at shoulder level as you demonstrate. Instruct the subject to close his eyes and visualize to the best of his ability that he is holding a bucket by the handle in his left hand. Tell your subject to visualize this bucket to the best of his ability as you now suggest that you are slowly pouring sand into it. The operator keeps describing this as the bucket becomes heavier and heavier. Keep this description up and even elaborate on the general theme (the more descriptive and convincing and emphatic the better) for a few minutes until the subject's arm has lowered considerably, at which time you ask him to open his eyes.

If the subject is suggestible, his arm will have lowered considerably and he will generally be surprised when he opens his eyes, hence building belief in you and hypnosis. With a very suggestible subject, his right arm may go up into the air to counterbalance the imagined weight. With some subjects, their left hand will rise instead of lower. This is either a sign of resistance (doing the opposite of what is suggested) or of suggestibility (the subject's hand rises in an attempt to hold up the imagined weight). By quizzing the subject afterwards, the operator can generally determine which is the case.

An important consideration is handling failure. If you are working with a group of more than three or four people, some will almost always respond favorably. If you are working with an individual, however, what do you do if the subject does not respond or responds negatively? One recovery technique is to not ask your subject to open his eyes, but, instead, to relax and lower his arms first. The operator then asks him to open his eyes and quizzes him as to how he felt, i.e. did he feel his arm get heavier and could he visualize the bucket? If not, you know you had better not use induction or deepening techniques that call for visual imagery. This recovery technique prevents the sense of total failure on the part of the subject because without opening his eyes he is not sure where his arms really were. He becomes doubly unsure when you praise him by saying he did well.

A modification of this technique is to have the subject sitting and use just his left arm. If he responds well you may at that time, if the circumstances warrant it, continue with the arm drop induction.

Hand Levitation

Seat the subject(s) with both hands resting flat on a table, desk, arms of the chair, or his legs as you demonstrate. Instruct the subject that he can do this with eyes open or closed, or if he begins with eyes open he may close them at any time. The operator then continues with the hand levitation protocol in Chapter 4 until the subject's hand, if suggestible, floats off of the table. At this point the operator can either discontinue the test and praise the subject or, if appropriate, continue with the hand levitation induction.

If the subject fails to respond, discontinue the levitation suggestions and ask him how his hand felt, i.e. "Did it feel different? Did it get lighter? Could you visualize the balloon?" Any different feelings are a positive indication, whereas no difference will indicate low suggestibility or resistance.

Postural Sway

The authorities in hypnosis generally agree that this is the best of all suggestibility tests. The subject(s) is asked to stand with his feet together, arms at his side, and eyes closed. If in a group, have the people work in pairs so that each person has someone who can catch or steady them if they sway too far. If working with one subject, the hypno-investigator stands to the side of the subject so that he can provide support both in front and back if necessary. The operator continues with the postural sway protocol in Chapter 4 until the subject, if suggestible, is swaying substantially. Suggestible people will begin to sway rather quickly.

If you intend to continue with the postural sway induction if working with a single subject and you obtain an adequate response, be sure to have him standing in front of a large easy chair or recliner so that it will support him comfortably when he falls.

If the subject responds poorly by swaying very little or even standing rigidly upright, he is either relatively unsuggestible or actively resisting.

Miscellaneous Tests

1. Sleeptalkers and especially sleepwalkers are generally natural somnambules. Therefore, ask each audience of potential subjects if any of them fall into either of these categories.

2. A variation of the postural sway test is to stand behind a prospective subject and ask him to let himself fall backwards against your waiting hands. If he lets go enough and has sufficient trust in the operator he will most likely prove to be a good subject. On the other hand, the subject who lacks confidence in the operator and who steps back to break his fall will usually prove to be unsuggestible.

3. An excellent test of suggestibility is the olfactory ammonia test. When testing a group of people, the operator comes prepared with an ammonia bottle filled with water. When ready for the test, he explains that peoples' sensitivity varies a great deal and to demonstrate this fact, he will open this bottle of ammonia and see who smells it first. He continues to suggest that it will rather quickly pervade the room and those with a keen sense of smell will detect it soon. He asks those who smell it to raise their hands immediately. To add realism, the operator may "wince" at the aroma as he

uncaps the bottle and steadily back away as it gets "stronger." This continues for approximately one minute at which point several hands should be up. The operator then recaps the bottle and makes a mental note of those with raised hands.

4. A positive correlation has been established between hypnotic susceptibility and the amount of sclera or white of the eye visible as a person simultaneously gazes upward as high as possible and slowly closes his eyelids. In an individual test, the operator sits or stands at eye level with the subject and asks him to roll his eyes up as high as possible with lids open, and then to slowly close his lids as he continues to look upward. The greater amount of white of the eye showing between the lower border of the iris and the lower eyelid, the greater the person's susceptibility.

5. The operator asks the seated members of a group to pick a spot on the ceiling and to stare and concentrate on it. He then continues with suggestions of heaviness and tiredness of the eyes for several minutes until some peoples' eyes are closed (see "Eye Fixation" in Chapter 4 for appropriate suggestions). As all people will not be influenced by the suggestions and close their eyes, the operator tells the others to close them. He continues by saying, "Now for those of you who could no longer hold your eyes open and had to close them, I want you to now notice that your eyes are becoming even heavier and tireder and they are stuck tightly shut." The operator continues with eye catalepsy suggestions and then challenges the subjects to open them (see "Eye Catalepsy" in Chapter 4 for appropriate suggestions). Those who cannot open their eyes will be good subjects.

Appendix 5

NAME _____DATE OF BIRTH _____
        Last   Middle   First

ADDRESS _____PHONE Home _____
                                                  Work _____

R E L E A S E

I, _____, hereby
                               (Print Full Name)

forever release and save harmless the City of Great Falls, any member of the Great Falls Police Department, and the Chief of Police of all causes of action, charges, or liability by reason of my volunteer participation as a hypnotic subject. I hereby voluntarily consent to undergo a hypnosis interview.

      Dated this ____ day of _____, 198__.

                                                 _____

Witness: (Signature)

_____

_____

PREINDUCTION QUESTIONNAIRE:

1. a. Are you now seeing or have you seen a medical doctor or psychologist within the past five years?
   b. Have you ever had any form of seizure in your lifetime?
2. Have you had any emotional or stress problems in your past medical history, more especially, the past six months?
3. Do you now or have you had heart problems?
4. Do you now or have you had problems with your breathing?
5. Have you used any form of medication during the past six months?
6. Do you have any problems sleeping at nights?
   (i.e. heavy dreaming, nightmares, etc.)
7. Can you visualize readily with your eyes closed?
8. Do you have a fear of high or low places or of a possible floating feeling?
9. Have you ever been hypnotized?
10. What is your favorite color?   Fragrance?
11. What is your favorite place to get away from stress?
    (i.e. the mountains, a place to escape to in your mind, etc.)
12. Do you have any visual problems?

The above questions are answered true and correct to the best of my knowledge.

                                               _____
                                                Signature

A COMPLETE HYPNO-INVESTIGATION TRANSCRIPT: THE CASE OF DEBBIE

THE FOLLOWING is a verbatim transcript of a live demonstration given before a class of law enforcement officers being instructed in forensic hypnosis. The subject is a twenty-one-year-old female who has volunteered to undergo a time regression to an automobile accident five years prior in which she sustained severe lacerations on her face. The actual cause of the accident was never determined and this fact was a continual annoyance to the subject. Her desire to undergo hypnosis was to relive the incident so that she might be able to determine what happened.

This transcript is offered as an illustration of how a hypno-investigation is conducted from the preinduction through the postinduction. Its purpose is to give the reader a specific example of a preinduction talk and to illustrate how the induction, deepenings, tests and challenges, and time regression all blend together in seeking maximum depth and information obtained.

Although this is not a criminal case-related session, the techniques are the same and it will prove equally informative and illustrative had the subject been a crime victim or witness. The reader is encouraged to pay particular attention to the preinduction talk, the sequence of testing, challenging, and deepening, as well as the revivification and hypermnesia techniques. It may be helpful to refer to Table II in Chapter 4 to understand the sequence of techniques used.

The transcript begins immediately after the operator is introduced to the subject by a mutual acquaintance.

TRANSCRIPT

Operator. Hello Debbie. It's nice meeting you. My name is Whitney Hibbard, and I am one of the hypnosis instructors teaching this class of law enforcement officers techniques of hypno-investigation so that they can use it on volunteer victims and witnesses to refresh their memories. Please be seated, Debbie, and make yourself comfortable. You know, we certainly appreciate your volunteering for this as it will be very beneficial for the class and also for you. Before we begin, I'd like to explain something about myself and about hypnosis so that you have a clear understanding of what you are about to undergo. I was trained in clinical hypnosis approximately five years ago in the clinical psychology graduate department of the University of Montana. Since that time, however, I have specialized in the use of hypnosis in criminal and civil investigations, such as this case with you. Now, before I explain to you something about hypnosis I'd like you to read this release form and sign it if you understand it and are in agreement. The release is really a formality, and the city requires that it be done, even though hypnosis is completely safe. *(She reads and signs it.)* Now, on the reverse I'd like you to read and answer these questions *(see "Release and Preinduction Questionnaire" in Appendix 5.)* These questions just let me know a little more about you, what is the best technique for me to use, and if there is anything important that I should be aware of, such as if you are under the care of a doctor of any kind. *(Debbie reads and answers the questions and there are no contraindications.)* Okay, I see that you say you have no known health problems or psychological problems for which you are being treated and nothing as a result of the accident, right?

Debbie: Well, at the time I had eighty stitches in my face, but I had no long-term problems.

Operator: Okay, that's good. You're lucky that whoever worked on your face did an excellent job because I couldn't even tell until you mentioned it, and still I can hardly see it. How did you feel at the time? *(The operator wants to get an indication of the degree of trauma experienced at the time of the accident so he'll know how much to dissociate her during the regression.)*

Debbie: Well, I didn't feel too much as it all happened so fast. I was pretty scared, though, because blood was pouring all over my face and I didn't know how my friends were.

Operator: Let me assure you right now, Debbie, that you won't have to relive any of that trauma. Okay?

Debbie: Okay, that's good. *(She sighs with relief.)*

Operator: Have you ever been hypnotized, Debbie?

Debbie: No.

Operator: Have you ever seen anyone hypnotized, such as at a stage show or on TV or a movie?

Debbie: No I don't think so, except maybe on TV once.

Operator: Okay. I'd like to take just a few minutes to tell you about hypnosis, because there are so many misconceptions and outright misinformation about it, largely engendered by Hollywood and stage hypnotists. You know how, even if you haven't actually seen it, hypnotized people are depicted as or believed to be in a state of unconsciousness or sleep and can be made to do things against their will because they are under the control of the all-powerful hypnotist. Well, all this is simply untrue. You will find that you will be very much aware of everything as you will not be asleep or unconscious, and as such, you will know everything that's going on and therefore are actually in full control. I cannot, even if I wanted to, make you do something against your will, so you won't do or say anything that you don't want to, and you can come out at any time by yourself, if for any reason you should want to or get concerned. Hypnosis is really a cooperative process, and I just serve as the guide. All you have to do is just let yourself go and listen to my voice. Hypnosis is really a letting go process where you become completely relaxed both physically and mentally. So I don't want you to do anything or not do anything, but just let it happen. You might find that your body will tend to work automatically or without effort, and that's a good sign, so let it happen and don't fight it. Also, your body may feel a little differently, such as heavy and numb, or it might buzz a little or tingle. It might even feel light and floaty, or maybe like it's not even there. Whatever feelings you have, just let them develop and magnify as they are good signs. Also, you might find that you'll feel a little different psychologically. Some people experience a spinning sensation, or a float- ing feeling, and others a spiralling down sensation, and others just get kind of drowsy and relaxed. So, if you feel any of these or any other way just let it happen. Don't let it concern you because it's completely natural and a sign that it's working. On the other hand, you may not feel any different, so don't be disappointed if you don't. Some people go into very deep levels of hypnosis but don't feel any differently. Hypnosis is experienced different- ly by everyone so just let happen what may. I'll also ask you to try not to analyze or figure out what I'm doing. Okay?

Debbie: Okay, but I really thought people were kind of out of it under hypnosis.

Operator: No, they aren't at all. In fact, a lot of people, even though they were deeply hypnotized will say immediately upon coming out that they don't think they were hypnotized because they didn't feel any different. Even such physiological measures as the EEG, base metabolism rates, and the patellar reflex which is the knee jerk reflex test, among other mea- sures, all show that hypnosis is more similar to the waking state than to sleep. Hypnosis is a normal and natural experience that every normal person can experience at least to some degree. In fact, people are hypno- tized at least twice per day, right before waking and immediately before going to sleep. That twilight zone between waking and sleep is very similar to some people's experience of hypnosis. You know those times when you've been mesmerized by the white lines running down the highway when driving for long stretches, or being totally absorbed in a good book or movie. Well, those experiences are similar to hypnosis. Also, I'd like to stress that in no way is hypnosis dangerous. It is actually completely safe and there is no record of anyone being hurt in anyway by competent professionals. I might also add that hypnosis is a very creative and benefi- cial tool that can be used to help people for such things as curing bad habits, such as smoking, nail-biting, drinking, or overeating. It is also often used by obstetricians for painless childbirth, and by dentists and doctors for drugless dental work and surgery. Its uses are almost limitless, and, if you're interested, I can teach you self-hypnosis afterwards. Any questions?

Debbie: What if I can't come out, or if you have to leave?

Operator: That's another fear that a lot of people have, but the fact is that you can easily come out even on your own, and you can stop at any time. There is not one single case on record where a subject has not come out of hypnosis. The worst that can happen is that you will enjoy it so much that you won't want to come out when I tell you to, so, in that event, I'll just let you stay there until you're ready to come out yourself. Okay? Any other questions or concerns?

Debbie: Well, what will I say under hypnosis?

Operator: Ah, yes. That's another big fear that most people have. People associate hypnosis with uncontrollably telling all their deepest darkest secrets, but let me assure you that that is not the case. Remember now that you are actually in control and are aware of everything so you won't say anything that you don't want to. Furthermore, the whole purpose of this session is just to go back to that agreed upon incident of the car wreck, so that's all I'll ask you about. Agreed? *(She nods.)* Another common associated fear that people have is that they will act or look funny under hypnosis, but you won't at all. In fact you will look just like you have your eyes closed and are resting, and that is all.

Debbie: Will I remember everything?

Operator: Oh yes! Most certainly. In fact, I make sure that you will by giving you a suggestion to that effect before bringing you out. If you want to forget the accident, though, I can leave that decision up to you before bringing you out. Do you want to remember it or forget it? *(In a case facing litigation or prosecution, this alternative should not be given the victim or witness. This particular case was not being litigated so the choice was offered to the subject.)*

Debbie: I want to remember it.

Operator: Okay, that's the way you'll have it then. Let me ask you something. Can you concentrate and visualize well? I mean, if I ask you to concentrate on something specific or ask you to visualize something in your mind's eye that I describe to you, could you picture it clearly?

Debbie: Yes, I think so. I have a good imagination.

Operator: That's good. You see, intelligent, mature people who can concentrate and visualize well and who are motivated make the best hypnotic subjects. You are obviously all of these so I'm certain we'll be successful. Actually, hypnosis always works, but the degree to which it works depends largely on you, so just let yourself go and follow what I say as best you can, but without trying too hard. We'll also take as much time as we need, okay?

Debbie: Good.

Operator: Okay, Debbie, would you tell me the events leading up to the accident, the specific date, time, and your age, as well as exactly what you want to remember?

Debbie: Well, it happened on the night of April 19, 1974, which was a Friday night. At that time I was sixteen-years-old; I'm now twenty-one. On that night we stopped at the Wrangler Bar on Tenth Avenue South to pick up a bottle of wine or something, and headed from there to a party at George's house. I think we headed east on Tenth to probably Nineteenth Street where we would have turned left to head up to 1st Avenue South, but at about the intersection of Nineteenth Street and Sixth Avenue South we jumped the curb and hit a tree.

Operator: Who's "we?"

Debbie: Oh. I was sitting in the passenger's seat and my friend Bobbie, who introduced us, was in the middle, and Janet was driving. What I want to try to figure out is exactly why it happened. I can't remember much just before or at the time of the accident, but I thought if I could go through it again I'll know why.

Operator: I'm sure you'll make a very good subject, and we shouldn't have any trouble taking you to the exact event so you can really examine exactly what happened. You see, everything that is taken in through the senses is permanently stored in the brain, but that the vast majority of that information is stored at a subconscious level, either because it's not important enough, we didn't consciously attend to it at the time it was experienced and taken in, or in some instances due to the traumatic nature of the incident, the material may actively be repressed by the person. So, in effect, the mind serves or functions as something like a giant computerized videotaped recorder, taking in and storing everything. Through hypnosis we can turn our attention and consciousness inward to the point where we can reactivate those memories and bring them to awareness. *(If the case were being litigated and therefore audio and videotaped, the operator at approximately this time would explain the reason and necessity for recording. In this instance, however, the operator explained the videotaping in the following manner.)* The reason we're taping this, Debbie, is because we'd like to save the tape as a training film so that the class can review and critique it later. Do you mind?

Debbie: No, that's fine.

Operator: Now the technique that I'm going to use is an actual regression to the time of the accident, but we'll dissociate it somewhat so that you will not actually have to relive it. Instead, you will view it as it actually happened, but you will not get personally or emotionally involved in it. In other words, it will be like you're standing apart from it and just watching it, very objectively and in a detached and unemotional manner. And in the technique I'll use, you will also find that we can slow down the action, stop it if we want to in order to look more closely, or even back it up. I'll also have you stop the action before you hit the tree because there's no need reviewing that part. Alright?

Debbie: That's good.

Operator: Ready to begin?

Debbie: Sure.

Operator: Before we do, can you tell me what kind of wine or whatever it was you bought, and what you and your friends were wearing? *(The operator is looking for some specific information that cannot be recalled in the awake state so he can verify the regression.)*

Debbie: No I can't.

Operator: Before we begin, do you need to use the lavatory or do you want a drink of water or something?

Debbie: A drink of water would be nice. *(She goes to the fountain. Ideally, glasses and a pitcher of water should be at arms length for both subject and operator.)*

Operator: Okay, Debbie, if you'd be seated again we'll begin. Are you ready?

Debbie: Yes.

Operator: Oh, I may also touch you occasionally, such as placing my hand on your shoulder *(the operator reaches out and places his hand on her nearest shoulder as he watches her nonverbal reaction.)* Do you mind?

Debbie: No, that's fine.

Operator: Any other questions?

Debbie: No, I don't think so, but I have a difficult time relaxing so I'm not sure I can be hypnotized.

Operator: That's fine. You don't have to be able to relax in order to be hypnotized. In fact, there's an excellent technique that works well for tense people, so I'll use that. Now before you go into hypnosis you ought to be as comfortable as possible, because you'll be sitting there for approximately forty-five or fifty minutes, so I don't want you to be uncomfortable in any way, as that will tend to distract you. I would prefer if you would uncross your ankles and put both feet flat on the floor for the reason that sometimes when they're crossed, the circulation is reduced and they might go to sleep or cramp. I want you to realize, however, that if you need to get more comfortable and move during the session you may do so and it won't affect your depth. Now, I'd also prefer that you put your hands flat on your legs. Now, to see how relaxed you are, I'm going to pick up your left arm by the wrist so just let me have it. Let the arm be totally relaxed. *(The operator has picked up the arm and it is fairly tense as gauged by the degree of muscle control. The operator then lowers the arm to her leg. Due to the muscle tension and the subject's admission that she's a tense person, the hand levitation induction is indicated.)* Okay, that's fine Debbie. Now, as you sit there comfortably with your hands resting lightly in your lap, what I'd like you to do is to fix your gaze on your left hand. As you fix your gaze on that hand, also fix your concentration and attention on it. In doing so, you can become very aware of all the feelings and sensations in that hand. While you're doing this, just continue to breathe easily, naturally, and deeply, and listen to the sound of my voice. You're probably aware of the hand resting lightly on your leg. You can feel its weight there. I'm sure you can feel the texture of your pants and probably the temperature of your leg, and I'm sure you can feel the temperature of the hand, and possibly the temperature of the air in the room. Occasionally, you may even feel a slight puff or breeze of air across the hand. You are also keenly aware of the position of each finger in relation to the other fingers, and the color and shape of the hand. Whatever those feelings and sensations are, you can become very aware of them by gazing and concentrating on that hand. We know that there's a great deal of muscular movement throughout our bodies and particularly in the minute muscles of our hands. By gazing and concentrating on that hand and that feeling, that movement tends to manifest itself. Now we know from experience that sooner or later that movement will manifest itself, and it could be in any one of those fingers. It could be in the little finger. There, it *is* the little finger! The little finger moved a little bit. Now, you'll notice an interesting thing as you concentrate on that feeling, because it will tend to magnify, and it will also tend to spread. It's almost as if that feeling, that feeling of lightness magnifies to the point that that finger wants to straighten up and lift upwards, as if it wants to float upwards. That's it, you just let yourself go, your body has a tendency to work automatically, and that's a good sign. That's what we both want. Continue now to gaze and concentrate on that hand and all those feelings and sensations, but particularly that movement in the little finger. That's it, it moved a little while ago, tended to twitch a little, felt a little differently. That feeling, as you continue to gaze and concentrate on it, will tend to magnify, will tend to spread. That's it, you're doing fine, Debbie, just let yourself go; just let it happen. You're becoming more and more relaxed. That finger, now, that feeling, spreading. There, the ring finger moved a little bit. You'll notice another interesting thing, that that movement, that feeling, will tend to spread even more. It's already spread over into the ring finger which just moved a little bit, and now it will tend to spread back into the hand and over into the middle finger, and spread over into the index finger, and over into the thumb and back into the whole hand. The whole hand is getting lighter and lighter, as if it wanted to float upwards. The whole hand, getting lighter and lighter. I can see it lifting from your leg, as it gets lighter and lighter and floats upward, and that's what we both want. Your body has a tendency to work automatically, and the longer you gaze and concentrate on that hand, the lighter it gets. Getting lighter and lighter, as if it wanted to float upwards. Floating upwards now, getting lighter and lighter, and that feeling and that lightness are spreading back, spreading back more and more into the whole forearm. Spreading back now and floating up. The whole hand, the whole forearm getting lighter and lighter and floating upwards, as if a force were pulling it up. Floating up now as it gets lighter and lighter. Your body working automatically as the hand floats up, getting so light, getting so light, that it moves up by itself, without effort. Now, as you continue to gaze at that hand, I want you to imagine something, as best you can, in your mind's eye. I want you to imagine that somewhere near the ceiling of the room there's a large balloon of your favorite color. Attached to that balloon is a string, and that string descends down and is tied around your wrist, right here. *(The operator pulls up slightly on her wrist.)* I'm going to start filling that balloon with helium, and as I do, it gets larger and larger. And the larger it gets, the lighter it gets and it starts floating upward, and as it does, it starts pulling on that string, it starts pulling on that string around the wrist, p–u–l–l––i–n–g up, getting bigger and bigger, and the bigger it gets, the lighter it gets and it starts pulling up, p–u–l–l–i–n–g that hand up, higher and higher, p–u–l–l–i–n–g harder and harder and floating up. *(Her hand is approximately at shoulder level.)* That's good, and now I want you to imagine something else, Debbie. I want you to imagine that your head and the hand are like two magnets, and your head being the larger magnet attracts the hand towards it. It's almost as if you can see and feel the lines of force between your head and the hand, and the elbow is flexible and bends and the hand starts pulling towards your face, starting to pull towards your face, and when the hand finally touches, you'll close your eyes and go into a very deep state. You might have noticed that your eyes are having a tendency to get kind of heavy and tired and drowsy, almost as if they wanted to blink. *(Her eyes blink for the first time.)* That's it. Blink occasionally, and the longer you gaze at that hand, the more it pulls towards your face, and the harder it pulls towards your face, the heavier and tireder the eyes become. You know that when it touches, but not before, the eyes will close and you'll go way down. About 3 inches away and moving closer. The eyes getting s–o h–e–a–v–y and t–i–r–e–d as the hand pulls closer. And the head moves ever so slightly down to meet the hand. Almost touching and getting ready to go way down! Almost touching, ALMOST TOUCHING, TOUCHING, going **D–E–E–P, D–E–E–P, D–E–E–P.** *(The operator simultaneously does the single shoulder press with one hand while preparing to catch her hand with his other one. Her hand, upon touching her face, lets go and drops into the operator's hand.)* Now as I lower the hand slowly to your leg, you go even deeper relaxed. Going deeper and deeper with each movement down. And when it touches you'll be twice as deep as you are now. Effortlessly drifting deeper relaxed with each movement down and getting ready to go way down. Almost touching, touching, going d–e–e–p, d–e–e–p, d–e–e–p. That heavy tired, drowsy feeling going all through you, going all through your arms, all through your head, and all through your body, as you go deeper and deeper relaxed. Effortlessly, you become deeper and deeper relaxed.

You've probably noticed that the eyes are very heavy and tired and drowsy, and so relaxed. They're s–o h–e–a–v–y. It's almost as if a force is pulling them down, as if they were as heavy as lead, as if they were glued tightly shut. Now, as you hold your eyes tightly shut, I'd like you to roll your eyeballs back up into your head a little ways as if you were looking at the top of your forehead. That's it, now hold that position. And you'll notice that the longer you hold that position, the heavier and tireder the eyes become, and the more they stick shut, as if they were glued tightly shut, so tightly shut, you won't be able to open them, and that's what we both want. That's a good sign. So tightly shut, you won't be able to open them. Go ahead and try to open them, Debbie. Go ahead and try hard! Try and open the eyes! But the harder you try, the more they stick! Alright, that's fine, you've done very well. Now, let the eyeballs relax and return to their normal position. That's it. See how the eyes are so heavy and tired and relaxed that you cannot open them, and that's a good sign.

Now we're going to do something that will take you deeper. In a moment I am going to count backwards from twenty to one. As we go through this process, any other noises that you may hear you can either just ignore, or they may even help you to go deeper, such as the hum of the video recorder. Now, in a moment, I will count backwards from twenty to one. As I count backwards, I will synchronize each count with each exhale. So with each count backwards, you will go deeper and deeper relaxed. Let yourself go deeper with each exhale. By the time I reach one, you will be twice as deep as you are now. Alright, getting ready to go deeper, twenty, nineteen, . . . If you need to move in any way or straighten up to get more comfortable, feel free to do so as it won't affect your depth.

Okay Debbie, you're doing fine. Now we're going to do something else that will take you even deeper. I'm going to pick up the left arm by the wrist. That's it, you just let me have it. Alright now, in a moment, I'm going to count from one to twenty, and as I do, with each count, the arm will become more and more relaxed. As it does, it will become heavier and heavier. With each count, the arm will become more and more relaxed and heavier and heavier. By the time I reach twenty, it'll be so relaxed, so heavy, it'll be like a dead weight, like a wet dishtowel. At that time I'll let it go and it'll just drop to your lap with a thud, and your whole body will just drop down with it. Ready now, counting, one, two, three, four, five, that's it, just let me have it, let all those muscles in that whole arm relax more and more, so that the arm becomes heavier and heavier with each count. Six, seven, eight, nine, ten. That's it, I can feel it, the whole arm letting go, all those muscles relaxing completely, becoming more and more relaxed. The arm is getting heavier and heavier. Eleven, twelve, thirteen, fourteen, fifteen, three quarters of the way there, it's getting heavier and heavier, I can feel it. You know when we reach twenty, it'll be so relaxed and so heavy that it'll be like a dead weight, and I'll drop it at twenty, drop it to your lap, and your whole body will just drop down with it into a very deep state, and you're getting ready to go all the way down, sixteen, seventeen, eighteen, nineteen, and all the way, twenty! (The operator drops her arm to her lap.) You're going deeper and deeper relaxed. That's fine, Debbie, you're doing very well.

Now we're going to do something else with that same arm that will help to take you even deeper, because we're trying to get deep enough to where we can obtain what we both want most, and that is the recall of that event that we decided upon. Alright, now I'm going to pick up that arm again as you just let me have it, and as I pick it up, you can think, feel, and imagine yourself going deeper and deeper relaxed with each movement of the arm upwards, drifting deeper and deeper relaxed, drifting deeper and deeper relaxed, with each motion upwards. *(The arm is extended straight out at shoulder level.)* That's it. Now I want you to make a fist with the left hand. Make a fist, make a tight fist. That's it, tighter and tighter. Now we're going to do something interesting as you're sitting there that will help you to go even deeper. I'm going to gently stroke the left arm with my hand, and, as I do, the arm will become stiffer and stiffer with each stroke of my hand. The muscles will tighten more and more, getting tighter and tighter, with each stroke of my hand. The muscles getting tighter and tighter. I can feel it — the shoulder muscles are getting tighter and tighter. The forearm is getting tighter and tighter. If you really wish to go deeper, the arm will get tighter and tighter. So tight, it's almost like the arm is a bar of steel. The elbow is locked, and it's like a bar of steel. So stiff, so locked, so tight, you won't be able to bend it, and that's a good sign. So stiff, so locked, you won't be able to bend it! If you really wish to go deeper, you won't be able to bend it. That's it. The elbow's locked! The whole arm is locked! Go ahead and try and bend it, Debbie! Go ahead and try! Try hard! Alright, that's fine. Now, let me have the arm, and as I take it, the muscles relax. Relaxing more and more, the whole arm relaxes, and we lower it to your lap. As we do, you can think, feel, and imagine yourself drifting deeper and deeper relaxed. With each motion down, going deeper and deeper relaxed. That's it. So relaxed and so comfortable, it feels so good to let that arm relax. You're doing fine, Debbie. You see how the arm can actually work automatically, and that's a good sign.

Alright, Debbie, as you sit there I want you to listen to the sound of my voice. You can actually drift deeper and deeper relaxed, just from the sound of my voice, because it's really so very simple and easy to effortlessly let yourself drift deeper and deeper relaxed. Let yourself drift further and further away on the sound of my voice. Just let yourself go completely, neither helping or resisting, but let it go all through you. A vague pleasant numbness pervading your body, so pleasantly heavy — kind of a dreamy, drifty, drowsy feeling, so relaxed and so comfortable. With each breath, with each beat of your heart, with each minute that rolls by, you go deeper and deeper relaxed. It's so easy to concentrate on the sound of my voice, feeling safe and secure and comfortable, as you effortlessly drift further and further away.

Now, in a moment, I want you to imagine something as best you can in your mind's eye that I'm going to describe to you. I want you to imagine a staircase, but it's unlike any that you've ever seen before. It's as if this staircase was just kind of floating in the middle of a fluffy cloud, just kind of suspended in midair. You and I are standing at the head of this staircase, and you look down and see that there are twenty stairs. These stairs are carpeted in a thick, plush carpet of your favorite color. You're standing there in your bare feet. You can feel that carpet around your feet and around your toes. *(Her toes move.)* I'm standing to one side and to the other side is a hardwood bannister, and you place your hand on that bannister, and you can feel its smooth, hard texture. *(Her fingers move slightly.)* When you can visualize this scene as best you can, signal me by raising this finger. *(The operator touches her left index finger and she promptly raises it.)* Okay, we're standing on the twentieth stair, and in a moment we're going to step slowly down together to the first stair. With each step down, you will feel that carpet around your feet and in your toes, and you will feel your hand slide down that bannister. With each step down you will go deeper and deeper. By the time we reach the bottom you will be much deeper than you are now. Alright, you're getting ready to go deeper, stepping down now from the twentieth stair, down to nineteen, and eighteen, seventeen, sixteen, and fifteen, and we pause for a moment. *(The operator synchronizes the counting with her exhaling.)* You feel your hand sliding down the bannister and feet on the carpet as you do deeper relaxed with each step down. Going down further now to fourteen, thirteen, twelve, eleven, and ten, and we pause for another moment. We're halfway there, and you know that when we reach the bottom you'll be much deeper than you are now. Nine, eight, seven, six, five, three quarters of the way there and getting ready to go all the way down. Four, three, two, and one, going **D–E–E–P,**

D–E–E–P, D–E–E–P. *(The operator uses the single shoulder press.)*
Now that you're at the bottom of the stairs you look over to the side and you see a large intricately carved oak door with a brass doorknob. Now, in a moment you're going to walk over to that door and you will open it, and, on the other side, you will find one of your favorite places, that place in Sprague, Washington. *(This was determined by her response to question #11 on the Preinduction Questionnaire.)* Alright, you're walking over to that door, that's it, walking over to the door and you place your hand on that large brass doorknob. *(Her fingers move slightly again.)* Now you open that door, and, on the other side, you see that favorite place, that campground, that picnic area in Sprague, Washington. In just a moment I'm going to have you step through that door into the scene and I'll leave you there for approximately two minutes, and, during that time, I just want you to enjoy yourself and whatever you are feeling and experiencing and be willing to take yourself deeper, and involve yourself as much as you can in that scene. You have a feeling of no worries, no anxieties, just enjoying yourself to the fullest. At the end of that two minutes, I want you to be as deep as you can go this time, as deep as you want to go this time. Also during this time, we are going to change the videotape, but you can just relax as you enjoy this scene as you take yourself deeper. And at the end of that two minutes, I'll speak to you again. Alright, stepping through that door into your favorite scene. That's it, now just enjoy that, immerse yourself in that scene and those feelings and remembrances and take yourself deeper. Begin. *(The two minutes pass and the videotape is changed. Thirty minutes have lapsed.)*
Now that you are completely relaxed, we need to make sure that your mind is completely relaxed before we can move on to what we both want most, and that is the time regression, so that you can recall that event that we decided upon. To do that, I want you to imagine something in your mind's eye, something that I am going to describe to you. I want you to imagine a blackboard. It can be any blackboard. It can be one you're familiar with or one you've never seen before. You can see written on that blackboard the numbers from 100 back to one. You may want to place those in rows, so there are five rows of twenty numbers, all the way from 100 all the way back to one. Now, if you can see those numbers on that blackboard, signal me by raising this finger. *(The operator touches her left index finger and she promptly raises it.)* Alright, that's good. Now, in a moment, what I want you do to, when I tell you to begin, is to call off those numbers, out loud, from 100 backwards. What I want to do is with each number that you call off, I want you to pick up an eraser and erase that number off the board and out of your mind. And we'll do that all the way back to number ninety-seven, but when you reach ninety-seven, I'll have you erase that number and all the rest of the numbers off the board and out of your mind, so that your mind will be a blank, and you won't be able to find any other numbers. *(Pause)* You can talk now. Call off the first number, Debbie. "100" Pick up that eraser and erase that number off the board and out of your mind, so that all you see is a smudge there. *(Her hand moves slightly as*

she picks up the imaginary eraser.) "99." Erase it off the board and out of your mind. "98." Erase it off the board and out of your mind. Now, that last number you'll be able to find. "97." *(Her voice gets softer.)* Now erase it and all the rest of the numbers off the board and out of your mind. That's it, erase all the rest of the numbers off of the board and out of your mind so that your mind is a complete blank, so that you won't be able to see or find any other numbers and so that your mind will be a blank and that's what we both want. You can't see any other numbers. You can't find any other numbers, and that's a good sign. What's the next number, Debbie? Do you see any other numbers? "No." Okay, that's fine, Debbie. You see, you've not only made your body completely relaxed, but your mind also completely relaxed. Now we can successfully proceed to what we both want most, and that is the regression.

We're going to achieve that by doing a very similar thing to what you just did. In a moment, I'm going to have you again imagine that blackboard, imagining yourself in front of that blackboard and on that blackboard you will see the numbers from twenty-one back to sixteen. Now, place yourself again in front of that blackboard and you can again see some numbers on that blackboard. The numbers twenty-one back to sixteen. Can you see those numbers? If you do, nod your head. *(She nods.)* Okay. Now, these numbers, Debbie, represent your ages twenty-one back to sixteen, back to the age to which you are going to return. I want you to know that as long as I talk to you, you will remain as deep as your are now, and you may even wish to go deeper, and no matter how deep you go, you'll always be able to hear my voice. Now, in a moment, I'm going to have you pick up that eraser again, and erase those numbers, those ages, as I call them, off the board and out of your mind, so that you temporarily forget all those memories and experiences that you normally remember from each of those ages. As we go back, you will grow younger and younger, and the memory of previous ages will increase, so, that by the time we reach the age of sixteen, you will temporarily have forgotten all those memories and experiences and everything that happened to you after that age. So, by the time we reach the age of sixteen, you will think as you thought at the age of sixteen, you will act as you acted at the age of sixteen, you will see what you saw at the age of sixteen, in fact, you will be sixteen years old. We're going to go back to the night of April 19, 1974, a Friday night when you were sixteen years old, and you'll find yourself outside of the Wrangler Bar. I want you to know that I will accompany you on this trip, and I will be somebody who may be present at that time, someone you like and like to talk to, and you can see me in that other person, or I may just be a voice you hear, but, if for any reason you should lose contact with me, all I'll have to do is to touch your hand and shoulder and you will immediately come back to where you can hear my voice. Also, anytime I want you to go deeper all I'll have to do is press down on your left shoulder. If for any reason you should become concerned, just reach out to me with your hand and we'll stop and straighten things out. Or if you feel you need to go deeper, just tell me. Do you understand? *(She nods.)* Everything that you relive at the age of sixteen, that night of April 19, 1974, you will have actually lived before. You are not to imagine or invent anything; just describe to me everything as it actually occurred. If for any reason you wish to open your eyes, you can do so, but the only things you will see are the things that you actually saw that night. Also, if you do happen to open your eyes, that will not awaken you and in no way will it affect your depth. After you have completed reliving that event that we agreed upon, at that point I will bring you back to your present age and then awaken you. But during the time that you relive this experience at 16 years old, you will have temporarily forgotten all about where you are and your present age, and you will actually relive everything that you experienced on that night, being totally unaware of where you are at this point. Alright, now I want you to again see yourself standing in front of that blackboard, and you can see those numbers, your ages from twenty-one back to sixteen. Now, as I call off the numbers, you erase that age, that number, off the board and out of your mind. Now, number twenty-one, the age of twenty one, erase it off the board and out of your mind, temporarily forgetting all those memories and experiences from that age on, and growing younger. The number twenty, the age of twenty, memories from prior years coming back. Nineteen, erasing it off the board and out of your mind, and going back to the age of eighteen, erasing it off the board and out of your mind, becoming younger and younger, and those memories from prior years increasing. Now seventeen, erase it off the board and out of your mind. Now you are sixteen-years-old, Debbie, and you find yourself on the night of April 19, 1974. It's a Friday night, and you find yourself outside of the Wrangler Bar and you're with your friends, Janet and Bobbie. Now I want you to describe to me everything that you see. Everything that's happening. What's happening now, Debbie, where are you? *(The operator attempts a revivification of the events leading up to the crash to test for depth and detail of information.)*

Debbie: Well, we're sitting in the car at the Wrangler Bar. I just got a bottle of wine.

Operator: What kind of wine?

Debbie: Strawberry. Oh geez, I just spilled it on my sweater! My mother's going to be angry.

Operator: What color is your sweater?

Debbie: It's white.

Operator: Now what's happening?

Debbie: Well, we pull out of the parking lot on to Tenth Avenue heading east. Now we're approaching Nineteenth.

Operator: Where are you all sitting?

Debbie: I'm sitting on the passenger's side, Bobbie is in the middle, and Janet is driving.

Operator: What are all of you wearing? *(The operator tests for the degree of revivification by seeing if she can see what she could not recall during the preinduction.)*

Debbie: Well, I'm wearing a white sweater and pants, brown pants. Bobbie is wearing a skirt and blouse, but I can't see exactly what Janet is wearing. *(Obviously, the revivification is not complete.)*

Operator: Go ahead and look around Bobbie so that you can see Janet clearly and tell me what she's wearing if you can, but don't try too hard if you can't see it.

Debbie: Well, I think she's wearing a dark shirt and pants, but I just can't see her clearly.

Operator: Okay, that's fine Debbie. Just don't try too hard; all that information is stored in your memory, and the more you relax the easier it will come to you. Let's continue on down the road now. Where are you now? *(At this point the operator would normally have deepened the subject further before proceeding in an attempt to get as complete a revivification as possible, even if it necessitated two or more sessions. For the purposes of the demonstration, however, he continued.)*

Debbie: We just turned left onto Nineteenth street and we're heading north. Now we're stopped at a stop sign.

Operator: Before you proceed any further, Debbie, what I want you to do is just remain stopped there for a moment and we're going to do something a little different. What I want you to do now as you're stopped at that stop sign is to imagine yourself sitting in the back seat of the car. It's as if a part of you separates and moves to the back seat so that you see an image of yourself, or someone who looks like you, sitting in the front seat. You see Bobbie sitting in the middle and Janet in the driver's seat. So, it's as if you are looking at yourself from the back seat of the car. Can you see that? Can you do that, Debbie? *(She nods.)* And now, from this position you will be able to describe to me out loud, everything that is occurring as it occurs. You can do this objectively and unemotionally in a detached manner, so that you can report to me everything that is happening without becoming emotionally involved. You can do an interesting thing, and that is, when I ask you to, you can actually slow down or even stop the action, as if you were stopping a movie and just looking at one particular scene, so you can look at it in detail and describe it in detail. If, for any reason, you should lose contact with me, all I have to do is touch your hand and shoulder, and you'll immediately come back to where you can hear me. Do you understand? "Umhum." *(Even though the revivification is not complete, the operator changes to hypermnesia by dissociating the subject. This is a safety precaution because as she approaches the impact she may spontaneously revivify it.)* Alright, now we're on nineteenth, heading northward, and I just want you to describe to me exactly what's happening, all very objectively and unemotionally as you watch it from the back seat. You are not to get emotionally involved or relive it, okay?

Debbie: Um hum. Well, we're traveling up Nineteenth, and now we're approaching the intersection of Seventh Avenue South.

Operator: Okay, now as you go through the intersection and approach Sixth Avenue South, slow the action down so that you can see everything that's happening as you look over the front seat. What's happening now?

Debbie: Well, they're talking and laughing and just kind of playing around.

Operator: What are they saying?

Debbie: I'm not sure.

Operator: Go ahead and listen in and tell me what they're saying if you can in fact hear them. If you can't hear them just tell me.

Debbie: Okay, now I can hear them. Janet is wondering who's at the party, and they're trying to decide if they should even go.

Operator: Look through the front windshield and tell me what you see.

Debbie: Well, there's a white house on the corner, the right corner, and a brick house beyond that, I think. It's kind of dark. There's only one car parked on the street on the right side.

Operator: Are there any cars either in front or behind you, or coming towards you?

Debbie: No, we're the only one. Oh no! We just swerved to the right, jumped the curb, and now we're heading across the lawn and there's a tree right in front of us!

Operator: Stop the action right there Debbie! There's no need to keep going. All we're interested in is the events leading up to the accident. Okay?

Debbie: Okay, good. *(She sighs with relief.)*

Operator: Now, Debbie, I'd like you to back up the action to the point just before you veered off and look around to see why.

Debbie: I don't see why. There's nothing in the road.

Operator: Is there an animal or car or anything like that that you swerve to miss?

Debbie: No there's not.

Operator: Where's Janet looking?

Debbie: She's looking at me and Bobbie.

Operator: Where are you looking?

Debbie: At Janet.

Operator: Now move the action right up to the time where the car veers off and look what Janet's doing.

Debbie: She's laughing, and, my God, she just turns the wheel! She did it on purpose! *(Pause)* She was just playing around and must have wanted to drive through the yard, but she hit the tree.

Operator: Okay, Debbie, you've done very well, but now I'm going to give you just a minute or so to examine that incident leading up to the crash, but not the crash itself, to see if there's anything else that you see that may have contributed to or caused the accident. When you are satisfied that you've seen and re-examined everything, signal me by raising this finger. *(The operator touches her left index finger. Approximately one minute passes when she signals.)* Did you see or find anything else, Debbie?

Debbie: No. I'm sure that's why it happened, but I just can't believe that she'd do it, but she did.

Operator: Okay, Debbie, you've done very well, but now I want you to merge that dissociated part of you that's in the back seat with the image of you in the front seat, so that you are in one piece again. So that you are completely whole and normal in every way. Okay? Have you done that? *(She nods.)* Okay. Now I want you to leave that scene and go **d–e–e–p, d–e–e–p, d–e–e–p.** *(The operator does the single shoulder press to deepen the subject and break her involvement with the scene.)* Now, Debbie, what I want you to do is to again see yourself standing in front of that blackboard, and you see the number sixteen, which represents the age you are now. Can you see yourself in front of the blackboard and can you see that number on it? "Um hum." Okay, now in a moment I'm going to again call off some numbers, your ages, and, as I do, you will see them reappear on the board. As those numbers reappear, all the memories and experiences of that age that you normally remember will come back. Alright, look at the board now and see the number, the age, seventeen reappear. You're getting older, and all those memories and experiences that you normally remember are coming back. The number eighteen, the age of eighteen, reappear, and now the age of nineteen, and you're getting older. Now the age of twenty, getting older, and all those experiences and memories that you normally remember are coming back. Now the age of twenty-one, and you're now back to March 21, a Wednesday, 1979, twenty-one-years-old, in the sheriff's office, and it's 4 PM.

Now in a moment, Debbie, I'm going to bring you out, and I'm going to do that by counting from one to five, and when I reach five, you'll open your eyes, be wide awake, alert, refreshed, relaxed, and feeling good all over. You'll find that you will sleep very deeply and profoundly tonight and awaken refreshed in the morning as a result of this experience. You'll also find that you'll have very vivid, colorful, and pleasant dreams that you'll be able to remember in the morning. The next time you are hypnotized you will be able to go deeper faster, and easier, because you're familiar with this experience now, but you'll only be able to be hypnotized when you want to and by a qualified person like myself, or in the event that you learn self-hypnosis. Also, that part of you that was in the back seat will now be completely merged with your true self, so that you will be normal in every way, and you will also remember everything that you experienced during this session. You can also see and remember all those numbers that you were able to temporarily erase off of the blackboard and out of your mind. Do you understand? "Um hum." Alright, you're able to come up now, coming up a little ways to one. Feelings starting to come back in your body, coming up a little more to two, feelings coming back more and more. You might want to start moving around a little, take a deep breath or two. Coming up a little more to three, all the feelings starting to come back, coming back more and more, that's it, moving around a little, coming up a little more to four, straightening up now, moving around a little, that's it, getting ready to come all the way up, coming all the way up to FIVE! How do you feel? Are you awake?

Debbie: Yes, I think so.

Operator: What's your name?

Debbie: Debbie. *(She laughs a little.)*
Operator: Do you want to stand up and stretch a little?
Debbie: Yah.
Operator: How about a drink of water?
Debbie: Okay. My mouth is a little dry. *(She goes to the fountain.)*
Operator: Do you feel awake and normal?
Debbie: Yah, but I feel a little tired.
Operator: That's completely normal. In fact, most people experience some kind of hangover effect, but it will dissipate quickly. What did you think of this experience?
Debbie: Well, it was kind of weird. You know it was kind of like I was fluctuating in and out of it, like sometimes I could see it clearly and other times I couldn't.
Operator: Yes, that's very normal. Most people seem to experience a regression that way. Who was I during the regression?
Debbie: Well, you were just kind of a voice in my head. I didn't really know where it was coming from nor did I really care.
Operator: I'll tell you what, Debbie, I'd like to take just a couple of minutes to quickly run through everything I did because there are literally dozens of different techniques and combinations of techniques that work differently for different people, so it's largely a matter of finding, through trial and error and through your experience just what works best for you. So in case you want to do another session I'll know better what to do with you as far as techniques. What did you think of the hand levitation, you know, when your hand got light and floated up?
Debbie: That was kind of neat. I didn't think it'd happen, but it got light and felt real numb. I also didn't think my eyes would close when it touched my face as you said, but they did.
Operator: How did you feel when the hand finally touched and I pushed down on your shoulder?
Debbie: I felt like I was sinking at that time.
Operator: Good. That's a good sign. Okay, then I had you try to open your eyes, but you couldn't. What did you think of that?
Debbie: I thought for sure that I'd be able to and that it'd embarrass you, but I couldn't. It kind of surprised me.
Operator: Next I had you count backwards to yourself from twenty to one, synchronizing each count with your exhaling.
Debbie: Yah, I liked that. I could feel myself sinking further on each count.
Operator: Good. Then I did what we call the rapid arm drop where I picked up your arm by the wrist and counted to twenty as it got heavier with each count.
Debbie: Yah, I could feel it getting heavier but I don't know if it really took me deeper.
Operator: Okay, that's fine. How about the arm catalepsy. You know, when I picked up your arm and gently stroked it as it got stiffer.

Debbie: That amazed me! It automatically got so stiff I couldn't bend it, and I really tried.

Operator: Did that concern you at all?

Debbie: No, I thought it was interesting. It convinced me that something was happening.

Operator: Then I just talked to you for about a minute.

Debbie: I liked that. It's so soothing, and I don't have to do anything but just listen.

Operator: Okay. How about the staircase and through the closed door to your favorite place?

Debbie: Both were good. I could see them real clear.

Operator: Could you feel the carpet and bannister?

Debbie: Oh yah!

Operator: Did you know your toes and fingers moved?

Debbie: Did they?

Operator: Yes, you really seemed to be enjoying it. Then I had you erase the numbers off the board and out of your mind. What was that like?

Debbie: That was kind of interesting not being able to remember those numbers.

Operator: You can remember them all now can't you?

Debbie: Oh yah.

Operator: Good. Then we went into the regression.

Debbie: That was neat because I could sort of feel myself getting younger and a lot of scenes were flashing before my eyes with each year that we went back. At times, though, I just couldn't see things as clearly as I'd like to have. It was kind of like I wasn't totally there, but part of me was still here. You know?

Operator: Yes, a lot of people experience it that way but you did very well, especially for the first time. If you think there's anything to be gained by doing another session I'm sure you'll go deeper and can experience it more totally. Could you experience yourself clearly in the back seat?

Debbie: Yah, pretty much.

Operator: Okay, Debbie, any questions?

Debbie: Could I have moved without bringing myself out? I mean at one point I wanted to change position but was afraid to, even though you told me I could in the very beginning.

Operator: Oh yes. Most people believe, as you did, that you can't or shouldn't move as it might bring you up, but actually you can move and we encourage you to. Well, we certainly appreciate you volunteering for this and I hope it was worthwhile for you.

Debbie: Thank you. *(The operator walks her outside and follows up with a phone call the next day to see if she has any questions and to make certain there were no negative aftereffects. Furthermore, many subjects will remember additional details after the hypnosis session, so the hypno-investigator should make it a practice to follow up with all victims and witnesses.)*

Appendix 7

CHECKLIST

Preparation and Preinduction

1. Secure setting against noise and interruptions. Make the subject as comfortable as possible, both physically and emotionally.
2. Remove misconceptions and allay fears and anxieties:
   (a) loss of consciousness, (b) surrender of will, (c) nonawareness and nonremembrance, (d) revelation of secrets, (e) fear of not being dehypnotized, etc.
3. Emphasize naturalness of hypnosis, e.g. highway hypnosis, twilight zones, etc.
4. Emphasize positive nature of hypnosis.
5. Stress the need for concentration, cooperation, and passivity, i.e. "Don't try to do anything or not do anything, but just let yourself go. Just let it happen and neither help nor resist. Hypnosis always works, but the degree to which it does work depends on your ability to concentrate and cooperate."
6. Describe in simple terms what the subject is supposed to do and how he might feel. Stress the tendency of the body to work automatically and the need to let any feelings develop.
7. Get details of the event, time, location, etc. for regression. Explain recording.

Protocol

1. Induction:
2. Eye Catalepsy
3. Deepening:
4. Arm Drop, Eye Flinch, Arm Catalepsy
5. Deepening:
6. Suggested Amnesia
7. Time Regression: Hypermnesia or Revivification

Protocol Continued

Present	Regressed	Critical Details of Event:
Age:		1.
Time:		2.
Date:		3.
Location:		Information Forgotten:
Questions to Ask:		1.
1.		2.
2.		3.
3.		

8. Return to Present Age (Progression)

Awakening

1. "In a few moments I am going to count from one to five and with each count you will gradually come more awake so that when I reach five you will open your eyes and be wide awake, alert, refreshed and relaxed, and feeling good all over."
2. "Tonight you will sleep very deep and profound, awakening refreshed in the morning, and you'll have very vivid, colorful, and pleasant dreams that you'll remember in the morning."
3. "The next time you are hypnotized you will go deeper, faster, and easier because you are now familiar with this experience, but you will only be able to be hypnotized when you want to and by a qualified person like myself or in the event that you learn self-hypnosis."
4. "You will also remember everything that happened during this session and everything that you were able to recall (or re-experience)."
5. Restore numbers if suggested amnesia was used.
6. "Coming up now, one, coming up a little more to two, . . . "

INVESTIGATIVE HYPNOSIS REPORT

TYPE OF CRIME _____ DR. NUMBER _____

DATE REPORTED ___–___–___ DATE/TIME OF OCCURRENCE ___–___–___ _____ Hrs.
          mo day yr   mo day yr

LOCATION OF CRIME _____

SUBJECT'S NAME _____ DOB ___–___–___ VICTIM _____
                                              mo day yr

HOME ADDRESS _____ HOME PHONE _____ WITNESS _____

BUSINESS ADDRESS _____ BUSINESS PHONE _____

OCCUPATION _____

PRIMARY INVESTIGATOR _____

HYPNO-INVESTIGATOR _____

DATE OF SESSION _____–_____–_____ BEGINNING TIME _____ Hrs.
              mo   day   yr ENDING TIME _____ Hrs.

LOCATION OF SESSION _____

PERSONS PRESENT DURING SESSION _____

PURPOSE OF SESSION (include info. subject asked to remember): _____
_____
_____

INDUCTION TECHNIQUES UTILIZED _____
_____

DEEPENING TECHNIQUES UTILIZED _____
_____

CHALLENGES & TESTS CONDUCTED _____
_____

POSTHYPNOTIC SUGGESTIONS GIVEN _____
_____

ESTIMATED LEVEL OF TRANCE: ____ Light ____ Medium ____ Deep

EVALUATION OF SESSION: No Value 1   2   3   4   5   Valuable

AUDIO TAPE NUMBERS _____ VIDEOTAPE NUMBERS _____

OBSERVATIONS AND SUGGESTIONS FOR FUTURE SESSIONS: _____
_____
_____

HYPNOSIS SESSION EVALUATION*

		PRE-HYPNOSIS	DURING HYPNOSIS	POST HYPNOSIS	VERIFICATION
DATE/TIME					
SUSPECT	SEX/AGE/RACE				
	HEIGHT/WEIGHT				
	HAIR/EYES				
	SPEECH				
	CLOTHING				
	PHYSICAL ODDITIES (marks, scars, tatoos)				
WEAPON	TYPE/MODEL/CALIBER				
	COLOR/SIZE/LENGTH				
	HOW USED				
VEHICLE	YEAR/MAKE/MODEL				
	BODY STYLE/COLOR				
	UNUSUAL CHARACTERISTICS				
	LIC. NO./STATE				
	INTERIOR				
	EXTERIOR				

COMPOSITE MADE: _____ YES _____ NO
*Use additional page for continuation if necessary.
Use a separate page for each suspect.

Appendix 9

POLICE DEPARTMENT
GREAT FALLS, MONTANA
GENERAL ORDER

Date of Issue	Effective Date	Amends:
May 1, 1979	May 1, 1979	
		Rescinds:

Subject:

INVESTIGATIVE HYPNOSIS

Introduction

Investigative hypnosis will be used only in connection with alleged criminal offenses once the preliminary reports and investigations have been completed. It will not be used for noncriminal or private purposes, except for authorized training and recertification procedures. The services of the hypno-investigator will be provided, without charge, to any law enforcement agency requesting assistance in a criminal investigation. All investigative hypnosis sessions must be authorized by the Chief of Police or, in his absence, his designated representative.

The objective of hypno-investigation is to assist volunteer victims and witnesses in recalling facts and details that have been forgotten. Investigative hypnosis has proven to be a highly successful investigative aid used to enhance the recall of victims and witnesses to crimes. Its use should be considered in cases where victims or witnesses have sketchy or conflicting recall of events and details, or when they may have actively repressed the incident due to the emotional trauma of the crime event.

A hypnosis interview is not a truth establishing procedure and is no substitute for a thorough police investigation and interview. It should only be regarded as a supplement to the investigative process.

Any violation of the following policies and procedures may be grounds for voiding certification and authorization of a hypno-investigator.

Procedures – The Primary Investigator

When requesting a victim or witness to undergo hypnosis, the primary investigator shall stress that the procedure is entirely voluntary. The hypno-investigator will then thoroughly explain the process prior to the session. No attempt shall be made by any person other than the hypno-investigator to explain the procedure, except to express complete confidence in the results. The investigator will not give any misleading statements regarding the hypnosis procedure.

The hypnosis session can be quite lengthy and must be administered under relaxed circumstances in the proper setting. The primary investigator should be present during the entire procedure so adequate time must be allowed to ensure a session without interruption.

It will be the hypno-investigator's responsibility to audio and/or video record the entire session. He shall retain custody of all tapes, since these are confidential, and will enter them into evidence. Personnel who are not a part of the investigation will not have access to any tapes.

Prior to hypnosis, the primary investigator will take a full statement from the victim or witness regarding his knowledge of the crime event in question. This statement must be reduced to writing.

When a case in which hypnosis was utilized is transferred to the County Attorney's Office, that office will be informed by the investigator that hypnosis was used. Where an arrest has been made or is imminent in a criminal proceeding, no witness or victim may be hypnotized without the consent of the County Attorney and Chief of Police.

All hypno-induced evidence must be corroborated by the primary investigator before search or arrest warrants are obtained.

Procedures – The Hypno-Investigator

The hypno-investigator must ensure that the subject's physical and mental welfare are totally protected. It will be the hypno-investigator's responsibility to maintain confidentiality and to ensure the subject's comfort and safety during the session. Under no circumstances will a subject under hypnosis be displayed for public amusement or for the amusement of departmental personnel. No photographs or videotapes are to be taken except those used for evidentiary or educational purposes with consent of the subject. Use of therapeutic treatment or diagnosis of illnesses will not be allowed. Emotional rewards, however, can be offered as this practice is an acceptable and ethical procedure during hypnosis, i.e. instruction in self-hypnosis, suggestions to help deal with crime-related stress, etc.

The hypno-investigator will be responsible for written records on each session to include a log of names, completion of a Preinduction Questionnaire and Release form, and an Investigative Hypnosis Report/Hypnosis Session Evaluation form. These records are considered confidential and their dissemination is restricted to those personnel conducting the investigation.

Once authorized by the Chief of Police or, in his absence, his designated representative, a criminal case-related hypnosis session will be conducted by a hypno-investigator selected by the above or the Chief of Detectives. Rotation of hypno-investigators is encouraged. A hypno-investigator has the privilege to decline to hypnotize a subject if he feels that another hypno-investigator is better suited to the particular subject or case in question.

Persons Not to Be Hypnotized

No suspect or potential suspect in any criminal matter will be considered for hypnosis sessions. The procedure will be restricted to victims and witnesses in criminal cases. Persons under the age of eighteen will not be considered unless a written release is received from a parent, guardian, Juvenile Court Judge, or person having jurisdiction over the minor. If a subject becomes a suspect at any time, the session must be terminated immediately.

Those persons who are known to have mental disorders or who are below average intelligence are not to be considered for the procedure. Subjects will be screened through their responses to the Preinduction Questionnaire. In addition, women who are in a state of advanced pregnancy are not to be hypnotized without their doctor's permission. Subjects under the care of a physician, psychiatrist, or psychologist should not be hypnotized without prior approval of their doctors.

Administering the Hypnosis Sessions

The hypno-investigator, the primary investigator and subject must expect the initial procedure to take approximately two hours. It is not unusual to deal with a subject who will require two or more sessions to reach the proper depth to achieve positive results, but, if additional sessions are required, they will normally be shorter in length. A prehypnosis interview will be conducted by the hypno-investigator so that all misconceptions and questions can be explained and answered.

A hypnosis session must be conducted in a quiet and comfortable atmosphere secure from interruptions and with all efforts being made to ensure the subject's comfort. If necessary and only under unusual circumstances, the hypno-investigator may conduct the session at the subject's home or other location, although this is to be discouraged. All sessions should be held at the subject's convenience. Recognizing the hypersuggestibility of a hypnotized person, extreme caution will be used in obtaining a truthful and accurate narration or re-experiencing of the events under question, being very careful to ask no leading, accusatory, or suggestive questions.

Ethics

The training of police hypnotists is a relatively new and controversial development in criminal justice. It is therefore imperative that hypnosis only be used in a strictly professional manner within the confines and according to the procedures outlined in this document. To ensure its professional use only, the practice of hypnosis will be governed by the following ethics enforced by the Certification Board:

1. Hypnosis will not be used for noncriminal or private purposes.
2. Under no circumstances will a subject, under hypnosis, be displayed for public amusement or for the amusement of departmental personnel.
3. Under no circumstances will hypnosis be used for personal aggrandizement or for the fulfillment of personal desires.
4. Use of therapeutic treatment or diagnosis of illnesses will not be allowed.

5. At all times, the emotional and physical well-being of the subject is of paramount importance, and it is the responsibility of the hypno-investigator to ensure and protect the best interests of the subject, including his civil rights.
6. In all ways and at all times the hypno-investigator will utilize his skills as a professional and as a representative of the Great Falls Police Department.

Certification of Hypno-Investigators

A hypno-investigator must have completed a professional course of no less than forty hours instruction on hypnosis and criminal investigation. Upon completion of the above requirement, the hypno-investigator must then be authorized by the Chief of Police before he can conduct hypnosis sessions for the Department. Such authorization will be granted by the signing of an authorization form to be kept in the hypno-investigator's personnel file. Once this requirement is fulfilled, the hypno-investigator will be required to recertify the first six (6) months after the original certification and every year thereafter. If the hypno-investigator fails to recertify within any of the designated periods, he will not be allowed to use hypnosis for police investigative purposes and his Hypno-Investigation Authorization Form will be withdrawn from his personnel file. If the hypno-investigator wishes to continue, however, appropriate arrangements may be made with the Certification Board.

Certification Board

This Board will consist of a certified hypno-investigator and the Chief of Police or his designee.

Each twelve months starting November 1, 1979, the hypno-investigator will be required to appear before the Certification Board or videotape a session for review by the Board to demonstrate as a minimum the following techniques in the designated sequence:

1. Preinduction
2. Induction
3. Deepening Technique
4. Eye Catalepsy
5. Deepening Technique
6. Arm Catalepsy
7. Deepening Technique
8. Suggested Amnesia
9. Time Regression: Hypermnesia or Revivification
10. Seal and Awakening

The hypno-investigator must show in the Hypno-Investigator's Practice Log having hypnotized at least one subject every month. This will be checked by the Certification Board prior to recertification testing. Case-related hypnosis sessions will count towards recertification.

If the investigator fails any portion of the above tests he will not be allowed to function as a hypnotist until all phases are passed as a complete unit. The Certification Board's decision is final and will forward a copy of its findings to the Chief of Police and the Chief of Detectives.

Record of Subjects Hypnotized

The Hypno-Investigator's Practice Log will be kept in the training office to be used as a log for persons hypnotized for practice purposes. Each hypno-investigator will enter all subjects hypnotized by name, date, techniques used, estimated depth, special considerations or reactions, and the location of the session. This log must be kept up to date and will show at least one hypnosis session per month. Each hypno-investigator will observe this log to determine the frequency of use of practice subjects and if there are any special considerations or reactions of the subject to be used.

Summary

The purpose of recertification is to ensure that the Hypno-Investigator stays current in the various techniques of hypno-investigation and sharpens his skills through continued experience. It is most important that all of the certification/recertification guidelines are adhered to, and, if for any reason the above requirements are not fulfilled, he will not be allowed to function as a hypno-investigator for the Great Falls Police Department.

Revision

The above certification requirements may be re-evaluated by the Chief of Police at the request of any certified hypno-investigator, and revised only after personal consultation with each and every certified hypno-investigator in the Department. A copy of any revisions will be forwarded to the County Attorney and Sheriff.

HYPNO-INVESTIGATION AUTHORIZATION FORM

This is to certify that _____ has completed a recognized course of no less than forty (40) hours instruction on hypnosis in criminal investigation and is hereby authorized to serve in the capacity of a hypno-investigator for the Great Falls Police Department.

It is recognized that any violation of the Department's policies and procedures governing Investigative Hypnosis may be grounds for the voiding of this authorization.

An authorized hypno-investigator's failure to meet the recertification requirements as specified in the said policies and procedures will result in the automatic voiding of this authorization.

Dated this _____ day of _____, 19____.

_____
Chief of Police

HYPNO-INVESTIGATOR'S PRACTICE LOG

Hypno-Investigator's Name	Subject's Name	Techniques Used	Estimated Depth	Observations & Suggestions for Future Sessions	Location & Date of Session

NAME INDEX

SUBJECT INDEX

E

Effeminate male subject, 55
Eidetic imagery, 283–284
Eidetikers, 283–284
Electronic brain wave synchronizers, 130
Elliotte v. State, 248
Emmett v. Ricketts, 238
Emmett v. State, 238
Emotional readiness, 84
Empathy, 88
Enhanced recall (*See* Hypermnesia)
Enthusiastic hysterical female subject, 52
Erotic dreams, 79
Ethical Hypnosis Training Center, 5, 23
Expectancy, 39, 67
Expectations, 36, 84
Extraverbal communication, 37
Extraverbal suggestion, 91
Eye blink, 97–98
    confusion technique, 113
    general instructions and method, 97
    pen or pencil, 97
    verbalization, 97–98
Eye catalepsy, 69, 75, 148, 151–153, 324
    considerations, 153
    direct, 151–152
    indirect, 152
    recovering, 152–153
Eye closure (*See* Closing of eyes)
Eye fixation, 64–66, 68, 93–97, 148, 324
    considerations, 96–97
    digital watch, 97
    dynamic method, 122
    general instructions and method, 93–94
    hypno-disc, 97
    pen or pencil, 93–97
    resistance, dealing with, 122
    strobe light, 97
    verbalization, 94–96
    wrist watch with sweep hand, 97
Eye flinch, 148, 153
Eyeball-set, 151–152
Eyewitnesses, fallibility of, 291

F

Fabrication, 242
Facilitation, 39

Failure, dealing with, 187–190
Fantasized hand levitation, 124–125
Fear of failure, 119–120
    recognition of, 120
Federal court cases, 250
Federal court system, 220–221
Feedback from subject, 7, 73–74
Field of consciousness, restriction of, 64
Firewalking, 31
First impressions, significance of, 54–55
Flashbacks, 288
Flexibility of operator, 92
Floating sensation, 142
Following subjects, 66
Forcing confessions through hypnosis, 14–15
Forensic hypnosis (*See also specific topics*)
    additional uses of, 298–300
    approaches to, 194–196
    authorization form, 353
    conflict of interest, 196–197
    defined, 3, 12
    discovery stage, 21–22
    independent clinicians, 195
    introduction to, 3–27
    persons who should practice, 12
    police hypnotists, 195–196
    practical aspects, 193–219
    primary objective, 3
    program within law enforcement agency,
        establishment of, 193–194
    purpose of, 57, 193
    report, 346–347
    research project to evaluate merits of,
        193–194
    room for, 57–60 (*See also* Hypnosis Session)
    transcript, 326–343
Forensic hypnotists and clinical hypnotists
        distinguished, 13–14
Forgetting, reasons for, 288–289
    acute trauma, 289
    brain damage, 289
    context, 289
    deterioration, 289
    interference, 289
    repression, 289
Format of book, 4–5
Foundation of basic knowledge of hypnosis,
        28–63
Fractionation, 132, 143–145, 148, 160, 306